The V*a*KE Handbook

Moral Development and Citizenship Education

Series Editors

Wiel Veugelers (*University of Humanistic Studies, Utrecht, The Netherlands*)
Kirsi Tirri (*University of Helsinki, Finland*)

Founding Editor

Fritz Oser†

Editorial Board

Nimrod Aloni (*Kibbutzim College of Education, Tel Aviv, Israel*)
Marvin Berkowitz (*University of Missouri–St.Louis, USA*)
Horst Biedermann (*St. Gallen University of Teacher Education, Switzerland*)
Maria Rosa Buxarrais (*University of Barcelona, Spain*)
Helen Haste (*University of Bath, UK/Harvard University, USA*)
Dana Moree (*Charles University, Prague, Czech Republic*)
Clark Power (*University of Notre Dame, USA*)
Jasmine Sim (*National Institute of Education, Singapore*)
Joel Westheimer (*University of Ottawa, Canada*)

VOLUME 18

The titles published in this series are listed at *brill.com/mora*

The V*a*KE Handbook

Theory and Practice of Values and *Knowledge Education*

Edited by

Sieglinde Weyringer, Jean-Luc Patry, Dimitris Pnevmatikos
and Frédérique Brossard Børhaug

BRILL

LEIDEN | BOSTON

Cover illustration: Photograph by Dimitris Pnevmatikos

All chapters in this book have undergone peer review.

The Library of Congress Cataloging-in-Publication Data is available online at https://catalog.loc.gov

Typeface for the Latin, Greek, and Cyrillic scripts: "Brill". See and download: brill.com/brill-typeface.

ISSN 2352-5770
ISBN 978-90-04-51543-7 (paperback)
ISBN 978-90-04-51544-4 (hardback)
ISBN 978-90-04-51545-1 (e-book)

Copyright 2022 by Koninklijke Brill NV, Leiden, The Netherlands.
Koninklijke Brill NV incorporates the imprints Brill, Brill Nijhoff, Brill Hotei, Brill Schöningh, Brill Fink, Brill mentis, Vandenhoeck & Ruprecht, Böhlau and V&R unipress.
All rights reserved. No part of this publication may be reproduced, translated, stored in a retrieval system, or transmitted in any form or by any means, electronic, mechanical, photocopying, recording or otherwise, without prior written permission from the publisher. Requests for re-use and/or translations must be addressed to Koninklijke Brill NV via brill.com or copyright.com.

This book is printed on acid-free paper and produced in a sustainable manner.

Contents

Series Editor's Foreword XIII
    Wiel Veugelers
Preface XIV
List of Figures and Tables XVI
Notes on Contributors XVII

PART 1
VaKE Values and *Knowledge Education* – Introducing the Approach

1. What Is VaKE? 3
   Sieglinde Weyringer, Jean-Luc Patry, Dimitris Pnevmatikos and Frédérique Brossard Børhaug

2. VaKE: Theory, Prototype, and Variations 12
   Jean-Luc Patry and Sieglinde Weyringer

PART 2
Recommendations for VaKE Practice

3. Planning, Preparing and Doing a VaKE Course 45
   Sieglinde Weyringer and Dimitris Pnevmatikos

4. How to Write a Dilemma Story 57
   Sieglinde Weyringer and Dimitris Pnevmatikos

5. Tools and Techniques Used in VaKE 67
   Sieglinde Weyringer and Jean-Luc Patry

6. Awareness of Teacher Roles in VaKE and Capitalizing on Them for Teacher Training 78
   Martina Nussbaumer

PART 3
VaKE in Different Educational Settings

SECTION 1
VaKE in School Education

7   Challenges in Primary Education with VaKE   91
         Alexandra Reichenwallner

8   VaKE+: Fostering Learning Performance in Cognitive Heterogeneous Classes in Lower Secondary Schools   101
         Alfred Weinberger and Martina Nussbaumer

9   Values *and* Knowledge Education Meets Conceptual Change for Science Education   111
         Dimitris Pnevmatikos and Panagiota Christodoulou

10   Implementing Value Education in Teaching Units for Newly Arrived Immigrant Pupils in France   120
         Marco Brighenti and Frédérique Brossard Børhaug

SECTION 2
VaKE in Higher Education and Training

11   Training of In-Service Teachers for VaKE   133
         Alfred Weinberger, Dimitris Pnevmatikos and Lydia Linortner

12   Using VaKE with Secondary Science Pre-Service Teachers in Australia   142
         Karen Marangio and Rebecca Cooper

13   Experience in Working with VaKE in the Georgian Higher Education Space   153
         Izabella Petriashvili, Ekaterine Shaverdashvili, Ina Baratashvili and Tamar Mosiashvili

14   Exploring Diverse Cultural Positions in Multicultural French and American Higher Education Student Groups Using VaKE   162
         Grazia Ghellini

CONTENTS   IX

SECTION 3
VaKE in Nonformal Education

15 Promoting the Idea of European Citizenship with VaKE   175
    Sieglinde Weyringer

16 Training of Integration Competences for Female Asylum Seekers and
    Refugees with VaKE   187
    Sieglinde Weyringer, Jean-Luc Patry and Natascha Diekmann

17 "Equal Right to Talk": Fostering Hospitality and Intercultural Dialogue in
    the University of Sanctuary 'Mellie' Project through VaKE   199
    Julie Daniel and Veronica Crosbie

18 The Values *and* Knowledge Education in Transformative Learning   211
    Dimitris Pnevmatikos and Jean-Luc Patry

PART 4
VaKE for Specific Topics

19 Improving Language Skills in EFL Classes through VaKE   223
    Mariam Kilanava

20 VaKE in Teaching the Hearing-Impaired   230
    Lydia Linortner

21 When Value and Moral Are Problematic Concepts: Using VaKE in an
    Intercultural Management Context   236
    Bénédicte Legué

22 Bridging Teaching, Coaching and Interculturalism through VaKE   243
    Jimena Andino Dorato

23 Creating Moral Dilemma Stories for Intercultural Education   252
    Frédérique Brossard Børhaug and Helga Bjørke Harnes

24 VaKE in Healthcare: Using VaKE in Different Healthcare Settings   260
    *Lydia Linortner, Jean-Luc Patry, Dimitris Pnevmatikos, Rachel Eichler
    and Mirjam Tonheim Augestad*

PART 5
Practical Extensions of VaKE

25 Meaningful Teaching Using Moral Dilemmas: From VaKE to DBM   273
    Roxana G. Reichman

26 The VaKE Model through the Lens of a Computer-Supported Collaborative Learning Environment   283
    Tamar Meirovitz and Liat Eyal

27 Civic Media as a Multicultural Dialogue: The Dilemma of Arab and Jewish Students via Documentary Filmmaking in Israel   294
    Evanna Ratner

28 MAaKE – Moral Action *and* Knowledge Education: Considerations on a Practical Model for Moral Action Based on VaKE   300
    Sieglinde Weyringer

PART 6
Research Principles and Prospects for VaKE

29 The Justification of the Double Assignment   319
    Jean-Luc Patry and Alfred Weinberger

30 RAC3 Thinking: Selected Thinking Styles Nurtured with VaKE   331
    Sieglinde Weyringer and Dimitris Pnevmatikos

31 Assessment in VaKE Studies   344
    Jean-Luc Patry and Alfred Weinberger

32 Research Designs for VaKE Studies   359
    Jean-Luc Patry

33 Transdisciplinarity and Trans-Domain Approaches in VaKE   370
    Jean-Luc Patry, Natascha Diekmann and Sieglinde Weyringer

PART 7
Afterthoughts to VaKE

34 Afterthoughts to V*a*KE   393
   Jean-Luc Patry, Sieglinde Weyringer, Frédérique Brossard Børhaug and Dimitris Pnevmatikos

   Index   405

Series Editor's Foreword

Where can we find moral education in schools? This question is not that easy to answer. It looks like it is everywhere, but it is not easy to find.

A lot of the research on moral education focuses on the school culture, on interpersonal relationships of teachers and students, and between students. Regarding the role of the teacher, the teacher is presented as a role model; in how the teacher shows values and interacts with the students. What is often missing in research on moral education is full attention for the content of education, the curriculum.

The V*a*KE approach really addresses values in the curriculum. It is about teaching and learning of values in schools, embedded in the curriculum. It shows how teachers work with values in their concrete educational practices. In more than 10 years the V*a*KE approach has been developed, implemented, and spread. A strong network of researchers has been working together in all kind of activities. Interesting are the different scientific foundations in the V*a*KE community: philosophy, psychology, sociology, pedagogy, and educational studies.

I first learned about V*a*KE in the symposium of the SIG Moral and Democratic Education of the European Association of Learning and Instruction (EARLI) in Greece, in 2008.

And there was a symposium at the EARLI conference in Amsterdam in 2009. V*a*KE started at the University of Salzburg, in the research group of Jean-Luc Patry, but has now important links with other European countries. In particular Norway, Greece and France. There has always been a strong link between V*a*KE and the EARLI SIG Moral and Democratic Education; several former SIG coordinators (Patry, Pnevmatikos, Weinberger) are at the heart of the V*a*KE-movement. It is great that they finish the handbook in the year that the SIG is 25 years old.

Sometimes I was joking: is V*a*KE vague? This handbook shows how a large group of international researchers work with the concept in different educational settings, with different theoretical perspectives and with different research methods. Central is the focus on a critical engagement with moral values in the curriculum. So, I will say: don't be vague ask for V*a*KE.

Wiel Veugelers
Series Editor *Moral Development and Citizenship Education*

Preface

Values without knowledge are blind; knowledge without values is irresponsible – although we were not always aware of that, this principle, and the need to provide education that helps overcome both blindness and irresponsibility has driven us to develop VaKE, to use it in practice, to adapt it to new populations, conditions, topics, and to improve it. We have also presented VaKE at conferences, written papers in journals, book chapters and booklets in several languages. Very often, we were asked to conceive a comprehensive text about VaKE. With the present handbook, we comply with this wish. We asked many researchers and practitioners to write about VaKE, and this is what turned out. The handbook is not comprehensive in that it covers all relevant issues about VaKE; for this, VaKE has evolved too much, and it is used more often than we know of. Nevertheless, the handbook gives a fairly representative picture of the current state of VaKE with respect to its theoretical underpinning, its practical application, and its future perspective, as far as this can be judged. The thirty authors from nine countries testify to the dissemination of VaKE, and the scope of topics addressed to confirm the theoretical richness and the widespread usefulness of the approach. There are plenty of individual experiences of very different kinds reported by the different authors; all of them converge, it seems, to the statement that VaKE is a valuable tool.

For us, the four editors, the decision to edit a book on theory and practice of the didactical approach VaKE – Values *and* Knowledge Education was not an easy one, primarily because this handbook is not the result of an international project: The chapters present and share the single and individual experiences, considerations on modifications, and follow-up ideas of the authors using VaKE with very diverse groups of learners. These experiences have been established very individually over a very long timeline and under very diverse conditions and objectives of the learning process. Such a manifoldness could have been to become growing points to the need for a stable theoretical base, which is also included in this handbook.

The handbook is addressed at practitioners who want to know about VaKE and possibly to use it, as well as at researchers and people interested in the theoretical foundation and research issues related with VaKE. The different groups of readers will start with different chapters within this handbook. With this handbook, we try to stimulate and motivate to look also at the other side of the coin: Practitioners to read about the theory because to apply VaKE successfully, a minimal understanding of this background is essential, and the theoreticians to relate to the practical experiences (and their outcomes) with VaKE.

This aim is shared by all authors. We want to thank all contributors for their willingness to transfer their narrated experiences into a written form, their accuracy regarding the work and deadlines, and their motivation to continue using VaKE. We also thank the editor of the book series on Moral Development and Citizenship Education, Wiel Veugelers, for his encouragement, support, and constructive feedback – we have tried not to be vague about VaKE in this handbook. Furthermore, we thank the staff at Brill, in particular John Bennett, Henriët Graafland and Jolanda Karada, for their passion and constructive attitude when it came to overcoming editorial obstacles.

Figures and Tables

Figures

2.1 Theoretical background of V*a*KE (adapted from Patry et al., 2013, p. 564).   20
5.1 The Values and Development Square (adapted from Schulz von Thun Institut, 2020, p. 1).   68
5.2 Potter Box (based on Guth & Marsh, 2005, p. 264).   69
17.1 Artifact from Mellie participant group, illustrating reasons for demonstrating for climate change response.   205
21.1 Sikh dilemma and retroactions in RH recruitment (© B. Legué, 2018, with kind permission of the student).   238
28.1 Field of potential components of action.   303
31.1 The five pages of the WALK questionnaire used by Pnevmatikos and Patry (2012).   349
32.1 2*2 latin square as a base for the cross-over design.   363
32.2 Prototypical cross-over design.   364
33.1 Trans-Domain Approach (TDA) as the relationships between general theory (GT), domain-specific theories (DT), domains, and research topic.   371

Tables

2.1 Distinction of descriptive and prescriptive statements on two levels.   16
2.2 Stages of moral judgment (adapted from Kohlberg, 1972, p. 14f.).   24
2.3 Prototypical steps in V*a*KE.   29
7.1 A V*a*KE process at primary level (V*a*KE-pr).   97
28.1 Prototypical course of MA*a*KE based on Rubicon model and V*a*KE-*dis*.   311
31.1 Prototypical items for a Lesson-Interruption Method questionnaire.   345
33.1 Different types of TDAs of values, as addressed in dilemmas.   380

Notes on Contributors

Ina Baratashvili
is English language teacher in courses on general and academic level at Tiblisi State University, Georgia. She participated in Erasmus+ projects (DOIT, CURE, ASSET). Her fields of interest are teaching/assessment methodologies. She is the author of textbooks for young learners.

Marco Brighenti
has been departmental administrator in the Academic Center for Education for New Arrivals and Travellers' Children (CASNAV) for the past ten years. He taught French in Laos and history, geography, and citizenship education in a suburb of Paris.

Frédérique Brossard Børhaug
is Professor of Education at VID Specialized University and NLA University College, Norway. Her research deals with intercultural and anti-racist education for promoting more inclusive educational practices for all in respect with the nature/biodiversity.

Panagiota Christodoulou
is a PhD candidate at the Department of Primary Education at the University of Western Macedonia, Greece, and Vice-Secretary of the AVaKE-Association. Her interest is on initiating conceptual change through exploitation of innovative approaches, e.g., VaKE.

Rebecca Cooper
is Senior Lecturer in the Faculty of Education, Monash University, Australia. Her research interests include considering how science teachers and science teacher educators develop pedagogical knowledge and pedagogical content knowledge throughout their career.

Veronica Crosbie
is Assistant Professor in Migration, and Intercultural Studies in Dublin City University. She is the Director of the DCU University of Sanctuary Mellie programme and is currently Chairperson of the Universities of Sanctuary Ireland Committee.

Julie Daniel
is a PhD candidate and scholarship holder in Dublin City University. Her research focuses on storytelling to promote social inclusion for forced migrants. She is also the coordinator of the DCU University of Sanctuary Mellie programme.

Natascha Diekmann
is a PhD candidate at the Department of Educational Research at Paris-Lodron University Salzburg, Austria. Her scientific focus is on education for sustainable development (master thesis at the University of Bielefeld, Germany) and adding values to sustainability education (dissertation).

Jimena Andino Dorato
is Certified Coach (ICF), Certified Mediator and Master in Business Law, France. In four countries and four languages she has combined her coaching approach with her passion for sharing knowledge, accompanying leaders, students, and migrants in their intercultural journey.

Rachel Eichler
is Senior Lecturer, and Director of vision therapy clinics at Hadassah Academic College, Israel. Her research interests are on Optometric education, specifically active learning, and reflective practices. She has gained diverse experience teaching with V*a*KE.

Liat Eyal
is Senior Lecturer at Levinsky College of Education, Israel. Her focus is on educational innovation, hybrid pedagogy and learning technologies in higher education. She directs a program for academic digital leadership and learning design.

Grazia Ghellini
is free-lance Intercultural Communication Trainer and instructor in France. She is currently teaching Business Ethics at the Montpellier Business School, and Interactive Pedagogies and English as a Medium of Instruction at the University of Montpellier, France.

Helga Bjørke Harnes
is Assistant Professor in the social sciences, and PhD-student in teacher education at NLA University College, Norway. Research interests are intercultural education, Values *and* Knowledge Education (V*a*KE), and the concept of 'historical empathy' in educational practices.

Mariam Kilanava

is affiliate Associate professor at European University, Georgia. She was the Head of the Innovative Teaching Methods Training Center. She is a trainer on the innovative teaching/assessing methods in higher education and works at the International Students Admission Office.

Bénédicte Legué

has worked as a manager in the creative industries as well as a teacher and trainer in intercultural studies. She publishes scientific articles on intercultural professional and psychosocial practices.

Lydia Linortner

is a PhD candidate at Paris-Lodron University Salzburg, Austria, and member of the current AVaKE Executive Committee. She combined VaKE with the Tact approach and implemented VaKE in several fields (curriculum for the hearing impaired, training of optometrists and other health care professionals, Teacher Manual for Israeli universities).

Karen Marangio

is Lecturer in the Faculty of Education, Monash University, Australia. Her research relates to science education, including developing pre-service teacher pedagogical knowledge and teaching science in integrated ways to explore its value, complexity, and relevance in society.

Tamar Meirovitz

is Lecturer and teacher educator at Beit Berl College and Mofet R & D Institute, coordinator of Erasmus+ project CURE at David Yellin College, all in Israel. Her research interests are mentorship, dilemmas in teacher education, educational leadership, and digital instruction.

Tamar Mosiashvili

is researcher and Invited Lecturer at the Innovative Education Research Center of Ilia State University, Georgia. As a former high school teacher, she is interested in researching, writing and teaching about connections between settings in teacher policies and practices in schools.

Martina Nussbaumer

is a PhD candidate and former scientific assistant in a research project on VaKE at Paris-Lodron University Salzburg, Austria. Her research interest is on constructivist teaching and learning, moral development, and moral action.

Jean-Luc Patry
is University Emeritus Professor at Paris-Lodron University Salzburg, Austria. He is a founding member of the Association for Values *and* Knowledge Education (AV*a*KE). His research fields include moral education; social interaction in education, particularly situation specificity; theory of science; theory-practice relationship; research methods, etc.

Izabella Petriashvili
is Associate Professor, Faculty of Psychology and Education Sciences, Ivane Javakhishvili Tbilisi State University, Georgia. She was Fulbright Visiting Scholar at North Eastern Illinois University, Chicago, IL, USA. Her research interests are on English language teaching methodology, online teaching, and Values *and* Knowledge Education.

Dimitris Pnevmatikos
is Professor of Developmental Psychology at the University of Western Macedonia, Greece. He is a founding member and currently the President of the Association for Values *and* Knowledge Education (AV*a*KE). His research interests include among others moral development and education, conceptual change, and values education.

Evanna Ratner
is Professor at Gordon Academic College, Haifa University, Israel. She is head of the Film and Media Studies at the Arts Department in the Ministry of Education in Israel; involved in teacher preparation and media literacy; and an expert in "Dialogue through Media" and Peace Education.

Alexandra Reichenwallner
studied at Paris-Lodron University Salzburg and University College of Education of the Diocese of Linz, Austria. She is specialist in social science research methods; teacher for children with special needs; currently working at a primary school and teaching children in the German support class.

Roxana G. Reichman
is Senior Lecturer at Gordon Academic College, Israel, head of the MEd Department of Educational Administration and Organization, and head of the program for retraining academics to teaching. She is an expert in educational administration and comparative education.

NOTES ON CONTRIBUTORS　　　　　　　　　　　　　　　　　　　　　　　　XXI

Ekaterine Shaverdashvili
is Professor of Education at Ilia State University, Georgia, and head of the Innovative Educational Research Center. She worked as the director of the Research Centre for Language Didactics and as an expert in the department of the National Curriculum in the Ministry of Education, Georgia.

Mirjam Tonheim Augestad
is Assistant Professor of Nursing at VID Specialized University, Norway. Her research focus is on the impact of chatbots and artificial intelligence to provide information for patients within cancer care.

Alfred Weinberger
is Professor in Education at Linz, Austria. He studied educational research at Paris-Lodron University Salzburg, Austria, and habilitated at the University of Leipzig, Germany. His research focus is on moral education, constructivist learning and teaching, and teacher education.

Sieglinde Weyringer
is founder and current general secretary of the AVaKE Association, retired Senior Lecturer at the Department of Educational Research at Paris-Lodron University Salzburg, Austria. Her interests are in research and practice of values and citizenship education, high ability studies, and organizational development.

PART 1

VaKE Values and *Knowledge Education – Introducing the Approach*

CHAPTER 1

What Is V*a*KE?

Sieglinde Weyringer, Jean-Luc Patry, Dimitris Pnevmatikos and Frédérique Brossard Børhaug

1 Introduction

Our newspapers are full of news addressing conflicting values with contradictory stakeholder positions, interests, and values. Examples are climate crisis opposing biodiversity and economic prosperity, and Corona pandemics opposing health and social and economic consequences. These issues share two characteristics. They consist of value conflicts that cannot be satisfied simultaneously, and the need to understand conflictual views by developing complex factual knowledge in order to avoid superficial and short-sighted judgments like in conspiracy theories.

Furthermore, in our rapidly changing and pluralist world, citizens are increasingly confronted with situations and problems in which alternative, mutually exclusive options and solutions are potentially acceptable. Different values usually support alternative solutions, and all may be endorsed by (parts of) society. For instance, regarding the examples mentioned above, in the Corona related discourse, there is a complex trade-off between the economy and public health, with regard to how strict restrictions should be and for which regions, areas of activity, and groups of citizens (e.g., Lin & Meissner, 2020). Similarly, the climate crisis concerns the present and the future generations' living, economic prosperity and overall systemic resilience and adaptability. However, although the fact that climate change is a real threat and is increasingly acknowledged, little has been done to fight global warming because this might jeopardise the economy (Trump's policy was a prototype, see Bunch, 2020). Different stakeholders thus defend strongly opposing interests and compete for power.

We believe that decisions in such conflictual situations should be based on evidence, analytical thinking, and values reflection. A key strategy in any decision-making is thus to make explicit in what way each possible solution to a complex problem is linked with sets of values and knowledge, and the decision of which solution to choose becomes a matter of prioritising one set of values/knowledge over another. Reflection and decision-making are not only fundamental for experts, but also crucial to citizens who have to decide in antinomic situations in everyday life and should justify, accept and implement their decisions. Hence, all citizens should be prepared to understand these processes and decide competently. In education, then, a key question is *how do we prepare citizens for handling complexity using knowledge and value reflection*?

2   VaKE as an Innovative Teaching Approach

Unfortunately, in dominant teaching approaches, values and knowledge are often taught separately. If values are addressed at all, they are usually taught the same way as the curricular contents: After being told what knowledge to learn, the students are informed what moral dimension of this knowledge has to be learnt without delving further into complexity. For instance, when students are taught about technology and the need for hyper-connected devices, they might hear a discourse-friendly narrative on digital technology and human progress without looking deeper into relational impact for less privileged humans and between humans and nature. Then, the students acquire insufficiently the skills and procedures to judge by themselves the appropriateness of different options in complex circumstances where different values compete. Furthermore, decisions that entail morality are frequently influenced by the emotions that individuals experience. For instance, for participating in the 'Fridays for Future' demonstrations, the decision rests on the participation of friends as much as on one's own moral conviction (Wallis & Loy, 2021). In our experience, it is not enough to inform students about the importance of knowledge-based evidence in their decisions. It is also necessary to experience ambivalent emotions as critical thinkers and to reflect on the activated psychological mechanisms.

VaKE offers an innovative teaching-learning method that permits addressing the above issues in a more sophisticated and appropriate way. It combines values education in the sense of fostering moral judgment, and active, self-directed learning of knowledge from the acquisition of knowledge to analysis, synthesis, and evaluation. The letters "V" and "K" in the acronym *VaKE* indicate the two pillars of the method, which are *values* and *knowledge*, and the letter "E" stands for *education*. The letter "*a*" in italics denotes the combination and relationship between the two pillars of the method, namely the Values Education *and* Knowledge Education.

A VaKE workshop starts with a well-structured dilemma story where a protagonist has to decide on an issue; whatever option the protagonist chooses, she or he will break some moral norms. The participants in the workshop have to decide which option the protagonist should prefer. The dilemma is structured to facilitate participants to identify themselves with the protagonist who has to make the decision. Thus, the protagonist's dilemma becomes the participants' dilemma. Furthermore, the dilemma is conceived in such a way that for its discussion, it is necessary to use some knowledge. An example for a dilemma is the following:

> Emilie (…) teaches 18 year 7 pupils at a small, rural school. Most of them have lived their whole lives in the small town where the school is, four have moved from other places in the country. One of them is Saida, born in Somalia and brought up in Bergen, Norway. She has been in the class for two years, does well at school and speaks Norwegian. Emilie is about to plan the following month's teaching in the social sciences and wants to cover the learning aims: the use of maps, to understand the interrelatedness of natural resources and ways of life, comparison between countries in Europe and countries on other continents, and migration. She has an idea for a project that will fulfil many of the competence aims: What if she asks the pupils to compare Norway and Somalia? The next day, Emilie mentions the project to Saida, and Saida spontaneously answers: "Do we have to?" Emilie replies, "Well, we don't have to, why?" "There is so much about war and piracy and starvation when they talk about Somalia in the media. I want the others to think I am from Norway".
>
> *Should Emilie go through with a project of comparison that emphasizes Saida's Somali background?* (see Chapter 23 in this handbook).

The moral norms and values at stake are for instance: care, to address difficult issues, to ensure the integrity of the girl, to show empathy, belonging in a multicultural state, wellbeing, inclusive practices, seeing opportunities instead of challenges. The necessary knowledge base refers for instance to young (Somali) immigrants in Norway, geographical identity, media treatment of Somalia and bullying in school.

The dilemma triggers argumentations, critical thinking, and reflections. Students are looking for evidence to support or defend the expressed or even hypothetical arguments. In the end, they conclude with one or two decisions and relevant actions. They acquire the planned knowledge effortlessly while becoming aware of the cognitive mechanisms and procedures to follow to come to safe conclusions. They acknowledge that different values are behind the suggested solutions. They learn, thus, to connect the decisions or solutions with the ethical issues.

VaKE has similarities with many other teaching methods. However, VaKE is a unique teaching-learning method as it combines different approaches. On one hand, addressing dilemmas to moral education is not new. Several current methods take advantage of dilemma discussions to address moral issues and values. On the other hand, however, VaKE goes beyond values education by combining it with inquiry-based learning, i.e., the participants ask questions about knowledge (that they need to discuss the dilemma) and search autonomously for answers. Hence, a typical moral dilemma is not necessarily an appropriate dilemma for VaKE. Rather, through VaKE dilemmas, participants should be moved to acquire new knowledge according to the group's scope and use this knowledge in their decisions and actions.

Workshop leaders (e.g., teachers) can apply VaKE flexibly and adapt the method to their own or their audience's needs. The method proposes a series of steps that have been shown to be effective in class settings. This series of steps can be modified in order to serve the particular needs of the class. In this handbook, the reader will find numerous variations of VaKE and examples of implementing VaKE in different educational settings.

3   Why Should I Use VaKE?

As an educator you might ask yourself: *Why should I use VaKE?* In our days, an educator in any setting has many teaching-learning methods available. Is there any reason to implement VaKE instead of another method? Regardless of the teaching method, some people indeed find a way to learn what the educator expects him or her to learn. Many of them are motivated to do this for instrumental reasons, such as to pass the class, to have an excellent evaluation or to get a diploma or a formal qualification. In contrast, VaKE is a method that motivates students through self-determination (Ryan & Deci, 2017) to engage in the dilemma and to look for the relevant information to support one or another option in a collaborative effort. Thus, participants discuss appropriate moral justifications and search for information, they construct their own moral and knowledge framework to support or reject the discussion's arguments, and they get feedback from their peers whether this framework can be considered as valid. And often, in the end, the educators acquire new knowledge as well. Participants also benefit from learning procedural knowledge on how to formulate and support arguments, test hypotheses, distinct beliefs from evidence, become more analytical and critical thinkers, become more open-minded and seek for the truth. They also learn to solve real problems improving their creativity and connect the solutions with concrete actions in the community. Finally, VaKE shows how one can connect knowledge education with ethical issues, one of the recommendations in most (if not all) national curricula (e.g., Pnevmatikos & Patry, 2014) and one of key challenges for the 21st century.

Evidence for all of the above mentioned is documented in the chapters of the present handbook. However, this evidence does not permit the claim that VaKE is the only approach that satisfies these conditions; but we do not know of another one. We also do not claim that VaKE should replace all traditional teaching and education; rather, we consider it as one additional didactical choice in the educator's practice to be used when judged appropriate.

4 How and for What Audiences Can I Use VaKE?

Educators can use VaKE whenever they want, considering the needs of their classes and their curricula. It is recommended to start progressively using VaKE. The use of VaKE on an everyday basis in school might demand modifications in curricula. However, in training or lifelong education, VaKE could even be the primary teaching method.

VaKE has been used in various educational settings, both within formal and non-formal education, as it is documented in the chapters in this handbook. The method has been used in primary and secondary education for many different subject matters or intradisciplinary settings (Part 3, Section 1). VaKE has also been used at the university level (Part 3, Section 2) and in training across many disciplines or lifelong education in diverse settings (Part 3, Section 3). With some transformations, the method has also even been used in kindergarten classes (e.g., Linortner, 2008). Thus, there are just a few limits to the age groups or disciplines that one could use the method. One is that the participants must be able to follow arguments and to argue themselves, be it even on a low level. Secondly, for using the method effectively it is necessary to formulate an appropriate dilemma for the particular group of learners, which is not always easy to achieve. However, many indicative examples of dilemmas from diverse pedagogical settings are given throughout this handbook.

As with any didactical method, educators need to be trained to prepare and implement VaKE in their own educational settings. Throughout this handbook, many tips are given. Our strongest advice is to start with preparing a good dilemma story (see Chapter 4) that will trigger discussions in the group and lead participants into the acknowledgement that they lack the necessary information to make a safe decision. Workshop leaders should be creative when formulating dilemma stories that will motivate and lead participants to seek evidence-based knowledge and performative values reflection. For the first time using VaKE, it is also recommended to follow the prototypical sequence of steps. After having experienced the method several times, educators can make necessary adaptations and changes if needed for the particular group. Many examples are provided here that show variations in their implementation.

5   What Are the Scientific Bases for VaKE?

VaKE is a theory-based teaching-learning method that is based on the idea that students construct their concepts (moral judgment; knowledge) in their interaction with their social environment. Psychological theories in alignment with this idea are used to support the foundation of the method, and several scientific traditions are combined into a single theoretical framework. It includes the constructivist theories of Piaget (i.e., the distinction of assimilation and accommodation; Piaget, 1985), Kohlberg (moral judgment development, Kohlberg, 1984; dilemma discussion method, Blatt & Kohlberg, 1975), from Vygotskian tradition (i.e., the zone of proximal development; Vygotsky, 1978), from framework theories (i.e., conceptual change approach; Vosniadou, 2012), social domain theories (i.e., mixed-domain situations where different values compete, Nucci, Turiel, & Roded, 2017; Turiel & Banas, 2020), and transformative learning (Mezirow, 2009); all of these theories are described in this handbook. Moreover, throughout this handbook, the reader will find teaching methods that stress problem-based learning, inquiry-based learning, and collaborative learning.

At last, VaKE has been implemented and tested in many different disciplines, educational settings, and countries. The research studies showed that VaKE systematically triggers the students' motivation, facilitating the acquisition of the expected knowledge even with complex concepts in science, mathematics, and engineering (see for instance Chapter 9 in this handbook).

6   The Current Handbook

Although many journal articles, books and book chapters addressing the method of VaKE as a whole or specific issue thereof have been published, the present handbook is the first systematic and comprehensive presentation of the Values *and* Knowledge Education method. Many VaKE courses have been implemented in the last fifteen years around the world, among others, in Australia, Austria, France, Georgia, Germany, Greece, Ireland, Israel, and Norway. All these experiences show the dynamic of this teaching-learning method. Participants and educators involved in a VaKE course often express their enthusiasm for the method. Moreover, in times of an uncertain future, complex issues that link science with its ethical aspects is one of the critical challenges for the 21st century. For many of them, there is no time to waste. However, most teachers acknowledge that they do not know how to do this (Gruber, 2009; see also Chapter 10). This handbook is written to help educators by offering a theory-based and successfully evaluated method to meet some of our era's challenges.

But this handbook is not only about combining scientific knowledge and values reflection. VaKE is also an important teaching-learning method that stimulates and motivates the participants. For those educators who are looking for new insights to implement in their teaching, this handbook will offer a new set of options and hope because it might be only the starting point to discover, understand and implement a new method. Practitioners and researchers are also invited to join the VaKE family, the Association of Values and Knowledge Education (AVaKE), a worldwide non-profit organisation aiming to exchange ideas and spread the method and to establish a research community to test and expand the method (see VaKE.eu).

Last but not least, we want to mention that there are different ways to read this handbook. The most typical one would be starting from the first chapter until the last chapter. However, the reader might start from another chapter. For instance, you may prefer to know the theory behind the method in more detail and to do research studies with or for VaKE. In Part 6, the authors focus on some essential and indicative aspects and present several research principles and prospects recommended for designing and testing the effectiveness of implementing VaKE in an area beyond those presented elsewhere in this handbook.

Another reader might be more interested in general practical recommendations. In Part 2, much concrete advice and tools are presented in order to prepare and implement participant learning in VaKE courses effectively. Although the concept of the teacher is mainly used here, teachers are pedagogues which may stand in many diverse pedagogical contexts, not only at school, and this Part intends to englobe this larger group as well as their addressees.

Part 3 addresses different interests in practice at different levels of education, such as primary and secondary school levels, in Part 3, Section 1. The design of school teaching is linked both to teaching principles (e.g., adaptation to the level of development of the learners) and to institutional and systemic framework conditions (e.g., timetable, curriculum, legal requirements). These guidelines also apply to the use of VaKE in school classes. Therefore, VaKE is recommended to complement traditional teaching, not as a substitute for best established didactic and methodological approaches and practices. Due to these conditions, adaptations of the prototypical course of VaKE are recommended or necessary.

In higher education (Part 3, Section 2), the audience (Universities, University Colleges) differs in important ways from the pupils in primary and secondary school. First, the students have more elaborate subjective theories, both with regard to values (stage of moral judgment; the reflection of values in general and their own values in particular) and to knowledge (particularly, specific knowledge that they have dealt with in their studies). Second, the aim of using VaKE is often not only to provide values and knowledge education with respect to some particular set of topics but also – and often primarily – to empower the students to use VaKE themselves as teachers or workshop leaders of their pupils. Since many of the authors in this handbook work in teacher education, there are also many studies in this field.

Due to its adaptability, VaKE suits well to non-formal education as well (see Part 3, Section 3). This last subsection provides diverse examples of VaKE implemented in broader pedagogical contexts.

In Part 4, the focus is on using VaKE in diverse educational settings for specific topics, on the analyses, whether and how VaKE can be used or needs to be adapted for that, and on the experiences with VaKE. The flexibility of VaKE is shown concerning the topic (language teaching; intercultural education), specific participants (students with particular characteristics, like hearing impaired students), students with particular conceptions of the role of values, intercultural students and participants from health care

The use of VaKE also encourages further independent developments and radical implementation in and adaptations of established research and teaching activities. The articles in Part 5 present selected models and ideas beyond VaKE. Furthermore, they want to broaden the horizon for future thematic priorities in the research and practice of VaKE.

The book can also be read with a specific focus such as intercultural education (Chapters 10, 14, 18, 23, 27); science education (Chapter 9), health (Chapters 20, 24), citizenship matters (Chapters 15, 16), assessment (Chapter 31) and many other topics.

The handbook thus is written as a *hypertext*; using the index at the end of the handbook might help the readers to navigate through it.

All texts are originals and specially written for this book

We wish you a profitable and enjoyable reading!

References

Blatt, M. M., & Kohlberg, L. (1975). The effects of classroom moral discussion upon children's level of moral judgment. *Journal of Moral Education, 4*(2), 129–161. doi:10.1080/0305724750040207

Bunch, E. (2020). *7 things to know about Trump's perspectives and policies regarding climate change*. New York, NY: Well + Good. Retrieved April 5, 2021, from https://www.wellandgood.com/donald-trump-climate-plan/

Fridays for Future. (2021). *Fridays for future*. Retrieved April 5, 2021, from https://fridaysforfuture.org

Gruber, M. (2009b). Barriers to value education in schools – what teachers think. *Newsletter from EARLI SIG 13 Moral and Democratic Education, 5*, 23–30.

Kohlberg, L. (1984). *Essays on moral development: Vol. 2. The psychology of moral development*. San Francisco, CA: Harper & Row.

Lin, Z., & Meissner, C. M. (2020). Health vs. wealth? Public health policies and the economy during Covid-19. Working Paper 27099. Cambridge, MA: National Bureau of Economic Research. Retrieved April, 5, 2021 from http://www.nber.org/papers/w27099.

Linortner, L. (2008). *VaKE im Kindergarten* [Unveröffentlichte Bachelorarbeit]. Paris Lodron Universität Salzburg.

Mezirow, J. (2009). An overview on transformative learning. In K. Illeris (Ed.), *Contemporary theories of learning* (pp. 90–105). London, UK: Routledge.

Nucci, L., Turiel, E., & Roded, A. D. (2017). Continuities and discontinuities in the development of moral judgments. *Human Development, 60*(6), 279–341.

Piaget, J. (1985). *The equilibration of cognitive structures: The central problem of intellectual development*. Chicago, IL: University of Chicago Press.

Pnevmatikos, D., & Patry, J.-L. (2014). Combining values and knowledge teaching through the dilemma's discussion. In E. Katsarou & M. Liakopoulou (Eds.), *Instruction and "Bildung" issues in multicultural school environment: Unit 3, students' psycho-social support: Psychological and sociological approaches* (pp. 555–575). Thessaloniki: Ministry of Education.

Ryan, R. M., & Deci, E. L. (2017). *Self-determination theory: Basic psychological needs in motivation, development, and wellness*. New York, NY: The Guilford Press.

Turiel, E., & Banas, K. A. (2020). The development of moral and social judgments: Social contexts and processes of coordination. *Eurasian Journal of Educational Research, 85*, 23–44. https://dergipark.org.tr/en/pub/ejer/issue/52308/684952

Vosniadou, S. (2012). *International handbook of science education* (2nd ed.). Dordrecht, The Netherlands: Springer.

Vygotsky, L. S. (1978). *Mind in society: The development of higher psychological processes*. Cambridge, MA: Harvard University Press.

CHAPTER 2

V*a*KE: Theory, Prototype, and Variations

Jean-Luc Patry and Sieglinde Weyringer

1 Introduction

Values *and* Knowledge Education (V*a*KE) is a constructivist teaching-learning approach that combines values education and knowledge acquisition. It starts with a moral dilemma discussion (values education) that leads to inquiry-based learning (knowledge acquisition). A moral dilemma is a situation in which the protagonist has to choose between two (moral) values; whatever he or she does, he or she will break one of the values; in some dilemmas, e.g., from history or literature, the issue is whether the protagonist is guilty or not, or whether he or she was entitled to act as he or she did. In V*a*KE, in addition to addressing moral values, the dilemmas are conceived in such a way to trigger questions relating to knowledge.

To get a first impression of V*a*KE, let us look at the following example (from Weinberger, 2006). The students, grades 5 and 6, were presented the following dilemma:

> *The nuclear power plant*
> Family Bauer lives in a small Austrian town (...). The father, a building worker, is unemployed (...). The mother cares for the household and for the three children Mario (13), Tina (12) and Peter (3). Peter suffers from a life-threatening disease and needs expensive medication. (...) If the father does not find work soon, Peter's life will be jeopardized.
>
> They learn that close to the city, a (...) nuclear power plant is going to be built. The works will start in two months, and building workers are wanted. (...)
>
> What should the family do? (translated from Weinberger, 2006, p. 52)

The question is whether the father should take the job or not. Values education (in the sense of Blatt & Kohlberg, 1975) is addressed through the opposing values. Those attached to taking the job are, among others, that the family can survive, and Peter can get his medication. In contrast, a refusal of the employment offer would comply with values like avoiding the threats of nuclear power plants. The dilemma leads to knowledge questions, such as functioning and risks of nuclear power plants, which the participants then search to answer through inquiry-based learning (e.g., Furtak et al., 2012). After that, the moral dilemma discussion will continue on a higher level, with a better knowledge foundation, e.g., on the accident in Chernobyl, on radioactivity and ensuing health hazards. The procedure of dilemma discussion and search for information can be repeated if necessary. Finally, there is a synthesis (in the example, a role-play of a discussion panel with proponents of the nuclear power plant) and a generalization (here: a discussion on the nuclear power plant in Three Miles Island and the nuclear policy in Austria with the plant in Zwentendorf which had been built, but following a public vote, was never activated).

This chapter presents the theories that underlie VaKE, the steps that are proposed for implementing VaKE, and variations that have been developed for specific purposes and audiences. In Part 2, the central concepts of VaKE and their relationships are explained. Then, the specific theoretical underpinning of VaKE is presented. Next, the steps of prototypical VaKE processes are discussed. We finish with some conclusions.

2 Basic Concepts

In this section, we define and explain the basic concepts that will be used in the presentation of the different issues of VaKE. A first set deals separately with the concepts that underlie the argumentation in general, without explicit reference to VaKE. Then, the two key concepts of VaKE, *knowledge* and *values*, and their relationships will be presented.

2.1 *Constructivism*

The general framework underlying all of our work is *constructivism*. Since many different types of constructivism have been developed in educational theory and research (e.g., Phillips, 1995), and since we have some specific concepts of constructivism (Patry, 2016), it is necessary here to explain some key issues that will be used later on.

The premise of constructivism is that learning is an active construction process by the learner and not a "passing on" of information (Foerster, 1972). This means that people build *subjective theories* and check them for *viability*. These two terms need to be clarified ahead of discussing constructivism.

Viability is a concept that has replaced truth in the constructivist theory building. Glasersfeld defines viability as follows.

Simply put, (...) an action, operation, conceptual structure, or even a theory, is considered 'viable' as long as it is useful in accomplishing a task or in achieving a goal that one has set for oneself. Thus, instead of claiming that knowledge is capable of representing a world outside of our experience, we would say that knowledge is a tool within the realm of experience. (1998, p. 24)

This means that a person has a *viability criterion*, i.e., a set of conditions that the concept has to fulfil to be regarded as viable. He or she has to check whether the concept meets the viability criterion; we call this the *viability check* (Patry, 2014a; Weinberger, 2006).

In the example of the nuclear power plant, the viability criterion is whether an argument is seen as contributing to the discussion and pertinent. An argument is viable for a participant of the VaKE process if he or she is satisfied with the justification given for the respective option, even if he or she may not agree with this position. For instance, although being against nuclear power plants, he or she agrees that Peter's health is an important issue, even if he or she thinks that other viable arguments – against nuclear power plants – are more important.

Subjective theories in the sense of Groeben et al. (1988) are complex aggregates or networks of cognitions which refer to one's interpretations of oneself and the world which are claimed to be viable. Such networks can be interpreted as systems of generalized[1] statements, consisting of subjectively relevant elements referring to presumed facts or values (including cognitions about situations, goals, possible actions, etc.) and argumentative relations between these elements. They have the same functions for the individual as scientific theories have for the scientific community, namely description, explanation, prediction, guidance for action, and representation and justification of values and norms (Patry & Gastager, 2017). In contrast to scientific theories, they are not explicit, but need to be reconstructed (ibid.), and the viability checks focus not on critical evaluation, but rather on uncritical confirmation of hypotheses (Furnham, 1988; Perrez, 1991).

In the dilemma discussion, at the beginning, the participants had very different subjective theories about nuclear power plants, their risks, and their potential impact on health. They first read a book about the spread of radioactivity following the Chernobyl accident to have at least some common knowledge base. Their subjective theories about the values were also different; for instance, some think that providing energy from whatever source has a high priority, whereas others think the source of energy matters very much.

In constructivism, learning and development mean that the person changes his or her system of subjective theories with respect to the phenomenon as perceived (e.g., he or she has a more differentiated subjective theory about the impact of radioactivity on health than before the VaKE process), provided that it is seen as viable. Based on Piaget's theory (e.g., 1985), this process can be described as follows:

1. Any *perception* is theory dependent (Hanson, 1958); e.g., the interpretation of the dilemma depends on how much a participant already knows about nuclear power plants. Arguments about the societal impact of nuclear power plants, however, might not be understood due to initial lack of comprehension of societal relationships.
2. *Judgment of viability*: Only if the perceived content is considered relevant and viable under the given circumstances, will the information be further proceeded; e.g., for most people, arguments related to health issues – whether Peter's disease or health hazards from radioactivity – are seen as highly relevant, but the preferred arguments may be different.
3. *Assimilation*: If the information fits the subjective theory, it will be integrated; this is what Piaget called *assimilation*. If the participant already knows something about radiation, he or she can distinguish different types of radiation, including gamma radiation.
4. *Disequilibrium*: If assimilation is not possible, there is a disequilibrium (in the terms of Piaget), i.e., a contradiction between different parts of the system of subjective theories; the person then has two possibilities:
    a. He or she can say that the phenomenon belongs to another realm or domain than the actual subjective theory, and the two domains (the one from the original subjective theory and the one with the new phenomenon) are seen as independent from each other,[2] which may lead to situation specificity (Patry, 2019): In one situation one domain is viable and another domain in the other. For instance, in the (new) context of nuclear power plants, radiation is seen as dangerous, in the context of medical diagnosis, which the participant has experienced, e.g., with his or her dentist, X-rays are seen as beneficial. That X-rays are also radiation and dangerous is not recognised.
    b. Or the person will change the subjective theory (*accommodation* in terms of Piaget). For instance, since X-rays are invisible, people tend not to suspect they are dangerous; when confronted with the fact that X-rays are radiation and with the evidence of diseases obviously caused by radioactivity, they change their subjective theory about the visibility of danger sources.[3]

2.2   Is and Ought

As VaKE is dealing with values and knowledge, we need to distinguish Is and Ought: *Is* refers to facts or descriptive statements, *Ought* to norms or prescriptive statements. We take a non-naturalistic stance: Descriptive and prescriptive statements are clearly distinct, and one cannot draw a conclusion from one to the other (Hume, 1739/1896, pp. 244f.). In particular, the fact that something is the case cannot be used as justification for regarding a norm as justified – this would be the naturalistic fallacy which we reject (see Morscher, 2018).

The system used in the following is represented in Table 2.1. On one hand, there are Is and Ought statements (columns), on the other scientific and subjective theories (rows). The scientific discourse addresses empirical research (cell 1 in Table 2.1) and ethics (cell 2); the persons' beliefs can be about Is (knowledge, 3) and about Ought (values, 4). If a person expresses a value statement, hence, he or she says what he or she believes is (morally) required (cell 4). Scientists' descriptions of these beliefs are descriptions of what a person's values are (cell 1). A person's knowledge, in contrast, is the set of a person's beliefs about what is the case and relations between these phenomena (3).

2.3   Knowledge

Knowledge education is one part of VaKE; this refers to the education towards cell 3 in Table 2.1: In a general sense, knowledge means that the person has some information about facts, contents, etc. in his or her subjective theories; he or she is able to do something with this information and is aware of it (meta-cognition). Taxonomies of knowledge can be found in the classical taxonomy

TABLE 2.1   Distinction of descriptive and prescriptive statements on two levels (the numbers refer to the text)

	Knowledge	Values and norms
Scientific statements	(1) Empirical research (Descriptive theories and data)	(2) Ethics (Principles as guidelines for morally good decisions and actions; normative)
Subjective theories	(3) Knowledge (Contents, facts; descriptive)	(4) Values convictions (Material and immaterial values/tangible and intangible assets; descriptive when described by researchers; normative from the perspective of the person)

of cognitive educational objectives by Bloom et al. (1956) and its extension by Anderson et al. (2001). In simplification of the cognitive process dimension, three levels can be distinguished. The lower level refers to the dimensions; remembering, understanding, and applying, which means dealing with the knowledge itself, while the higher levels are analysing and creating (or synthesising), which means going beyond the core knowledge. The third level, evaluation, is distinguished from the second level because it addresses values, which are a topic of its own in VaKE.

We assume that the learners consider the acquired knowledge (of any taxonomic type) as viable for some purpose, that is, it satisfies some viability criteria from the point of view of the learners. This does not mean, however, that their peers necessarily share this viability judgment. Furthermore, the means used for viability checks (Patry, 2014a) may be more or less appropriate, as mentioned above about subjective theories. One aim in VaKE, then, is to provide opportunities for appropriate viability checks through using reliable sources and social problem solving (see Section 3.1).

2.4 *Values*

Values are defined as statements about what is *desirable*, what is good or bad etc. In our concept of values, we include norms, i.e., binding prescriptions about what *should* be the case (e.g., what one should do). They are, first of all, the response to one of Kant's (1787/1998, p. 677, A805/B833) key questions in philosophy: "What should I do?". Secondly, they can be responses to questions like "What is good?", "What is beautiful?", etc. For the discussion, we must distinguish the *philosophical* claims and the ethics (cell 2 in Table 2.1), which are independent from whether someone believes in them or not, from what people actually *believe* about what should be done, what is good or beautiful, etc. The latter are the subjects' subjective theories (cell 4 in Table 2.1), and statements about those are descriptive as they deal with the question "What is the case?" with respect to the subjects' belief systems (cell 1). For instance, from an ethical point of view, saving lives has a higher priority than economy, which may lead to question the ethical viability of nuclear power plants (cell 2); for an employee in the plant, however, the personal economic benefits of working in the plant can be perceived as more important than the risks of a nuclear catastrophe, hence his or her subjective hierarchy of the values in the dilemma may differ from the ethical one (cell 4), and this is described by a scientist who interviewed the worker (cell 1).

A subject's values (cell 4) are ideas and basic attitudes about what a good life is; they are also used by them as an orientation for their decisions and actions. In this understanding, values are given a function of meaningfulness. Meaning and value are inseparably linked and related to each other: What makes sense is valuable and vice versa. The aspect of will comes to the fore: Values become imaginary points of reference for human action. They give support to the human being and at the same time they anchor the person in the social group with which she or he shares these ideas. For Higgins and Gordon (1986, p. 268), values are an expression of individual identity. In his or her values, one can recognise the image a person has of him- or herself, as well as who he or she wants to be.

Countless classification systems can be found in the scientific literature. For our further theoretical argumentation as well as for the practice of V*a*KE, four aspects are emphasized: (1) the distinction between material and immaterial values; (2) the diverse categories of conflict related to a dilemma; (3) the phenomenon of the individual hierarchy of values or, in other words, the setting of value priorities in the practice of daily decisions; and (4) the phenomenon that several distinct values can be relevant in the same situation.

(1) To put it simply, *material values* can be mapped with numbers. A higher number usually represents an added value – in a comparison this connotes "better than". As the name suggests, these values are connected with matter, quantity, size, etc. For *intangible values*, an extensive field for systemization possibilities is spreading: moral and non-moral (Lickona, 1991), instrumental and terminal (Rokeach, 1973), theoretical, utilitarian, aesthetic, social, individualistic and traditional (Spranger, 1928), power, achievement, hedonism, stimulation, self-direction, universalism, benevolence, tradition, conformity, security and super-grouping (Schwartz, 1992), religious, social, aesthetical, ecological, technical/functional, psychological, egocentric, economic, scientific, educational, profession-specific, democratic, political, European, national, culture-specific, society-specific, social-class-specific, civic, human/universal, traditional, individual, collective, deontological, emotional, etc. values.

Values of some kind (e.g., immaterial, or deontological ones) per se are not "better than others", "good" or "bad", "right" or "wrong", "positive" or "negative". An appropriate assignment is only suitable in the sense of an evaluation, i.e., to what extent it is appropriate to consider a certain value in the search for a conflict solution. An example is caring for one's child versus egocentrism: On security training courses, one is instructed first to care for oneself, and only afterwards for one's child; in contrast, in an emergency situation caring for the child might prevail.

(2) *Classifications* describe and possibly prescribe directions of thought, which in turn establish rules according to which assignments can be made. For our concern – the theoretical foundation of V*a*KE – it is irrelevant to which category a certain value can be assigned (e.g., human dignity, the protection

of life, etc.). Rather, the premise in V*a*KE is that a value can be viewed under several directions of thought (e.g. the protection of life seen from a religious, democratic, human rights or societal point of view), and depending on these, different decision options arise – in V*a*KE this is one category of conflicts related to the dilemmas (Yang, 2017; see Legué, Chapter 21 in this handbook: value registers in the sense of Heinich, 2017). Another category of dilemma conflict is opposing values, e.g., protection of a minority and economic development: Both values are seen from a socio-cultural point of view.

(3) This example leads to the third aspect: the *value hierarchy* or values priorities. Concepts of personality and identity are constructed by the establishment, awareness, and constitution of an individual values system, which enables a person to decide what actions are valuable and how they wish to be. Theoretical concepts of "moral character" (Plato, Aristotle) and "habitus" (Bourdieu, 1977) address the ideal that follows specific principles or a set of values regardless of situational constraints, i.e., on a highly abstract level. The demands of everyday life require, on a much more concrete level, a variability of priorities depending on the situation (Patry, 2018, 2019).

(4) Finally, we can hold *several values simultaneously* in the same situation; many of these values cannot be achieved or respected simultaneously (antinomies of values). Life, and particularly education, are full of antinomies, one can even say that antinomies are characteristic for education (Winkel, 1988; Schlömerkemper, 2006; Patry, 2012a). The moral dilemmas in moral education and as starting points of V*a*KE are based on such antinomies (see the health of Peter vs. threats of nuclear power plants). Since different subjects may have different value hierarchies, they can hold varying and contradicting priorities with respect to the options of the protagonist in a given dilemma.

3   Theoretical Background of V*a*KE

In this section, the theoretical background that led to the development of V*a*KE is presented. The knowledge of this theory is not only necessary for the researchers, but also for the practitioners because V*a*KE is not a recipe to be followed blindly, but a method that needs to be adapted to specific conditions, provided that it is done in agreement with the theory (see also Section 4 below for some adaptations that have been used). Furthermore, the theory is required to understand the relationship with the other theories and the integration thereof into the V*a*KE framework.

Our experience with moral education in the Kohlbergian tradition (e.g., Oser et al., 1991) confirmed previous experiences that dilemma discussions

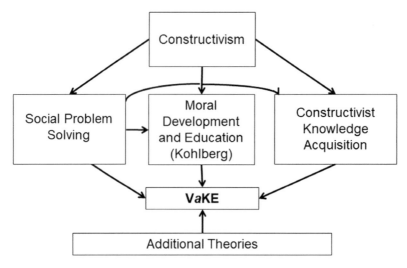

FIGURE 2.1 Theoretical background of V*a*KE (adapted from Patry et al., 2013, p. 564)

are highly motivating (see also Krebs & Denton, 2005). In the tradition of Blatt & Kohlberg (1975), the dilemma discussions were mainly with artificial dilemmas. In contrast, Aufenanger, Garz and Zutavern (1981, pp. 108–1 34) used dilemmas related to curricular content (e.g., historical episodes). Within the knowledge acquisition framework, approaches were developed based on dilemma discussions that focused uniquely on knowledge, and the aim to have an impact on moral competence was explicitly rejected (Bohse, 1982). Combining these different approaches led us to conceive V*a*KE (Patry, 2000), based on several theories which are connected, as presented in Figure 2.1 and which will be discussed below. Constructivism has already been explained above (Section 2.1) and will not be repeated here.

3.1 Social Problem-Solving

The discussions in the V*a*KE process are a special case of social problem-solving. They are social because the dilemma discussions are done in groups, and they are problem-solving since the dilemma story poses problems for which the participants look for solutions. However, the problem is not such that there is one and only one appropriate, or even a presumably best solution. The key issue is that the participant must be satisfied with the proposed denouement, i.e., consider it as viable, and therefore, in agreement with the constructivist perspective, different participants may have different viability criteria and thus be satisfied with different denouements; this includes which option for the protagonist of the dilemma the participant chooses, but also the argumentations, i.e., the justifications for (and against) this decision. This requires a special discussion with respect to problem-solving.

Social or collaborative problem-solving refers here not only to factual issues (e.g., answering factual questions), which is the traditional topic of the problem-solving discussions, but also to values or moral issues and their justification (normative from the point of view of the decider).

In human problem-solving, the problem has to be identified (e.g., Bailey & Im-Bolter, 2020), which determines the viability criterion; then a process of trial and error with three elements follows: variation of possible solutions, evaluation and selection of the solution that satisfied the viability criterion best, and retention of this best solution (e.g., Popper, 1972; Campbell, 1960, 1982). These four elements, (1) identification of the problem, (2) variation, (3) evaluation and (4) selection, retention will be discussed in detail.

(1) *Problem identification*. According to constructivism, the same stimulus constellation can be perceived and interpreted differently by different people (see above). For a fruitful dilemma discussion, it is important that the participants have a common understanding of the key issues in the dilemma. Since the dilemma is a moral one, this means that the values at stake in the dilemma must be clarified – at least some of them, as in the course of the discussion, the participants might identify further values that the creator of the dilemma had not anticipated. Furthermore, if the workshop leader or organiser pursues a certain goal (e.g., to fulfil curricular requirements), he or she has to ensure that the participants have an understanding of the dilemma that refers to this goal.

For the knowledge part, the identification of the problem is simpler: The participants ask questions, i.e., the problems are not given by outsiders; rather, these are genuinely the participants' own issues, coming from their own discussions, so that the context of the questions are well known. Misunderstandings or misinterpretations, hence, are less likely than if the problems are external, as it is typical for direct teaching situations.

(2) *Variation* means that many possible solutions to the problem are proposed. These variations are done on the base of one's subjective theories; people might focus on certain types of solutions but can also be triggered by peer propositions to change the focus, as in brainstorming (Osborne, 1956, p. 298ff.: "joint ideation"). In the dilemma discussion, the participants come up with different value issues and hierarchies and different justifications for them.

In the case of knowledge acquisition through VaKE, there are two issues:
- There are several questions to which the participants search for possible answers. The questions may be related to each other, or completely independent. In the dilemma on the nuclear power plant, the focus was on atomic

power (How many people die in an explosion? How high is the risk of an accident? What are the protection measures? How is the technical equipment of a nuclear power plant? What happened exactly in Chernobyl?; etc.) but also on health (What is the impact of radiation? Which organs are most concerned?; etc.).
- Maybe the participants find different answers to the same question (e.g., when they look up homepages from contrary interest groups, e.g., promoters of nuclear power plants and Greenpeace). These differences show how important it is, that in the process the information that was gathered by the groups is exchanged in the whole class. This way, the different perspectives are combined, and contradictory results are recognised and show the students the necessity for viability checks, which includes the judgment of the trustworthiness of the respective (internet) sources. This is part of critical thinking.

(3) The *evaluation* is the most important step in the problem-solving process because it is this that leads to learning. The proposed denouements are checked for viability. While one can distinguish many types of viability checks (Patry, 2014a), only a few are used in VaKE, in particular the social, the argumentative and to a lesser degree the communicated viability check:
- Social viability check: The concept is discussed with peers. Within these discussions, viability criteria are provided and applied (in the sense of feedback) which support or challenge the individuals in their argumentative viability check.
- Argumentative viability check: The arguments provided give good reasons why a statement should be viable. This is the most important viability check in VaKE. A condition is that the arguments can be integrated into one's system of subjective theories by assimilation or accommodation, another is whether the argument is convincing.
- Communicated viability check: Someone informs the protagonist that a concept is viable (and maybe why: argumentative viability check). The search for information in the knowledge acquisition phase of VaKE is exactly this: One looks for information whose viability one assumes; one issue here is the viability of the source, i.e., whether one can trust the communicated viability check, as addressed above.

The social viability check can also be seen within the framework of social constructivism (Vygotsky, 1978).[4] We cannot here deal in detail with this approach and its application to VaKE, but just mention the crucial issues and additional thoughts, using our own terminology as developed above:

- The process is one of co-construction, which means building subjective theories beyond those the individual participants had before working together that have a common base shared by the participants (collaborative learning, see Chapter 30 in this handbook).
- While subjective theories typically are not made explicit, the discussion in VaKE groups forces the participants to formulate them so that they can communicate them to others. In the Vygotskian perspective, making one's own thinking explicit contributes to constructing one's own knowledge (Webb, 2009, p. 3).

(4) The final step in the problem-solving process is *retention*: The participants keep the propositions with positive evaluations. Retention is enhanced by using the new insights in further dilemma discussions.

3.2 *Moral Development and Moral Education*

With Turiel and Gingo (2017), we assume that to moral and social development, reasoning is central but emotions are part of it, without giving reasoning a minor or no role; morality is a distinct domain of thought which develops through social interactions; and moral decisions entail coordination of different considerations and goals embedded in social situational contexts (p. 210).

Moral education can be done in many different ways (e.g., Oser, 2001; Nucci & Narvaez, 2008; Schuitema et al., 2008). According to these authors, the most successful teaching approaches are those that are not based on trying to convey certain values (indoctrination) or becoming aware of one's values (values clarification); rather, approaches based on moral judgments proved to be effective.[5] In these approaches, not the values as such are at stake, but *how people argue in favour or against values* (e.g., justified decisions in dilemma situations), in the tradition of Kohlberg (summarized in 1981, 1984). This is also the moral education approach on which VaKE is based.

Kohlberg has adapted Piaget's principles of assimilation and accommodation to moral judgments and their development. When confronted with a dilemma, the students argue in favour or against a certain option; however, it is possible that the problem cannot be solved to the individual's satisfaction (the argument is not viable) and a disequilibrium in the individual's moral cognitive structure ensues. For re-equilibration, the individual has to invent new argumentation principles (possibly based on the peers' stimulation) which he or she estimates to be more viable (accommodation).

Since Kohlberg developed his theory, there have been substantial scientific developments (e.g., Nucci & Narvaez, 2008; Zizek, Garz, & Nowak, 2015), among others the neo-Kohlbergian concept (e.g., Rest et al., 2000; Thoma,

2014). We acknowledge the differences; however, since with respect to VaKE as an intervention method, none of these differences are crucial as they deal with assumptions that are not at stake, we can build on the general principles of Kohlberg.

Kohlberg (1972) has proposed a series of six stages of moral argumentation, which individuals successively reach, although only a few achieve the highest stages (according to Lind, 2008, this categorization is still helpful, even if not supported by empirical research). These stages are given in Table 2.2. The postconventional stages are more advanced (in a normative ethical sense), and hence it is normatively justified to educate for this (Kohlberg, 1971).

Kohlberg's (1972) statement that the "main experiential determinants of moral development seem to be the amount and variety of social experience, the opportunity to take a number of roles and to encounter other perspectives" (p. 15), is still viable. This is concretized in the approach by Blatt and Kohlberg (1975) who proposed dilemma discussions to foster the development of the moral competence, which includes creating disequilibria and social viability checks.

TABLE 2.2   Stages of moral judgment (adapted from Kohlberg, 1972, p. 14f.)

Level	Stage
Pre-conventional: Typical of young children and delinquents; decisions are made largely on the basis of self-interest and material considerations	1. Orientation to punishment and reward, and to physical and material power 2. Hedonistic orientation with an instrumental view of human relations. Beginning notions of reciprocity, but with emphasis on exchange of favours
Conventional: Most of the adult population operates on these stages	3. "Good boy"/"good girl" orientation; seeking to maintain expectations and win approval of one's immediate group: morality defined by individual ties of relationship 4. Orientation to authority, law, and duty, to maintain a fixed order, whether social or religious, which is assumed as a primary value
Postconventional: Characteristic for 20 to 25% of the adult population	5. Social-contract orientation, with emphasis on equality and mutual obligation within a democratically established order 6. Morality of individual principles of conscience that have logical comprehensiveness and universality

This method has been quite successful (e.g., Schläfli et al., 1985; Lind, 2003, 2016; Thoma, 2006; etc.). It can be considered as social problem-solving (see above) triggered by disequilibria following dilemma confrontation and discussions.

In addition to the focus on justice (roughly: all people have to be treated equally; a deontological concept) as in Kohlberg's theory, other value systems as discussed above in Section 2.4 can be taken into account, such as morality of care (Gilligan, 1982) whose focus is that each person deserves to be cared for in cases of need, i.e., one is responsible for the well-being of someone with whom one has a special relationship, or teleological concepts. In contrast to the typical dilemmas used in the tradition of Blatt and Kohlberg (1975), most VaKE dilemmas refer to several moral value systems, and hence all of them are addressed in the discussions. We assume that in these cases, the impact of dilemma discussions is not only on justice, but also on the other moral domains.

3.3 *Knowledge Construction*

Knowledge acquisition, or in terms of constructivism, knowledge construction, is usually seen as the core task of school education. Glasersfeld (e.g., 1995), Reitinger (2013; Reitinger et al., 2016) and many other researchers have applied constructivism to knowledge acquisition through disequilibrium and accommodation. Baviskar et al. (2009) formulated four criteria for constructivist teaching: (a) eliciting prior knowledge; (b) creating cognitive dissonance; (c) application of the knowledge with feedback; (d) and reflection on learning.

Inquiry-based learning environments as probably the most prominent representatives of constructivism comply with these criteria. The National Research Council (quoted from Settlage, 2007, p. 465) defines inquiry with five additional essential features: (e) an activity focused upon an investigable question; (f) an investigation that emphasizes the use of evidence: (g) the formulation of explanations from evidence; (h) connecting of explanations to that of the larger scientific community; and (i) the effective and justifiable communication of conclusions.

In VaKE, the inquiry-based learning of knowledge occurs in four steps:
– The participants ask questions (see issue e) based on the recognition that they lack knowledge to discuss the dilemma (a and b);
– they search in groups for answers to these questions using any source they can find (particularly the internet and the teacher who answers upon request; f and g);
– they exchange the gathered information so that all participants are on the same level and inconsistent information can be identified and taken into consideration in further discussions (e.g., by considering reasons for inconsistencies; c and i).
– The newly acquired knowledge is used in the further dilemma discussions (h).

Reflecting on learning (d) is not addressed explicitly in the proposed steps, but experience shows that the participants often mention this issue when reflecting on the method.

Furtak et al. (2012) carried out a meta-analysis of inquiry-based science teaching studies and emphasized three key findings (p. 324f.): (1) There is a positive effect on student learning; (2) teacher-led activities were more effective than student-led activities, and (3), "this meta-analysis has illustrated how a refined model for an instructional approach can yield more nuanced interpretations of the effects of that approach on student learning" (ibid.). VaKE was not included in the meta-analysis. It can be regarded as a "refined model", and our studies (many of which are reported in this handbook) show in general that VaKE leads to at least as much learning as in control groups with traditional teaching, and very often to clearly better learning results and on a higher level (analysis and creation in the taxonomy of Anderson et al., 2001). In contrast to the results of Furtak et al., the teacher-student interaction is not crucial (except if the teacher serves as an information source); we assume that the participants' focus on the task as a consequence of the motivation triggered by the dilemma discussion, reduces the need for teacher support.

However, different students may react differently when confronted with inquiry-based teaching (Cairns & Areepattamannil, 2019). And also, possibly not all topics can be addressed with VaKE. Furthermore, many teachers complain that VaKE is quite time-consuming. While some of these issues can be accounted for (see, for instance, Weinberger, 2006, with respect to students with different abilities; Chapter 8 in this handbook), it seems appropriate to consider that inquiry-based teaching should not be used as the unique teaching-learning approach for knowledge acquisition (see also Teig et al., 2019, based on PISA; Settlage, 2007); rather, we consider VaKE as one method among others. A succession, and possibly combination, of different methods seems appropriate.

3.4   *Additional Theories*

Research on VaKE (e.g., Patry et al., 2013; Pnevmatikos et al., 2016; see also this handbook) has shown the necessity to integrate additional theories beyond the ones discussed above. There are many theoretical frameworks that can be linked with VaKE. We cannot go into detail, but only provide some topics; each of them is a research programme of its own, so we restrict ourselves to just mentioning some of them as key words and if necessary, key references, without claiming to be comprehensive. Among the theoretical frameworks that have already been addressed in discussions about VaKE, one can mention theories referring to the following topics (in alphabetical order): the "Authentic Inner Compass" (Assor, 2019); conceptual change (Vosniadou, 2013); creativity; critical thinking; discourse pedagogy (Oser, 1986); gender-related issues; giftedness; intelligence; interest; perspective taking; problem-based learning; self-determination (Ryan & Deci, 2017); situation specificity; and many more. Some of them have already been mentioned above, and some are addressed in other chapters in this handbook.

Other relevant topics have not yet been tackled within the VaKE framework, but this can easily be done. For instance, it would be important to contrast VaKE with other methods, such as the so-called Socratic method, with which it is often confounded. Further aspects include culture related issues; dialogic processes (Wegerif, 2011); emotions; flow (Csikszentmihalyi, 1990); higher order thinking; individualized and web-based learning; the interaction between formal, non-formal and informal learning; learning in groups; meta-cognitions; personal development and identity; wisdom; and many more. In fact, any theory that is not diametrically opposed to constructivism may contribute to a further analysis, understanding, and development of VaKE.

Two special and related issues are the concept of moral atmosphere and the Just Community approach to moral education (Kohlberg, 1985; see Power & Higgins-D'Alessandro, 2008); the latter "aims to promote moral development and moral responsibility through the organization, practices, and culture of the school itself" (ibid., p. 230). While we did not have the opportunity to use VaKE in an institution that practices the Just Community or has a high moral atmosphere, we think that they are fully compatible with VaKE and that VaKE might add some substantial value to them, just as they can highly benefit VaKE as they would provide a moral embedding that is completely in line with it.

This is just a tentative list. When we present VaKE in a scientific community, researchers often suggest that their predilected theory may apply. We can usually agree with that, but we cannot integrate all of these theories into the system. On the other hand, this experience shows the theory-integrative power of VaKE.

In addition to the theories that address VaKE as a method or process, practitioners using VaKE need to refer to the theories underlying the topics addressed in the dilemma, e.g., the respective scientific disciplines.

Finally, there are several meta-theoretical frameworks that play a role. We have already mentioned constructivism and the meta-ethical non-naturalism, and we can also refer here to transdisciplinarity (see Chapter 33 in this handbook) and to issues of integrating different theories (Patry, 2013, 2014b), as well as to critical multiplism and the priority of theory over methods (Patry, 2012b), etc.

4 VaKE Procedures

As mentioned above, VaKE is not a recipe, but conceived in such a way that it can be adapted to the specific conditions of implementation (target audience, time restrictions, research question, etc.). Therefore, when presenting the steps of VaKE, we call them "prototypical" (in the sense of Rosch: Mervis & Rosch, 1981) since they are possible operationalizations of the theory presented above, but other ways may be suitable as well. We present in this section two approaches that have been frequently used and are referred to throughout this handbook: the standard prototype and VaKE-*dis*. Furthermore, we refer very briefly to some adaptations that have been used.

4.1 *The Standard Prototype*

The standard prototype – usually simply called "VaKE" – consists of a series of eleven steps (plus a preparation). The overview is presented in Table 2.3. The different steps are as follows:

– *Preparation and clarification*: If it is the students' first experience with VaKE, they need to be prepared since most of them are not familiar with open teaching and the freedom it provides. They must be informed about the principles of VaKE (including the eleven steps) and learn to deal appropriately with each other, to argue and to focus on arguments and not on the person who utters it, to search for information on the internet and elsewhere, etc.
– *Introducing the dilemma*: The dilemma is presented in a form adequate for the target group, and the teacher ascertains that the students know what values are at stake.
– *First decision*: The students have to communicate what they think is the appropriate option of the dilemma (e.g., what the protagonist should do). This decision is taken with the students knowing very little and based on their common knowledge (subjective theory); it is the first opportunity to recognise that they should base their decisions more on justifications and facts.
– *First arguments (dilemma discussion)*: The students argue in favour and against the different options to the dilemma. This includes a
– first moral viability check with respect to the justifications – possibly with ensuing disequilibrium.

The steps 1 to 3 correspond to the dilemma discussion in the Blatt and Kohlberg (1975) tradition.
– *Exchange of experiences and missing information*: The group experiences concerning the results of the argumentation are exchanged, although the dilemma discussion may not be finished yet. In particular, the participants

TABLE 2.3 Prototypical steps in VaKE

	Step	Action	Group
0	Preparation of the students and pupils	Introduce discussion rules and search competence, etc.	Class
1	Introduce dilemma	Understand dilemma and values at stake	Class
2	First decision	Who is in favour, who against? (Voting)	Class
3	*First arguments* (*dilemma discussion*)	Why am I in favour, why against? Do we agree with each other? (moral viability check)	Groups
4	*Exchange experience* and **asking about missing information**	Exchange of arguments; what do I need to know further to be able to argue?	Class
5	**Looking for evidence**	Obtain the information, using any source available!	Groups
6	**Exchange information**	Inform the other students about your constructions; is the information sufficient? (content related viability check)	Class
7	*Second arguments* (*dilemma discussion*)	What is my decision now? Why? Do we agree with each other? (moral viability check)	Groups
8	**Synthesis of information**	Present our conclusions to the whole class (moral and content viability check)	Class
9	*Repeat 4 through 8 if necessary*		
10	*General synthesis*	Closing the sequence capitalizing on the whole process	Class/ Groups
11	*Generalization*	Discussion about other but related issues, or act based on the results of the discussions	Class/ Groups

Note: in italics: values education; in bold: knowledge education (according to Patry et al., 2013, p. 265)

think about what kind of knowledge is necessary to be able to discuss the dilemma more deeply. The students set their individual learning goals (e.g., dangers of a nuclear power plant, radioactivity).
- *Looking for evidence*: The students organise themselves to gather the necessary information and to exchange the evidence they have acquired, while the teacher is a manager and counsellor of the whole endeavour; if clearly stated in this phase, the teacher can also serve as source of information and respond to the students' content questions as an expert among others.
- *Exchange of information*: After this phase of information acquisition, there is once again a phase of exchange of information in the whole class so that all students have the same level of knowledge. This includes a viability check of the acquired knowledge with respect to its contribution to addressing the dilemma.

Steps 4, 5 and 6 correspond to the constructivist knowledge acquisition.
- *Second arguments (dilemma discussion)*: With this new knowledge in mind, the students turn back to the dilemma discussion itself, as in step 3.
- *Synthesis of information*: There then follows a general discussion with the presentation of the results (current state of the negotiations). This can be done in anticipation of the task to be performed in Step 10.
- *Repeat 4 to 8 if necessary*: If the knowledge base is not yet sufficient, steps 4 to 8 are repeated, with additional material and internet research and eventually with a new focus (e.g., to satisfy curricular needs); this can be done several times, depending on the time constraints of the course and interest of the participants.
- *General synthesis*: The final synthesis addresses the current state of the problem discussion (including, if appropriate, new problems) of the group. This can be done in didactically sophisticated ways such as through role plays – possibly with perspective change – writing a newspaper, etc. (see Chapter 5 in this handbook).
- *Generalization*: The generalization consists in dealing with similar issues to broaden the perspective. Very often, this does not need to be conceived; rather the students do it spontaneously. Sometimes they decide to act in a certain way (e.g., writing letters to newspapers or politicians, collecting money for a certain cause, etc.).

4.2   VaKE-dis

To put a special focus on the *reflection* in VaKE, Weyringer (2008) developed an extension of the prototypical process: VaKE-*dis* (VaKE – *differentiated, individualized,* and *specified*). This extension results from experiences in the Platon Youth Forum (see Chapter 15 in this handbook). The special circumstances, especially the linguistic and cultural heterogeneity of the groups, made an adaptation absolutely necessary.

The concept emphasises the possibilities of variation in order to be able to respond in a *differentiated* (d), *individualised* (i) and *specified* (s) way to different groups of learners and their learning needs, learning interests, and developmental objectives:

- The course of instruction is *differentiated:* Different methods of acquiring knowledge and documenting learning progress are integrated. The change of perspective is bindingly highlighted as part of the method.
- The learning and development process is *individualised:* The introduction of reflection/foresight phases ensures that each learner has time to reflect on the points of view expressed and then can consider individually which opinion he or she wants to represent in the future dilemma discussion.
- The version is *specified* because the procedure for the implementation can be specifically adapted to the respective learning group, to the intended learning objectives, and to the existing framework conditions.

Compared to the prototypical VaKE version (see Table 2.3), VaKE-*dis* contains
- differentiation of the prototypical course: the integration of a preparation phase (step 0) and four phases of reflection and foresight for the individual learner before and after the decisions and discussions (steps 2 and 3);
- three didactic additions: the possibility to postpone decisions ("don't know" as the third option for decision), binding implementation of the change of perspective, feedback as a viability check;
- a methodological extension: the integration of methods, tools, and techniques for ensuring the learning and teaching outcome and the educational goals (for details, see Chapter 5 in this handbook).

Findings show that these additions support and promote the processes of personality and consciousness development in particular (Weyringer, 2008).

5 Adaptations

VaKE is not only used in schools and universities. In many of these fields, VaKE can be applied following roughly the prototypical steps or VaKE-*dis*. This is possible because VaKE is a flexible concept: It can be adapted to specific requirements, depending on the particular needs and circumstances, without digressing from the theoretical background. Furthermore, VaKE teachers or workshop leaders have much freedom, which is different in the different steps (in function of the roles, see Nussbaumer, Chapter 6 in this handbook).

One can distinguish different kinds of adaptations: different dilemmas, adaptations to specific conditions, adaptations for research purposes, and situative adaptations.

(a) The choice of the dilemma leads to a focus on specific issues. For instance, Diekmann (2020; see also Chapter 33 in this handbook) used dilemmas addressing consumption and sustainable development, and Linortner et al. (Chapter 24 in this handbook) used several dilemmas specific to medical professionals. The formulation of an appropriate dilemma does not only depend on the topic of interest, but also on many other conditions; hence the dilemma construction is one of the most difficult issues in VaKE, and Chapter 4 in this handbook is dedicated to this question. Because the dilemmas need to be conceived specifically for the target audience and the slightest change may be important, we emphasise that dilemmas provided by, for instance, published lists of dilemmas – which are often asked for by practitioners – can only serve as a template to be adapted to the specific needs under the particular circumstances.

(b) The conception of a VaKE workshop may differ in relation with conditions that are already known beforehand. We can mention the following variations which are addressed in other chapters of this handbook or in other publications:

- VaKE-Tact: Some steps are added to the prototypical VaKE to address practical issues that pre-service professionals may encounter in practical situations, and actually some of them have encountered during their internship (Linortner & Patry, 2015).
- VaKE-pr: Demetri (2015) adapted VaKE to the needs of primary students that takes into account their age-related competences with respect to social and argumentative strategies, moral judgment, and reading abilities (see Chapter 7).
- VaKE has been used – and adapted – repeatedly to work with migrants of different kinds, as documented in the chapters by Weyringer et al. (Chapter 16 in this handbook), Brighenti and Brossard Børhaug (Chapter 10), and Crosbie and Daniel (Chapter 17). Since the conditions were very different, the adaptations of VaKE differed as well.
- VaKE for hearing impaired students: Linortner (2014) formulated a VaKE structure that takes into account that hearing-impaired students have a

particular challenge to communicate with each other (see Chapter 20 in this handbook).
- VaKE and action: While in many studies, the students spontaneously took action after a VaKE process, in several studies, VaKE was changed so that moral actions were explicitly included and fostered.
- VaKE and the Dilemma Based Model: Reichman (2017) provide a combination of VaKE and a Reflective Cycle (see Chapter 25 in this handbook).
- VaKE and media: Capitalizing on Computer-Supported Collaborative Learning (CSCL), Meirovitz and Eyal (Chapter 26 in this handbook) provide computer-based tools to support the different steps of VaKE with concrete internet sites.

Many more adaptations of VaKE have been proposed. It is not possible here to deal in detail with them. We explicitly welcome such adaptations, provided that they comply with the theoretical framework presented above. However, the logo of VaKE is a trademark and may only be used if accredited by the rightful owner, the Association of Values *and* Knowledge Education (AVaKE; see VaKE, 2020).

A special topic is conceiving VaKE for workshop leaders: They must experience VaKE themselves, but also know the theory; details are given in the chapter by Nussbaumer (this handbook, Chapter 6). In addition to the workshops themselves, we vividly recommend to implement a supervision and counselling structure after the end of a workshop, and to organise cooperation between participants who implement VaKE so that they are not lone fighters, but act in teamwork with mutual support and counselling. A particularly important common activity would be the joint development of specific dilemmas which then can be adapted to the specific needs.

(c) VaKE can be varied to satisfy specific needs of research. VaKE is an intervention method, which can be used as treatment in experimental or quasi-experimental studies (see Chapter 32 in this handbook). Instead of comparing VaKE – in whatever version – with traditional teaching, one can compare different conceptions of VaKE to study specific research questions. We want here to refer only to VaKE+ (Weinberger, 2006), where steps addressing explicit viability checks are added to the prototypical VaKE steps; details of this approach are given in Chapter 8 (this handbook).

(d) Finally, the open structure of VaKE may require spontaneous changes because of the reactions or wishes of the participants. With Schön (1991, p. 135), one can say that "the situation talks back": In social interactions, one can never fully anticipate what is going to happen, and hence the workshop leader has to decide autonomously what to do and to improvise. While no research and no theory can describe exactly to the last detail how to act, the workshop leader is required to respond to the situation in agreement with the theory. This has been discussed in terms of pedagogical tact (Gastager & Patry, 2018).

An example for this is the discussion of the Sikh dilemma by Ghellini (Chapter 14 in this handbook) and Legué (Chapter 21): Unexpectedly, the French students addressed the issue of morality and moral education itself, which they saw with suspicion given the culture of secularism in their country. Hence, the discussions moved from the dilemma at stake to the discussion of the method itself, which needed an appropriate adaptation from the teacher, the requirement of the theory being to be transparent about the method – in the particular case, to emphasize that the approach is not an attempt to indoctrinate, which would have been rightly criticized by the students (not only because it was against the secularist doctrine) – but focuses on the *justification* of values, which in contrast to indoctrination would be welcomed.

Furthermore, in certain steps, the participants make decisions: They decide on the questions to be searched (step 4, Table 2.3), what sources they want to search (step 5) and how to proceed in the different synthesis steps (steps 8, 10, 12), and they participate in the decision-making in all other steps as well – in fact, the steps formulated in Table 2.3 are such, that often the participants decide themselves what to do next without being aware that this is in agreement with the next step and fits the concept perfectly. On the other hand, when the participants' decisions are asked for, the workshop leader can make propositions, as well as participate in the decision making, and take responsibility in the implementation.

In both of these issues, the situation talks back, and the participants' co-determination imply that no two V*a*KE processes are similar, even if the conditions are highly similar. This will be discussed, among others, in the study with migrants (Chapter 16) where eleven workshops were implemented – and each of them was very different from the others, although always in compliance with the theoretical framework.

All these adaptations, from (a) to (d), are based on our experiences. They comply with the practical needs of the respective fields. However, they also imply specific problems. The first one has already been mentioned repeatedly, but because of its importance, we will say it again: V*a*KE is not a recipe to be applied blindly. Secondly, comparisons are difficult. For instance, assessments of the acquired knowledge are challenged by the fact that one cannot anticipate what the participants will actually learn (although, if necessary, it is possible to some degree to control for this, see Chapter 3 in this handbook). In Chapter 31 there is a description of how one can deal with this problem.

6   Conclusions

VaKE could have a positive impact in many different fields where social problems can be dealt with using education instead of repression, prohibition, and segregation. We do not contend that such problems could be solved through the use of VaKE, but they could be attenuated. We do not have experience in all possible fields, as there are so many, and the responsible people are not usually aware of the possibilities of VaKE. We try to promote VaKE and inform responsible people. But we are often perceived as trying to sell a new "magic wand" to solve problems. This misinterpretation can only be controverted by referring, on one hand, to the sound theoretical background (see above, Section 3 in this chapter), and on the other, to the empirical research body which in the meantime has grown to be quite substantial, as the present handbook documents. However, both the theory and the empirical research are quite complex, and to convey them requires the willingness of the responsible authorities to engage into such endeavours, which cannot be expected from all of them; also, results cannot be expected to occur overnight.

We have succeeded in some domains, though, to convince the respective authorities or individual practitioners that VaKE is an appropriate method, and they either used it – after some training – or they commissioned us to do so. One must also mention, however, that VaKE aims at autonomous people who engage in the social discourse and take responsibility, and this does not please all authorities; but this is only a suspicion based on our experiences, and we do not want to create new conspiracy theories in this regard.

Overall, VaKE has grown to be a sound and well-founded approach that deserves to be seriously examined in any field, and all of the VaKE teams will be happy to support any effort to implement it appropriately.

Notes

1   Not idiosyncratic, not valid for only one occasion, but for several situations, times, behaviours, or other facets – but also not necessarily universal, i.e., for all situations, times, behaviours, etc. statements.
2   This is a new approach compared to Piaget; this development was required by the experience that under some conditions – which still need to be determined in detail – there is no accommodation but both domains are accepted independently (Gastager, 2003).
3   A comparable framework with respect to knowledge related to science is the conceptual change theory (Vosniadou, 2013; application to VaKE by Pnevmatikos & Christodoulou, 2018; Chapter 9 in this handbook).
4   In previous publications on VaKE (e.g., Patry et al., 2013, p. 564), we used the reference to social constructivism and Vygotsky instead of "social problem-solving". It is important to

emphasize that we use here Vygotsky's or Neo-Vygotskyan concepts as heuristic and not as rigid framework.
5 Based on Kohlberg, two additional methods must be mentioned but cannot be discussed here: moral exemplars and Just Community (Snarey & Samuelson, 2008).

References

Anderson, L. W., Krathwohl, D. R., Airasian, P. W., Cruikshank, K. A., Mayer, R. E., Pintrich, P. R., Raths, J., & Wittrock, M. C. (Eds.). (2001). *A taxonomy for learning, teaching, and assessing: A revision of Bloom's taxonomy of educational objectives.* New York, NY: Longman.

Assor, A. (2019, November). *Nurturing students' and teachers' inner compass as a key task in autonomy-supportive education* [Paper]. The international workshop "The teacher's voice: Agentic engagement and self-determination among MIT participants: A multicultural perspective", Project Proteach. Kaye Academic College of Education, Beer Sheva, Israel.

Aufenanger, S., Garz, D., & Zutavern, M. (1981). *Erziehung zur Gerechtigkeit. Unterrichtspraxis nach Lawrence Kohlberg.* München, Germany: Kösel.

Bailey, K., & Im-Bolter, N. (2020). My way or your way? Perspective taking during social problem solving. *Journal of Applied Developmental Psychology, 66,* 101087.

Baviskar, S. N., Hartle, R. T., & Whitney, T. (2009). Essential criteria to characterize constructivist teaching: Derived from a review of the literature and applied to five constructivist-teaching method articles. *International Journal of Science Education, 31,* 541–550.

Blatt, M. M., & Kohlberg, L. (1975). The effects of classroom moral discussion upon children's level of moral judgment. *Journal of Moral Education, 4*(2), 129–161.

Bloom, B. S., Engelhart, M. D., Furst, E. J., Hill, W. H., & Krathwohl, D. R. (Eds.). (1956). *Taxonomy of educational objectives – The classification of educational goals – Handbook 1: Cognitive domain.* London, WI: Longmans, Green & Co.

Bohse, J. (1982). Inszenierte Dramenlektüre: Der Prozess gegen Karl von Moor und Moritz Spielberg. Modell für einen "produktions"- und "handlungsorientierten" Literaturunterricht am Beispiel von Schillers "Räubern". In G. Haas (Ed.), *Literatur im Unterricht. Modelle zu erzählerischen und dramatischen Texten in den Sekundarstufen I und II* (pp. 205–267). Stuttgart, Germany: Reclam.

Bourdieu, P. (1977). *Outline of a theory of practice.* Cambridge, UK: Cambridge University Press.

Cairns, D., & Areepattamannil, S. (2019). Exploring the relations of inquiry-based teaching to science achievement and dispositions in 54 countries. *Research in Science Education, 49*(1), 1–23.

Campbell, D. T. (1960). Blind variation and selective retention in creative thought as in other knowledge processes. *Psychological Review, 67*, 380–400.

Campbell, D. T. (1982). The "blind variation and selective retention" theme. In J. M. Broughton & D. J. Freeman-Moir (Eds.), *The cognitive-developmental psychology of James Mark Baldwin* (pp. 87–97). Norwood, NJ: Ablex.

Csikszentmihalyi, M. (1990). *Flow: The psychology of optimal experience*. New York, NY: Harper & Row.

Demetri, A. (2015). *Kombination moralischer Werterziehung mit konstruktivistischem Wissenserwerb in der Grundschule. Das Unterrichtsmodell VaKE in der Grundschule*. [Dissertation]. Kultur- und Gesellschaftswissenschaftlichen Fakultät der Universität Salzburg.

Diekmann, N. (2020). Adding values to education for sustainable development with Values and Knowledge Education. *Menon, Online Journal of Educational Research, 5th Thematic Issue,* 30–40. Retrieved April 4, 2021, from http://www.edu.uowm.gr/site/system/files/menon_issue_5th_special_052020.pdf

Foerster, H. v. (1972). Perception of the future and the future of perception. *Instructional Science, 1*(1), 31–43.

Furnham, A. F. (1988). *Lay theories. Everyday understanding of problems in the social sciences*. Oxford, UK: Pergamon Press.

Furtak, E. M., Seidel, T., Iverson, H., & Briggs, D. C. (2012). Experimental and quasi-experimental studies of inquiry-based science teaching: A meta-analysis. *Review of Educational Research, 82*, 300–329.

Gastager, A. (2003). *Paradigmenvielfalt aus Sicht der Unterrichtenden. Subjektive Theorien über Handeln in "traditionellen" und konstruktivistischen Lehr-Lern-Situationen*. Lengerich, Germany: Pabst.

Gastager, A., & Patry, J.-L. (Eds.). (2018). *Pädagogischer Takt: Analysen zu Theorie und Praxis*. Graz, Austria: Leykam.

Gilligan, C. (1982). *In a different voice: Psychological theory and women's development*. Cambridge, MA: Harvard University Press.

Glasersfeld, E. V. (1995). *Radical constructivism: A way of knowing and learning*. London, UK: The Falmer Press.

Glasersfeld, E. v. (1998). Why constructivism must be radical. In M. Larochelle, N. Bednarz, & J. Garrison (Eds.), *Constructivism and education* (pp. 23–28). Cambridge, UK: Cambridge University Press.

Groeben, N., Wahl, D., Schlee, J., & Scheele, B. (1988). *Das Forschungsprogramm Subjektive Theorien*. Tübingen, Germany: Francke.

Hanson, N. R. (1958). *Patterns of discovery: An inquiry into the conceptual foundations of science*. Cambridge, UK: Cambridge University Press.

Heinich, N. (2017). *Des valeurs. Une approche sociologique*, Paris, France: Éditions Gallimard.

Higgins, A., & Gordon, F. M. (1986). Arbeitsklima und sozio-moralische Entwicklung in zwei arbeitereigenen und selbstverwalteten Betrieben. In F. Oser, R. Fatke, & O. Höffe (Eds.), *Transformation und Entwicklung* (pp. 252–296). Frankfurt/Main, Germany: Suhrkamp.

Hume, D. (1739/1896). *A treatise of human nature* (Reprinted from the original edition in three volumes and edited, with an analytical index, by L. A. Selby-Bigge) Oxford: Clarendon Press. Retrieved April 4, 2021, from https://people.rit.edu/wlrgsh/HumeTreatise.pdf

Kant, I. (1787/1998). *Critique of pure reason* (P. Guyer & A. W. Wood, Trans. & Eds.). Cambridge, UK: Cambridge University Press. Retrieved April 4, 2021, from http://www.strangebeautiful.com/other-texts/kant-first-critique-cambridge.pdf

Kohlberg, L. (1971). From is to ought: How to commit the naturalistic fallacy and get away with it in the study of moral development. In T. Mischel (Ed.), *Cognitive development and epistemology* (pp. 151–235). New York/London: Academic Press.

Kohlberg, L. (1972). A cognitive-developmental approach to moral education. *Humanist, 32*(6), 13–16.

Kohlberg, L. (1981). *Essays on moral development. Vol. 1: The philosophy of moral development. Moral stages and the idea of justice.* San Francisco, CA: Harper & Row.

Kohlberg, L. (1984). *Essays on moral development: Vol. 2. The psychology of moral development.* San Francisco, CA: Harper & Row.

Kohlberg, L. (1985). The just community approach to moral education in theory and practice. In M. Berkowitz & F. Oser (Eds.), *Moral education: Theory and application* (pp. 27–8 6). Hillsdale, NJ: Erlbaum.

Krebs, D. L., & Denton, K. (2005). Toward a more pragmatic approach to morality: A critical evaluation of Kohlberg's model. *Psychological Review, 112*, 629–649.

Lickona, T. (1991). *Educating for character: How our schools can teach respect and responsibility.* New York, NY: Bantam Books.

Lind, G. (2003). *Moral ist lehrbar: Handbuch zur Theorie und Praxis moralischer und demokratischer Bildung.* München, Germany: Oldenbourg.

Lind, G. (2008). The meaning and measurement of moral judgment competence revisited – A dual-aspect model. In D. Fasko & W. Willis (Eds.), *Contemporary philosophical and psychological perspectives on moral development and education* (pp. 185–220). Cresskill, NJ: Hampton Press.

Lind, G. (2016). *How to teach morality. Promoting deliberation and discussion, reducing violence and deceit.* Berlin, Germany: Logos.

Linortner, L. (2014). "Gehört sich das?" Adaption von VaKE für die Gehörlosenbildung. Unveröffentlichte Master These an der Universität Salzburg, Fachbereich Erziehungswissenschaft.

Linortner, L., & Patry, J.-L. (2015). *Teaching manual, module 1: VaKE-Tact – Values and Knowledge Education and agogical tact* [Unpublished paper]. Life-Long Learning in Applied Fields (LLAF), Project 543894 – TEMPUS-1-2013-1-IL-TEMPUS-JPHES, Group 4: Learning to Be, University of Salzburg.

Mervis, C. B., & Rosch, E. (1981). Categorization of natural objects. *Annual Review of Psychology, 32*, 89–115.

Morscher, E. (2018). Metaethics and moral education. In A. Weinberger, H. Biedermann, J.-L. Patry, & S. Weyringer (Eds.), *Professionals' ethos and education for responsibility* (pp. 17–27). Leiden, The Netherlands: Brill.

Nucci, L. P., & Narvaez, D. (Eds.). (2008). *Handbook of moral and character education*. New York, NY: Routledge.

Osborne, A. F. (1956). *Applied imagination. Principles and procedures of creative thinking* (8th printing). New York, NY: Scribner's Sons. Retrieved May 24, 2020, from https://b-ok.cc/book/3486334/cf74o4

Oser, F. (1986). Moral education and values education: The discourse perspective. In M. C. Wittrock (Ed.), *Handbook of research on teaching* (3rd ed., pp. 917–941). New York, NY: Macmillan.

Oser, F. (2001). Acht Strategien der Wert- und Moralerziehung. In W. Edelstein, F. Oser, & P. Schuster (Eds.), *Moralische Erziehung in der Schule: Entwicklungspsychologie und pädagogische Praxis* (pp. 63–8 9). Weinheim, Germany: Beltz.

Oser, F., Patry, J.-L., Zutavern, M., Reichenbach, R., Klaghofer, R., Althof, W., & Rothbucher, H. (1991). *Der Prozess der Verantwortung – Berufsethische Entscheidung von Lehrerinnen und Lehrern*. Bericht zum Forschungsprojekt 1.188-0.85 und 11.25470.88/2 des Schweizerischen Nationalfonds zur Förderung der wissenschaftlichen Forschung. Freiburg, Switzerland: Pädagogisches Institut der Universität.

Patry, J.-L. (2000). Werterziehung und Wissensbildung – lässt sich das vereinigen? In C. Metzger, H. Seitz, & F. Eberle (Eds.), *Impulse für die Wirtschaftspädagogik. Festschrift zum 65. Geburtstag von Prof. Dr. Rolf Dubs* (pp. 423–440). Zürich: Verlag des Schweizerischen Kaufmännischen Verbandes.

Patry, J.-L. (2012a). Antinomien in der Erziehung. In C. Nerowski, T. Hascher, M. Lunkenbein, & D. Sauer (Eds.), *Professionalität im Umgang mit Spannungsfeldern der Pädagogik* (pp. 177–187). Bad Heilbrunn, Germany: Klinkhardt.

Patry, J.-L. (2012b). Über die Methodenvielfalt hinaus: Kritischer Multiplizismus am Beispiel von VaKE. In M. Gläser-Zikuda, T. Seidel, C. Rohlfs, A. Gröschner, & S. Ziegelbauer (Eds.), *Mixed Methods in der empirischen Bildungsforschung* (pp. 65–77). Münster, Germany: Waxmann.

Patry, J.-L. (2013). Beyond multiple methods: Critical multiplism on all levels. *International Journal of Multiple Research Approaches, 7*, 50–65.

Patry, J.-L. (2014a). Die Viabilität und der Viabilitäts-Check von Antworten. In C. Giordano & J.-L. Patry (Eds.), *Fragen! Antworten? Interdisziplinäre Perspektiven. Freiburger Sozialanthropologische Studien* (pp. 11–35). Vienna, Austria: Lit.

Patry, J.-L. (2014b). Rivalisierende Paradigmen in der Erziehungswissenschaft: Das Beispiel der Situationsspezifität. In S. Kornmesser & G. Schurz (Eds.), *Die multiparadigmatische Struktur der Wissenschaften* (pp. 103–144). Wiesbaden, Germany: Springer VS.

Patry, J.-L. (2016). Thesen zur konstruktivistischen Didaktik. *journal für lehrerInnenbildung, 16*(2), 9–17.

Patry, J.-L. (2018). Situation specificity of discourse. In A. Weinberger, H. Biedermann, J.-L. Patry, & S. Weyringer (Eds.), *Professionals' ethos and education for responsibility* (pp. 41–61). Leiden, The Netherlands: Brill.

Patry, J.-L. (2019). Situation specificity of behavior: The triple relevance in research and practice of education. In R. V. Nata (Ed.), *Progress in education* (Vol. 58, pp. 29–144). Hauppauge, NY: Nova.

Patry, J.-L., & Gastager, A. (2017). Subjektive Theorien. In A. Kraus, J. Budde, M. Hietzge, & C. Wulf (Eds.), *Handbuch Schweigendes Wissen. Erziehung, Bildung, Sozialisation und Lernen* (pp. 92–106). Weinheim, Germany: Beltz/Juventa.

Patry, J.-L., Weinberger, A., Weyringer, S., & Nussbaumer, M. (2013). Combining values and knowledge education. In B. J. Irby, G. Brown, R. Lara-Alecio, & S. Jackson (Eds.) and R. A. Robles-Piña (Sect. Ed.), *The handbook of educational theories* (pp. 565–579). Charlotte, NC: Information Age Publishing.

Perrez, M. (1991). The difference between everyday knowledge, ideology, and scientific knowledge. *New Ideas in Psychology, 9*, 227–231.

Phillips, D. C. (1995). The good, the bad, and the ugly: The many faces of constructivism. *Educational Researcher, 23*(7), 5–12.

Piaget, J. (1985). *The equilibration of cognitive structures: The central problem of intellectual development.* Chicago, IL: University of Chicago Press.

Pnevmatikos, D., & Christodoulou, P. (2018). Promoting conceptual change through Values *and* Knowledge Education (V*a*KE). In A. Weinberger, H. Biedermann, J.-L. Patry, & S. Weyringer (Eds.), *Professionals' ethos and education for responsibility* (pp. 63–74). Leiden, The Netherlands: Brill.

Pnevmatikos, D., Patry, J.-L., Weinberger, A., Linortner, L., Weyringer, S., Maron, R., & Gordon-Shaag, A. (2016). Combining values and knowledge education for lifelong transformative learning. In E. Panitsides & J. Talbot (Eds.), *Lifelong learning: Concepts, benefits, and challenges* (pp. 109–134). New York, NY: Nova Science.

Popper, K. R. (1972). *Objective knowledge. An evolutionary approach.* Oxford, UK: Clarenton Press.

Power, F. C., & Higgins-D'Alessandro, A. (2008). The Just Community approach to moral education and the moral atmosphere of the school. In L. Nucci & D. Narvaez (Eds.), *Handbook of moral and character education* (pp. 230–247). New York, NY: Routledge.

Reichman, R. G. (2017). *Dilemma-Based Model (DBM): Effective teacher and learning in higher education* [Paper]. The conference on higher education pedagogy, Blacksburg, VA.

Reitinger, J. (2013). *Forschendes Lernen: Theorie, Evaluation und Praxis in naturwissenschaftlichen Lernarrangements*. Kassel, Germany: Prolog-Verlag.

Reitinger, J., Haberfellner, C., Brewster, E., & Kramer, M. (Eds.). (2016). *Theory of inquiry learning arrangements. Research, reflection, and implementation*. Kassel, Germany: Kassel University Press. Retrieved April 4, 2021, from http://dx.media.org/10.19211/KUP9783737601450

Rest, J. R., Narvaez, D., Thoma, S. J., & Bebeau, M. J. (2000). A neo-kohlbergian approach to morality research. *Journal of Moral Education, 29*(4), 381–395.

Rokeach, M. (1973). *The nature of human values*. New York, NY: The Free Press.

Ryan, R. M., & Deci, E. L. (2017). *Self-determination theory: Basic psychological needs in motivation, development, and wellness*. New York, NY: The Guilford Press.

Schläfli, A., Rest, J., & Thoma, S. (1985). Does moral education improve moral judgment? A meta-analysis of intervention studies. *Review of Educational Research, 55*, 319–352.

Schlömerkemper, J. (2006). Die Kompetenz des antinomischen Blicks. In W. Plöger (Ed.), *Was müssen Lehrerinnen und Lehrer können? Beiträge zur Kompetenzorientierung in der Lehrerbildung* (pp. 281–308). Paderborn, Germany: Schöningh.

Schön, D. A. (1991). *The reflective practitioner. How professionals think in action*. Hants, UK: Ashgate.

Schuitema, J., ten Dam G., & Veugelers, W. (2008). Teaching strategies for moral education. A literature review. *Journal of Curriculum Studies, 40*(1), 69–89.

Schwartz, S. H. (1992). Universals in the content and structure of values: Theoretical advances and empirical tests in 20 countries. *Advances in Experimental Social Psychology, 25*, 1–65.

Settlage, J. (2007). Demythologizing science teacher education: Conquering the false ideal of open inquiry. *Journal of Science Teacher Education, 18*(4), 461–67.

Snarey, J., & Samuelson, P. (2008). Moral education in the cognitive development tradition: Lawrence Kohlberg's revolutionary idea. In L. Nucci & D. Narvaez (Eds.), *Handbook of moral and character education* (pp. 53–79). New York, NY: Routledge.

Spranger, E. (1928). *Types of men* (P. J. W. Pigors, Trans.). Halle (Saale), Germany: Max Niemeyer Verlag. (Original work published in 1914)

Teig, N., Scherer, R., & Nilsen, T. (2018). More isn't always better: The curvilinear relationship between inquiry-based teaching and student achievement in Science. *Learning and Instruction, 56*, 20–29.

Thoma, S. J. (2006). Research using the Defining Issues Test. In M. Killen & J. G. Smetana (Eds), *Handbook of moral psychology* (pp. 67–92). Mahwah, NJ: Erlbaum.

Thoma, S. J. (2014). Measuring moral thinking from a neo-Kohlbergian perspective. *Theory and Research in Education, 12*(3), 347–365.

Turiel, E., & Gingo, M. (2017). Development in the moral domain: Coordination and the need to consider other domains of social reasoning. In N. Budwig, E. Turiel, & P. Zelazo (Eds.), *New perspectives on human development* (pp. 209–228). Cambridge, UK: Cambridge University Press. doi:10.1017/CBO9781316282755.013

VaKE. (2020). *Values and Knowledge Education.* Retrieved July 4, 2020 from VaKE.eu.

Vosniadou, S. (Ed.). (2013). *International handbook of research on conceptual change* (2nd ed.). New York, NY: Routledge.

Vygotsky, L. S. (1978). *Mind in society: The development of higher psychological processes* (M. Cole, V. John-Steiner, S. Scribner, & E. Souberman, Eds.). Cambridge, MA: Harvard University Press.

Webb, N. M. (2009). The teacher's role in promoting collaborative dialogue in the classroom. *British Journal of Educational Psychology, 79,* 1–28.

Wegerif, R. (2011). Towards a dialogic theory of how children learn to think. *Thinking Skills and Creativity 6*(3), 179–190.

Weinberger, A. (2006). *Kombination von Werterziehung und Wissenserwerb. Evaluation des konstruktivistischen Unterrichtsmodells VaKE (Values and Knowledge Education) in der Sekundarstufe I.* Hamburg, Germany: Kovač.

Weyringer, S. (2008). *VaKE in einem internationalen Sommercampus für (hoch) begabte Jugendliche: Eine Evaluationsstudie* [Unpublished dissertation]. Paris Lodron Universität Salzburg.

Winkel, R. (1988). *Antinomische Pädagogik und Kommunikative Didaktik. Studien zu den Widersprüchen und Spannungen in Erziehung und Schule* (2nd ed.). Düsseldorf, Germany: Schwann.

Yang, S. (2017). A commentary reflection of moral psychology based on embodied cognition. *Ethics in Progress, 8*(2), 59–68.

Zizek, B., Garz, D., & Nowak, E. (Eds.). (2015). *Kohlberg revisited.* Rotterdam, The Netherlands: Sense.

PART 2

Recommendations for VaKE Practice

∵

CHAPTER 3

Planning, Preparing and Doing a VaKE Course

Sieglinde Weyringer and Dimitris Pnevmatikos

1   Introduction

"Good instruction and good results depend on proper planning". This motto also applies to a teaching-learning process that is designed using VaKE.

In this chapter, we will address practical issues of planning, preparing, and doing a VaKE course. We will especially highlight differences in standard class management and lesson planning. The first section of this chapter aims to present commonalities from the abundance of different paradigms and theoretical approaches from contemporary lesson planning. It describes how to make these elements usable for the planning of school lessons or training with the VaKE method. The second section deals with and illustrates the requirements teachers and learners face when carrying out a VaKE lesson; it also provides specific recommendations for their actions. The use of selected instruments and tools (see Chapter 5 in this handbook) will also be recommended in this chapter. Links to theoretical basics will be provided, however, without an in-depth discussion. Therefore, the chapters will only include a minimum of references.

The application of VaKE is not limited to school education, as will be shown in Part 3, Section 3 in this handbook. Also, the practice experiences on which this chapter is based have been gained in a variety of different learning environments and contexts. Therefore, we will use terms broader than those relevant to the school system: learner instead of student or pupil; course, training instead of lesson or subject; moderator and/or trainer additional to a teacher.

2   Planning VaKE Course – A Symbiosis of Diverse Existing Pedagogical Approaches

Constructivist didactics and competence orientations are two current paradigms for lesson planning and design. *Constructivist teaching* aims at nurturing a thinker and an autonomous learner, who asks questions, investigates facts for possible answers, and seeks reasons and arguments for preferring one answer or solution (e.g., Fosnot, 1989). It focuses on the process of knowledge acquisition which considers the individual cognitive, affective, and emotional constitution of the student. Accordingly, there is a need for a certain degree of freedom in teaching, in which independent and autonomous acquisition of knowledge is possible for the learner. Therefore, the planning considerations are a critical issue within this paradigm. This paradigm has been criticized for its arbitrariness and overwhelming personal responsibility concerning the learning result (e.g., Künkler, 2016).

Competence orientated teaching, on the other hand, puts the focus on the outcome of the learning process, which should be transferred and applied in the situational demands of a concrete problem solution (e.g., Bachmann, 2018; Oser et al., 2006). Thus, the content of a lesson is in the background of learning efforts – it becomes a means for competence development. Although the existing diversity concerning scientific definitions of the term "competence" leads to diverse heuristics of lesson plans, we will mention here only a few components. Based on existing resources, competence is an interacting interplay of knowledge ("I know"), abilities and skills ("I can"), attitudes and values ("I will"), and external resources ("I may") (e.g., Furrer, 2009; Weinert, 2001). This paradigm received critics for the economization of education, namely that knowledge acquisition and content learning only aim at serving the needs of markets and economy; the development of individual personality, some critics say, is not in the focus of school education anymore (e.g., Liessmann, 2006, 2014).

Acknowledging the reported critics on the two paradigms – constructivist teaching, as well as competence-oriented teaching, we, however, argue that both have components that are useful for the preparation of a VaKE course.

3   Necessary Components for Planning

Doing VaKE for the first time is a new experience for all; the acceptance and approval of all groups of people involved (e.g., students, parents, colleagues, and/or legal guardians) is crucial, and clear and open communication should go along with the VaKE course. This will also promote trust and confidence between students and teachers, which are two basic prerequisites for successful learning (Tschannen-Moran, 2014; Van Maele & Van Houtte, 2011).

On the VaKE site,[1] we provide a form for course planning, which has proven to be supportive in many cases. In the following, we will highlight some of the aspects mentioned in the form and address specificities related to them.

3.1 Looking Carefully at the Characteristics of the Learner Group

A VaKE course can be conducted with any group of participants. However, adaptations and/or restrictions might be necessary due to the characteristics of the group and to the learning environment. Nevertheless, a minimum group size of five people is recommended, while a group between 15 and 20 people is considered as ideal. In larger groups, there might be a problem with the noise level (see Chapter 14 in this handbook). The group might be homogeneous or heterogeneous in terms of age, gender, language, social or religious and cultural backgrounds, etc. Note that when the group is heterogeneous, or the participants have specific characteristics, adaptations, extensions, or changes in the order of the implementation steps may be necessary.

In formal education, every teacher has detailed knowledge of the dominant characteristics of his or her learning community. For instance, as the teachers know the grade of the school class, it can be expected that they have information on the age of the participants, their prior knowledge on the topic, the skills that are available among the students, the number of students in the class, the distribution of the learners across gender, social backgrounds, etc. Most of the teachers are also quite aware of some hidden characteristics of the class, such as the learners' motivation and interest towards the topic, their value priorities, and attitudes within the group.

In contrast, in non-formal educational settings, the trainer usually lacks this type of information. When the trainer starts planning, he or she may have vague information on age, number, why the people participate in the course, and other relevant details. Participation in non-formal education is mostly voluntary. Therefore, the motivation boost of the VaKE story must be particularly strong so that the participants get involved and stay with it until the end of the course. Besides that, age groups share common areas of interest, specific professional groups may also share an interest in specific topics. In groups with heterogeneous interests, it is advisable to allow sufficient time at the beginning of the course, on the one hand, to ask about the expectations of the participants, and on the other hand to focus on the specific components of the VaKE process (e.g., pro-contra debates, teamwork, etc.) to join in.

3.2 Defining Goals and Objectives

The second important aspect of planning considerations concerns the intended learning goals and outcomes. These must be made explicit in the planning. As in other teaching methods, planning a VaKE course demands to set goals within Vygotsky's zone of proximal development (Vygotsky, 1978) and how the teacher/trainer might support and facilitate the learners' knowledge acquisition and development. Vygotsky's approach is recommended for an application not only in school teaching. With their studies, scholars could underpin the continued validity of the theory and the positive effects of its practical application in adult education (e.g., Chaiklin, 2003; Shah & Rashid, 2017).

The setting of objectives does not only concern the field of knowledge but also includes thinking of ethical values and aspects which constitute the dilemma in the VaKE story.

The group's specific characteristics and the particular educational settings indicate the starting point. Sometimes, the acquisition of some particular knowledge as a part of a curriculum or professional development needs, determines the priority of the knowledge over the values. In this case, the teacher or trainer should be able first to answer questions in the same way as they do when planning a traditional lesson. For instance, the teachers formulate the learning goals and outcomes in terms of knowledge, skills, and competences in alignment with the curricula descriptions. Also, taxonomies of writing learning objectives provide respective guidance (e.g., Anderson & Krathwohl, 2013; Bloom & Krathwohl, 1956; Krathwohl, Bloom & Masia, 1964). In any case, however, the teacher must be open to accept that the participants learn other things – both with regard to content as well as to values – than initially planned. It is his or her decision to decide whether and how strongly he or she sticks to the goals formulated at the beginning.

The question of knowledge goals when planning a VaKE course in non-formal education is often more challenging than in formal education settings. With the knowledge that adult education is primarily driven by interest, an experienced trainer can anticipate the expectations and needs of the participants for the conception of the dilemma story. However, this anticipation also carries the risk of failure as the following experience shows: A voluntary teacher training seminar organised during the summer holidays offered VaKE as an innovative didactical approach to problem-solving. The trainer chose a problem of classroom management – assuming that this is an area of teacher interest. However, the participants rejected the story with the argument that they were "on holiday", and they wanted to work on the fictive and funny problem dealing with the question of whether a nearby lake should be covered by a huge dome similar to the construction of an indoor swimming pool. Furthermore, they did not want to experience themselves the approach but wanted a presentation of the method by the trainer. So, the trainer was more or less forced to throw his planning overboard. This example demonstrates that moderating a VaKE course may provide surprises for teachers and trainers due to the high level of autonomy and responsibility for learning outcomes given to the learners.

The values domain could also be the starting point for planning. However, it is more challenging to define the outcomes in the values domain compared to the knowledge domain. For instance, it is not easy to provide definitions for justice or care values. Nevertheless, for planning, it is crucial to identify possible values that support and justify the different points of view in a dilemma and to find a specific definition for each and the possible personal meaning for different individuals. The main goal of values education is to clarify the personal attitude towards a given problem: it is not the value *per se* that is under discussion, but to what extent one value as a point of reference contributes to having a more viable solution for the dilemma and for the problem that the protagonist will have to another value. Since every dilemma has (at least) two opposing points of view, it helps the trainer to think and reflect about the conflict of values already during the planning stage, specifically which ethical values support the respective point of view.

Therefore, the trainer could formulate in a way how predefined values could support each standpoint. The moral developmental theories (e.g., Kohlberg stage theory, Kohlberg, 1984) might help the trainer to choose the proper values for the particular group of participants, having in mind the Vygotskian principle already mentioned. For example, preparing a V*a*KE course for a group of young adolescents, the trainer might use predefined values that support the two opposite standpoints related to family and friendship: e.g., to obey the family or to follow the friend. Preparing a V*a*KE course for a group of professionals, the trainer might use predefined values that support the opposite standpoints related to justice and care: e.g., to act based on the obedience of rules or to overpass them to help a family person. The choice of the values that support the different standpoints becomes crucial for the success of a V*a*KE course. When learners have a dilemma whose values in the competition are similar to those they are currently confronted with in their lives, they may identify themselves with the protagonist of the dilemma and see the dilemma as their own. In other words, the trainer should predefine the values that will be discussed but not expect outcomes as in the knowledge acquisition because in the values domain, it is not easy to link an answer with the assessments "right/wrong" or "good/not good".

Summarising the comments so far, the objective of the course should be the acknowledgment that different standpoints are supported by different values and to discuss the explanatory power of each value for the common good. Furthermore, the values discussion needs additional preparation, and the trainer should consider the potential risks when implementing a V*a*KE course in a group. The risks might be that some members will not be comfortable with explicit disclosure when they support one or the other standpoint. The acknowledgment of the risks by the trainer might trigger transformations of the original goals and objectives.

Beyond the knowledge and value domains, by implementing VaKE in a group, one could also set goals and expect outcomes regarding the skills and working techniques. A VaKE course offers a large selection of opportunities to practice skills and techniques that have already been learned (e.g., in a phase prior to the VaKE unit) or to learn new ones. The trainer could set goals for communication (e.g., asking questions), argumentation (e.g., formulate arguments), reflections (e.g., how did I change the standpoint I was in favour of?), or even more complex skills such as critical thinking skills. A recent qualitative study (Pnevmatikos, Christodoulou & Georgiadou, 2019) provided evidence that a VaKE course implemented in a higher education institution triggered all specific skills that have been described as components of critical thinking and dispositions (e.g., Facione, 1990). Additionally, the trainer could integrate goals for particular techniques such as how to write a summary of a text, how to quote, how to make a digital presentation, how to conduct and record an interview, or how to use the computer. Finally, one could set among the goals of a VaKE course skills for the nature of knowledge (e.g., how to justify the knowledge) and distinguishing the beliefs from evidence.

3.3   Finding a Relevant and Effective Dilemma Story

The dilemma story is the initial trigger of the entire learning process during a VaKE course. It should motivate the learners for continuous, deepening, and, above all, independent learning, and it should be possible to reach explicit learning goals and outcomes. A separate chapter within this handbook pinpoints the characteristics of a VaKE dilemma story and guidelines on how to write such a story (see Chapter 4). For the sake of completeness, only the essential design points are highlighted here below.

Current topics that are discussed in newspapers and the media, plays, dramas, novels, but also events in everyday life are suitable and may give ideas. A VaKE dilemma story must explicitly address two domains: knowledge and values. For the knowledge area, the reference to curricular requirements (in school education) or thematic requirements (in non-formal education) is at the core of the planning by the teacher or the trainer – as we described in the previous section. Working on the story, the learners may also explore their personal interests on additional topics. Both areas of knowledge, the curriculum, and the personal interest, receive an equivalent status of importance and must be made explicit. This equal importance can have the consequence that at the end of a VaKE course, students may have additional and/or different expertise than the teacher/trainer.

Concerning the domain of values, it is more difficult for the planning to determine which values could or should be involved (see above the example on family or friendship). If values are strictly specified, there is a risk of indoctrination and manipulation. Using additional didactical tools and introducing specific methods for sensitizing value consciousness (e.g., Potter Box or Values Square in Chapter 5) may offer possibilities to avoid this risk.

It must also be possible to relate a V*a*KE dilemma story to the assessment of learning outcomes. This includes the newly acquired knowledge and the reflection on the learning process as a whole: on possible effects and consequences, on follow-ups, and possible areas of learning transfer (see Chapter 32).

3.4   *Additional Components of Classroom Management*

As the overall responsibility for reaching the intended learning outcomes remains with the teacher or trainer, the usual structural elements of classroom management, possibly adapted to the specific conditions of a V*a*KE process, have to be selected and implemented: time management for the individual steps, useful practice skills and techniques, supportive material, equipment, media, and specific sources of information.

As for the discussions, the search for information and the creation of a summarising final product may happen in small groups, different social forms of learning become relevant for planning considerations.

A very detailed planning supports the teacher in moderating and guiding the interest-based individualization of the learning process, which the students are responsible for, and at the same time allows to maintain a controlling overview of the individual learning paths. It must be emphasized, however, that given the open structure of V*a*KE, planning is a flexible tool and not a rigid corset, even more so than in regular teaching.

4   Rules in V*a*KE Discussion and Debate

Debates and discussions are challenging when becoming intervention tools for learning processes, particularly because most students are not acquainted with open teaching as practiced in V*a*KE. Further, factual knowledge must be retrieved very quickly from memory – this requires a high activation of explicit (not tacit) knowledge. Furthermore, active participation leads to an increase in the emotional state of mind – this requires the concentrated coordination of external perceptions and inner states of arousal.

Depending on the level of cognitive and affective development of the participants, certain behaviours may be acceptable from the point of view of optimal discussion while others would be unknown or inappropriate, e.g., behaviours of emotional control. Cultural peculiarities must also be taken into account.

Therefore, it is necessary to agree on appropriate discussion rules in advance. A poster of "Do's and Don'ts", visible for all discussants, can support the quality of the discussion, preferably based on a common decision instead of ordered by the teacher, since if the students participate in the decision-making, they are more committed to complying with the rules. The following list emphasises the basics:

- As a prerequisite, all fruitful discussions must be led by mutual esteem and appreciation.
- Critiques are expressed on ideas, not on people: This is the most important rule. All participants are equal, and the status or other people's characteristics, as well as their behaviours, and eloquence skills, play no role. Only the estimated viability of the expressed arguments must be taken into account.
- Any statement must include the position that is defended and its justification. It is not sufficient, for instance, to simply say that one disagrees or that one prefers one option of the protagonist over the other, but one must say *why* one disagrees or prefers that option.
- The group does not need to come to a final agreement about what the protagonist of the dilemma should do.
- Feedback must be specific, descriptive (not evaluative), and factual. The peers must understand it. The feedback must not be personal, but in a way that one would accept if receiving feedback in that manner.
- Encouragement of participation: The discussion climate must be inclusive and invite all participants to take part.
- Asking for clarification in case of poor understanding: Participants might misunderstand each other. To enhance understanding, one might ask the participants first to repeat what the other person has said before responding.
- No sanctions are applied: Everyone can say whatever he or she wants with respect to the topic (not the person) without any risk of negative consequences. In particular, the utterances must not be graded.
- No interruption of the argument: Any person must be given the possibility to give a complete account of his or her concept without, however, becoming excessive.
- No monopolization of the discussion as there is a continued steady focus on the topic, no excessive repetition of an argument.
- Showing respect to opposing standpoints: The arguments must be considered carefully; rejections must be justified with arguments, not simple opposition.

- Any participant can change his or her position at any time without the risk of being judged as inconsistent.
- Active participation, not only listening to the debate.

The teacher is required to act in three different roles during the discussions, namely (1) moderating the discussion if necessary; (2) as one participant among others, expressing his or her own opinion, or an argument that might have been missing so far, or that can provoke further reflection (e.g., moral arguments on a higher stage than the ones expressed so far); and (3) supporting the weaker students if it is evident that they have difficulties to express themselves. Under certain conditions, the teacher can take the role of 'the devil's advocate' (see Chapter 5 in this handbook).

Discussions can be organised in diverse forms, e.g., group work, fishbowl, round table, jigsaw, plenum. Information search is usually done by individuals or in small groups of not more than three unless the task requires larger groups. Overall, the rules must be handled flexibly within the principles underlying VaKE.

5 Preparing the Class for a VaKE Course

As the responsibility for the individual learning process should be shifted more and more over to the learners, a comprehensive and detailed introduction to the method and the process is required. The teacher must allow enough time for this, especially if such a project is being carried out for the first time.

This preparation is called step 0. General information on the VaKE approach is addressed, especially about learner-centeredness and its consequences for activation. Explicitly, the step-like structure of the procedure has to be explained. Furthermore, it needs a clear statement on the differences to the traditional teaching-learning approach concerning the roles of a teacher, on the non-existence of the "right-wrong" evaluations when presenting arguments, and if applicable on the tools and the criteria for final assessment of the learning outcomes regarding the intended curricular objectives.

In particular, when applied to school and formal education, clear information must also be provided in advance on the two types of learning objectives and outcomes: on curriculum-based knowledge relevant to assessment, as opposed to that which can be acquired on the basis of personal interest.

As with value education, it is of utmost importance to emphasize that the aim is not indoctrination, i.e., conveying values, but arguing (see Chapter 21 in this handbook).

If VaKE recommended tools and techniques are intended to be used, it is appropriate to make the participants familiar with and train their utilization in advance.

6 Conducting a VaKE Course for the First Time

In short, the teacher/trainer activities concentrate on three levels: (i) on a meta-level (i.e., introducing and explaining the next VaKE steps); (ii) on the management level (i.e., moderating the discussion, organizing the work, paying attention to the time, focusing on the learning goals and outcomes, giving support); and (iii) as an option on the involvement level (i.e., becoming a participant of the process or an expert upon request in the information search step). Each level needs a symbol for recognition, so the learners can distinguish on which level a specific teacher/trainer activity is performed.

For the first implementation, it is advisable to follow the prototypical sequence of steps. However, a possible unforeseen group dynamic must not be overlooked and should be taken into account.

The following components are central for the implementation in general – the strict order of the steps is of secondary importance: taking a standpoint, discussion, reflection, decision for/against a proposal, its justification by presenting arguments, search for information, change of roles or perspectives, shared conclusion, summary in a final product, appropriate and useful additions. One must mention however, that the participants often decide spontaneously and without knowing about the prototypical steps to address the next task, particularly in the transition from dilemma discussion to question asking. Related experiences have driven the creation of various versions of the prototypical course (e.g., VaKE *dis,* VaKE-pr, etc.). A poster with the applied version visible for the whole group supports efforts to keep control of the process and follow the steps. It is also possible to start by integrating only individual steps into regular lessons and progressively adding more and more steps, provided this is done in agreement with the theory underlying VaKE.

7 Conclusions

Planning a VaKE course, preparing the class, and implementing the course is challenging for the trainers and teachers as well as for the learners because it does not correspond to the traditional ideas and experiences of a learning process. Teachers are afraid of losing control, and learners miss a clear order on what to learn. To start with VaKE requires some courage, trust, and the acceptance of the possible failures, from both trainers and learners.

The advantage of trying VaKE is that it is possible to reshape the relationship between trainers and learners. VaKE opens for new perspectives on people, it renews the dynamics of learning processes where knowledge and values are actively combined, and it encourages trainers to think about their own professional actions. Since the open spaces for individual interests and development can lead to unpredictable learning pathways, the planning principle can be as follows: Prepare for as many contingencies as possible, involve the learners, and learn from failures!

Note

1 www.VaKE.eu

References

Anderson, L. W., & Krathwohl, D. R. (Eds.). (2013). *A taxonomy for learning, teaching, and assessing: A revision of Bloom's taxonomy of educational objectives*. Boston, MA: Allyn & Bacon.

Bachmann, H. (Ed.). (2018). *Competence oriented teaching and learning in higher education – Essentials*. Zürich, Switzerland: hep Verlag.

Bloom, B. S., & Krathwohl, D. R. (1956). *Taxonomy of educational objectives: The classification of educational goals, by a committee of college and university examiners. Handbook I: Cognitive domain*. New York, NY: Longmans, Green.

Chaiklin, S. (2003). The zone of proximal development in Vygotsky's analysis of learning and instruction. In A. Kozulin, B. Gindis, V. Ageyev, & S. Miller (Eds.), *Vygotsky's educational theory and practice in cultural context* (pp. 39–64). Cambridge, MA: Cambridge University.

Facione, P. (1990). *Critical thinking: A statement of expert consensus for purposes of educational assessment and instruction* (The Delphi Report). Retrieved August, 8, 2020, from https://www.researchgate.net/publication/242279575_Critical_Thinking_A_Statement_of_Expert_Consensus_for_Purposes_of_Educational_Assessment_and_Instruction

Fosnot, C. T. (1989). *Enquiring teachers, enquiring learners: A constructivist approach for teaching*. New York, NY: Teachers College Press.

Kohlberg, L. (1984). *The psychology of moral development: The nature and validity of moral stages* (Essays on Moral Development, Vol. 2). New York, NY: Harper & Row.

Krathwohl, D. R., Bloom, B. S., & Masia, B. B. (1964). *Taxonomy of educational objectives, Book II. Affective domain.* New York, NY: David McKay Company, Inc.

Künkler, T. (2016). *Konstruktivistische Didaktik: Theoretisch plausibel?* In J.-L. Patry & I. Schrittesser (Eds.), Konstruktivistisches Denken – theoretisch unbehaust? *Journal für LehrerInnenbildung, 2,* 18–27.

Liessmann, K. P. (2006). *Theorie der Unbildung. Die Irrtümer der Wissensgesellschaft.* Vienna, Austria: Paul Zsolnay.

Liessmann, K. P. (2014). *Geisterstunde: Die Praxis der Unbildung. Eine Streitschrift.* Vienna, Austria: Paul Zsolnay.

Oser, F., Achtenhagen, F., & Renold, U. (Eds.). (2006). *Competence oriented teacher training: Old research demands and new pathways.* Rotterdam, The Netherlands: Sense Publishers.

Pnevmatikos, D., Christodoulou, P., & Georgiadou, T. (2019). Promoting critical thinking in higher education through the Values and Knowledge Education (VaKE) method. *Studies in Higher Education, 44*(5), 892–901.

Shah, T., & Rashid, S. (2017). Applying Vygotsky to adult learning. *Journal of Social Sciences, Government College University Faisalabad, 8,* 1–13.

Tschannen-Moran, M. (2014). The interconnectivity of trust in schools. In D. Van Maele, P. B. Forsyth, & M. Van Houtte (Eds.), *Trust and school life: The role of trust for learning, teaching, leading, and bridging* (pp. 57–81). Dordrecht, The Netherlands: Springer Science+Business Media. https://doi.org/10.1007/978-94-017-8014-8_3

Van Maele, D., & Van Houtte, M. (2011). The quality of school life: Teacher-student trust relationships and the organizational school context. *Social Indicators Research, 100,* 85–100.

Vygotsky, L. S. (1978). *Mind in society: The development of higher psychological processes.* Cambridge, MA: Harvard University Press.

Weinert, F. E. (2001). Vergleichende Leistungsmessung in Schulen – eine umstrittene Selbstverständlichkeit. In F. E. Weinert (Ed.), *Leistungsmessungen in Schulen* (pp. 17–31). Weinheim, Germany: Beltz.

CHAPTER 4

How to Write a Dilemma Story

Sieglinde Weyringer and Dimitris Pnevmatikos

1   Introduction

The dilemma story is at the heart of the V*a*KE approach because it is intended to initiate the critical examination of the evaluation and moral justification of decisions as well as the process of acquiring knowledge. It must have the potential to trigger interest and curiosity among the participants. Using dilemma stories in ethical or moral research, education or training has a long tradition. We will only mention a few examples here: the "Heinz dilemma" on moral justification by Kohlberg (1981), and dilemma stories on care developed by Gilligan et al. (1971) are very prominent. Since then, numerous studies have shown that using dilemma stories nurtures positive effects on the development of moral argumentation and moral thinking (Blatt & Kohlberg, 1975). Dilemma stories also are used for training courses on ethics in organisations (Kvalnes, 2019); Viz (1990) proposes narrative stories – non-abstract moral dilemmas and real-life dilemmas are recommended (Balakrishnan, 2011). Dilemmas are used to motivate the learning process (Bohse, 1982) from children in primary school (Settelmaier, 2006) to adults in advanced training seminars (Lind, 2016). However, constructing and writing a dilemma story suitable for V*a*KE and introducing it to the learning group is always a pedagogical challenge. This chapter is an attempt to accompany the teacher when elaborating a V*a*KE dilemma story, firstly by describing the essentials of a V*a*KE dilemma story in contrast to similar types of stories, secondly by presenting a checklist, thirdly by presenting hints on the creation of a story suitable for a specific learner group, and finally on its introduction in a V*a*KE course.

2   Dilemma, Problem, or Case Story?

Although the dilemma approach and problem-based learning share many similarities, they are not identical. Therefore, the differences between a dilemma, a problem, and a case story need to be highlighted. A dilemma is a conflict that cannot be totally resolved – a temporary decision can be found, but the dilemma will continue. For a dilemma, what is at stake is that two alternative decisions are in conflict. In philosophy, dilemmas (e.g., the prisoner's dilemma) are common. Additionally, the philosophers express the dilemma as a *paradox* (e.g., Buridan's donkey), as *aporia* (e.g., Socratic dialogue in Protagoras) or as *antinomy* (e.g., in the work of Kant). Philosophers also use stories in which the conflicted solutions are more than two. When the choice has to be made between three options, it is called *trilemma*, and for more than three options, it is called *polylemma*.

When people try to resolve the *dilemma*, they choose one specific decision at a particular moment. However, deciding for that action or judgment does not entail that it is the only correct option and that the other is wrong. If this happens, the story would not be considered to be a dilemma. As such, a dilemma presupposes that the person perceives the two alternatives as both to be correct, and hence the two alternative decisions to conflict with each other. The conflict arises because the values associated with every course of action and every judgment in play are considered by the person as important. Thus, a dilemma is about value priorities, and no matter how the person decides, in any case, the decision will violate one of the involved values. Therefore, when the person suggests a solution to the specific situation and takes action, it may resolve the conflict for the person, but it does not necessarily resolve the dilemma. In addition, in order to solve the conflict by the individual, a reorientation and restructuring of the personal value system might be required; this would lead to a different set of priorities, which may make the conflict resolution possible.

For a *problem*, in contrast, a final "right" solution can be found. When a solution is found, the problem no longer exists for the person involved. Similar problems may appear, yet the problems will not be exactly the same.

Due to these characteristics, the debate on a dilemma story often focuses on conflicting values, whereas facts do not play a crucial role. Thus, in schools, seminars, and training courses, dilemma stories are used in lessons on religion, ethics, and philosophy. In a problem story, the relationship between values and facts is the opposite. Knowledge about related facts based on viable evidence found by research is essential for the solution, while considerations and assessment based on ethical orientation are not in explicit focus – in short: dilemma story – focus on values, problem story – focus on facts and knowledge. Thus, the problem stories became famous in didactics for all the subject matters. Hence, diverse didactic teaching approaches have been developed using problem-based approaches (e.g., Bruner, 1961, for a starting point).

Another type of problem-based approach is the *case* story. In its centre, there is a person, and the question is: "What did the protagonist do to achieve the present result?" The central approach is limited to the case analysis and is at most expanded by considering how a better result could have been achieved. Working with case stories is a preferred method in business training and training in health care, jurisdiction, psychotherapy, and others (e.g., Afsouran et al., 2018).

All three story types (dilemma story, problem story, case story) provide characteristics for the concept of a specific VaKE dilemma story, which will be described in detail in the next section.

3 VaKE Dilemma Stories – A Mixture of Different Story Types

A VaKE dilemma story can be characterised as a mixture of the three story types described above. The VaKE dilemma story is about a fictional person whose nature is described in concrete terms. One can also use historical figures or people from literature (e.g., Aufenanger et al., 1981). The protagonist is faced with a specific situation in which he or she must choose between two or more options for what he or she should do. Each of the options of action is acceptable and supported by values. However, no matter how he or she decides, in any case, the decision violates a moral value that is important to the person. Therefore, such a story does not imply that one option is good or right, and the other is bad or wrong. Furthermore, the VaKE dilemma story must end with the following question "What should the protagonist do and why?" By identifying themselves with the individual protagonist, the participants are asked to answer *what* the person should do and *why*. Thus, they argue in favour or against a particular behaviour option that is suggested by the story. The teacher can also allow the participants to postpone the decision by saying, "I do not know for the time being". In any case, the moral issues and ethical values at stake are included in the argumentative discussions, as each participant must explain why she or he thinks a particular solution is better than the other.

A VaKE dilemma story, however, moves beyond the frame of only discussing the moral-ethical aspect of the story because it also integrates the necessity to use factual knowledge in the argumentation about the conflict. The overall objective is that the learners acknowledge that their first answers are based on beliefs, emotions, stereotypes, or lack of relevant evidence-based knowledge before they move further and develop a value decision with an evidence-based knowledge background. We recall that the diverse activities within the different steps of a VaKE course provide good opportunities for searching for relevant information and assessing its validity based on scientific evidence and analytical thinking.

4   VaKE Dilemma Story – The Essential Elements

The brief description of the essential components allows the process for writing a dilemma story; it is also crucial to have a clear view of these aspects before starting to write a good VaKE dilemma story. Furthermore, because it is challenging to write a compelling dilemma story, it is recommended when implementing VaKE for the first time that the teacher/trainer starts with a dilemma story that was used in other similar educational settings (learning goals, knowledge, or context).

The starting consideration for a VaKE dilemma story is the question "What specific knowledge should the participants have acquired after the course?" often explicitly defined in the curriculum by the specific learning outcomes. So, a VaKE dilemma story should lead the participants to construct the relevant knowledge defined by the curricula. The story should also trigger a dynamic discussion and contribute to reflections on involved values. Additionally, the participants will search for the evidence that may support their arguments, and this working process should be relevant for both the curricular and educational aims of the course as well as for the personal interests of the participants. Otherwise, the VaKE process runs the risk of not being successful. The guidelines of constructivist teaching-learning approaches are relevant for the VaKE course design as well (e.g., the role of prior knowledge; the new knowledge demands an enrichment or reconstruction of the prior knowledge; skills and procedural knowledge necessary for the construction of the new knowledge).

Another crucial aspect when writing a VaKE dilemma is to allow the participants to identify themselves with the person who has the dilemma in the story. This refers to the need for *personalisation* of the dilemma. For example, a dilemma a lawyer has in his or her professional work might be irrelevant on a training course with teachers or care professions. On the other hand, this dilemma story might provide a very successful learning process for a group of lawyers. Sharing some characteristics with the person having the dilemma enables the participants on a VaKE course to identify themselves with the person and suggest a solution as if they were in the protagonist's shoes. Thus, it is crucial to consider the characteristics of the participants prior to the VaKE course and to describe the person in the dilemma story as having some common characteristics with the participants. Thus, the person in the dilemma story should resemble the participants. For example, writing a story for children in which a father has a dilemma does not seem as relevant as presenting a child of the same age who has a dilemma. One should use concrete names but avoid using names that connect the person with real and known people or institutions (e.g., *Mr. James,* the director of *our* school ...). Instead, fictive names and institutions should be used (e.g., *Mr. Jonathan who is the director of a school* ...). As V*a*KE is a student-centred method, regardless of their age, the students are expected to construct and expand both their value reflection and their knowledge base. It is then crucial to be aware of the students' moral characteristics. Moral developmental stage theories (e.g., Kohlberg, 1981) could help to give a hint for whom teachers/trainers prepare a V*a*KE dilemma story. A dilemma addressing societal issues, which would require at least stage 4, would then not be appropriate for fourth graders, whereas a group-focused dilemma (stage 3) would be. Furthermore, and in the same vein, the context should be similar to the participants', so a dilemma story prepared for the pre-adolescents with a conflict between obedience to the family and solidarity in friendship is suitable. In contrast, a dilemma story with a conflict between friendship and a romantic relationship is more relevant for adolescents. Moreover, a dilemma of whether a woman should have an abortion or not should hardly be a dilemma for young male adolescents. Also, a dilemma story that deals with the conflicting choices between professional and family duties is more suitable for adults than for children.

The dilemma story should also provide a fair amount of information. A massive story with much irrelevant information or a short story lacking the necessary information disorient the participants, thus hindering an effective development of knowledge and value reflection. Furthermore, they might be unnecessary and lead participants to search for information beyond the course's scope. One must also consider how much the students know already, not to provide them with redundant information.

Moreover, the dilemma story should have cultural validity. For instance, a dilemma story that refers to a testamentary inheritance could be a suitable dilemma in some learning settings; however, it might be irrelevant in others as, for instance, in some Muslim contexts where there is no traditional testamentary inheritance. The dilemma story should also have a broad horizon, welcoming many different points of view (e.g., ecological, economic, social, health, and aesthetic issues).

A teacher or workshop leader must always be aware that a topic of the dilemma might touch a participant particularly. Any event presented in the dilemma story can evoke memories about some events and trigger an emotional reaction. A dilemma on abortion, for instance, might have a substantial impact on a woman who has had an abortion. With children, it might be possible that the dilemma discussion can create conflicts when family practices may differ from what is discussed in school. The teacher should consider potential conflicts that participants might experience and be prepared on how to manage some upcoming reactions, uneasiness, and questions. In this context, it is also crucial that the dilemma story does not explicitly address a problem experienced by the participants. For instance, if there has been a particular event (e.g., discipline problems in class, stealing or lying, bullying, cheating) and the teacher wants to address the issue in a VaKE unit, the dilemma should be formulated in such a way that the link to this event must not be obvious, but the transfer of the learning outcome to real life and/or to similar problems can be performed. This means other protagonists and other circumstances must be described. The transfer will be done by the participants and can be triggered, if necessary, in the last steps of VaKE.

5 How to Write a VaKE Dilemma Story – A Preliminary Checklist

The following checklist aims to facilitate the educators to reflect on their writing of dilemma stories and help them to evaluate potential modifications. We mention some questions that the teachers and trainers need to ask themselves.

1. *Knowledge*: What is the knowledge that the learners will seek to solve the dilemma situation? What part of the expected learning objectives can be covered during a VaKE course? As mentioned, the dilemma should trigger class discussions and work activities that include evidence-based knowledge in alignment with the learning objectives (i.e., the knowledge part). If not, the educator should reflect on what she or he should modify and what changes are needed in order to have a promising dilemma story.

2. *Values*: What are the conflicting values involved that are most likely to support the two alternative decision options of the dilemma? Because a dilemma story is about a person who is in a decision-making situation, the dilemma should end with, at minimum, two alternative courses of action, or two judgment options that simultaneously represent two different and conflicting sets of values, and the learners must decide *for* or *against* the action presented at the end of the story. Although the value positions conflict with one another, the participants may see one position or both as irrelevant. So, the educator should carefully consider whether and how the opposing values will be received by the group of learners. If the participants perceive the values as being equally important, the opinion might be split in the discussion group, with approximately equal numbers supporting the opposing solutions, which will trigger stimulating discussions. The educator should ask him or herself: what changes should I do to highlight the conflict of values and trigger good learning?

3. *Personalisation*: Is the dilemma appropriately personalised in terms of names, ages, and what other elements support the dilemma's cultural and

ecological validity? The dilemma story should have current relevance to life, and the topic addressed should be known and relevant in everyday life. However, it is important to mention that a V*a*KE course is not equivalent to a therapeutic situation where concrete personal problems and/or conflicts within the learning group are dealt with. For instance, in the case of bullying in class, the V*a*KE dilemma story should not address this particular issue because this problem cannot be solved within a teaching-learning situation, and personal problems disrupt the learning process. Thus, the educator should ask: What changes should I make, and for which elements of the dilemma story in order to meet the group's characteristics appropriately?

4. *Awareness of the problem and routine to select a solution:* Do the learners combine previous experience with problems similar to the dilemma story and find a satisfying solution? If yes, the learners will probably not experience the story as a value conflict, and they will not think about different possibilities to handle the conflict. For instance, if the conflicting values address the decision between a well-paid job offer from a company that produces environmentally harmful pesticides and a low-paid job in an environmental protection organisation, it can be assumed for example, that chemistry students will handle the conflict differently than unemployed adults, or environmental activists, or managers of a chemical company, or a person who is not interested in this issue at all.

5. *Narrative style*: Is the dilemma story written in an engaging style? Remember that the protagonist should be portrayed very lively in his or her thoughts, feelings, and motivations, and minor modifications in the story's content can intensify or weaken the dilemma. For example, the question "Should the woman have an abortion or not?" can be valued differently with the combined information that the woman is about to get a promotion or has wanted a child for a long time. One can regulate the focus of a dilemma towards one or the other option with subtle changes. However, if dilemmas from literature or history are used, such adjustments cannot be made.

6. *Unintended negative effects:* Are there any adverse effects and consequences possible due to the dilemma story or the use of V*a*KE? As such, can controversial discussions disunite the group and endanger the collaboration? The educator should be prepared for this possible situation and reflect on how to manage such situational dynamics.

7. *Modifications of the story:* Is it convenient to present the story as a sequel? As the V*a*KE course can span over several learning meetings, the story can be presented as a series of sequels. If more meetings are necessary, the educator should consider the possibility of dividing the dilemma into parts that might include surprises comparable to everyday life. One can conceive the

continuation of the dilemma differently depending on the participants' chosen option. These inputs will most probably influence decision-making behaviour, reasons, and argumentative reflections.

6 How to Use the Wider Context for Creating a Suitable Dilemma Story

As mentioned, the unique characteristics of the respective learning group and the educator's learning intentions are decisive for researching topics for a dilemma story. However, a distinction must be made between the specific curricular objectives which are binding for teaching and the broader learning field, which is also crucial for researching information and for the individual learner's goals.

Example: The learning field is history, in particular, Europe during the First World War; the topic is the British Empire and the question: "Should Britain grant asylum to the Russian tsar family?", this was the Prime Minister's dilemma. The curricular objectives might concentrate on the historical data of people and the negotiation of possible contracts. In contrast, the broader learning could focus on the Russian Revolution and the role of the British government in giving asylum to Russian Marxists, and the personal interest is in the life of Lenin.

The chosen dilemma could also be related to the current daily situation. Daily and weekly newspapers and news reports are therefore particularly suitable for finding a good topic.

Example: A VaKE discussion in spring 2007 about the awarding of the Nobel Prize in Literature to Omar Pamuk. Question: "Should Omar Pamuk be brought to justice for his statements about the genocide against the Armenian people?" This would be the Turkish Public Prosecutor's Dilemma – Topics: Literature, History, Geography, Human Rights, European Union, Politics, or Legal Systems.

Newspapers provide many examples of dilemmas that might trigger effective dilemma stories. In addition, films and autobiographical stories are suitable sources of inspiration for dilemma stories. World literature can be used in literature lessons since almost all literary works contain dilemmas or are based on dilemmas. In history, dilemmas can also be found in every epoch, based on decisions made by individuals. In science and technical teaching, the dilemma stories can highlight more or less well-known dangers and misuse possibilities of science: nuclear power plants; advantages and risks of vaccinations; social problems in the case of identification technology; ecological destruction of nature and human genetic changes, etc. Often, several of these areas are addressed simultaneously, mostly across scientific disciplines (see Chapter 33 in this handbook).

7 Conclusion

The presented instructions for writing a V*a*KE dilemma story are based on the diverse and concrete experiences that were had by many authors of this handbook. However, each teacher or trainer must find his or her way to accomplish this task. It is worth noting that a well-written story does not always imply a successful V*a*KE process. Furthermore, based on our experience, it also can be said that the repeated use of the same dilemma story in different groups does not necessarily lead to the same results (see Chapter 14 in this handbook). The reception of the story, thus, is to a great amount decisive, not only the redaction of the dilemma story. Consequently, the story is an essential impetus for a V*a*KE course's success, combined with carefully prepared planning and skillful moderation of the course.

References

Afsouran, N. R., Charkhabi, M., Siadat, S. A., Hoveida, R., Oreyzi, H. R., & Thornton III, G. C. (2018). Case-method teaching: Advantages and disadvantages in organizational training. *Journal of Management Development, 37*(9/10), 711–720. doi:10.1108/JMD-10-2017-0324

Aufenanger, S., Garz, D., & Zutavern, M. (1981). *Erziehung zur Gerechtigkeit: Unterrichtspraxis nach Lawrence Kohlberg*. München, Germany: Kösel.

Balakrishnan, V. (2011). *Real-life dilemmas in moral education*. Kuala Lumpur, Malaysia: University of Malaya Press.

Blatt, M.M., & Kohlberg, L. (1975). The effects of classroom moral discussion upon children's level of moral judgment. *Journal of Moral Education, 4*(2), 129–161. doi:10.1080/0305724750040207

Bohse, J. (1982). Inszenierte Dramenlektüre: Der Prozess gegen Karl von Moor und Moritz Spielberg. Modell für einen "produktions"- und "handlungsorientierten" Literaturunterricht am Beispiel von Schillers "Räubern". In G. Haas (Ed.), *Literatur im Unterricht. Modelle zu erzählerischen und dramatischen Texten in den Sekundarstufen I und II* (pp. 205–267). Stuttgart, Germany: Reclam.

Bruner, J. S. (1961). The act of discovery. *Harvard Educational Review, 31*(1), 21–32.

Gilligan, C., Kohlberg, L., Lerner, J., & Melenky, M. (1971). Moral reasoning about sexual dilemmas: The development of an interview and scoring system in United States. In

Commission on Obscenity and Pornography, *Technical report of the Commission on Obscenity and Pornography* (Vol. 1; pp. 141–174). Retrieved September 10, 2020, from https://books.google.at/books?hl=de&lr=&id=DuMpAQAAMAAJ&oi=fnd&pg=PA141&ots=Jdhikk8bTM&sig=67TKU1bgFYZLDB55ZRzmHpzUXqI&redir_esc=y#v=onepage&q&f=false

Kohlberg, L. (1981). *Essays on moral development, Vol I: The philosophy of moral development.* San Francisco, CA: Harper & Row.

Kvalnes, O. (2019). *Moral reasoning at work: Rethinking ethics in organizations* (p. 145). Cham, Switzerland: Springer Nature. doi: 10.1007/978-3-030-15191-1

Lind, G. (2016). *How to teach morality: Promoting deliberation and discussion, reducing violence and deceit.* Berlin, Germany: Logos.

Settelmaier, E. (2003, March 23–26). *Dilemmas with dilemmas: Exploring the suitability of dilemma stories as a way of addressing ethical issues in science education* [Paper]. The annual meeting of the National Association for Research in Science Teaching, Philadelphia, PA. Retrieved September 10, 2020, from https://eric.ed.gov/?id=ED476253

Vitz, P. C. (1990). The use of stories in moral development: New psychological reasons for an old education method. *American Psychologist, 45*(6), 709–720. doi:10.1037/0003-066X.45.6.709

CHAPTER 5

Tools and Techniques Used in V*a*KE

Sieglinde Weyringer and Jean-Luc Patry

1   Introduction

V*a*KE is open to many different tools, instruments, and intervention techniques that can be used to achieve the teaching goals. This chapter intends to highlight some that have proven useful in the implementation of V*a*KE. They support the development of diverse competencies, including non-curricular aspects, such as, from the students' perspective, critical thinking; collaboration in heterogeneous teams; communication skills; argumentation; etc. From the perspective of the teacher or trainer, one can mention classroom management; variability of teacher's role; flexible switching between frontal and open teaching; and others.

The selection of methods will present a short description each and proposals for their application. This compilation does not claim to be complete, mandatory, or exclusive. The proposed list is expandable. Other techniques and tools not mentioned here have a similar potential to support the learning process. It is always up to the teacher to decide on their use, preferably in agreement with the students, either against the background of the success experienced in his or her own teaching practice or out of interest to try something new that has been shown to be useful in other studies. It is also quite possible to propose methods not described here but that follow the same logic.

Within a V*a*KE course, the listed tools, instruments, and techniques primarily serve as educational interventions, not for assessment, although the information gained this way can also be used for that purpose. The range includes tools and techniques for sensitizing for immaterial values; stimulating knowledge and ideas; knowledge management; stimulating empathy and debate; and final synthesis.

2   Tools for Sensitizing for Immaterial Values

Values education is a central aim of a V*a*KE course, which mainly occurs during the dilemma discussions (see Chapter 2 in this handbook). Besides that, there are several tools that can be used to raise awareness of values and that fit well into VaKE processes. Two methods are presented here: the Values and Development Square and the Potter Box.

2.1   The Values and Development Square

Schulz von Thun (1998; Schulz von Thun Institut, 2020) developed an instrument to study the way of thinking about personal values that trigger individual communication patterns and habits: the Values and Development Square (see Figure 5.1). It raises awareness for differentiation in the interpretation and evaluation of perceptions and behaviours. Its origins go back to Nicolai Hartmann (1926), who created the synthesis of value antinomies with the strength of each value. First, a value (1 in Figure 5.1) is presented and distinguished from its positive countervalue (2), like friendliness and its positive countervalue, reserve. A second dimension, the negative extremes of these two values, is integrated into the model, e.g., friendliness put to its extreme, becomes exuberant lack of distance (3), and reserve becomes brusque rejection (4). The idea is that a value can unfold its positive and constructive effect only if it is in dynamic and balanced tension with its positive countervalue, otherwise it degenerates to devaluing exaggeration.

In practice, starting from a predetermined value, e.g., friendliness, the participants are encouraged to express polarizing reflections, namely: What can be the positive countervalue? and: What are exaggerations of the respective values, in the sense of "too much of the good"? Several relationships are given between the four corners: between 1 and 2 a positive stress relationship; between 1 and 3 as well as between 2 and 4 devaluing exaggerations; between 1 and 4 as well as between 2 and 3 contrary contrasts; and between 3 and 4 negative overcompensations. Problematic developments are in the diagonal: If the positive tension (1–2) is not in balance, friendliness exaggerates either to exuberant lack of distance or to brusque rejection.

In VaKE courses, we may use this square for raising awareness about values and for the fact that in daily life, each consideration on the moral viability

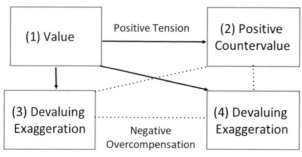

FIGURE 5.1   The Values and Development Square (adapted from Schulz von Thun Institut, 2020, p. 1)

of action options is grounded in pondering between alternatives. According to our experience in VaKE courses, participants sometimes have problems talking about their values: Either they have never explicitly thought about their values preferences, or they reject sharing this very intimate aspect with others; in some cases, they also misinterpret discussions about values and their justification with the attempt to indoctrinate them.

The Values and Developmental Square can trigger value awareness without exposing the personal value preferences. Stimulated by the dilemma and possibly after the debate on pros or cons of a possible solution, the group is asked, "Which value could justify this particular decision?" Several values will be nominated by the participants and documented on a poster. Even in this first round, the participants realize that diverse values can be attributed to a behaviour option for the protagonist of the dilemma. The other three values in the model will be named in the same way. The result is a specific list of values for each pole created by the participants. It makes obvious, both the heterogeneity of the group as well as the individuality of the person with respect to values.

2.2   The Potter Box

In the case of ethical dilemmas, decision-making is very difficult. But when the dilemma is broken down into its components, it may help define the situation and bring the conflicting values, principles, and loyalties to stage. This allows the identification of overlaps and discrepancies between the competing elements. Potter (1965, cited in Guth & Marsh, 2005, p. 264) developed an instrument to show these interdependencies: the Potter Box (Figure 5.2).

The process of clarification begins at the definition and continues anticlockwise:

Definition is the clarification of the situation: As good as possible (i.e., with all personal abilities) the learner should describe and find out what he or she

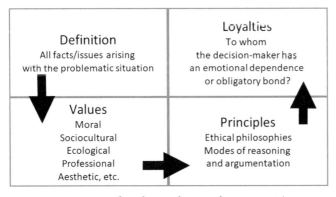

FIGURE 5.2   Potter Box (based on Guth & Marsh, 2005, p. 264)

knows and does not know and with whom he or she would have to talk in order to get the additional information.

In the next step, the learner should clarify for him- or herself which *values* are involved in the dilemma, trying to rank the values (which value(s) is/are judged most important).

Principles are, on the one hand, models of justification for the hierarchy of values determined by the situation; on the other hand, they propose guidelines for action, towards which a person can direct his or her activities, e.g., ethical codes issued by organizations or professions. There are also personal value principles, which are then considered as personal ethical codex. Codes which have proved useful in the course of human history can serve as reference points, e.g., the principle of the golden middle according to Aristotle, the principle of the golden middle way according to Confucius, Kant's categorical imperative, Mill's principle of usefulness, Rawls' veil of the ignorance or the agape principle of the Judeo-Christian tradition. This list can be supplemented by other principles, e.g., from the Muslim cultural sphere. The learner may deepen the knowledge about these different approaches and may determine which is the principle they prefer in the concrete case.

Loyalties refer to all the protagonists of the dilemma between whom bonds or dependencies can be assumed. The learner has to decide by a sequence, who of them deserves loyalty.

In a next step, the learners consider whether the established hierarchy of values, the preferred principles and the established series of loyalties are compatible with each other. Inconsistencies will become evident in this comparison. If the learner believes that he or she chooses the right decision, he or she should check it by a further situation analysis, whether it relates honestly to the situation or is based on something else, e.g., on sympathy.

The Potter Box does not provide answers to dilemmas, but its use allows the identification of overlaps and discrepancies between the competing elements. This way, the Potter Box provides a basis for the justification of the decision.

Both tools, the Potter Box and the Values and Development Square, provide lists of values as the result of their application on a concrete problem, conflict, or dilemma. The knowledge and understanding of values are wrested from abstraction and latent or tacit knowledge and become concrete. In order to deepen this process of becoming aware of values, the next step could be to consider assigning them to value categories. This exploration seems significant with regard to the category of "ethical-moral value", concrete, to ask whether a specific value (e.g., friendship, or parental care) can be assigned to this category.

3 Techniques and Tools for Stimulating Knowledge and Ideas

Since in social problem solving, we cannot seize all content stored in long-term memory, it may be necessary to stimulate the access to knowledge and values bases that do not come to mind immediately when someone is confronted with a dilemma. The proposed techniques and tools are brainstorming, mind-map and the WALK.

3.1 *Brainstorming*

This technique, developed by Osborne (1956), aims at fostering creativity of people in a group. After being informed about specific questions and tasks, the group members spontaneously state ideas that could be viable. The process is moderated by a trainer and goes through two phases: first finding ideas and recording them visibly for all, followed by sorting and evaluating all results for viability. Associating, imagining, capturing, and combining ideas already expressed are welcome. Accepting all proposals without critics or comments is a basic rule in the first phase. In the second phase, all ideas are presented by the moderator and then sorted according to their problem relevance and by subject areas. Finally, the group or invited experts are asked to assess the chosen elements for viability.

Especially after the presentation and clarification of the dilemma story, this technique has proven itself useful as a warm-up for the discussion. Using brainstorming in a VaKE course enables the separation of value and knowledge elements.

3.2 *Mind-Map*

Similar to a cognitive map, the mind-map is a graphical representation that shows the relationship between the different aspects of a theme. These aspects are formulated as keywords that are linked with lines. The display can be changed and extended. These changes can be handled flexibly in line with the progress of knowledge acquisition and the increase in sensitivity to the problem.

In a VaKE project, two different types of mind-maps can be produced: personal and group mind-maps. Both contain information on areas of knowledge and values. The first type includes the personal interests and focal points in the examination of the problem. This mind-map is compiled and further developed in the phases of reflection. The second type represents the problem area according to the focus set by the group. It visualizes all aspects found to be relevant to the defence of the position taken. This mind-map serves as orientation and support during the discussion. Again, it can evolve in the course of the work, and hence document the progress and help in knowledge and/or value management of the course.

In the progress of the course, these mind-maps can be extended, supplemented, or corrected. All mind-maps together show the entire field of knowledge that was defined during the learning process. They can be created either on paper (particularly flip charts) or with a computer programme. At least the group mind-maps are to be exposed to all participants during the work process and thus made available to the whole group.

3.3   The WALK – W Assessment of Latent Knowledge

In this section, we describe how the WALK is used as an intervention tool to make tacit knowledge visible and to raise awareness of the values involved. WALK is the abbreviation for "W Assessment of Latent Knowledge". The "W" comes from the kind of questions that address all the important information about a phenomenon, namely, Who? What? When? Where? Why? and How? Everyone possesses hidden knowledge – the latent knowledge. It is knowledge that we have stored somewhere in our long-term memory that is not immediately available for the short-term memory, or that is not available in the present situation. It may also be a vague idea or feeling that has not yet been concretized. These factual contents cannot be used for discussion and argumentation for which participants do not recognise their relevance and/or because the necessary details are not spontaneously available or reconstructed. These details can be found and produced with the W-questions.

The WALK can be used for assessment and evaluation purposes, as described in Chapter 31 in this handbook, but also as information. In the WALK, typically, pictures are used as stimuli to evoke the latent knowledge, but other stimuli can be used as well. When using the WALK for intervention purposes, the choice of the stimuli is quite flexible; it should relate to crucial and particularly sensitive parts of the dilemma.

It must be clarified before starting the VaKE course whether this tool will be used for evaluation or intervention purposes to avoid confusion. It is important to clearly separate and distinguish between these two uses. It is also possible to use the WALK as an intervention technique to prepare the students for using the WALK as an assessment tool – but in this case, a comparison with the control group in which this intervention has not been applied is not possible.

Just like brainstorming, the W-questions increase the sensitivity to the conflict and the problems associated with it. In addition, they stimulate creativity and lead to further questions with which detailed areas of the problems can be viewed and analysed. The tool enables very individual ways of working on a problem. Learners can pursue their interests; this stimulates them to organise the search for information and knowledge themselves. The WALK can also be kept like a work diary accompanying the V*a*KE project; in that case, this tool becomes a documentation of the individual learning process.

4 Tools and Techniques for Knowledge Management

Knowledge needs not only to be retrieved from memory, but the contents that have been gained – either from information reconstruction or through information search – need to be organised for further discussions and for the records. For this, Portfolios and World Cafés are among the techniques that can be used. One could mention many more techniques that can be used at wish and that we do not want to discuss in more detail here:
– Text-processing: Capturing, reading, marking and highlighting texts, particularly the internet pages found in the information search;
– Communication: Making a transcript or recording of the process, conducting an interview or a survey;
– Presentation: Designing a worksheet, a PowerPoint presentation or a poster, giving a lecture;
– Library: Handling of catalogues, finding a book after the signature, knowing and using virtual libraries, collecting useful links;
– Computer: Using the device professionally, mastering different programmes, copying data, back up data, creating a data collection, managing data;
– Internet: Knowing reliable services, particularly search engines (mostly, the participants know only Google; there are more professional engines, beginning with Scholar.Google), knowing search strategies, checking the quality of data sources;
– Group work: Dividing tasks into sub-tasks, distributing task packages, integrating into the group, contributing to the common result.

4.1 *Portfolio*
A portfolio is a collection of all the work and contributions that have been collected over a longer period on a topic or in a process and that have been assessed as important for working on a problem. The structure of a portfolio is rather hierarchical, either according to a chronological order or according to the importance of each aspect and topic. The portfolio can also be used for performance assessment; in contrast to traditional grading, portfolio assessments are more flexible, and in particular the participants keep the ownership of their product as they can use it in further activities, for instance, in job applications, as a document of their achievement (Häcker, 2007).

In a V*a*KE project, similarly to the mind-maps, two different portfolios can be created: one personal and one common to groups or the entire class, i.e., to all participants together. The group or class portfolio represents the knowledge acquired by the entire learning group. It records how the learners have dealt with the issue and the results they have achieved. All working documents, documents from the Internet, own texts, contributions, pictures, voting results, protocols, and summaries of the discussions as well as personal opinions are digitally stored in a separate folder available to the whole learning group.

The personal portfolio can only be viewed with permission of the owner. For performance assessment this type should only be used if a clear agreement was given at the beginning of the V*a*KE course.

4.2   World Café – Knowledge Café

Sitting in a relaxing atmosphere at a café table and talking about crucial issues: This idea is at the origin for several "Café"-approaches, like the World Café (The World Café, 2020) and the Knowledge Café. This method serves for knowledge exchange and problem exploration. The process has a clear structure: Several tables with different questions related to a core theme, limited numbers of people (guests) per table, one permanent host per table, guests changing table after a fixed time limit, documentation of discussed issues on paper on the table, and selective report of the results to the whole group are some suggestions in order to organise such discussions.

In a V*a*KE course this approach can also be introduced to continue the discussions with an invited audience from outside at the end of the course.

5   Stimulating Techniques

The work on a V*a*KE dilemma aims, among other things, at the development and maintenance of empathy and participation in debates. Two methods, role-play and 'devil's advocate', are presented that can stimulate related competences.

5.1   Stimulating Empathy: Role-Plays

Slipping into someone else's shoes facilitates a change of perspective without indoctrinating requirements. There are plenty of approaches, of which well-established concepts and methods like psychodrama and sociodrama (Moreno, 1973, 1977), forum theatre (Boal, 1993) and others can give ideas for adaptations to a V*a*KE course. One can also enact the dilemma and use the stop-and-go technique: The action is interrupted by the spectators, who ask questions to the protagonists. We have also had good experiences with mock trials, panel discussions, political debates, team meetings, etc., since as in dilemma discussions, these aim at judging a behaviour.

When using role-plays, some rules must be followed. First, it is essential to clearly distinguish and not to confound the situation of the workshop and the situation played in the role-play, as the participants act *as if* they were another person in the latter. Only if this distinction is strictly enforced by the workshop leader is it possible for the participants to express safely an opinion that in real life they would not defend, but they try out to put themselves into the shoes of another person. This differentiation is supported by the use of requisites and of names for the role-played protagonists that do not overlap with the names of the participants. And in any case, there must be an extensive debriefing in which the participants report their experiences, emotions, relations to the other players (on the level of the role-play, not of the workshop!), and the conclusions for the topic at stake. The developing dynamic of the role-play is difficult to anticipate in complex role-plays.

5.2 *Stimulating Debate: Devil's Advocacy Technique*

It is possible in a V*a*KE discussion that an overwhelming majority opts for the same position. As a result, the debate seems to be superfluous and consequently, interesting aspects might not be taken into account. While one can assume that even if the participants agree on the action the protagonist should take, they usually disagree on the justification for this action; in this case, a discussion will result anyway. Furthermore, the devil's advocacy technique has the potential to rekindle the debate.

The role of the devil's advocate can be taken on by the moderator, by a nominated participant or by an invited expert. The task here is to criticize the view defended by the majority, to identify its weak aspects, such as failures, false assumptions, wrong information, unobserved and disregarded consequences, etc.

When taking on the role as the devil's advocate, it may be appropriate to make clear that the argument is provided in this role and not as a personal conviction. This can be expressed by formulations like "did you consider the possibility that …?" or "One could also think of … because of …". In general, role-plays are a possibility for bringing arguments into the discussion that challenge the prevailing opinion without being identified with the position.

6 Final Products

A V*a*KE process should end with a common product. Usually, the participants decide together what they want to produce at the end; this also depends on the specific circumstances. For instance, some V*a*KE procedures end with a presentation for a larger group (for the parents, within the school, performances of different kinds, etc.); this presentation can take many different forms, from a role-play to a presentation of the arguments using different presentation modes (e.g., PowerPoint presentations, video sequences, posters, and flip charts, etc.), or even discussions with the audience using appropriate techniques (e.g., a World Café).

Other end products are only for the participants. Besides the forms already discussed above (e.g., group mind-map, group portfolio, role-play), one can use different techniques like creating a newspaper or a newspaper article, a broadcast, or another form of media, etc. Very often, the participants make propositions, which should be accepted if they comply with the principles of V*a*KE.

7 Conclusions

The tools offered here are to be seen as options that can be used according to the concrete objectives and process. In any case, time constraints will not allow the use of all the tools presented here, and this also holds for specific audiences and possibly for the subject matter and curricular regulations. The tools themselves can also be adapted to the specific needs – we have tried here to provide some indications in this regard, but the user is invited to conceive new approaches, for which the list of tools can serve as a model.

References

Boal, A. (1993). *Theater of the oppressed*. New York, NY: Theatre Communications Group.
Guth, D. W., & Marsh, C. (2005). *Adventures in public relations: Case studies and critical thinking*. Boston, MA: Pearson Education.
Häcker, T. (2007). *Portfolio. Ein Entwicklungsinstrument für selbstbestimmtes Lernen: Eine explorative Studie zur Arbeit mit Portfolios in der Sekundarstufe* (2nd ed.). Baltmannsweiler, Germany: Schneider-Verlag Hohengehren.
Hartmann, N. (1926). *Ethik*. Berlin, Germany: De Gruyter.
Moreno, J. L. (1973). *The theatre of spontaneity*. New York, NY: Beacon.
Moreno, J. L. (1977). *Psychodrama Vol. I*. New York, NY: Beacon.
Osborne, A. F. (1956). *Applied imagination: Principles and procedures of creative thinking* (eighth printing). New York, NY: Scribner's Sons. Retrieved May 24, 2020, from https://b-ok.cc/book/3486334/cf7404

Potter, R. B. (1965). *The structure of certain American Christian responses to the nuclear dilemma* [Ph.D. dissertation]. Harvard University. Retrieved May 24, 2020, from https://dash.harvard.edu/handle/1/32749952

Schulz von Thun, F. (1998). *Miteinander reden. Teil 2: Stile, Werte und Persönlichkeitsentwicklung.* Reinbek bei Hamburg, Germany: Rowohlt.

Schulz von Thun Institut. (2020). *Das Werte- und Entwicklungsquadrat.* Retrieved May 24, 2020, from https://www.schulz-von-thun.de/die-modelle/das-werte-und-entwicklungsquadrat

The World Café. (2020). *World café method.* Retrieved May 24, 2020, from http://www.theworldcafe.com/key-concepts-resources/world-cafe-method/

CHAPTER 6

Awareness of Teacher Roles in V*a*KE and Capitalizing on Them for Teacher Training

Martina Nussbaumer

V*a*KE is a constructivist teaching method which combines value education and knowledge construction (see Chapter 2 in this handbook; Patry et al., 2013). Experience shows that it is difficult to integrate V*a*KE properly in the regular school system (e.g., Weinberger, 2006) because the teachers are not used to acting in the way required in the respective steps. For this reason, in the first section, an explicit formulation of the teacher roles within each step of V*a*KE is established and focused on teacher training. This should lighten the implementation of V*a*KE, which is studied in a small research investigation (Section 2). In the third section, some recommendations for teacher training for V*a*KE are made, and the chapter closes with some conclusions.

1   Teacher Roles in V*a*KE

Although V*a*KE is based on the principles of constructivism, the usual constructivist teacher roles (e.g., Brügelmann, 1997) are not sufficient for V*a*KE. These roles are:
- The teachers challenge the learners' experience, thinking and judgments by (a) asking them questions ("What are the consequences of your decision?", "Which ethical principles are at stake?"); (b) showing alternatives ("What do you think about this argument?", "What would you think about this way?"); and (c) expressing doubts ("Does this also work, if …?", "Your friend has a different solution").
- The teachers are critical companions of the learning process.
- The teachers provide learning opportunities.
- What learners learn is their responsibility.
- The teachers hold a restrained role – the learners are in the foreground.
- The teachers shift over responsibility for learning to the learners without giving up their own responsibility for teaching.

These constructivist teacher roles can be used as a basis; however, they need to be extended for V*a*KE because of the specificities of the different steps in a V*a*KE process (see Chapter 2 in this handbook), and in accordance with the theory of situation specificity. Situation specificity means that relevant features (parameters) of the behaviour of the same person may differ in different situations (Patry, 2000, 2011, 2019); in the context of the present study, roles address requirements that teachers should fulfil to comply with the theoretical principles underlying V*a*KE.

In the different steps in V*a*KE (in the theory of situation specificity they are equivalent with situations), these requirements are different, and hence the teachers may have to act differently in these situations with regard to specific behaviour features. One of these features is guidance, which plays an important role in education – the more application and self-construction of knowledge is aimed at, the less teacher-guided should it be (e.g., Dubs, 1995, p. 43). However, teachers are familiar primarily with the traditional educational concept with high guidance and hence have problems to teach with low guidance.

To conceive the teacher roles in V*a*KE, all relevant theories (constructivist teacher roles, underlying theories for the steps in V*a*KE, situation specificity) must be put together in a cone. Based on these theories, in the different steps of V*a*KE-*dis* (step 0 for clarification, then 16 steps; Weyringer, 2008; see Chapter 2 in the handbook) the teachers have different roles, which may also differ within one step, i.e., the teacher may have to practice different roles or change her role *within* one step. The following roles can be distinguished (see also Weyringer, Patry, & Weinberger, 2011):

– Decider (D): Deciding on how to proceed, etc.
– Expert (E): Participating in the information research step as an expert from whom the students can get the information they ask for.
– Facilitator (F): Guiding the learning to help the students.
– Initiator (I): Initiating activities according to the steps.
– Learner (L): Participating in the discussions on the same level as the students.
– Mediator (Me): (a) Acting as an advocate for the students who need it; (b) providing his or her own contribution; (c) advocatus diaboli (see Chapter 5 in this handbook).
– Moderator (Mo): Making sure that the discussion rules are kept.
– Observer (Ob): Observing the situation in class and the students, at what step of V*a*KE they are and what is going on.
– Organiser (Or): Making available what is necessary for a learning situation, providing the opportunity to learn.

In the different steps, the roles can be described as follows:

(0) Clarification: The teacher must *decide* (D) whether to use a VaKE process and what competences (social, cognitive, etc.) the participants need to acquire before successfully performing such a process, and she or he has to *initiate* (I) the acquisition of these competences with any reasonable means, with a particular focus on constructivist approaches.

(1) Introduce the dilemma: The teacher *decides* (D) whether the VaKE process will be done with a dilemma she or he has written him or herself or with one decided by the students. In both cases, she or he *initiates* (I) the dilemma by conceiving the way how the participants are familiarized with it. This can be done by simply exposing the dilemma, or by using some media or other means (e.g., role-plays, see Chapter 5 in the handbook). The teacher then *moderates* (M) the presentation of the dilemma, e.g., by organizing (Or) the role-play, by choosing (D) and implementing (Or) the media, etc.,

(2) Reflection: The teacher asks the students questions like "What do you think about the dilemma?", "What is your opinion?", "Which values are at stake?" (I) and *facilitates* (F) the reflection if needed. Steps one and two of the WALK (see Chapter 5 in the handbook) can be used (I, Or). The teacher then *observes* (Ob) the students.

(3) First decision: The teacher *initiates* (I) the first decision of the students. Who is in favour, who is against the respective options in the dilemma, and who cannot decide yet? She or he then *moderates* (M) the students' decision process and maybe formalizes the decision on a poster (Ob).

(4) First dilemma discussion: After the decision, the teacher *initiates* (I) the dilemma discussion by asking the students "*Why* are you in favour, why against?", *moderates* (Mo) the discussion and *observes* (Ob) the students, and if the discussion rules are fulfilled, may act as *mediator* (Me). Often, she or he is also a learner (L).

(5) Reflection: The same roles as in step (2) with the focus on "What do I think about it now?" (I, F, Or, Ob).

(6) Exchange experience, missing experience: The teachers *initiate* (I) the discussion about what information is missing if necessary (often this happens spontaneously), and *facilitates* (F) the learning process by *moderating* (Mo) the exchange of arguments. Then, the teacher *organises* (Or) the task to be done by the students for the next step.

(7) Looking for evidence: The teacher *observes* (Ob) the information research of the students and helps the students as a *facilitator* (F) if necessary. If requested by the students, she or he takes on the role of an *expert* (E) for information research.

(8) Exchange of information: The teacher *initiates* (I) that the students exchange the information they have gathered and *moderates* (Mo) the

discussion. If the students are autonomous, the teacher is in a restrained role as an *observer* (Ob) and *facilitator* (F), the information shared is usually new to the teacher (L).

(9) Synthesis of information: The teacher *initiates* (I) and *facilitates* (F) the students' conclusion presentations by proposing them presentation techniques, and if necessary, participates in the organisation (Or) of the activities. She or he then *observes* (Ob) the process.

(10–12) The steps are equal to the previous ones (2–4).

(13) The teacher decides (D) whether a repetition of steps 5 to 12 is appropriate (possibly with the participation of the students).

(14) Same as step 5 (I, F, Or, Ob).

(15) General synthesis: The teacher *initiates* (I) and *facilitates* (F) the students by finding a final form for presenting the results. She or he then *observes* (Ob) the process.

(16) Generalization: The teacher *initiates* (I) and *moderates* (Mo) the discussion about related topics and organises if necessary (Or); maybe she or he provides inputs for further projects (E). In general, she or he *observes* (Ob) the process.

2   Study on Teacher Roles in VaKE

In a pilot study in 2014 (Nussbaumer, 2022), the following hypothesis was tested: With special training on teacher roles in VaKE, the teachers are better able to implement VaKE than without such training. The volunteer teachers received training on VaKE with a general theoretical input on VaKE, an explicit theory input on teacher roles and the implementation of VaKE, and to finish, a workshop on dilemma story writing.

The research expectations were as follows: (i) The teacher training and the implementation strategies will change teaching practices. (ii) The teachers become facilitators and place the responsibility for learning on the students instead of trying to transfer values and knowledge. (iii) This effect is sustainable, and the teachers become independent of the research support. (iv) The teachers are aware of their roles in a VaKE class compared to their roles in a traditional class. (v) The teachers think that students are differentiating the teacher actions of the same teacher in different settings (traditional class vs. VaKE class).

Two additional questions need to be asked: (vi) What are the difficulties occurring in the implementation of VaKE?; and (vii) How can VaKE training courses be improved?

To answer the research interest questions, expert ratings, a LIM-questionnaire (see Chapter 31 in this handbook; Patry, 1997) and qualitative interviews were conducted. The sample was 28 students and one teacher of a school class. The LIM-questionnaire was used twice for students and teachers. The first measure time (T1) was after the first dilemma discussion (step 4 in VaKE-*dis*) and the second (T2) was after the first information research phase (step 7 in VaKE-*dis*). A qualitative interview with two teachers (1 male, 1 female) was conducted. It consisted of a guideline with general questions about VaKE classes compared to traditional classes with a focus on (1) lesson planning; (2) interaction with students; (3) experiences with VaKE in general; and (4) teacher roles in VaKE. After transcribing the interviews, a definition of the difficulties within VaKE was established.

The results of the judgments of the students and teachers to the two measuring times per construct were as follows: From the point of view of the students, the teacher *guidance* is declining from T1 to T2, but from the point of view of the teacher the guidance is the same; students as well as the teacher estimate *instruction* as decreasing from T1 to T2; *freedom* was hypothesized to increase from T1 to T2 but this is not the case, neither for the teacher nor for the students. Hence, the teacher is not giving students enough freedom for constructivist learning; the students' *cooperation* is decreasing from the teacher's and the students' points of view.

These results do not go along with the intention of VaKE since the higher the step in VaKE, the more freedom students should notice and the less the teacher guidance should be – less teacher guidance leads to more freedom. Only the constructs instruction and teacher guidance in the estimations of the students are according to constructivist teaching. On the basis of the students' judgments, the teacher is not totally fulfilling a constructivist teaching method. The teacher's and the students' judgments are very diverse. Due to not totally fulfilling the intention of VaKE and the diversity between the students' and teacher's judgements, interviews with two teachers were conducted to understand why this was the case and determine how to improve VaKE training.

The results of the *interviews* show several difficulties within VaKE: External inhibitors are the curricular goals and the pressure on the teacher to achieve them, the standards of education and the school leaving examinations, as well as joint tests and exams in different classes. Moreover, because of the organisation in schools, there are difficulties to properly integrate VaKE in classes; the 50-minute lesson and class schedules are not compliant with VaKE. For example, after 50 minutes of ethics and a short break, a 50-minute biology class with a different teacher is scheduled. The students might have been involved in a moral discussion within VaKE in the ethics class, which they have to interrupt because of the scheduled change of the subject matter (Nussbaumer, 2022).

The teachers also mentioned some difficulties when implementing VaKE, particularly with the conception of the dilemma story. Finding a dilemma story in general is very hard, particularly in subjects like information technology, and writing a dilemma story is very time-consuming: They said they could not use the same text for all classes, it must be adapted, and the dilemma and curriculum must fit together, which sometimes is very hard to fulfil. Moreover, it must be a pertinent dilemma, i.e., one that is interesting for the students. In any case, some of them might work well, but they always have to be adapted more or less according to the students and subject. VaKE is not predictable and requires "situative competence" to a much larger extent than in traditional a class. It is also more challenging in VaKE to guide the students without giving the solution – or even accepting that there is not a one and only solution. Overall, VaKE is very time-consuming in dilemma construction and in implementation. The teachers also reported that if the VaKE process gets stuck, the teachers also get lost. Finally, not every topic is suitable for VaKE (Nussbaumer, 2022).

For the students, there are also many difficulties to deal with. They do not like too many VaKE projects in a row – twice is already too much. If they have too many open lessons, as in VaKE, they wish for traditional classes. Furthermore, if VaKE lasts too long, they ask for a break. Sometimes, students are quickly convinced by other arguments because they are not engaged and do not care. It can also occur that the students are overstrained, confused, feeling lost and helpless. They then need instructions, and they call for it. This is accentuated by the ability differences between the learners (Nussbaumer, 2022).

The interactions between teachers and students show that the students know that the teachers act differently in traditional classrooms compared to VaKE classes: They do not give a solution to their questions. This is confirmed by the results of the LIM-questionnaire. Students are able to reflect the teachers' behaviour and can differentiate their tasks.

Asked explicitly about the teacher roles in VaKE, the teachers distinguish the following roles: group-leader, observer, answering questions, providing students with key questions, supporting students, moderator, coach, secretary, evaluating role. Teachers also mentioned that the teacher is always present, walks around, totally engaged and convinced by the method, and that the moderation role is very present through all steps. Compared with the roles formulated theoretically, the teachers' differentiation is less sensitive (Nussbaumer, 2022).

3   Improvement of Teacher Training in VaKE

The study provides some suggestions for improving training for teachers for their own teaching with VaKE. First of all, it is necessary that the teachers take part in a whole VaKE process. To begin with, they should observe a whole VaKE course. They then should be involved in certain steps as participants, so that they know the "feeling" of a participant. It is important to do VaKE-steps for example in role-plays, where they can also take the students' role (see Chapter 5 in this handbook for role-plays).

Teachers need suggestions for topics for dilemma stories and how to write such stories, maybe in collaboration with colleagues. It would be helpful to have a pool of pertinent and practicable dilemma stories for certain subjects in school – not to be copied but used as an impulse to generate one's own story. It is preferable to start with an "easy" dilemma story which does not need much effort to adapt to the specificities of the class, and then to implement.

Teachers also need practicable tools if they get stuck in a VaKE-process. They need to know how to deal with difficulties. They have to be very sensitive about the VaKE process and the steps within it. Maybe if they keep the students posted during the steps of VaKE, it will not get stuck so easily. In any case, in agreement with the principles of constructivism, it is important to be transparent in this regard. One possibility is to address the problems directly in the class, thus allowing the students to express their own perception of the situation and to jointly look for a solution. In this case, the teacher has the role of a moderator and a mediator – it is important that she or he articulates his or her needs and does not aim less than the students.

As it has been emphasized repeatedly, the theory of VaKE is important; hence, it would be the best on a VaKE training course to have a half-day of theory about the concept and the theory behind it, and a half-day VaKE in practice by joining another teacher doing VaKE, including the preparation, implementation, debriefing and reflection. If possible, this should not be done with the teacher's own students but rather with a different class and maybe a different subject matter.

Finally, it is highly recommended to form tandems where two (or more) teachers within the same school help and support each other in the conception and implementation of VaKE. In the same vein, it is recommended to stay in touch with the VaKE experts, i.e., to establish a tutoring and supervision system – not in the sense of control, but in the sense of critical friends (Nussbaumer, 2022).

4   Conclusion

Implementing VaKE properly is sometimes very challenging for the teachers, but also for the students. The present chapter focused on the difficulties and challenges in using V*a*KE. For training and research purposes, it is very important to identify them, so that in the long run, teachers can overcome them and successfully use V*a*KE. Overall, however, teachers as well as students really like working with V*a*KE, as the experiences in the present study, as well as those reported in other chapters of this handbook show. Taking these challenges and problems as well as the specific roles in the different V*a*KE steps into account, V*a*KE can become an even better method to combine value education and knowledge construction.

References

Brügelmann, H. (1997). *Die Öffnung des Unterrichts muss radikaler gedacht, aber auch klarer strukturiert werden.* Retrieved August 19, 2020, from http://www.zvm.tu-dresden.de/die_tu_dresden/fakultaeten/erzw/erzwibf/sp/forschung/ganztagsschule/Hans% 20Brgelmann.pdf

Dubs, R. (1995). *Lehrerverhalten: Ein Beitrag zur Interaktion von Lehrenden und Lernenden im Unterricht.* Zürich, Switzerland: Verlag des Schweizerischen Kaufmännischen Verbandes.

Nussbaumer, M. (2022). *Weiterentwicklung der VaKE-Methode: Funktionen der Lehrperson als situationsspezifisches Verhalten.* Manuscript in preparation.

Oser, F., Patry, J.-L., Zutavern, M., Reichenbach, R., Klaghofer, R., Althof, W., & Rothbucher, H. (1991). *Der Prozess der Verantwortung: Berufsethische Entscheidungen von Lehrerinnen und Lehrern.* Research report from the Pedagogical Institute of the University of Freiburg, Switzerland.

Patry, J.-L. (1997). The lesson interruption method in assessing situation-specific behavior in classrooms. *Psychological Reports, 81*, 272–274.

Patry, J.-L. (2000). Kaktus und Salat – Zur Situationsspezifität in der Erziehung. In J.-L. Patry (Ed.), *Situationsspezifität in pädagogischen Handlungsfeldern* (pp. 13–54). Innsbruck, Austria: Studienverlag.

Patry, J.-L. (2011). Methodological consequences of situation specificity: Biases in assessments. *Frontiers in Psychology, 2*(18), 1–17.

Patry, J. L. (2019). Situation specificity of behavior: The triple relevance in research and practice of education. In R. V. Nata (Ed.), *Progress in education* (Vol. 58, pp. 29–144). Hauppauge, NY: Nova.

Patry, J.-L., Weinberger, A., Weyringer, S., & Nussbaumer, M. (2013). Combining values and knowledge education. In B. J. Irby, G. Brown, R. Lara-Alecio, & S. Jackson (Eds.) and R. Robles-Piña (Sect. Ed.), *The handbook of educational theories* (pp. 565–580). Charlotte, NC: Information Age Publishing.

Weyringer, S. (2008). *VaKE in einem internationalen Sommercampus für (hoch)begabte Jugendliche: Eine Evaluationsstudie* [Dissertation]. Paris-Lodron University Salzburg.

Weyringer, S., Patry, J.-L., & Weinberger, A. (2011). Teaching VaKE: Experiences with teacher trainings. In D. Alt & R. Reingold (Eds.), *Changes in teachers' moral role. From passive observers to moral and democratic leaders* (pp. 165–180). Rotterdam, The Netherlands: Sense.

PART 3

VaKE in Different Educational Settings

∴

SECTION 1

VaKE in School Education

CHAPTER 7

Challenges in Primary Education with VaKE

Alexandra Reichenwallner

1   Introduction

The VaKE (Values *and* Knowledge Education) teaching model is well implemented in lower and upper secondary schools (Patry & Weinberger, 2004; Weinberger, 2009; Weinberger, Patry, & Weyringer, 2009; Weyringer 2008; Gastager & Weinberger, 2013; Ali, 2006; Patry et al., 2013). There is also already some experience in primary education in Austria (Demetri, 2015; Guggenberger, 2011; Hörtenhuber, 2008; Linortner, 2008). These experiences indicate that VaKE cannot be used with first graders in the same way as with the secondary level, but that the concept needs to be extended.

The development of such an extended concept of VaKE will be presented here. It is based on the experiences from five small studies and takes into account research knowledge on the developmental state of the children in that age group, the question being whether the children have already acquired the necessary skills for practicing VaKE, such as empathy and change of perspective, the abilities of problem-solving, critical thinking, and reasoning, independent learning, presentation competences and communication skills. Children entering primary school in Austria have not yet developed any of these skills or have done so only partially in kindergarten. To address these skills, some of the learning methods proposed by Klippert (2001, 2002, 2007; Klippert & Müller, 2012) are combined with VaKE to form the extended concept which is called VaKE-pr. This model will be described in this chapter.

2   The Need for Extension

The core difficulties encountered in the implementation of VaKE in primary education are the following: (1) identifying the protagonists of the dilemma story, (2) formulating arguments, (3) discussing the dilemma story, (4) developing knowledge independently, and (5) presenting results.

One reason for these difficulties is that children around the age of six may not yet have developed the appropriate skills, abilities, and competences from a developmental psychological point of view (Flammer, 2009; Keller, 1990;

Keller & Becker, 2008; Klein, 2008; Koch, 2001; Levin, 2005; Lindemann, 2006; Oerter & Dreher, 2002; Oerter, Altgassen, & Kliegel, 2006; Von Glasersfeld, 2001). However, their availability is considered a basic prerequisite for successful learning with V*a*KE (Weinberger, 2006; Weinberger, Patry, & Weyringer, 2008; Weyringer, 2008). In order to be able to identify with protagonists, the children should be able to take on other perspectives. Critical thinking and the ability to solve problems help the children to argue. In order to be able to effectively discuss with each other, the children need communication skills. So, aiming for children to be able to acquire knowledge independently, they should be able to learn independently. To present the final results, especially in groups, the children need experience in teamwork and lots of practice. Precisely, these skills still need to be developed and promoted with children at the primary level. For this reason, an adaptation of the original V*a*KE concept is necessary for effective implementation.

In order to develop such an adaptation, the research presented here consists of three steps: In the first step, five small practice-based studies were carried out, which focused on identifying the specific difficulties that can arise when V*a*KE is used at the primary level. Based on the results of these studies, in the second step, constructivist methods and exercises are presented that allow children in primary school to learn in a constructivist way and to overcome the difficulties. These methods ground in the concept of method learning according to Klippert (2001, 2002, 2007). Since V*a*KE means constructivist learning, Klippert's methods are one way among many others to work with for effective adaptation. When children are familiar with Klippert's methods, it can facilitate learning with V*a*KE, even if some skills are not yet fully developed. In the third step, the chosen methods of Klippert are integrated in the prototypical steps of V*a*KE.

3   Studies as a Basis for the Adaptation of V*a*KE

All five studies were conducted in a small rural primary school[1] in Upper Austria. Due to changing conditions (school class merging through a school cooperation), there was also a lively change of the participating children. In the first two studies, it was a cross-year integrative class at primary level 1 (first and second class), which was managed integratively. This means that children with special educational needs were taught together with the children being assessed regularly. In this case, there were three children in the first grade and one child with serious behavioural problems in the second grade. There was also a child in this class who was assigned to the preschool level. In the third and fourth study, a second-grade integration class with three integration children took part. As a result of the above-mentioned school cooperation, the children of the first grade of three schools were brought together in the following school year to form a single-year class. Thus, the second-grade class included some children who had already had experience (study one and two) and children without experience. The fifth study was held in a fourth class, which was also managed in an integrative manner (now five children with special educational needs) (Demetri, 2015). These were the same children as in studies three and four. Due to a change of school location and further changes in class composition, no study could be conducted for the third grade. Despite the many changes, 16 children were in the classes throughout.

The aim of these studies was to find out what difficulties are associated with the use of VaKE at the primary level. The method chosen was participatory observation. The observations were made undercover by the special education teacher, who was the researcher. The unstandardized observations were recorded in subsequent thought protocols. In order to obtain results as authentic as possible, the children were not informed that their behaviour was being observed. Since there was no agreement of the educationalists to make audio or video recordings, the observation could only be made directly. The observations for each of these small studies were documented and reflected upon. The insights gained in this way were again incorporated into the planning of the next study.

In these five small studies, the results showed that children in primary school need a lot of practice to develop the necessary skills and abilities. The children had problems putting themselves in the role of the protagonists (1). The observations showed that the children had difficulties above all when the situation of the protagonists did not correspond exactly to their own horizon of experience. From this, it can be concluded that the dilemma story should correspond to the children's experiences. Since the children had difficulty imagining the situation of the protagonists, it was also difficult for them to argue their decisions (2). Many of the children were not able to answer more detailed questions, and they took on the arguments of others, sometimes literally. This also led to the next difficulty, namely that it became difficult to get the discussion going on (3). The arguments were strung together, and little reference was made to previous speakers. The conclusion is that the children need more practice in actively listening and paraphrasing the statements of previous speakers. Especially in the first study, the children found it difficult to present their final results despite intensive practice (4). A practicable solution was to change the general conditions. Instead of presenting the end products frontally, a circle of chairs, in the middle of which they put their products, was chosen, which was known and familiar to the children. And finally, problems with independent learning could be observed, especially in the first four studies (5). The children needed help with the implementation of the work assignments and, especially in the first VaKE project (nature conservation), support in dividing the assignments within the group.

The question now arises on how these difficulties can be overcome as much as possible in order to use VaKE effectively at the primary level. The concept of method learning from Klippert (2001, 2002, 2007) provides a good starting point for this. In order to enable the children to filter out information from the texts more easily, important preliminary skills such as marking should be introduced and trained. It seems to make sense that in the first two years the focus should be on conducting dilemma discussions. Several VaKE projects may take place in the remaining two years. In addition to the processed filtered information, the children should also be given the opportunity to carry out their own research. The regular and frequent exchange of information is important (Weinberger, 2006; Weyringer, 2008) and should be included in an adaptation as well as a period of reflection before each dilemma discussion (VaKE-*dis* in Chapter 2 in this handbook). If the children can test their arguments in a small group first, the discussion might not be so slow. Before the resulting developed adaptation of VaKE can be discussed, Klippert's methods of interest for VaKE are linked to the difficulties observed.

4   Klippert Methods Interesting for VaKE

Klippert (2007, p. 35) wants to use his methods to teach children to work independently. These methods must be practiced and understood. He considers it very important to learn elementary work, communication, presentation, and cooperation techniques, even at the primary level. For this reason, the Klippert methods are particularly interesting for VaKE. In VaKE projects, the children also have to work independently. With specific methods, children learn social competence, cooperation, and communication and to apply these competences in independent work. It is assumed that using these methods can help to overcome the described difficulties of VaKE in primary school learning.

In the Klippert exercise "Ego-Messages instead of You-Messages" the children are given the task of individually assigning cards with so-called You-Messages to the corresponding Ego-Messages. Regarding VaKE, this exercise should be carried out in small groups. The ability to interpret body language can help the children identify with others, including the protagonists of a dilemma story. Another beneficial method called "chain story" helps the children practice listening. Within the framework of VaKE, this exercise or method can be used to retell the dilemma story together with the children.

After the children had decided on the protagonists' options for action, it was often difficult for them to formulate their own arguments and to justify this decision. Klippert's snowball method offers a way for the children to formulate good arguments. In individual work, the children first try to find three reasons for themselves. They exchange these reasons with a partner and try to formulate three common reasons using these six arguments. They repeat this in a group of four. A similar method is "Think-Pair-Square". The children think again about formulating reasons for the decision in individual work. These are further exchanged and developed with a partner. In a group, all four arguments for the use in the plenum are examined once again.

This leads to the third difficulty of the discussion. The "Fishbowl" method can be helpful. Two to five children sit in the middle of a circle of chairs. The remaining children form a larger circle around them, so a double circle is formed. The children in the inner circle discuss the dilemma story and those in the outer circle listen. If a child from the outer circle wants to participate in the discussion, he or she sits on a free chair in the middle or stands behind a child in the inner circle. This child is allowed to finish formulating his or her thoughts and then makes room for the "new" child.

The fourth difficulty could be handled by open teaching methods such as weekly schedules and free work (Claussen, 1997). Also, Klippert considers the practice of elementary working techniques for independent or autonomous learning to be necessary (Klippert & Müller, 2012, p. 28). The children train the necessary techniques like marking, structuring, and excerpting. Another method is the learning pace. Here, tasks are solved by the children in several steps. The double circle method can also be used to work on learning contents, where already acquired knowledge is exchanged.

Another difficulty observed is the presentation of the final results. The method "reporter game" can help the children acquire more skills to develop their ability to present.

By training these methods intensively, the children also acquire additional skills to bridge the developmental deficits, which can enable the effective use of VaKE at the primary level. What an effective adaptation for the primary level can look like is shown below.

5 The Adaptation of VaKE for the Primary Level (VaKE-pr)

The basic prerequisite for effective adaptation of VaKE at the primary level is that the children first master skills and methods that can support them in coping with the addressed developmental psychological difficulties. Since experience has shown that children in primary level 1[2] in a V*a*KE project still have difficulties working independently in groups, even with a lot of practice in methods, the focus in the first two years of primary school is on dilemma discussions. At the same time, basic skills such as marking, recognizing simple structural patterns, creating tables, first look-ups, should be trained. In addition, the children must learn conversation rules and be given many opportunities to speak freely. In primary level 2,[3] the focus should be on V*a*KE projects. While the learnt methods are consolidated, communication training according to Klippert (2002) should take place including enough time for reflection.

In general, open, or at least partially open overall teaching is a promising framework condition for primary level education in which the V*a*KE method is applied. The weekly schedule instruction described by Claussen (1997) is an example of this. Several basic conditions are required, and they are also important for a V*a*KE course: the child is given the freedom to complete the tasks within several steps and within a time slot; the necessary working materials are provided, they are freely accessible and available to the children. Special order and communication systems are developed. In addition to V*a*KE projects and the methodological learning according to Klippert, open teaching is essential for the success of V*a*KE at the primary level.

In contrast to the existing prototypes and adaptations of a V*a*KE course (see Chapter 2 in this handbook) the V*a*KE-pr course has 18 steps, which are shown in Table 7.1 using Klippert's combined methods.

The most important changes are the general organization of a project due to the inclusion of Klippert techniques, and furthermore to shorten the individual steps. Here the children receive more precise instructions for working on the necessary knowledge. While children in higher school levels can acquire the knowledge more independently, children in primary school need even more instruction or smaller tasks that can be worked on independently in small groups. It is also important to exchange information after each individual information gathering phase.

This model is primarily used in primary level 2. An application in primary level 1 must be decided on a case-by-case basis. Since children in the first school year in particular are usually not able to write freely at the beginning, symbols and simple drawings should be agreed on for the reflection phase in order to record the decision. In order to be able to write down the first reasons for the decision, the children must also record them in pictures. The extent to which the reasons can be recorded in writing in the second school year depends on the children's competencies. It is crucial that the children are clearly told that neither spelling nor grammar mistakes are taken into account.

CHALLENGES IN PRIMARY EDUCATION WITH VAKE

TABLE 7.1 A VaKE process at primary level (VaKE-pr)

1. *Activation of previous knowledge (film, book, drawing, …)*,
   Brainstorming, Graffiti, Mind-map placemat, O: Plenary
2. *Image-based introduction to the dilemma story*
   Chain story for retelling the dilemma story, O: Plenary
3. *First decision – spontaneous decision with two coloured cards for pro/contra*
   Flash light, Mood barometer (How safe is the decision?), O: Plenary
4. *Reflection phase* and *search for arguments*
   Think-Pair-Square, O: Individual work
5. *Discussion with partners, searching and recording the best arguments*
   Knowledge lotto, Partner interview, O: Partner work
6. *Row of arguments, first discussion*
   Think-Pair-Square, Snowball method, O: Small group
7. *First dilemma discussion: Clarification of open questions, division of groups*
   Fishbowl, Think-Pair-Square, O: Plenary
8. Phase of information search and topic processing with provided material, possibly core work assignments for all, specialization for individual groups
   Learning pace, O: Small groups
9. Phase of the exchange: conclusion of each lesson/project unit with an exchange of information, short presentation of the results
   Double circle, Graffiti, O: Plenary
10. Creation of the agreed final product
    Reporter game, O: Small group
11. Exercise of the presentation, O: Small group
12. Presentation of the individual groups and end products
    Knowledge lotto, Reporter game, O: Plenary
13. *Second dilemma discussion (repeating the dilemma story)*
    Fishbowl, Think-Pair-Square, O: Plenary
14. *Second spontaneous decision with coloured cards (see step 3)*
    Flash light, Mood barometer, O: Plenary
15. Period of reflection (see step 4)
    Think-Pair-Square, O: Individual work
16. *Finding and capturing arguments*
    Partner interview, Knowledge lotto, Snowball method, O: Small group
17. *Third dilemma discussion*
    Think-Pair-Square, Fishbowl, O: Plenary
18. Connection of related topics, O: Plenary

Note: *Italics:* value education; standard print: knowledge acquisition; **bold:** Klippert methods; O: Form of organization

In primary level 2, VaKE projects can be carried out several times during the school year.

The more experience the children have had with this teaching method and independent learning, the more a project implementation can come closer to the possibilities at the secondary level. In general, regular application of the exercises and methods according to Klippert can not only enrich the general primary level teaching, but also provide the children with the key competences required for VaKE.

6   Conclusion

Although some difficulties were observed, it was shown that with some preparation, the VaKE teaching model can be effectively implemented at the primary level. Because of the similar basic principles mentioned above, methodological learning according to Klippert is suitable as a preparatory teaching concept. Nevertheless, it must be mentioned that this adaptation of VaKE (VaKE-pr) presented here, still needs to be evaluated in terms of its effectiveness.

Generally, for primary school, open or at least partially open overall teaching is a promising framework condition. For this purpose, it must be noted that the children need to learn collaborative learning and work, it cannot be obtained just by extrinsic support. For the success of VaKE at the primary level, additionally to VaKE projects and the method learning by Klippert, an open instruction in all school lessons is essential, otherwise children are overwhelmed by this teaching method.

Notes

1   In Austria, the primary school comprises four grades. The children start at around the age of six years old.
2   Primary level 1 in Austria includes the first and the second grade of primary school.
3   Primary level 2 in Austria includes the third and the fourth grade of primary school.

References

Ali, S. (2006): *The values and knowledge education (VaKE) approach in teacher preparing programs: Its impacts on teaching and moral judgment competences for pre-service primary school teachers* [Unpublished dissertation]. University of Salzburg, Austria.

Claussen, C. (1997). *Unterrichten mit Wochenplänen. Kinder zur Selbständigkeit begleiten.* Weinheim, Germany: Beltz.

Demetri, A. (2015). *Kombination moralischer Werterziehung mit konstruktivistischem Wissenserwerb in der Primarstufe. Das Unterrichtsmodell VaKE in der Primarstufe* [Unpublished dissertation]. University of Salzburg, Austria.

Flammer, A. (2009). *Entwicklungstheorien. Psychologische Theorien der menschlichen Entwicklung* (4th ed.). Bern, Switzerland: Huber.

Gastager, A., & Weinberger, A. (2013). Zur sozialen Perspektivenübernahme bei Wertekonflikten. Das Unterrichtsmodell VaKE – Values and Knowledge Education – bei Lehramtsstudierenden. In I. Benischek (Ed.), *Empirische Forschung zu schulischen Handlungsfeldern. Ergebnisse der ARGE Bildungsforschung an Pädagogischen Hochschulen in Österreich* (pp. 247–269). Wien, Austria: Facultas.

Glasersfeld, E. von (2001). Aspekte einer konstruktivistischen Didaktik. Geleitwort. In H. Schwetz, M. Zeyringer, & A. Reiter (Eds.), *Konstruktives Lernen mit neuen Medien. Beiträge zu einer konstruktivistischen Mediendidaktik* (pp. 7–11). Innsbruck, Austria: Studien-Verlag.

Guggenberger, A. (2011). *Kann das konstruktivistische Unterrichtsmodell VaKE auch an einer Förderschule erfolgreich durchgeführt werden?* [Unpublished Bachelor thesis]. University of Salzburg, Austria.

Hörtenhuber, B. A. (2008). *VaKE im Kindergarten* [Unpublished Bachelor thesis]. University of Salzburg, Austria.

Keller, M. (1990). Zur Entwicklung moralischer Reflexion. Eine Kritik und Rekonzeptualisierung der Stufen des präkonventionellen moralischen Urteils in der Theorie von L. Kohlberg. In M. Knopf &. W. Schneider (Eds.), *Entwicklung* (pp. 19–44). Göttingen, Germany: Hogrefe.

Keller, M., & Becker, G. (2008). Ein handlungstheoretischer Ansatz zur Entwicklung sozio-moralischer Kompetenzen von Kindern und Jugendlichen. In T. Malti & S. Perren (Eds.), *Soziale Kompetenz bei Kindern und Jugendlichen. Entwicklungsprozesse und Förderungsmöglichkeiten* (pp. 108–125). Stuttgart, Germany: Kohlhammer.

Klein, K. (2008). *Lernen mit Projekten. In der Gruppe planen, durchführen, präsentieren.* Mülheim an der Ruhr, Germany: Verlag an der Ruhr.

Klippert, H. (2001). *Eigenverantwortliches Arbeiten und Lernen. Bausteine für den Fachunterricht.* Weinheim, Germany: Beltz.

Klippert, H. (2002). *Kommunikations-Training. Übungsbausteine für den Unterricht* (9th ed.). Weinheim, Germany: Beltz.

Klippert, H. (2007). *Methoden-Training. Übungsbausteine für den Unterricht* (17th ed.). Weinheim, Germany: Beltz.

Klippert, H., & Müller, F. (2012). *Methodenlernen in der Grundschule. Bausteine für den Unterricht* (6th ed.). Weinheim, Germany: Beltz.

Levin, A. (2005). *Lernen durch Fragen.* Münster, Germany: Waxmann.

Lindemann, H. (2006). *Konstruktivismus und Pädagogik. Grundlagen, Modelle, Wege zur Praxis.* München, Germany: Reinhardt.

Linortner, L. (2008). *VaKE im Kindergarten* [Unpublished Bachelor thesis]. University of Salzburg, Austria.

Oerter, R., Altgassen, M., & Kliegel, M. (2006). Entwicklungspsychologische Grundlagen. In J. Hoyer & S. Knappe (Eds.), *Klinische Psychologie und Psychotherapie* (pp. 302–317). Berlin, Germany: Springer.

Oerter, R., &. Dreher, M. (2002). Entwicklung des Problemlösens. In R. Oerter & L. Montada (Eds.), *Entwicklungspsychologie* (5th ed., pp. 469–494). Weinheim, Germany: Beltz Verlag.

Patry, J.-L., &. Weinberger, A. (2004). *Kombination von konstruktivistischer Werterziehung und Wissenserwerb.* Retrieved August 8, 2014, from http://www.sbg.ac.at/erz/salzburger_beitraege/herbst2004/patry_weinberger_04_2.pdf

Patry, J.-L., Weinberger, A., Weyringer, S., & Nussbaumer, M. (2013). Combining values and knowledge education. In B. J. Irby, R. Brown, R. Lara-Alecio, & S. Jackson (Eds.), & R. A. Robles-Piña (Sect. Ed.), *The handbook of educational theories* (pp. 565–579). Charlotte, NC: Information Age Publishing.

Weinberger, A. (2006). *Kombination von Werterziehung und Wissenserwerb. Evaluation des konstruktivistischen Unterrichtsmodells VaKE (Values and Knowledge Education) in der Sekundarstufe 1.* Hamburg, Germany: Dr. Kovač.

Weinberger, A. (2009). Werterziehung in der Schule – Gängige Ansichten und ihre Widerlegung. In C. Seyfried & A. Weinberger (Eds.), *Auf der Suche nach den Werten. Ansätze und Modelle zur Wertereflexion in der Schule* (pp. 45–70). Wien, Austria: LIT.

Weinberger, A., Patry, J.-L., & Weyringer, S. (2008). *Das Unterrichtsmodell VaKE (Values and Knowledge Education). Ein Handbuch für Lehrerinnen und Lehrer.* Innsbruck, Austria: Studienverlag.

Weinberger, A., Patry, J.-L., & Weyringer, S. (2009). Werterziehung im Fachunterricht – Gelingensbedingungen für VaKE-Unterricht. In C. Seyfried & A. Weinberger (Eds.), *Auf der Suche nach den Werten. Ansätze und Modelle zur Wertereflexion in der Schule* (pp. 181–210). Vienna, Austria: Lit.

Weyringer, S. (2008). *VaKE in einem internationalen Sommercampus für (hoch) begabte Jugendliche. Eine Evaluationsstudie* [Unpublished dissertation]. University of Salzburg, Austria.

CHAPTER 8

VaKE+: Fostering Learning Performance in Cognitive Heterogeneous Classes in Lower Secondary Schools

Alfred Weinberger and Martina Nussbaumer

1   Introduction

The great majority of lower secondary school classes are characterized by heterogeneous student populations. Students differ in their values, religions, cultural backgrounds, prior knowledge, or cognitive abilities. This heterogeneity often turns out as a challenge for teachers. To ensure optimal learning performance for each student, the teachers need to adapt their teaching methods to the individual preconditions. VaKE (Values *and* Knowledge Education) draws upon heterogeneity in values, religion, and cultural backgrounds, which is conducive to an effective dilemma discussion. The discussion of different moral arguments based on heterogeneous worldviews can foster moral judgment development (Berkowitz & Bier, 2007).

For inquiry learning, the VaKE step that addresses knowledge acquisition, student heterogeneity in prior knowledge and cognitive abilities, demands adaptations to ensure optimal performance of individual knowledge construction. In inquiry learning, the learning setting is student-centred. In contrast to traditional teaching, the focus of the instruction is shifted from the teacher to the learner. Rather than being presented with knowledge, learners construct essential knowledge for themselves in a self-regulated way. Student-centred learning settings are less structured and less guided by the teacher than teacher-centred learning. In the latter explicit organization of information presentation and student support is provided which implies a high level of teacher guidance. Research shows that more able learners benefit more from student-centred, less structured learning than less able learners, whereas less able learners benefit more from teacher-centred, highly structured learning (aptitude-treatment interaction; Cronbach & Snow, 1977). According to the cognitive load theory (Sweller, 1988), less structured learning in a highly complex environment, such as VaKE, may generate a heavy working memory load that is detrimental to learning. This suggestion may apply particularly for less able learners and novices because they lack proper schemas to integrate the new information into their prior knowledge. Evidence shows that adequate teaching principles to structure student-centred learning can foster the performance of all students (Hmelo-Silver, Duncan, & Chinn, 2007). Considering these research results, this chapter focuses on the question of how inquiry learning in VaKE can be structured appropriately to ensure optimal conditions for knowledge construction for *all* learners.

2   Methods in VaKE+: Structured Viability Checks and Frequent Peer Feedback

Based on the constructivist learning principle *viability check* (see Chapter 2 in this handbook), Weinberger (2006) created the approach VaKE+, an adaptation of the prototypical VaKE. It includes frequent viability checks through peer feedback during inquiry learning to structure the student-centred learning. This allows high and low ability learners alike to benefit most from VaKE.

The *viability check* is a core element of the constructivist principles of learning. Viability means that our constructions serve the purposes to which they are put for.

Learners in VaKE perform a viability check to evaluate whether their moral argument or constructed knowledge meets this requirement. In other words, they perform a moral viability check to assess their moral argument and a content viability check to assess their constructed knowledge. Patry (2014, 2016) distinguishes between different methods of viability checks. In student-centred learning settings, peer feedback is an essential method of the viability check. For example, peers can give positive feedback (agreement), or negative feedback (rejection) to a learner's knowledge concept. The learner's reaction to this feedback depends on her or his viability criterion. The viability criterion is based on the situation and the individual goals. In VaKE the peers give feedback, either (1) whether the chosen criterion (e.g., different facts can contribute to discussing the dilemma) is appropriate, or (2) if the proposed concept is in agreement on the criterion, whether the construct is appropriate to achieve it. For example, students check their moral argument or acquired information by exchanging and discussing it with their peers. Each student gets feedback whether (1) her or his chosen criterion is appropriate (e.g., the moral argument or the researched facts initiate a discussion), or (2) her or his moral argument or acquired knowledge is an appropriate answer to the values conflict or her or his research question. For example, a criterion for a positive viability check of the moral argument can be that the argument is based on some moral principles (e.g., the Golden Rule). According to the constructivist learning theory, in case of a positive viability check, the learner is satisfied with her or his performance, whereas in case of a negative viability check, he or she will be rather unsatisfied and probably adapt her or his learning process. And this is independent of whether others are satisfied or not!

Based on research in cognitive science, on the classroom practices of master teachers and on cognitive supports to help students learn complex tasks, several teaching principles can be distinguished which structure the lesson and enhance learning (Rosenshine, 2012). To assist learners in constructivist and student-centred learning settings, *scaffolding* is considered as an effective teaching principle (Hmelo-Silver, Duncan & Chinn, 2007). With scaffolding, learners are provided successive levels of temporary support that help them reach higher levels of understanding (e.g., according to the taxonomy of Bloom, Engelhart, Furst, Hill, & Krathwohl, 1956) that they would not be able to achieve without assistance (Pea, 2004). Scaffolding and VaKE are rooted in social constructivism, particularly in Vygotsky's zone of proximal development, which is described as "the distance between the actual developmental level as determined by independent problem solving and the level of potential development as determined through problem-solving under adult guidance, or in collaboration with more capable peers" (Vygotsky, 1978, p. 86). In student-centred collaborative learning, peers can support each other's learning by giving appropriate comments within the zone of proximal development. These comments are labelled "peer feedback".

Peer feedback is expected to support the learning process by providing an intermediate check of the performance against the criteria, accompanied by feedback in strengths, weaknesses, and/or suggestions for improvement (Falchikov, 2001). Based on the social constructivist learning theory, quality criteria for feedback are appropriate to the assessment criteria, specificity, presence of justifications, presence of suggestions for improvement, and clear formulation (Gielen, Peeters, Dochy, Onghena, & Struyven, 2010), and one can assume that this also holds for the viability of the viability criterion itself. Feedback from peers can be more immediate and individualized than teacher feedback, particularly when students learn collaboratively (Topping, 2009). And students react differently to feedback from adults and peers; adults' feedback is perceived as authoritative but ill-explained, whereas peers give richer feedback that is open to negotiation (Cole, 1991). One can also assume that peers come closer to the zone of proximal development, whereas the teachers' feedback may be more ambitious than the zone of proximal development. Gibbs and Simpson (2004) describe several conditions under which feedback fosters constructivist learning. It should be (1) sufficient in frequency and detail; (2) focused on student performance, on their learning, rather than on students themselves; (3) timely in that it is received by students while it still matters; (4) adequate to the aim of the assignment and its criteria; (5) adequate in relation to the students' conception of learning, of knowledge, and of the discourse of the discipline; (6) attended to, and (7) acted upon. Peer feedback can improve group work (Salend, Whittaker, & Reeder, 1993). Further, evidence suggests that frequent feedback during the constructivist learning process is powerful (Thurlings, Vermeulen, Bastieaens, & Stijnen, 2013); learning takes place in small steps, feedback is timely, and learners can attend to and act upon it by perhaps quickly adapting their learning if needed.

The potential of frequent feedback to foster and structure learning is used in VaKE+. Peers give feedback several times during inquiry learning. On the one side, frequent peer feedback offers adequate support to less able learners because learning occurs in small steps and learners receive continuous formative assessment. On the other side, frequent peer feedback does not hinder the more able learners because student-centred learning is maintained. Frequent peer feedback during collaborative learning provides the learners with the possibility to continuously check the viability of their constructions.

In VaKE+, the learning process follows the steps of the prototypical VaKE (see Chapter 2 in this handbook), but steps 5 (Looking for evidence) and 6 (Information exchange) are implemented several times generating a learning-viability check-loop.

3 Empirical Research on VaKE+

The focus of the study on VaKE+ by Weinberger (2006) was on assessing the learning performance (knowledge gain, knowledge retention, and application of knowledge). A further objective was to assess whether a structured content viability check increases the learners' awareness of guidance. The hypotheses were that (1) VaKE+ compared to the prototypical VaKE improves the learning performance; (2) more capable learners achieve better learning results with the prototypical VaKE than with VaKE+ and less capable learners achieve better learning results with VaKE+ than with VaKE (aptitude treatment interaction); and (3) learner perception of guidance is higher in VaKE+ than in VaKE.

3.1 *Methods of the Study*

A cross-over design (see Chapter 32 in this handbook) was used. Two cognitive heterogeneous classes of 27 students (class A) and 26 students (class B) in a lower secondary school in Austria participated in the study. The experimental group was taught according to VaKE+ (three learning-viability check-loops) and the control group according to the prototypical VaKE (no systematic learning-viability check-loop). The research design consisted of two phases. In phase 1, class A was an experimental group and class B a control group. In phase 2, class B was the experimental group and class A the control group. In phase 1, the topic of the lesson was "nuclear energy" and in phase 2, it was "drugs". Each phase lasted seven units (one unit = 50 minutes).

Data collection and data analysis for assessing the central variable "learning performance" was based on a multi-method strategy. Three methods were used to examine the learning performance: (1) a teacher-made test, (2) student essays, and (3) the WALK (see Chapter 31 in the handbook). With the *teacher made test* (pretest, posttest, and follow up) knowledge gain and knowledge retention were assessed. The items in the first phase referred to the scales "economy" (9 items) and "ecology" (19 items). The items in the second phase referred to the scales "medicine" (12 Items) and "law" (9 items). With the *student essays* (posttest), knowledge application was assessed: Each student was asked to write a discussion related to the topic of the lesson that included pro and con arguments. Each argument should include knowledge acquired in the VaKE-lesson. With the *WALK* (posttest), knowledge application was assessed. The analysis focused on the quantity and quality of the formulation of the questions. Further, data collection methods were a traditional *intelligence test* (L-P-S; Horn, 1983), which was used to assess the cognitive abilities of the pupils, and the *LIM* (Lesson Interruption Method; see Chapter 31 in the handbook) which was used to examine the level of perceived guidance. It included four items to assess the variable "guidance" (e.g., "The teacher gave a lot of instructions in this lesson") and two items to assess the variable "viability check" (e.g., "I received peer feedback in this lesson"). With assessing the viability check the treatment construct validity was checked. The students responded on a five-point Likert scale ("1" = I don't agree, "5" = I totally agree).

3.2 Results

3.2.1 Testing of Hypothesis 1: Learning Performance

First, the results of the *teacher made tests* for the scales "economy" (first phase) and "law" (second phase) are reported. Similar results were obtained for the scales "ecology" (first phase) and "medicine" (second phase). There was a statistically significant interaction effect of Time (pretest vs. posttest vs. follow up) by Learning Condition (VaKE vs. VaKE+). Results of post hoc tests show that pupils who learn according to VaKE+ increase their test score significantly from pretest to posttest, whereas there is no significant difference between pretest and posttest with VaKE. Both classes increase their test score from pretest to follow up.

In the second phase, there was a statistically significant interaction effect of Time by Learning Condition. The results of post hoc tests show that pupils who learn according to VaKE+ increase their test score from pretest to posttest significantly whereas pupils learning according to VaKE do not increase their test score.

Second, the results of the student *essays* are reported. There was a statistically significant interaction effect Time (VaKE vs. VaKE+) by Depth of Knowledge (surface knowledge vs. detailed knowledge vs. reflected knowledge) by Class (class A vs. class B). Based on this result, single repeated measures ANOVAs were performed on each level of Depth of Knowledge. There was a statistically significant interaction effect Time by Class on surface knowledge. Surface knowledge was defined as knowledge which involves a base understanding of the subject. In class B the number of arguments which include surface knowledge increased in VaKE+, whereas in class A the number decreased.

There was no statistically significant interaction effect Time by Class on detailed knowledge. Detailed knowledge was defined as knowledge that involves a broad understanding in that details are mentioned. Both classes increased their detailed knowledge in VaKE+.

The interaction effect Time by Class was not significant for reflected knowledge. Reflected knowledge was defined as knowledge which includes examples or relationships between different pieces of knowledge. Both classes increased their number of arguments which included reflected knowledge in VaKE+.

Third, the results of the WALK are reported. The interaction effect Time (VaKE vs. VaKE+) by Quality of Question (type 1 question vs. type 2 question) by Class (class A vs. class B) was not significant. Summarized across both classes and both types of questions, the number of questions was higher in VaKE+.

The results of the teacher made tests, the essays and the WALK corroborate partly hypothesis 1: Compared with VaKE the learning performance (knowledge gain, application of knowledge) increases with VaKE+.

3.2.2   Testing of Hypothesis 2: Aptitude Treatment Interaction

A linear regression was carried out to test if the IQ predicted learning performance. In the first phase, the results indicated that there was a positive impact of the IQ on the test results with VaKE (explained variance: 10.8%), whereas there was no impact of the IQ with VaKE+ (explained variance: 0.6%). The IQ predicted learning performance of the WALK and essay in both learning conditions.

In the second phase, the results of the linear regression indicated that there was a moderate positive impact of the IQ on the test results in VaKE (explained variance: 9.6%), whereas there was a very small positive impact of the IQ on the test result with VaKE+ (explained variance: 2.1%). The interaction between intelligence and course type was not significant in both phases. The IQ predicted learning performance of the WALK and essay in both learning conditions.

The results corroborate partly hypothesis 2: As for the test, less capable learners achieve better learning results with VaKE+ than with VaKE. More capable learners achieve similar learning results in the tests with VaKE+ and VaKE.

3.2.3 Testing of Hypothesis 3: Perception of Guidance

In each class there were LIM observations from seven lessons from both main phases available, with four observed lessons from the first phase (topic: nuclear energy) and three observed lessons from the second phase (topic: drugs). For each class data from two lessons with viability check and five lessons without viability check were available. It was analysed whether there were mean differences between lessons with viability check and lessons without viability check.

First, the results for the scale "viability check" are reported which provide information about the construct validity of the study. The results show a significant interaction effect Time (lessons with viability check vs. lessons without viability check) by Class (class A vs. class B). In class B the pupils' perception of the viability check in lessons with viability check is higher than in class A. Post hoc tests reveal that in both classes the perception of the viability check is higher in lessons with viability check than in lessons without viability check. In lessons without viability check the perception of the viability check is similarly low in both classes. Summarized across both classes the perception of the viability check is higher in the lessons where the viability check was explicitly implemented than in the lessons without a viability check. This result indicates that the treatment validity was high.

For the scale "guidance", the interaction effect Time by Class was not significant. Summarized across both classes the perception of guidance is higher in lessons with a viability check than in lessons without a viability check. However, the guidance-rate is low according to the five-point rating scale of the LIM-questions.

4 Discussion

The question of this study was how VaKE can be used effectively in cognitive heterogeneous classes in lower secondary schools. VaKE+ includes frequent viability checks which structure constructivist learning. Based on a quasi-experiment which compares VaKE and VaKE+ including a multimethod research strategy, the central results are:

- VaKE+ increases the learning performance with respect to knowledge gain more than VaKE. The students acquire more knowledge according to the results of teacher-made tests.
- VaKE+ increases the learning performance with respect to the application of knowledge more than VaKE. The students use more detailed and reflected knowledge in essays and more additional knowledge in the WALK.
- Low ability learners benefit from VaKE+, high ability learners are not hindered in their learning by VaKE+ with structured content viability checks.
- Pupils perceive higher guidance in VaKE+.
- Pupils' perception of the viability check is higher in VaKE+ than in VaKE.

The central results show that structured viability checks can support learning in cognitive heterogeneous classes. They provide a useful method for scaffolding (Pea, 2004) based on frequent peer feedback (Gielen et al., 2010). However, the students have a higher perception of guidance, which is a characteristic feature of teacher-centred learning, in VaKE+, although overall on a very low level. A possible explanation could be that the teacher organised the viability checks according to the steps of VaKE+ which included a lot of instructions. Such instructions could be perceived as teacher guidance from the learner. The role of the teacher seems to be important in VaKE+, particularly the role of the organiser for each step, to ensure student-centred constructivist learning (see Chapters 2 and 6 in this handbook). VaKE+ is based on VaKE, thus the teacher roles are equal.

Regarding the viability check in steps 5 and 6 in VaKE+, the learners have to search for information and then exchange the information several times. The teacher acts as an observer, a facilitator and maybe as an expert (in step 5), and additionally as an initiator and a moderator (in step 6 and 7). It is actually a general aim of education and particularly in VaKE+ that the teacher participates in providing viability checks. The teacher's involvement does not mean to impose his or her own point of view (this would be indoctrination), but to provide arguments for or against certain standpoints, just like the learners.

For handling the necessary instructions regarding the structured viability checks in VaKE+, the more able learners could take over this task. The viability checks indicated by the more able learners may be subjectively perceived as feedback by the less able learners. According to Cole (1991), adult feedback is perceived as authoritative but ill-explained, whereas peers give richer feedback that is open to negotiation. The learners perceive more the instructions given by the teacher as teacher guidance (Nussbaumer, 2022). Maybe the teachers are not aware of the fact that learners are very sensitive about their behaviour. Maybe this has to be taken more into account when providing constructivist teaching or VaKE in general.

References

Berkowitz, M. W., & Bier, M. C. (2007). What works in character education. *Journal of Research in Character Education, 5,* 29–48.

Bloom, B. S., Engelhart, M. D., Furst, E. J., Hill, W. H., & Krathwohl, D. R. (1956). *Taxonomy of educational objectives: The classification of educational goals. Handbook I: Cognitive domain.* Philadelphia, PA: David McKay Company.

Cole, D. A. (1991). Change in self-perceived competence as a function of peer and teacher evaluation. *Developmental Psychology, 27,* 682–688.

Cronbach, L. J., & Snow, R. E. (1977). *Aptitudes and instructional methods: A handbook for research on interactions.* New York, NY: Irvington.

Falchikov, N. (2001). *Learning together: Peer tutoring in higher education.* London, UK: Routledge Falmer.

Gielen, S., Peeters, E., Dochy, F., Onghena, P., & Struyven, K. (2010). Improving the effectiveness of peer feedback for learning. *Learning and Instruction, 20,* 304–315.

Hmelo-Silver, C. E., Duncan, R. G., & Chinn, C. A. (2007). Scaffolding and achievement in problem-based and inquiry learning: A response to Kirschner, Sweller, and Clark, 2006. *Educational Psychologist, 42,* 99–107.

Horn, W. (1983). *Leistungsprüfsystem L-P-S.* Göttingen, Germany: Hogrefe.

Nussbaumer, M. (2022). *Weiterentwicklung der VaKE-Methode: Funktionen der Lehrperson als situationsspezifisches Verhalten.* Manuscript in preparation.

Patry, J.-L. (2014). Die Viabilität und der Viabilitäts-Check von Antworten. In C. Giordano & J.-L. Patry (Eds.), *Fragen! Antworten? Interdisziplinäre Perspektiven. Freiburger Sozialanthropologische Studien* (pp. 11–35). Vienna, Austria: Lit.

Patry, J.-L. (2016). Thesen zur konstruktivistischen Didaktik. *Journal für lehrerInnenbildung, 16*(2), 9–17.

Pea, R. D. (2004). The social and technological dimensions of scaffolding and related theoretical concepts for learning, education, and human activity. *The Journal of the Learning Sciences, 13*(3), 423–451. https://doi.org/101207/s15327809jls1303_6

Rosenshine, B. (2012). Principles of instruction. *American Educator, 36*(1), 12–39.

Salend, S. J., Whittaker, C. R., & Reeder, E. (1993). Group evaluation – A collaborative, peer-mediated behavior management system. *Exceptional Children, 59,* 203–209.

Sweller, J. (1988). Cognitive load during problem solving: Effects on learning. *Cognitive Science, 12,* 257–285. https://doi.org/10.1207/s15516709cog1202_4

Thurlings, M, Vermeulen, M., Bastiaens, T., & Stijnen, S. (2013). Understanding feedback: A learning theory perspective. *Educational Research Review, 9,* 1–15. https://doi.org/10.1016/j.edurev.2012.11.004

Topping, K. J. (2009). Peer assessment. *Theory into Practice, 48*(1), 20–27. https://doi.org/10.1080/00405840802577569

Vygotsky, L. S. (1978). *Mind in society: The development of higher psychological processes*. Cambridge, MA: Harvard University Press.

Weinberger, A. (2006). *Kombination von Werterziehung und Wissenserwerb. Evaluation des konstruktivistischen Unterrichtsmodells VaKE (Values and Knowledge Education) in der Sekundarstufe I*. Hamburg, Germany: Kovač.

CHAPTER 9

Values *and* Knowledge Education Meets Conceptual Change for Science Education

Dimitris Pnevmatikos and Panagiota Christodoulou

Policymakers highlight the need to prepare scientifically literate citizens who will be able to make informed decisions and act considering both the scientific knowledge and the ethical impact of their choices (Zeidler, Berkowitz, & Bennett, 2014). Still, it is an educational challenge to design instructional approaches that foster the development of better decision-makers. Values *and* Knowledge Education (V*a*KE) is an innovative instructional approach promoting scientific humanism, namely the ability to expose students to the ethical dimension of science apart from the conceptual and epistemological aspects (Pnevmatikos et al., 2016).

In this chapter, we argue that for V*a*KE to go beyond the standard procedure and be implemented successfully in science education, research on conceptual change should be considered. Instruction for a conceptual change in science education and V*a*KE share common principles. Hence, we present how the standard V*a*KE could be adopted to meet the dispositions of instruction for a conceptual change in science education. Finally, we provide empirical data to illustrate the effectiveness of V*a*KE in promoting conceptual understanding in science.

1 Conceptual Understanding in Science Education: The Conceptual Change Approach (CC)

A series of systematic reviews investigating the research trends in science education over the last two decades highlight the topic of conceptual change as one of the most frequently investigated (Lee, Wu, & Tsai, 2009; Lin, Lin, & Tsai, 2014; Lin, Lin, Potvin, & Tsai, 2019; Tsai & Wen, 2005). Although many CC models have been proposed over the years, a current systematic review (Potvin et al., 2020) investigated the support that 86 CC models have been received by the literature, eliciting Vosniadou's Framework Theory (Vosniadou, 2013) in the top two CC models with the most literature support. According to this model, young learners start the process of knowledge acquisition by forming naïve physics, namely, framework theories that allow the learners to explain natural phenomena. These framework theories differ from the scientific theories that explain the same phenomena. According to the Framework Theory, the two theories (i.e., the naïve theories and the scientific theories) have substantial structural and representational differences. The acquisition of the scientific theory is a cumbersome and slow process that demands the deconstruction of the naïve theory for a given concept and the construction of the new scientific theory. In their effort to change their naïve conceptual framework for a concept, the learners reconcile the new information in their existing conceptual structures and the ontological and epistemological presuppositions that support these theories. Through this process, the learners construct *synthetic models* that are alternative conceptual explanations known as *misconceptions*. The *synthetic models* have some internal consistency and explanatory value to the learner and, hence, they are difficult to abandon. Recent evidence shows that these naïve theories and the alternative synthetic models continue to exist even after acquiring scientific knowledge intervening in the exploitation of the scientific knowledge in the circumstances (Vosniadou et al., 2015, 2018).

2   Instruction for Conceptual Change in Science Education

Over the last two decades, many instructional approaches have been suggested to help the learners acquire scientific knowledge in science and mathematics. According to a recent review, instructors exploit multiple instructional approaches to promote CC, such as "cognitive conflict", "cooperative learning", "refutational texts", "experimentation", "models and modeling", as well as "inquiry-based learning" (Lin et al., 2016). Inquiry-based learning is a highly appreciated approach in science education as it integrates most of the preceding teaching strategies. At the same time, it effectively promotes conceptual, epistemological, procedural knowledge (e.g., Furtak et al., 2012) and sensitizes students around the ethical dimensions of science (Zeidler et al., 2014).

Moreover, Vosniadou and colleagues (2001) proposed a set of dispositions that instructors in science education should consider when designing a learning environment for CC. First, they suggested that scientific concepts should be examined in-depth rather than in breadth of curriculum coverage. At the applied level of instruction, the in-depth investigation of scientific topics takes place through the design of short topic-oriented Teaching-Learning Sequences (TLS) (Psillos & Kariotoglou, 2016). Second, they propose that teachers should consider the students' prior knowledge and possible misconceptions on the subject matter to facilitate the students' understanding of the limited explanatory power of their ideas. Third, they indicate that the sequence of the concepts introduced in learning and instruction is essential because the new knowledge should be introduced progressively to facilitate students in making changes and deconstructing their prior beliefs for the given concept before they reconstruct the new scientific knowledge. Fourth, they highlight the need to foster the students' metaconceptual awareness, namely, to render them aware of the limited explanatory power that their naïve physics has in the interpretation of a scientific phenomenon. At the applied level of instruction, collaborative learning, experimentation with physical or virtual manipulatives, and concept mapping could be considered. Fifth, they refer to the need to provide models and multiple representations to students to scaffold their perspective-taking and facilitate conceptual understanding. Sixth, they highlight the need to foster the sophistication of the students' epistemological beliefs. Scholars suggested the need for explicit instruction on the nature of models (e.g., Zoupidis et al., 2016) and the nature of science (Kuhn et al., 2008).

Other scholars stressed the need for motivating students to foster CC. Environments that are wealthy in opportunities for inquiry-based learning trigger students' interest in science topics (e.g., Loukomies et al., 2013).

Finally, to facilitate conceptual understanding, other scholars recommended the direct teaching of procedural knowledge such as explicit instruction on inferencing strategies (Christoforides, Spanoudis & Demetriou, 2016), or direct instruction on the Control-of-Variables Strategy (CVS) (Zoupidis et al., 2016).

3 Instruction for Conceptual Change in Science Education-Relations to VaKE

So far, we have tried (i) to underline the importance of CC in science education, (ii) to describe one of the most influential models of CC in science education, and (iii) to describe instructional approaches and the dispositions that should be met in instruction for CC in science education. We will now try to identify the convergence points between instruction for CC and VaKE, highlight their discrepancies and present a case study to describe how VaKE can be adjusted to promote CC effectively in science education.

On the one hand, both instruction for CC in science education and VaKE share in common the exploitation of inquiry-based learning, which is one of the applied theories integrated into VaKE addressing the Knowledge Education (KE) part of the approach (see Chapter 2 in this handbook). Inquiry in VaKE is perceived as a process where learners obtain information from any available source to meet their need for information stemming from the dilemma story (Patry, Weyringer, & Diekmann, 2019).

Further, instruction for CC has highlighted the integration of collaborative learning, which can foster the students' metaconceptual awareness. Likewise, collaborative learning is among the applied theories exploited in VaKE, which is integrated into VaKE regarding both knowledge and values education (Patry et al., 2013). Additionally, it is essential to highlight that during collaborative learning, students are able to check their knowledge or moral arguments for their viability (Patry, 2014). The explanatory power of the knowledge arguments and the sustainability of the moral arguments are evaluated through viability checks, and the students' reflective thinking is scaffolded.

The examination of an in-depth topic in CC for science education is in line with the VaKE approach. VaKE can be applied to any subject matter and level of education, examining topics thoroughly (Pnevmatikos et al., 2016). In this regard, when the KE part of VaKE is a topic related to the science education curriculum, the VaKE instruction can be implemented for a specific session or a short sequence of sessions.

Promoting motivation through instruction for CC is comparably essential for the VaKE approach, which offers various learning opportunities. The dilemma discussion triggers student interests on a specific matter, challenging their moral judgments and stimulating their need for an inquiry. Additionally, autonomous student learning is promoted as students have the control of the activities while the teacher is perceived as the facilitator of the learning process. Nevertheless, depending on the level of the students' familiarity with open inquiry environments, VaKE instructors can design more guided activities and materials for their students.

On the other hand, VaKE neither directly nor explicitly addresses some of the dispositions regarding the instruction of CC in science education. However, these dispositions can be addressed by adapting the KE of VaKE accordingly. For instance, instruction for CC in science education requires specific teaching strategies to facilitate conceptual understanding, such as experimentation, concept mapping, and exploitation of models and multiple representations. Although such activities are not directly or explicitly included in VaKE, they could be integrated into the KE steps, where students engage with inquiry. At the same time, the disposition for direct instruction of procedural knowledge could be met through the inquiry steps in VaKE.

Furthermore, VaKE, when applied in science education, does not consider prior student knowledge and misconceptions or the sequence of introducing the scientific concepts as suggested in the literature for CC. The first could be ameliorated through dilemma construction, while the latter through inquiry learning, where the teacher would guide the sequence of the topics' investigation. Finally, explicit instruction and sophistication of the students' epistemological beliefs in V*a*KE could be achieved during the dilemma discussion.

4 The Nanoscience-Nanotechnology Case: Adaptations to the V*a*KE Approach

In this section, we will present indicative adaptations that were implemented in KE in order to investigate the effectiveness of V*a*KE for promoting CC in science education. Although scarce data are examining the field of Nanoscience-Nanotechnology (N-ST) under the spectrum of CC, it was considered appropriate for three reasons. First, N-ST phenomena cannot be observed directly through everyday experience. Second, students could transfer their experience from the macroscale and microscale to the nanoscale, which nonetheless is inappropriate due to the different properties of nano-sized objects present in comparison to objects of other sizes. Finally, N-ST is an emerging field of activity with enormous ethical and societal issues for future citizens. Thus, V*a*KE could be an appropriate approach to exploit.

Preparing a V*a*KE dilemma requires identifying specific values and content, among others (for the preparation of the dilemma, see Chapter 4 in this handbook). The *Big Ideas of Nanoscience and Engineering* (Stevens, Sutherland, & Krajcik, 2009) offer a specific conceptual framework for introducing N-ST in education. To address KE, we selected the concepts (i) size and scale and (ii) size-dependent properties (i.e., hydrophobicity and absorption). Addressing concept (i) first would allow students to construct a new ontological category or recategorize objects depending on their size. Then, the introduction of concept (ii) could be facilitated, downsizing the chances that students would construct the misconception that specific properties (e.g., hydrophobicity) are related to all objects regardless of their size. Thus, the disposition of the sequence of the concepts' introduction is met.

Furthermore, considering the disposition for CC instruction regarding prior student knowledge and misconceptions, we infused "information" in the dilemma that would trigger student information search. For instance, regarding the size and scale concept, students in primary education have the misconception that the smallest object they can see is usually smaller than the smallest object they can imagine (Castellini et al., 2007). Thus, we integrated into the dilemma terms relatable to the new size category (e.g., nano-size, nanotechnology), which could trigger the discussion around the concept.

In order to address the KE part of the N-ST VaKE course, specific activities were designed in line with the CC literature. In particular, multiple representations and models, concept maps, discussion regarding the nature of the scientific knowledge, explicit instruction of the control of variables strategy, experimentation with physical manipulatives, and design of experiments were among the activities included addressing the two concepts of N-ST. On account of the adaptations, the actions students perform in the N-ST VaKE course differ from those in a standard VaKE unit (see Patry et al., 2013, p. 567 for the actions performed by students in a standard VaKE unit).

The N-ST VaKE course was implemented in three interventions to 44 sixth graders in primary education in Greece (21 female). Pre, post, and delayed post-tests assessed the students' level of conceptual understanding. Generative questionnaires were exploited to capture students' mental representation of the concepts according to the CC literature (Vosniadou, Skopeliti, & Ikospentaki, 2004); at the same time, students provided written arguments and moral judgments on values addressed by the dilemma (family/welfare vs. friendship/health), which were evaluated for moral development.

On the one hand, the results in values education revealed that students promoted their moral judgments taking into account a more global perspective (students supported the value of health). On the other hand, results indicated that students constructed new knowledge with respect to the introduced concepts; however, full conceptual change was not always achieved. Students constructed *synthetic models*, such as those materials with sleek surfaces at the macroscale, have bumps on the nanoscale that repel water. Although in this model, students categorized hydrophobicity as a property dependent on the size and scale of the object, they falsely categorized it as a property of materials with specific macroscopic characteristics. More information on the implementation and results of the VaKE N-ST course is provided elsewhere (Pnevmatikos & Christodoulou, 2018).

The literature on CC highlights that forming *synthetic models* is a typical outcome of the conceptual understanding procedure and results from the constructive use of learner learning mechanisms (Vosniadou & Skopeliti, 2017). During the implementation of the VaKE N-ST course, students faced difficulties regarding the experimentation with physical manipulatives and mainly when they employed the Control of Variables Strategy. Their difficulties were related to their inability to realize that a variable must be changed to test its influence; thus, the students failed to control for variables. Such difficulties are in line with the literature (e.g., Boudreaux et al., 2008).

5 Concluding Remarks

In this chapter, adaptations to the VaKE approach were presented, meeting the dispositions of instruction for CC in science education, proving its efficiency in promoting CC. Addressing the aspect of CC in science education renders VaKE into a powerful instructional tool in the crossbow of 21st-century instructors, which can foster knowledge acquisition and values education as well as cultivate scientifically literate decision-makers.

References

Boudreaux, A., Shaffer, P., Heron, P., & McDermott, L. (2008). Student understanding of control of variables: Deciding whether or not a variable influences the behavior of a system. *American Journal of Physics, 76*, 163–170. doi:10.1119/1.2805235

Castellini, O. M., Walejko, G. K., Holladay, C. E., Thiem, T. J., Zenner, G. M., & Crone, W. C. (2007). Nanotechnology and the public: Effectively communicating nanoscale science and engineering concepts. *Journal of Nanoparticle Research, 9*(2), 183–189.

Christoforides, M., Spanoudis, G., & Demetriou, A. (2016). Coping with logical fallacies: A developmental training program for learning to reason. *Child Development*, 1–21. doi:10.1111/cdev.12557

Furtak, E. M., Seidel, T., Iverson, H., & Briggs, D. C. (2012). Experimental and quasi-experimental studies of inquiry-based science teaching: A meta-analysis. *Review of Educational Research, 82*(3), 300–329.

Kuhn, D., Iordanou, K., Pease, M., & Wirkala, C. (2008). Beyond control of variables: What needs to develop to achieve skilled scientific thinking? *Cognitive Development, 23*(4), 435–451.

Lee, M. H., Wu, Y. T., & Tsai, C. C. (2009). Research trends in science education from 2003 to 2007: A content analysis of publications in selected journals. *International Journal of Science Education, 31*(15), 1999–2020.

Lin, J. W., Yen, M. H., Liang, J., Chiu, M. H., & Guo, C. J. (2016). Examining the factors that influence students' science learning processes and their learning outcomes: 30 years of conceptual change research. *Eurasia Journal of Mathematics, Science and Technology Education, 12*(9), 2617–2646.

Lin, T. J., Lin, T. C., Potvin, P., & Tsai, C. C. (2019). Research trends in science education from 2013 to 2017: A systematic content analysis of publications in selected journals. *International Journal of Science Education, 41*(3), 367–387.

Lin, T. C., Lin, T. J., & Tsai, C. C. (2014). Research trends in science education from 2008 to 2012: A systematic content analysis of publications in selected journals. *International Journal of Science Education, 36*(8), 1346–1372.

Loukomies, A., Pnevmatikos, D., Lavonen, J., Spyrtou, A., Byman, R., Kariotoglou, P., & Juuti, K. (2013). Promoting students' interest and motivation towards science learning: The role of personal needs and motivation orientations. *Research in Science Education, 43*(6), 2517-2539. https://doi.org/10.1007/s11165-013-9370-1

Patry, J.-L. (2014). Die Viabilität und der Viabilitäts-Check von Antworten. In C. Giordano & J.-L. Patry (Eds.), *Fragen! Antworten?* Zürich, Switzerland: Lit.

Patry, J.-L., Weinberger, A., Weyringer, S., & Nussbaumer, M. (2013). Combining values and knowledge education. In B. J. Irby, G. Brown, R. Lara-Alecio, & S. Jackson (Eds.) and R. A. Robles-Piña (Sect. Ed.), *The handbook of educational theories* (pp. 565-579). Charlotte, NC: Information Age Publishing.

Patry, J.-L., Weyringer, S., & Diekmann, N. (2019). VaKE intervention method: Education for democratic citizenship for female refugees. In E. Gutzwiller-Helfenfinger, H. J. Abs, & P. Müller (Eds.), *Thematic papers based on the conference "Migration, Social Transformation, and Education for Democratic Citizenship"* (pp. 191–205). University of Duisburg-Essen, Germany: DuEPublico. doi: 10.17185/duepublico/47792

Pnevmatikos, D., & Christodoulou, P. (2018). Promoting conceptual change through Values *and* Knowledge Education (VaKE). In A. Weinberger, H. Biedermann, J.-L. Patry, & S. Weyringer (Eds.), *Professionals' ethos and education for responsibility* (pp. 63–74). Leiden, The Netherlands: Brill Sense. doi:10.1163/9789004367326_005

Pnevmatikos, D., Patry, J.-L., Weinberger, A., Linortner, L., Weyringer, S., Maron, R., & Gordon-Shaag, A. (2016). Combining Values and Knowledge Education for lifelong transformative learning. In E. Panitsides & J. Tablot (Eds.), *Lifelong learning: Concepts, benefits, and challenges* (pp. 109–134). New York, NY: Nova Science.

Potvin, P., Nenciovici, L., Malenfant-Robichaud, G., Thibault, F., Sy, O., Mahhou, M. A., … Chastenay, P. (2020). Models of conceptual change in science learning: establishing an exhaustive inventory based on support given by articles published in major journals. *Studies in Science Education*, 1–55.

Psillos, D., & Kariotoglou, P. (2016). Theoretical issues related to designing and developing Teaching-Learning Sequences. In D. Psillos & P. Kariotoglou (Eds.), *Iterative design of teaching-learning sequences* (pp. 11–34). New York, NY: Springer.

Stevens, S. Y., Sutherland, L. M., & Krajcik, J. S. (2009). *The big ideas of nanoscale science and engineering*. Arlington, VA: NSTA Press.

Tsai, C. C., & Lydia Wen, M. (2005). Research and trends in science education from 1998 to 2002: A content analysis of publication in selected journals. *International Journal of Science Education, 27*(1), 3–14.

Vosniadou, S. (Ed.). (2013). *International handbook of research on conceptual change* (2nd ed.). New York, NY: Routledge.

Vosniadou, S., Ioannides, C., Dimitrakopoulou, A., & Papademetriou, E. (2001). Designing learning environments to promote conceptual change in science. *Learning and Instruction, 11*(4), 381–419.

Vosniadou, S., Pnevmatikos, D., Makris, N., Eikospentaki, K., Lepenioti, D., Chountala, A., & Kyrianakis, G. (2015). Executive functions and conceptual change in science and mathematics learning. In L. Carlson, C. Hoelscher, & T. F. Shipley (Eds.), *Proceedings of the 37th annual meeting of the Cognitive Science Society*, Pasadena, CA.

Vosniadou, S., Pnevmatikos, D., Makris, N., Lepenioti, D., Eikospentaki, K., Chountala, A., & Kyrianakis, G. (2018). The recruitment of shifting and inhibition in on-line science and mathematics tasks. *Cognitive Science, 42*(6), 1860–1886. https://doi.org/10.1111/cogs.12624

Vosniadou, S., & Skopeliti, I. (2017). Is it the Earth that turns or the Sun that goes behind the mountains? Students' misconceptions about the day/night cycle after reading a science text. *International Journal of Science Education, 39*, 2027–2051. doi:10.1080/09500693.2017.1361557

Vosniadou, S., Skopeliti, I., & Ikospentaki, K. (2004). Modes of knowing and ways of reasoning in elementary astronomy. *Cognitive Development, 19*(2), 203–222.

Zeidler, D. L., Berkowitz, M. W., & Bennett, K. (2014). Thinking (scientifically) responsibly: The cultivation of character in a global science education community. In M. P. Mueller, D. J. Tippins, & A. J. Stewart (Eds.), *Assessing schools for Generation R (responsibility)* (pp. 83–99). New York, NY: Springer.

Zoupidis, A., Pnevmatikos, D., Spyrtou, A., & Kariotoglou, P. (2016). The impact of procedural and epistemological knowledge on conceptual understanding: The case of density and floating–sinking phenomena. *Instructional Science, 44*(4), 315–334. doi:10.1007/s11251-016-9375-z

CHAPTER 10

Implementing Value Education in Teaching Units for Newly Arrived Immigrant Pupils in France

Marco Brighenti and Frédérique Brossard Børhaug

1   Introduction

This action research was initiated in 2016 and took place in the specific teaching context of UPE2A (*Teaching unit for newly arrived foreign language-speaking residents*) where VaKE was implemented. These teaching units are aimed at providing support and assistance to newly arrived foreign language-speaking residents schooled in France. UPE2A is regarded in Europe as an excellence-driven teaching device for socially innovative intercultural education (Cartaci, 2014, p. 102). In this chapter, we intend to investigate the implementation of values education in UPE2A teaching units at the secondary school level; as we shall see, it enabled teachers to reflect critically on their practice when teaching French as a second language. Firstly, the chapter offers a description of UPE2A's structures and mission. These teaching units update inclusion as a major democratic challenge although these units are seen as exceptional, temporary, and group-specific support programmes. Secondly, we will present the action research bearing on the implementation of VaKE-dis, and some of the key results, which were collected throughout 2016–2019. We unveil the problems that teachers encountered and present some remarks about our own role as mentors and researchers within the scope of this project. This chapter is developing further a work presented at an international conference (*International Association of Intercultural Education*) held in Angers (France) in June 2017 and published in a French article (Brighenti & Brossard Børhaug, 2018).

2   Presentation of UPE2A Teaching Units and Aims of the Research Project

For the 2017/2018 school year, the French Ministry of Education identified 64,350 foreign language-speaking residents enrolled in 9,300 schools. 88% of them were provided with language-learning assistance through a specific programme labelled *Teaching unit for newly arrived foreign language-speaking residents* (DEPP, 2019[1]). This schooling assistance programme is placed under the authority of the *Academic centers for the schooling of newly arrived foreign language-speaking residents or children from migrant or travelling families* (CASNAV[2]) whose mission has been detailed in two national memorandums (2002,[3] 2012[4]). These centers oversee UPE2A coordination for primary up to upper secondary schools and implement extra training and mediation actions (Brighenti, 2014).

This UPE2A designation indicates that the programme does not equate with ordinary classes, since newly arrived pupils must still be schooled in "regular"[5] classes. Furthermore, the programme implementation focuses on the individual skills of the pupil rather than the social and legal statuses or the origin of the family.[6] After initial assessment, schools arrange and provide each pupil with an individual schedule in line with their capacities and needs where the schooling takes place both in the ordinary class and in the special teaching unit; this arrangement aims to promote a better inclusion for the pupil.[7] Therefore, the UPE2A teacher has a class of pupils with discrepant levels and ages. Additionally, the teacher faces an incessant in-coming and out-going pattern because the pupils switch between the UPE2A class and the regular class. The class size also differs every hour (often from 7 to 20 pupils). This utter heterogeneity combined with the replacement of the class members from one period to the next, is a true daily challenge for the teacher, albeit indispensable for the pupils' effective inclusion (Brighenti & Brossard Børhaug, 2018).

This project aims at renewing teaching practices in the UPE2A teaching units placed under the authority of Essonne district's CASNAV. These units are often still looked at as "special classes for special pupils". This cliché is clearly problematic as the inclusion of each pupil becomes both an international (UNESCO, 2015) and national motto (French law passed on July 8 2013[8]). The VaKE project offers the opportunity to outreach this problematic vision and is an attempt to mentor teachers in the exploration and renewal of their teaching practice, in order to help pupils, elaborate, in their first and second languages, intercultural thinking skills that will sustain their cognitive and moral development (Brighenti & Brossard Børhaug, 2018).

We used the VaKE-*dis* version (Weyringer et al., 2012, p. 167) in order to promote the learner's reflective and proflective intellectual capacities (steps 2, 5, 10, 14) and two voting rounds (steps 3, 11). We believe that educational action must embed an "inspiring complexity" in "problem-situations" that are dealt with in class (Meirieu, 2010). It entails that it brings

> the subject in motion, drawn into active interaction between reality and own projects, both a process of de- and re-stabilization through the gaps

produced by the trainer, its successive representations: it is within this interaction that rationality is built, although often in an irrational manner. (Meirieu, 2010, p. 64, authors' translation)

Educators need to conceptualize the teaching tools in what Ouellet called an "intervention project". Such a project includes "strategies for effective pedagogical action and methodological indications to prepare pupils to confront ethnocultural pluralism" (Ouellet, 2008, p. 8, authors' translation).

3   Methodological Process

Our action research is based on qualitative methodology and analysis (Creswell, 2012, p. 212ff.). During the successive data collecting and encoding phases, the two authors made sure to adjust our support and assistance to the teachers with a desire to provide continuous feedback through personal and critical reflections from 2016–2019. Our sample is based on eleven volunteer teachers selected from the larger group of 29 UPE2A teachers in the district in 2016; however, one teacher left the group because of the heavy workload.

More specifically, we organised four seminars in 2016 (February, March, May, and December), two seminars in October and November 2017, a time for writing dilemmas in September 2017, as well as two class visits in November 2017, three class visits in October 2018 and two workshops in June, and November that year, as well as a three-day workshop in June 2019. Debates in the plenary session in 2016 were recorded and transcribed. In February 2016, we presented and tested V*a*KE with the whole group of UPE2A teachers (29), using two anonymized questionnaires for self-evaluation of their intercultural skills and values before V*a*KE (29 answers) and after V*a*KE (27 answers). An audio recording also was carried out. In March 2016, we organised a session with the volunteer teachers (11 teachers) and three other people outside the group. An audio recording and an individual questionnaire on the use of V*a*KE (relevance, possible difficulties in class – 11 answers) were implemented. In May 2016, we worked on the construction of the dilemmas with an audio recording. In December 2016, we started producing examples of dilemmas and dealt with questions from teachers about their viability. After the first visits in 2017, we elaborated a formal observation grid based on three categories; time used, pupil activities (e.g., Language1/L1; Language2/L2) use during searching and collaboration phases, body language, peer collaboration, emotions) and teacher activities (e.g., control and decentration, use of pedagogical tools, L1/L2 use in class, body language, emotions), we also decided to observe from different spots in the class. In addition, after workshops and class visits, the two authors held regular debriefings and were accompanied by two visiting researchers in 2017 and 2018. As mentioned, a former article mainly dealing with data collected in 2016 was published (Brighenti & Brossard Børhaug, 2018). Here, we briefly refer to some of its main conclusions and include further data collected during the workshops and class observations held in 2017 and 2018, as well as didactical tools developed by teachers in 2019.

4 Data Presentation and Discussion

We first present the main challenges encountered during the first phase of the action research project. Secondly, we discuss the role of mentoring and the role of the broader group in the course of the project. Eventually, we provide some pedagogical reflections and give some recommendations when using VaKE in intercultural learning settings.

4.1 Encountering VaKE in the First Phase of the Implementation: Challenges

Initially, we noticed the absence of explicit knowledge about a methodology for moral education in the teacher group, although moral education was considered by the teachers as just as necessary as knowledge education (Brighenti & Brossard Børhaug, 2018). This scarcity of methodological reflection might confirm a lack of initial training for this field of education, a situation that has already been singled out abroad (e.g., Weinberger et al., 2015). Furthermore, the teachers agreed to the relevancy of the VaKE method in their own teaching. However, despite their rising awareness, little progress was made in the dilemma design work in 2016–2017. We identified three challenges as reasons for the slow progress: the pupil's position, the teacher's stance, and their intellectual autonomy. More specifically, some comments reflected negative representations about the pupils' second-language proficiency as well as about their maturity and autonomy, features that the teachers deemed too weak for a VaKE session. Secondly, as VaKE challenges the teacher's traditional position and role (Weyringer et al., 2012), most of the teachers experienced at first, fears of losing power, authority, and control over the class. Some teachers also feared violent reactions and argued for cooled-off debates avoiding sensitive topics, in particular those dealing with colonization, religion and bodily integrity. In addition, the teachers struggled to write down dilemmas, which brought up numerous discussions and questioned the implementation of the method given the extreme heterogeneity found in UPE2A units. As mentioned, the heterogeneity is based on discrepant school levels, ages, and second-language proficiency for pupils on a permanent in-coming and out-going pattern (priority is given to the pupils' individual schedules). Such organizational issues are real and bear heavily on daily teaching practice, the teachers' leeway and no less on the implementation of a V*a*KE session. Eventually, during our discussions with the teachers, we observed unease around the concepts of law, authority, and controversy such as secularism (*laïcité*) and the implications they might entail in school practice[9] (Brighenti & Brossard Børhaug, 2018).

4.2 Role of the Mentor-Researcher and Role of the Group in the Development of Dilemma Stories and Didactical Tools

The teachers exhibited goodwill and commitment to the successive workshops. Nonetheless, their uneasiness and doubts shed in turn an interesting light on our role as mentoring researchers. During the first phase, we provided the whole group of UPE2A teachers with theoretical information on the method, we then had them experience a real V*a*KE session using a dilemma we had designed to that end during the first workshop in 2016. We provided guidance through the following workshops offering collaboration and discussion opportunities about dilemmas and we added an extra layer of methodology with visiting experts in 2017, organised class observations and a workshop in 2018. We also remained available, either physically or by email, to answer questions throughout the whole project until 2019.

We believe this continuous mentoring role played an essential part because it became clear that we had to adapt our support to overcome the difficulties faced by the teachers. The troubles were eventually defeated once the group itself agreed on a common dilemma and resorted to its collective resources to put difficulties aside. It was only by combining their efforts on a common dilemma that the teachers nurtured enough collective confidence to dare undertaking V*a*KE sessions in class. From there, class observations became possible. The teachers also developed didactical tools: the use of surveys outside the class, emoticons, art images, reflective drawings, lexical tanks, role playing games, the use of "the inclusion tree"[10] for assessing the pupils' feelings and position within the group, and diverse categorization/mapping tools where pupils reflected on relevant ideas and values. Such tools enabled teachers and pupils to foster knowledge acquisition and moral development and initiate to some extent a collaboration with other pupils and teachers in the school.

In 2019, this work also was formalized through a 3-day workshop where half of the group of teachers decided to develop didactical tools. These tools dealt with improving pedagogical activities that aim to promote pupil search skills in the knowledge construction phase. The teachers themselves chose this work theme because they had experienced that knowledge acquisition was an issue for the pupils and a pedagogical challenge in organizing the learning activities and the pupils' voice. At the same time, developing these tools was not limited to VaKE-sessions *per se*; they also wanted to use this work in other learning settings in regular classes. More specifically, the didactical tools dealt with raising awareness prior to a VaKE session (step 0) where pupils are trained to reflect on what they know or not about a thematic and what could characterize a good research activity from the pupils' point of view. They also were challenged to think about what valuable sources for valid knowledge are. This work attempted to compensate the need for search skills that are not always fostered as much as needed in class because teachers tend to transmit knowledge instead of getting pupils to search for it (Patry et al., 2013; Weyringer et al., 2012). As such, the teachers argued for the need to prepare pupils for knowledge acquisition, expanding the limited scope of learning French abilities to broader knowledge and search skills. As mentioned before, educational action must embed an "inspiring complexity" in "problem-situations" that brings the subject in motion, drawn into active interaction between reality and own projects, mobilizing the learner's intellectual and emotional capacities and exploration of the two dimensions (Meirieu, 2010). The group work of 2019 shows that the teachers were able to go beyond their initial anxiety, towards professional intellectual autonomy and the development of pedagogical teacher resources.

Eventually, we would like to mention that the teachers included the use of the first languages in the VaKE sessions. In one class for instance, we observed that 13 languages including French were spoken and many of these languages were spontaneously used in the research and discussion phases. In another class of non-writers and non-readers, we observed that some pupils reformulated the knowledge and values at stake in their first language. The teacher had decided in advance to organise the group work in dyads with the same linguistic background in order to consolidate the learning process in French through the first languages. A third example shows that the multilingual pupils also were open to other languages (not only their own or French) and manifested curiosity towards the other pupils' linguistic competencies and were comparing between languages and worldviews showing mediating and intercultural skills (Council of Europe, 2018). Translanguaging skills were also at stake although we did not explore this further in our project. This may confirm former research on VaKE, arguing that it is possible for non-native speakers to develop complex thinking in knowledge and value reflection in the target language as well as in first languages (Patry, Weyringer, & Weinberger, 2010).

4.3 Pedagogical Reflections and Recommendations

This project yielded new opportunities to reflect on professional actions in a critical and subtle manner, may these belong to teachers or accompanying mentor-researchers.

First, an educational programme where the VaKE-method is presented; during that phase we believe that the teachers should experience the VaKE-method by *themselves*, its potential, its limits, and the destabilizing process it entails, regarding both knowledge and value reflection (see also Chapter 6 in this handbook). For instance, we asked the teachers how they rated their own intercultural competence skills (attitudes, knowledge, and practice) before and after experimentation of VaKE at the end of the first workshop day (February 2016). Altogether, the teachers first were quite confident in terms of intercultural attitudes but undersold themselves concerning the outcome of the session regarding knowledge and practice, and eventually, seemed to realize their shortcomings. As such, VaKE raised their awareness in a powerful manner.

Secondly, as also stated in Chapters 4 and 6 in this handbook, we argue that the teachers have to develop their own dilemma stories, although it may be a long and difficult process. In our project, working on a common dilemma story became an effective springboard; the teachers were reassured. Then, they created individual or pair-working dilemmas that they presented to the whole group and implemented them in their own class.

Thirdly, we argue that a long-term and substantial academic support is fundamental through academic seminars, literature reading, visiting classes, and cooperative workshops allowing the emergence of good ideas and practices within and outside class. This support was especially crucial when the UPE2A teaching was challenged by the incessant in-going and out-going pattern as it posed an extra challenge in the implementation of the method. It helped to reflect on and define pedagogical activities that can be put in place before and during a VaKE class. One concrete example in the research-action was how to empower pupils in the ability to do effective research during the knowledge construction phase and with limited time in class. The teachers through the collaborative workshops held in May to June 2019, reflected on that matter; they bypassed stereotyped thinking and created concrete tools in order to give pupils pedagogical opportunities for consolidating their ability to participate in complex tasks. As in Chapter 6, we also argue that teachers need to work together when preparing a VaKE class, it may also include non-teacher professionals (social workers, school nurses etc.) in order to embrace complex societal dilemmas. We experienced this when a teacher and a social worker in our project focused on forced marriage and sexual mutilation. The pupils responded positively and actively. Due to the topic's sensitivity, the two adults collaborated greatly before and during the implementation. We observed that they became sufficiently confident in raising this sensitive issue in their class; one pupil during the V*a*KE session also told the educators that she had experienced an attempt from her family for forced marriage. We observed that the educators were able to listen to and responded genuinely to the pupil's voice. We understand this as a concrete example of ethical conduct. V*a*KE as such, was a lever for approaching a delicate value discussion and is an opportunity to consolidate professional skills.

5   Conclusion

We warmly thank the UPE2A teachers from the Essonne district for their relentless efforts within this action research stretching over four years. V*a*KE proved to be a valuable educational opportunity in these teaching units. We argue that the necessity of mentoring over the long term, along with a commitment to make room for real teacher freedom of action, can make a big difference when teachers are not acquainted with the V*a*KE-method in the first place. However, designing the mentoring function may vary and should be adapted to the local context. The teacher's freedom also should be concretized in the development of dilemma stories, didactical tools, and should be sustained by group work reflection and steady cooperation, which, nonetheless, should be consistent with the underlying theory. In our experience, when UPE2A teachers made pedagogical choices, they shared positivity and synergy that lifted both researchers and teachers, opening new paths of reflection and creation.

Notes

1   DEPP, Note d'information n°19.52, décembre 2019.
2   CASNAV: *Centres académiques pour la scolarisation des allophones nouvellement arrivés et des enfants issus des familles itinérantes et de Voyageurs.*
3   Circulaire n° 2002-063 du 20-3-2002.
4   Circulaire n° 2012-143 du 2-10-2012.
5   Circulaire n° 2012-141 du 2-10-2012.
6   Circulaire n° 2002-063 du 20-3-2002.
7   Circulaire n° 2012-141 du 2-10-2012.
8   LOI n° 2013-595 du 8 juillet 2013 d'orientation et de programmation pour la refondation de l'école de la République.
9   Chapters 6, 14, 21, and 22 in this handbook also discuss teacher roles, and challenges for creating a good dilemma and sensitive values such as *laïcité*.
10 A drawing found in a French textbook: (2016). *Sillages, Français 5ième, Manual de l'élève*. Paris: Editions Bordas.

References

Brighenti, M. (2014). La médiation des actes et des questions pour un enjeu capital, le nous. *Diversité, Médiation et médiateurs*, *175*, 83–90.

Brighenti, M., & Brossard Børhaug, F. (2018). Explorer l'enseignement des valeurs pour des élèves allophones: Une recherche action en UPE2A, Essonne. *CIRHILLA (Cahiers du Centre interdisciplinaire de recherches en histoire, lettres et langues et Arts)*, *44*, 51–66.

Catarci, M. (2014). Intercultural education in the European context: Key remarks from a comparative study, *Intercultural Education*, *25*(2), 95–104, doi:10.1080/14675986.2014.886820

Council of Europe. (2018). *Common European framework of reference for languages: Learning, teaching, assessment, Companion volume with new descriptors*. Strasbourg, France: Council of Europe.

Creswell, J. W. (2012). *Educational research. Planning, conducting, and evaluating quantitative and qualitative Research* (4th ed.). Harlow, UK: Pearson.

DEPP (Direction de l'Evaluation, de la Prospective et de la Performance). (2019). Retrieved February 15, 2021, from https://www.education.gouv.fr/64-350-eleves-allophones-nouvellement-arrives-en-2017-2018-8-sur-10-etaient-deja-scolarises-4913

Ministère de l'Éducation Nationale. (2002). *Modalités d'inscription et de scolarisation des élèves de nationalité étrangère des premier et second degrés*. Retrieved February 15, 2021 from https://www.education.gouv.fr/botexte/sp10020425/MENE0200681C.htm

Ministère de l'Éducation Nationale. (2012). *Organisation de la scolarité des élèves allophones nouvellement arrivés*. Retrieved February 15, 2021 from https://www.education.gouv.fr/bo/12/Hebdo37/MENE1234231C.htm

Ministère de l'Éducation Nationale. (2012). *Organisation des CASNAV*. Retrieved February 15, 2021, from https://www.education.gouv.fr/bo/12/Hebdo37/MENE1234234C.htm

Ministère de l'Éducation Nationale. (2013). *Loi n° 2013-595 du 8 juillet 2013 d'orientation et de programmation pour la refondation de l'école de la République*. Retrieved February 15, 2021 from https://www.legifrance.gouv.fr/jorf/id/JORFTEXT000027677984/

Meirieu, P. (2010). *Apprendre … oui, mais comment* (22nd ed.). Paris, France: ESF éditeur.

Ouellet, F. (2008). *Pédagogie de l'interculturel: Mettre en œuvre une pédagogie de la citoyenneté*. Communication présentée au séminaire « Culture, cultures: À l'épreuve de l'altérité, quelle(s) pédagogie(s) de l'interculturel ? Marly-Le-Roi, 29, 30 septembre et 1er octobre.

Patry, J.-L., Weinberger, A., Weyringer, S., & Nussbaumer, M. (2013). Combining Values *and* Knowledge Education. In J. B. Irby, G. Brown, R. Lara-Alecio, & S. Jackson (Eds.)

and R. A. Robles-Piña (Sect. Ed.), *Moral developmental theory. Series handbook of educational theories* (pp. 565–579). Charlotte, NC: Information Age Publishing.

Patry, J.-L., Weyringer, S., & Weinberger, A. (2010). Values and Knowledge Education (V*a*KE) in European summer camps for gifted students: Native versus non-native speakers. In C. Klaassen & N. Maslovaty (Eds.), *Professionalism of teachers* (pp. 133–148). Rotterdam, The Netherlands: Sense Publishers.

UNESCO. (2015). *Incheon declaration education 2030*. Paris, France: UNESCO.

Weinberger, A, Patry, J.-L., & Weyringer, S. (2015). Improving professional practice through practice-based research: V*a*KE (Values *and* Knowledge Education) in university-based teacher education. *Vocations and Learning, 9*, 63–84. doi:10.1007/s12186-015-9141-4

Weyringer, S., Patry, J.-L., & Weinberger, A. (2012). Values and knowledge education. experiences with teacher trainings. In D. Alt & R. Reingold (Eds.), *Changes in teachers' moral role. From passive observers to moral and democratic leaders* (pp. 165–179). Rotterdam, The Netherlands: Sense Publishers.

SECTION 2

VaKE in Higher Education and Training

∴

CHAPTER 11

Training of In-Service Teachers for VaKE

Alfred Weinberger, Dimitris Pnevmatikos and Lydia Linortner

1   Introduction

VaKE is a relatively new approach, and many in-service teachers have not been educated on how to use VaKE in their classes during their education in university. Thus, in most of the educational settings, there is a need for in-service teacher training courses to familiarise the teachers with VaKE. Most in-service teachers have a well-structured personal theory for many facets of the everyday school life (e.g., Darmawan et al., 2020) and what is functional with their students.

Thus, to integrate any new approach in their class, teachers should understand and be convinced that the new approach could be equally and even more efficient than the other approaches they regularly use in their class. In other words, it is crucial to convince the in-service teachers that VaKE has an added value for their teaching practices and the potential to solve problems that other teaching approaches do not. That is, as in-service teachers have their personal theory for the teaching practices that are efficient for their class, they need evidence that using VaKE in their classes will benefit their students more than traditional teaching if, as teachers, they implement VaKE in their classes. Previous studies suggested the need for three phases for training in-service teachers to adopt innovative practices in education (Kariotoglou et al., 2016). Similarly, based on our experience, we suggest here three phases for training in-service teachers with VaKE. These three phases are divided into several steps involving actions based on the Self-Determination Theory (SDT) by Ryan and Deci (2000). SDT claims that autonomy, competence, and social embeddedness enhances self-motivation, all of which foster learning. Thus, in a VaKE course, teachers must be given the possibility to experience autonomy, competence, and relatedness, which in turn can enhance the transition of VaKE into their classes. When teachers experience pressure, it is hard for them to offer autonomy and consequently, a constructivist teaching technique like VaKE. Control can foster student aversion, and their performance can decrease. Consequently, Martinek (2012) suggests need-satisfaction for teachers as one primary goal to break that negative circle system.

2   Phase 1: Familiarizing In-Service Teachers with VaKE

Training in-service teachers with VaKE might start with experiencing a VaKE course on topics where they can identify themselves with the character who should decide in a dilemma under discussion (for how to construct a dilemma, see Chapter 4 in this handbook). This starting point facilitates the in-service teachers to experience the dynamic of the VaKE approach. The reflection on their experiences as learners in this phase is necessary to facilitate teachers to capture the benefits and weaknesses of VaKE and to project them in similar situations with their students. This is a crucial phase of the training process, as teachers will be prompted to learn more about VaKE and how to implement it in their classes, or to decline any effort towards this. The first phase will motivate them to proceed to the second phase. For this first phase, the following steps have proved meaningful:

(1) *Presenting the central aims:* The teacher educator presents the central aims of VaKE emphasizing that these aims are one of the most critical aims in education (and school; e.g., these aims are stipulated in most of the curricula) and why it is important to combine them (*"Values without knowledge is blind; knowledge without values is irresponsible"*; see Chapter 29 in this handbook). It is of utmost importance to underscore that not the values as such are to be conveyed (which would be indoctrination), but that the *argumentation* in favour and against certain values in a given situation are at stake. Adequate examples from everyday life (e.g., climate change) show how important such a combination is. In-service teachers are asked to give further examples from their experience. Within the SDT theory in the first step, it is a possibility to reflect with the in-service teachers about how much and which of these central aims of VaKE or most important goals in educational curricula matches one's own goals. Thus, the need for autonomy of the novice teachers is considered.

(2) *Introducing the dilemma discussion method:* The in-service teachers get familiarised with the dilemma discussion method as an effective method of values education. The moderator presents a dilemma based on the everyday-life examples that she/he addressed in the first step (e.g., a dilemma based on climate change). In-service teachers realize that such moral dilemmas can only be solved appropriately with additional knowledge. The moderator particularly highlights the main conclusion of the teachers: "I need additional knowledge!" to show why learners are so motivated to learn with VaKE. However, the moderator must mention that this motivation depends on the relevance of the dilemma for the individual learner. One critical aspect of the SDT theory is that autonomy can also be experienced within an external impulse (Ryan & Deci, 2000). Through questioning one's basis of the opinion the external impulse to autonomous knowledge gain is given.

(3) *Doing a VaKE course:* The moderator performs a VaKE course with the teachers as learners according to the VaKE steps. Based on our experience, selecting an appropriate dilemma is crucial. It is possible to use either dilemmas which have already been used in classes, or to use dilemmas appropriate for adults (e.g., a dilemma about a current political problem such as climate change, migration). Providing option choices based on a pool of different dilemmas foster learners' motivation (Weinberger, Patry, & Weyringer, 2017). This is in line with SDT aiming at fostering learner's autonomy. When performing each step of VaKE, the teacher educator has two roles: The first role is the teacher role. In this role, he or she acts as if he or she were in the classroom and carrying out a VaKE course with students. The second role is the teacher educator role. In this role, he or she explains to the in-service teachers why the step is essential and how learning can be improved in this step. It is important to carefully distinguish between these two roles; otherwise, the in-service teachers get confused and do not learn appropriately what to do in each step. Special attention should be given to the implementation of the VaKE dilemma discussion. Teachers need good instructions, otherwise it might well happen that they do not foster a moral discussion but immediately proceed to the knowledge issues.

(4) *Reflecting on experiences:* After the completion of a full VaKE course, the in-service teachers reflect on their experiences as learners. They realize whether their personal theories are compatible with constructivist learning. They also ask about practical issues, such as the running time of a VaKE course, organization of group learning, or technical requirements. Against the often-heard statement from novice teachers that control is a necessity in school, the suggested remedy by Martinek is a reflective discussion within teachers about whether they want to be controlled and how these contributed to their competence development (Martinek, 2012, p. 13ff).

3 Phase 2: Theoretical and Practical Issues for Implementing a VaKE Course

After their first experience with VaKE, in-service teachers should be aware of the necessary theoretical and methodological foundations of the VaKE approach (see Part 1 in this handbook) and for the practical issues concerning how to design and implement a VaKE course in their class. Although this knowledge is necessary for the teachers to design and implement a VaKE course in their class, it is not sufficient, as people act based on their beliefs about their capabilities rather than on their actual capabilities (Bandura, 1986). Teachers who feel competent about performing a task are more likely to engage in implementing an innovative instructional approach in their class and are eager to spend their energy on this task (Pnevmatikos, 2016; see also Schunk, Meece, & Pintrich, 2012). To accomplish competence for implementing a VaKE course in their classes, teachers should have the opportunity to acquire some skills gradually through experience. Thus, there is a need for close collaboration between VaKE experts and novice teachers. This collaboration should not only aim at teachers to *'be'* competent but also to *'feel'* competent about implementing a VaKE course in their class. For this second phase, the following steps have turned out to be meaningful:

(1) *Learning about the theoretical background:* The teacher educator introduces the constructivist learning theory for knowledge education and the constructivist theory of moral judgment and moral education (dilemma discussion) by Lawrence Kohlberg.

(2) *Writing a VaKE dilemma story*: Against this theoretical background on moral education, the in-service teachers write an appropriate VaKE dilemma story for their class. The teacher educator introduces the main elements of a "good" dilemma story. Based on our experience, it is easier to write the first VaKE dilemma story in a small group with three or four teachers. Usually, the teachers do not have a problem finding a moral dilemma appropriate for their students. However, they often have a problem addressing the missing knowledge in the dilemma story. It is the teacher educator's task to support them in addressing the missing knowledge appropriately. After finishing the VaKE dilemma story in small groups, the teachers reflect on each story in the plenum (e.g., Is the moral dilemma clear? Is it a moral dilemma? Is the dilemma appropriate for the specific age level? Which additional knowledge is necessary?). Based on the feedback of the colleagues and the teacher educator, they adapt the dilemma story. In this step of phase 2, the third proactive need of teachers to have a feeling of embeddedness (Ryan & Deci, 2000) is fulfilled.

(3) *Planning a VaKE course:* The teachers plan a VaKE course on the basis of the new dilemma story. They consider for example, how the dilemma story can be presented appropriately (e.g., with fictional pictures of the protagonists, with a film clip), how the information search can be organised (e.g., allocating fact sheets, providing internet links), or which learning product students should prepare. These tools enrich the learning opportunities with a variety of meaningful choices (e.g., diversity of learning options, individual selection of learning aims and content as well as methods and media, social structure, and performance feedback); providing meaningful choices is one domain of autonomy fostering strategies to ensure an interpersonal atmosphere of support and understanding in class (Reeve, Deci, & Ryan, 2004). Based on our experience, the planning of a VaKE course in a small learning group (e.g., 3 or 4 persons) is

sensible because the joint preparation of a VaKE course is less labour-intensive and less time-consuming than doing it individually. We particularly suggest this procedure when planning the first VaKE course, otherwise, it might well happen that the amount of work is too much for one person which could be frustrating for the teachers. The teacher educator supports the process. After finishing the planning, each VaKE course can be presented in the plenum and evaluated by the teachers.

More details on the above three steps can be found in other chapters in this handbook. Here, we have just highlighted what it is essential to have in mind during phase 2.

4 Phase 3: Reflections

After the first implementation in class, it is critical for teachers to reflect on their VaKE course and to examine, comparing with their tradition in teaching, the pros, and cons of the VaKE approach. This will allow them to acknowledge the potential of VaKE and to reformulate their personal theories at least for some particular aspects. Hopefully, teachers will find some added value that the VaKE approach can have in various facets of their teaching and recognise that their practices up till now have been insufficient. For instance, in an in-service training course in Greece, teachers were asked to implement a VaKE dilemma discussion in their classes. After the implementation, they had time to reflect and to present their experiences to other teachers. In their reflections, the teachers claimed that the VaKE instruction had an added value for them. In the next paragraph, we will present some elements that Greek and Austrian teachers mentioned for the VaKE approach after their training and implementation of VaKE in their classes.

Knowledge and learning outcomes: Teachers acknowledged that their students acquired the necessary expected knowledge from the instruction. Interestingly, the teachers declared that their students remembered the acquired knowledge in the subsequent lessons, being able to transfer this knowledge in new circumstances. Moreover, they mentioned that students connected the acquired knowledge with sociocultural (e.g., the understanding that social groups have different values and interests for the same topic), affective (e.g., considering the emotional well-being) and epistemic (e.g., acknowledging the importance of evidence over beliefs, and facts over interpretations) aspects. More importantly, they acknowledge that in a dilemma situation, individuals decide based on their values. Thus, the teachers stressed that by using VaKE, they were able to broaden the teaching goals and the expected learning outcomes to other vital aspects of the instruction which their traditional teaching approaches failed to allow. A critical aspect for the teachers was that the implementation of VaKE enables their students to exercise some domain independent skills such as argumentation skills, discussion skills and reflection which are components of critical thinking skills.

Motivation: Teachers reported that their students continue the dilemma discussion in the break after the VaKE lesson and after school. They also reported from parents who said that after a VaKE lesson, their children wanted to discuss the dilemma in the family. This dilemma discussion in the family was often challenging for the parents because their children argued quite convincingly. It seems that they were able to integrate the acquired knowledge into their argumentation.

Teaching strategies: When teachers referred to the teaching strategies, they stressed that they adopted mainly a student-centred teaching strategy than a teacher-centred teaching strategy they used before. They benefited by using authentic situations and problem-based instruction. Students were engaged all the time in discussions, collaboration for providing solutions, explanations, and argumentations or in some cases designing and doing experiments. The teacher-centred teaching strategy was limited to teaching the process and to epistemic aspects, or to flourishing the discussion by asking questions and playing the 'devil's advocate'. It should be mentioned here that one teacher stated that it was challenging to implement VaKE in his class, considering VaKE as an inappropriate approach for Greek education. He said that he lost control of the class and he moved to a teacher-centred strategy in order to achieve the learning goals. When he informed the other teachers about the experience however, he noted that the method might not be suitable for him.

Classroom climate: Teachers referred to the implementation of VaKE in their class as an experience that students enjoyed and were motivated for learning. Students showed great enthusiasm, eagerness, willingness to participate and identified with the protagonist. They were motivated to collect additional information to decide about what the protagonist should do in the dilemma situation. In particular, students were prompted to learn the school knowledge and to seek the truth which is a valuable critical thinking disposition (Facione, 1990). Teachers stressed that this is evident even for students with low achievement motivation. Beyond this, students exercised their empathic concern, and being in the other person's position helped to improve their interpersonal relationships.

However, during the reflections, teachers also declared the problems which appeared when implementing VaKE. The *first* problem is that they are sometimes afraid of losing control in student-centred learning. To help them solve this problem, teachers must realize that in student-centred learning, students are responsible for their learning, and the teacher's responsibility is to provide the opportunity for this learning and to support it. Knowing that one is responsible for one's learning includes that the students prove what they have learned (e.g., by preparing a learning product). A *second* problem can be the lack of motivation by some learners. Lack of motivation can result from an inadequate dilemma story (e.g., a dilemma story which does not address the students' interests; to construct good dilemma stories see Chapter 4 in this handbook) or excessive demand with constructivist learning (e.g., a student is not able to organise his or her learning). In the latter case, it is essential to introduce VaKE in small steps, for example by showing the students how to search effectively for information, how to process information, or how to argue. Teachers should consider that students often have internalized a traditional role of learners, (as do teachers) which is based on the personal theory that the learner's responsibility is to do what the teachers ask them to do. It takes time to change this personal theory of the learners to learn effectively with VaKE. A *third* problem that can appear concerns the organization of learning in the classroom. Sometimes classrooms are small, and the numbers of students are high which exacerbates learning in small groups and might lead to excessive noise, or the classes cannot search for information on the internet. Learning in small groups can also take place outside the classroom. For example, students can learn in the hallway or any other room in school available. The information search can be done in books or other materials which can be prepared by the teacher (see Chapter 9 for an example in Science Education).

5   Conclusion

Training in-service teachers on VaKE is a necessary step to implement VaKE effectively. Teachers need to realize whether the constructive learning setting is compatible with their personal theories of learning. This can only be done by reflecting upon a VaKE course – in the role of the learner and in the role of the teacher. Our first conclusion is that teachers need to experience VaKE in both roles before they decide to implement it into their teaching strategies.

The teachers' experiences with VaKE regarding knowledge and learning outcomes, motivation, teaching strategies, and class climate are mostly positive. However, the planning and implementation of VaKE is time-consuming. Currently, teachers face a dense curriculum and their time available to implement VaKE is limited. Furthermore, it is also critical that teachers include VaKE in the teaching approaches they usually use in class. Collaboration can minimize the workload. Additionally, mutual reflections of VaKE teachers on their experiences with positive and negative effects of VaKE support them in their effort to implement VaKE successfully. It might be helpful if a VaKE expert sometimes joins these reflections and supports them in their ongoing effort to implement VaKE. Finally, it is easier for a group of teachers to represent VaKE in a school where teachers usually use traditional teaching methods. Our second conclusion is that collaboration between several teachers and with the VaKE expert is conducive to implementing VaKE successfully in a classroom and in a school.

References

Bandura, A. (1986). The explanatory and predictive scope of self-efficacy theory. *Journal of Social and Clinical Psychology, 4*(3), 359–373. https://doi.org/10.1521/jscp.1986.4.3.359

Darmawan, I. G. N., Vosniadou, S., Lawson, M. J., Van Deur, P., & Wyra, M. (2020). The development of an instrument to test pre-service teachers' beliefs consistent and inconsistent with self-regulation theory. *British Journal of Educational Psychology, 90*, 1039–1061. https://doi.org/10.1111/bjep.12345

Facione, P. A. (1990). *Critical thinking: A statement of expert consensus for purposes of educational assessment and instruction*. Millbrae, CA: Academic Press.

Kariotoglou, P., Avgitidou, S., Dimitriadou, K., Malandrakis, G., Papadopolulou, P., Pnevmatikos, D., & Spyrtou, A. (2016). The STED (Science Teachers EDucation) training program: Theoretical basis and application. *Educational Sciences (Epistimes tis Agogis), 4*, 96–122.

Martinek, D. (2012). *Selbstbestimmung und Kontrollreduzierung in Lehr- und Lernprozessen*. Hamburg, Germany: Kovač.

Pnevmatikos, D. (2016). Which teachers apply discovery learning and procedural knowledge in the natural sciences? The role of teacher's self-efficacy. In D. Psillos, A. Molochidis, & M. Kalleris (Eds.), *Proceedings from the 9th Panhellenic conference on science education and technologies in education* (pp. 114–120). Thessaloniki, Greece: Aristotles University of Thessaloniki. http://synedrioenephet-2015.web.auth.gr

Pnevmatikos, D., & Trikkaliotis, I. (2012). Procedural justice in a classroom where teacher implements differentiated instruction. In D. Alt & R. Reingold (Eds.), *Changes in teachers' moral role* (pp. 155–163). Leiden, The Netherlands: Brill Sense.

Reeve, J., Deci, E. L., & Ryan, R. M. (2004). Self-Determination Theory: A dialectical framework for understanding socio-cultural influences on student motivation. In D. M. Mclnerney & S. Van Etten (Eds.), *Big theories revisited* (pp. 31–60). Greenwich, CT: Information Age Press.

Ryan, R. M., & Deci, E. L. (2000). Self-determination theory and the facilitation of intrinsic motivation, social development, and well-being. *American Psychologist, 55*, 68–78. https://doi.org/10.1037/0003-066X.55.1.68.

Schunk, D. H., Meece, J. R., & Pintrich, P. R. (2012). *Motivation in education: Theory, research, and applications*. Boston, MA: Pearson Higher Education.

Weinberger, A., Patry, J.-L., & Weyringer, S. (2017). Autonomy-supportive learning with VaKE (Values and Knowledge Education) in teacher education. Fostering empathy and cognitive complexity. In J. Domenech i Soria, M. Cinta Vincent Vala, E. de la Poza, & D. Blasquez (Eds.), *Proceedings of the HEAd'17, 3rd international conference on higher education advances* (pp. 109–116). València, Spain: Editorial Universitat Politècnica de València. http://dx.doi.org/10.4995/HEAd17.2017.4978

CHAPTER 12

Using V*a*KE with Secondary Science Pre-Service Teachers in Australia

Karen Marangio and Rebecca Cooper

1   The General Science Method Unit

The General Science Education method units are part of the secondary science initial teacher education programme at Monash University and have a strong focus on developing the pedagogy of the pre-service teachers. We team teach the units: planning, teaching and critically reflecting on our teaching and our pre-service teachers' learning on an ongoing basis. We aim to offer significant collaborative learning experiences to open up productive and insightful discussions as to 'what is possible' in terms of teaching and learning science. Our intention is to encourage pre-service teachers to articulate their own views of science and science education, and we appreciate how their views influence their teaching of science. We ask them to monitor their own development as a teacher of science over the year.

The secondary science pre-service teachers come from a range of different pathways, some in their final year of a four-year undergraduate Bachelor of Education degree and others in a two-year Master of Teaching degree. Some pre-service teachers are changing careers and there is a mix of local and international students. Very few pre-service teachers come from rural parts of Australia. While all pre-service teachers have a tertiary science background, only a handful have studied earth and environmental science or were taught about socioscientific issues (SSIs) in their school education. Most have come from a traditional school science background, where science was taught in discrete disciplinary subjects, with limited emphasis on the nature and use of science in society, including the inter-, multi-, and transdisciplinary aspects of science and use in addressing personal, local, and global issues. We also recognise there is a tendency in schools to separate the teaching of knowledge education (content knowledge) from values education (students' moral stance) (Patry, Weyringer, & Weinberger, 2007). We take the view that if pre-service teachers have not experienced learning about the nature and values of science in their schooling nor thought about the complexities and potential sensitive, emotional and value laden aspects involved in teaching SSIs, then they are unlikely to feel comfortable to teach these aspects in the future. We believe offering a VaKE experience will make pre-service teachers open and willing to consider a VaKE-like strategy in their future teaching career.

2   Australian Curriculum Context

VaKE was first included in our units as a way to introduce SSIs and in response to major curriculum reform in Australia. The inaugural Australian curriculum introduced general capabilities to be taught in all studies, including 'Ethical understandings' that relates to understanding ethical concepts and issues, reasoning in decision making and actions and exploring values, rights and responsibilities (Australian Curriculum Assessment and Reporting Authority, 2015). There was also the introduction of a new science strand, 'Science as a human endeavour (SHE)'. SHE relates to the nature and development of science, and the use and influence of science, such as exploring how science is influenced by society and can be used to inform decisions and actions. SHE represents the applicability of science to personal, local, and global issues, including decision making and actions, and working towards developing scientifically literate citizens who can link content to the world beyond the classroom and contribute to the community. In particular, SHE endorses the teaching of SSIs, embedded within sociocultural contexts to work towards these scientific literacy goals (Zeidler & Sadler, 2011) and highlights the interrelationship between science and society (Sadler, 2004). SHE connects with the general capabilities including ethical understandings.

VaKE dilemmas that emphasise SSIs can sensitize students towards the ethical dimensions of science (Pnevmatikos et al., 2016). VaKE, as outlined by Patry et al. (2007), offers opportunities to encompass SHE and ethical understandings, along with disciplinary knowledge, through learners investigating dilemma stories. The knowledge acquisition is at least the same as traditional teaching methods (ibid.), and the richness of the task is that it is more likely to engage students in self-directed learning and learning with others and appreciate the complexities of social issues within our society.

Curriculum reform requires a significant shift in focus from "what" is taught in science classrooms to, importantly, "how" it is being taught. Curriculum reform is likely to be unsuccessful when teachers do not see the need to change or understand how to change their current ways of teaching (van Driel, Beijaard, & Verloop, 2001). Science teachers may not understand the intentions behind the new SHE strand in the curriculum and are therefore likely to overlook SHE in their teaching in favour of teaching science in traditional ways, focused more on the traditional content (Aubusson, 2011). The teaching of SSIs demands dramatic shifts from traditional science teaching (Fensham, 2011) where emotional and value-laden aspects of science are not explored. Similarly, most teachers are unlikely to be educated in VaKE, which requires the dilemma and procedure to be well planned and introduced in a way to stimulate interest and be well accepted by students (Patry, Weyringer, & Weinberger, 2008). Therefore, a VaKE experience in initial teaching education has the potential to inform pre-service teachers future teaching of science.

3   Setting up the VaKE Experience

Each year the General Science Method units are re-evaluated, including the VaKE experience, with a focus on providing a high-quality education for our pre-service teachers. Our second semester focuses strongly on values from a number of different lenses including the roles of personal, science, science education and societal values. VaKE enhances and extends these unit based 'learning to teach' experiences, and this section discusses the ways we currently incorporate VaKE into our unit to provide significant learning experiences for our pre-service teachers.

3.1   The Dilemma Story

The ways we use VaKE today builds on our previous work with science pre-service teachers (Keast & Marangio, 2015). The dilemma needs to be realistic, engaging, current and personable, but also needs to be something that the students are not entirely knowledgeable about so that there is a 'need to know more' before they make their own considered decision. The personable aspects create a situation where pre-service teachers can relate, empathise and/or feel compassion towards those at the centre of the dilemma. The sociocultural factors are important as they often inspire the 'need to know more' in the sense that SSIs are complex and complicated and value laden. These multifaceted considerations highlight the relationships between science and society.

Originally a dilemma (Appendix A) was created that draws on water issues (water is a precious commodity in Australia) and education (we assume our pre-service teachers will value education) but related to a remote part of northern Australia. The dilemma story is based on a rural family: their personal and financial situation and the aspirations of their child to continue with tertiary education in a major city. The family are asked to make a decision that concerns the irrigation of their land, a current political issue involving a variety of stakeholders including the irrigation lobby and environmental groups (Adamson,

2013; Wittwer & Banerjee, 2014). Scientific assessments for the water resources in the region also exist (for instance, Petheram, Watson, Bruce, & Chilcott, 2018). As with any good dilemma story, there is no clear answer, and the pre-service teachers need to analyse the situation and the science involved to make a judgement on what they believe should be done to 'solve' the problem.

3.2 Incorporating VaKE

VaKE is currently introduced in Week 2 Semester 2, following lectures and workshops discussing teacher values on student learning, core values of science, and the role of debate and argumentation in science education. We ask pre-service teachers to primarily take the role of a student (learning with VaKE), instead of the teacher role (learning to teach with VaKE) which mainly happens at the end of the semester. We adapt a lesson interruption method (see Chapter 31 in this handbook; Patry & Weinberger, 2004), following with a sequence of steps of decision making (make a decision), argumentation (exchange arguments and consider what further information is needed), look for evidence (search for new information), exchange new information (share and consider if new information is sufficient) and reflect on what this new information means for how they think of the dilemma (how does the evidence support their argument, what values are they prioritising) before making a new decision to repeat this series of steps. Argumentation and exchange of information allows pre-service teachers to check the viability of their arguments and communicate their ideas, consider different perspectives, and learn from and with each other.

3.2.1 Initial Decision

Pre-service teachers are presented with a dilemma story, as described earlier and in Appendix A. The original dilemma is still used, for reasons explained above, and the introduction of the dilemma story is structured very carefully to pique pre-service teachers' interest, which is critical for successful VaKE experiences (Patry, Weyringer, & Weinberger, 2008). For instance, the scene is set by using a geographical map of Australia and pictures to show the remote location. Pre-service teachers are asked to make a decision (YES or NO) and fill in the VaKE survey (Appendix B) that asks them for their current decision, the strength of this decision and the most important values that they identify as guiding this decision.

At this point, we make it clear to pre-service teachers that it is okay to change one's mind in the future. We are very conscious of holding back our views and opinions about the dilemma throughout the VaKE experiences so as not to influence the pre-service teachers in their decision making.

3.2.2 Initial Line Up and Group Assignment

The pre-service teachers then line up on a continuum based on the strength of their decision, from 'strongly YES' to 'strongly NO'. Close to equal numbers of YES and NO and a range of strengths are usually present, something we find each year and continues to surprise both us and our pre-service teachers. We briefly run a class discussion, asking for different reasons as to why they were standing on their particular position on the continuum, highlighting a range of knowledge and different values prioritised in this class. Values typically orientate towards economical, educational, environmental, health and welfare, personal and human rights, political and social influence priorities. This is typically an eye-opening experience for our pre-service teachers, and often creates the 'need to know more' to investigate the dilemma further.

Pre-service teachers are then assigned to groups of five to six based on their initial decision. Each group consists of pre-service teachers with differing views, ranging from 'strongly YES to 'strongly NO, with the hope that exploring different perspectives and values will challenge their own ideas. They carry out research, often in pairs or individually, and share their findings with the group. They continue to research further information, communicate their findings, and present arguments to justify their decisions.

3.2.3 Researching the Dilemma and Further Decision Making

In our Week 2 workshop, after some time investigating the dilemma and sharing the findings within their group, we ask the pre-service teachers a further two times to decide, justify their decision and highlight the values they prioritised via the V*a*KE survey (Appendix B). As mentioned earlier, pre-service teachers undertake a series of steps:
– decision making (make a decision),
– argumentation (exchange arguments and consider what further information is needed),
– look for evidence (search for new information),
– exchange new information (share and consider if new information is sufficient),
– reflect on what this new information means for how they think of the dilemma (how does the evidence support their argument, what values are they prioritising),
– before making a new decision and repeat this series of steps.

Importantly, we did not expect pre-service teachers to reach a consensus decision within their group, but we did expect them to offer claims and counterclaims, to try to understand the motives and values behind such decisions, consider what further information they need to know to make a more considered decision, brainstorm possibilities in terms of where to find such information, work together to search (typically online) and share new information. Often the groups will break up into smaller groups to search for different bits of information. Pre-service teachers are asked to consider how this information provides further evidence to support (or not) different claims within the group. In this way, we want respectful and considered discussions. Importantly, we aim to facilitate a classroom atmosphere where it is okay for pre-service teachers to change their mind to make more informed decisions.

In this workshop, most of the pre-service teachers are passionate about the issue and determined to find more information on this water and family issue, including sourcing news media articles, government (local, state, and federal) and science reports. It is worth noting that each year different group members often use the same report as evidence to argue different points of views (claims and counterclaims). Furthermore, the terms of reference on these reports are often discussed, particularly as they begin to see how the different reports are used by members of the class to justify different decisions. These discussions lead to deeper consideration around strengths and weaknesses of the evidence to support different arguments and underlying values that are prioritised.

Pre-service teachers continue working in their groups in preparation for our Week 12 workshop. At the end of Week 12, pre-service teachers are asked to make a final individual decision (VaKE survey, Appendix B). While drawing on their group's research (the new information sourced and arguments presented), they are responsible for their own individual decision. We prioritise their right to make and justify their own decision, rather than a group decision that often requires compromise, and occasionally leads to conflicts.

4 Reflecting on the VaKE Experiences as a Future Teacher of Science

Throughout the semester, especially at the end of the semester, we ask pre-service teachers to reflect on what the VaKE experience could mean for their future teaching of science. In the last workshop, we asked a number of questions such as:
– How does this VaKE experience compare to your own school science education experiences?
– In what ways does this VaKE experience get you thinking about the nature and values of science, and the purpose of secondary school science education? Explain.
– How likely are you to use a VaKE activity in your future teaching of science? What do you need to know and do in order to increase this likelihood?

The value and limitations and constraints with using a V*a*KE activity in science classrooms and in initial teacher education, including any other related ideas or information that they want us to know are discussed in depth. The likelihood that they will use V*a*KE in their science classrooms in the future and what they may do to increase this likelihood is then considered.

5   The Value of V*a*KE Experiences in General Science Method Units

V*a*KE offers a stand-out experience for our science pre-service teachers, one that gets them thinking deeply about the role of science and values in our society *and* the purpose of school science education. We continue to find that V*a*KE resonates in positive ways with the majority of pre-service teachers, in line with previous research with General Science units at Monash University (Keast & Marangio, 2015).

The majority of our pre-service teachers view the V*a*KE experience as promoting science-related aspects such as:
– the nature and values of science; and
– the use and benefits of science in our society.

In terms of teaching science, the V*a*KE experience invites pre-service teachers to explore a number of factors including:
– the ways science can be presented in classrooms,
– the relevance of science to students' personal and social lives,
– different perspectives and values within a group of pre-service teachers,
– the role of group work and collaboration, including the benefits of sharing different perspectives,
– teaching the role of evidence and values in decision making, and the importance of decision making, justifying, and communicating arguments,
– student-centered versus teacher-led teaching; and
– exploring their own values, they (as a teacher) bring into a classroom.

V*a*KE offers pre-service teachers a new teaching procedure to use when teaching science, and most, connected the V*a*KE experience as facilitating ways to teach science as a human endeavour (SHE) and general capabilities including 'ethical understandings', as part of the new Australian science curriculum (Australian Curriculum Assessment and Reporting Authority, 2015).

Most pre-service teachers are extremely positive about the experience, and many feel prepared to use a V*a*KE activity in the future. For a few, V*a*KE is such a big shift that more teaching experience and further opportunities to learn more about science teaching are necessary before they become comfortable with teaching and feel ready to teach VaKE. That said, not all pre-service teachers see the value in VaKE. Each year, a small number of pre-service teachers continue to hold traditional views of science, viewing science as factual, certain, unemotional, and value-free. At the end of the experience, these pre-service teachers view VaKE as an important activity, but not belonging in science classrooms, and thereby demonstrating that pre-existing understandings of the nature and values of science and science education impacted their VaKE experience. For these pre-service teachers, teaching with VaKE requires a dramatic shift in their beliefs and preferred ways of teaching and, without further support, they are unlikely to facilitate change from this experience.

In many ways VaKE is a new and confronting teaching strategy for our pre-service teachers, with many at first expecting to be shown the 'right way' to teach science and given the 'correct answers' to the dilemma. The VaKE experience can lead to a more complex view of science and their own values of science and science education. For successful teaching with VaKE, it is important that they understand the theory and are capable of adapting VaKE to their specific classroom context (Patry, Weyringer, & Weinberger, 2008). Follow up learning opportunities to extend and share their experiences once they start teaching would be very beneficial.

6   Implications for School Science Education

The VaKE activity is a unique and significant learning experience for our science pre-service teachers. As is often the case with practicing teachers, pre-service teachers are unlikely to have experienced VaKE-like activities in their own schooling (Patry et al., 2008), be educated in SSIs (Fensham, 2011), understand the science as a human endeavour strand (Aubusson, 2011) or deeply consider what it may mean to interweave the teaching of general capabilities, such as ethical understandings, in their science classrooms. VaKE demonstrates how these areas of the inaugural Australian curriculum can be interwoven and implemented in science education, helping pre-service teachers understand and appreciate ways they could change their current science teaching practice in line with curriculum reform, factors that can facilitate successful curriculum change (van Driel, Beijaard, & Verloop, 2001). Importantly, VaKE shows how science is very much a complex endeavour that is woven into our personal, local, and global world. VaKE facilitates the teaching of SSIs, highlighting the interrelationship between science and society (Sadler, 2004) and working towards building a scientific literate citizenry (Zeidler & Sadler, 2011).

In science education, V*a*KE shows just how vital it is to integrate approaches of teaching and learning science across the curriculum.

Every now and then a past pre-service teacher gets in touch with us to share their excitement with teaching V*a*KE. Sometimes it can take a couple of years before they get an opportunity to incorporate V*a*KE into their curriculum and/ or feel comfortable enough with their own teaching and knowledge to include a dilemma story; often they comment on taking small steps towards incorporating V*a*KE. As teacher educators, we feel that including V*a*KE is incredibly valuable, especially when it is inspiring our past pre-service teachers to incorporate V*a*KE into their classrooms, as this teacher comments:

> I have been eager to use V*a*KE for some time, and finally got the chance. Even though it was only a small class of Year 8 students, I found it effective. They enjoyed it, I really enjoyed doing it. Especially because [they] are at that age they start listening to the news. We were focused on energy and all the stuff in the news was on reliability of renewable energy in South Australia and Elon Musk. I saw it as an opportunity to get them to use evidence and think about the issues in different ways. One girl had struggled to engage in class but now could remember all the different views and the science. I will definitely work on more V*a*KE dilemmas in the future!

References

Adamson, D. (2013). The big issue: Northern irrigation: Dream or nightmare? *Irrigation Australia: The Official Journal of Irrigation Australia, 29*(3), 30.

Aubusson, P. (2011). An Australian science curriculum: Competition, advances, and retreats. *Australian Journal of Education, 55*(3), 229–244. https://doi.org/10.1177/000494411105500305

Australian Curriculum Assessment and Reporting Authority. (2015). *The Australian curriculum: Version 7.4*. Retrieved April 10, 2015, from https://www.australiancurriculum.edu.au/f-10-curriculum

Fensham, P. J. (2011). Knowledge to deal with challenges to science education from without and within. In D. Corrigan, J. Dillon, & R. Gunstone (Eds.), *The professional knowledge base of science teaching* (pp. 295–317). Dordrecht, The Netherlands: Springer. https://doi.org/10.1007/978-90-481-3927-9_17

Keast, S., & Marangio, K. (2015). Values *and* Knowledge Education (V*a*KE) in teacher education: Benefits for science pre-service teachers when using dilemma stories. *Procedia – Social and Behavioral Sciences, 167*(0), 198–203. https://doi.org/10.1016/j.sbspro.2014.12.662

Patry, J.-L., & Weinberger, A. (2004). Kombination von konstruktivistischer Werterziehung und Wissenserwerb. *Salzburger Beiträge zur Erziehungswissenschaft, 8*(2), 35–50.

Patry, J.-L., Weyringer, S., & Weinberger, A. (2007). Combining values and knowledge education. In D. N. Aspin & J. D. Chapman (Eds.), *Values education and lifelong learning* (pp. 160–179). Dordrecht, The Netherlands: Springer. https://doi.org/10.1007/978-1-4020-6184-4_9

Patry, J.-L., Weyringer, S., & Weinberger, A. (2008). Interaction of science and values in schools. In K. Tirri (Ed.), *Educating moral sensibilities in urban schools* (pp. 157–170). Leiden, The Netherlands: Sense Publishers.

Petheram, C., Watson, I., Bruce, C., Chilcott, C. (2018). *Water resource assessment for the Mitchell catchment.* CSIRO: EP186909. Australia: Commonwealth Scientific and Industrial Research Organisation (CSIRO). http://hdl.handle.net/102.100.100/86800?index=1

Pnevmatikos, D., Patry, J.-L., Weinberger, A., Linortner, L., Weyringer, S., Maron, R., & Gordon-Shaag, A. (2016). Combining values and knowledge education for lifelong transformative learning. In E. Panitsides & J. Talbo (Eds.), *Lifelong learning: Concepts, benefits, and challenges* (pp. 109–34). New York, NY: Nova Science.

Sadler, T. D. (2004). Moral and ethical dimensions of socioscientific decision making as integral components of scientific literacy. *The Science Educator, 13*(1), 39–48.

van Driel, J. H., Beijaard, D., & Verloop, N. (2001). Professional development and reform in science education: The role of teachers' practical knowledge. *Journal of Research in Science Teaching, 38*(2), 137–158. https://doi.org/10.1002/1098-2736(200102)38:2<137::AID-TEA1001>3.0.CO;2-U

Wittwer, G., & Banerjee, O. (2014). Investing in irrigation development in North West Queensland, Australia. *Australian Journal of Agricultural and Resource Economics, 59*(2), 189–207. https://doi.org/10.1111/1467-8489.12057

Zeidler, D. L., & Sadler, D. L. (2010). An inclusive view of scientific literacy: Core issues and future directions of socioscientific reasoning. In C. Linder, L. Östman, D.A. Roberts, P. Wickman, G. Erickson, & A. MacKinnon (Eds.), *Exploring the landscape of scientific literacy* (pp. 176–192). New York, NY: Routledge. https://doi.org/10.4324/9780203843284

Appendix A

Sam's Family Dilemma

Sam lives on a large cattle station some 50km west of Richmond near the Flinders River. The family farm barely makes a living these days, though once prosperous, the homestead stands as a monument to rich times, though the signs of disrepair and despair are obvious and everywhere. Sam at 16 would like to go to Brisbane or Sydney to study at university, but time away from the farm is expensive and means one capable hand absent.

There is hope. The recent news of the Queensland government allowing irrigation rights along the Finders River is welcome news for the family. Sam and the family are aware of the environmental problems with other river systems that have been overly irrigated, but the opportunity to access water and diversify into other food production rather than sparse cattle could mean wealth again for the family. The family has been planting native trees to maintain the soil condition more than their neighbours and have nagging doubts about the long-term impact of irrigation on the ecosystem.

If Sam wants to go to university, irrigation water rights may be the way to pay for it. Should the family irrigate? Yes, or no?

Appendix B

V*a*KE SURVEY   Participant Code: Survey Number (please circle)

1   2   3   4

V*a*KE uses a dilemma story, in this case Sam's family dilemma to irrigate and support his schooling. At this point in time, please answer the following questions.

1. Should Sam's family irrigate? What is our decision at this point in time? Yes or No Place a cross on the following line to identify the strength of your decision:

    I---------------------I---------------------I
    Strongly Yes   Strongly No

2. Why are you in favour (Yes) or against (No)? Give a brief reason for your answer.
3. Identify which values helped you make this decision.

CHAPTER 13

Experience in Working with V*a*KE in the Georgian Higher Education Space

Izabella Petriashvili, Ekaterine Shaverdashvili, Ina Baratashvili and Tamar Mosiashvili

1   Changes in Values Education in Georgia

After the collapse of the Soviet Union, the introduction of new values in Georgia and their inclusion as important educational elements in the educational process became top issues on the agenda.

In contrast to Western education systems of developed countries, the Soviet education system had a radically different approach to values education as it was completely based on one ideology, which was the "noble" aim of building Communism: "A university in a Socialist country is first of all an educational establishment training highly qualified specialists, brought up in the spirit of selfless service to the people who are building a Communist society" (Prokofiev et al., 1961).

However, the attitude changed after the breakup of the Soviet Union. During the transitional period and later it became of crucial significance to place major focus on values education that meant instilling progressive values in students, which is undeniably a corner stone for the country's rapid advance towards the establishment of a truly democratic system implying human rights protection, freedom of speech, social justice and equality and wellbeing/welfare of people.

After the rose revolution in 2003, the rapid changes of education reform initiated the development and approval of main documents regulating the teachers' preparation and professional development and National curriculum (Shapiro et al., 2007, p. 18). School curricula and teacher preparation programmes in universities, based on completely new values different from the Soviet educational goals, were developed, and the preparation of an important actor, the teacher, who could respond to new challenges, appeared on the agenda. The development of values as an extremely significant aspect for future teachers emerged as an important element in teacher preparation programmes, which is a prerequisite for the students' ability to formulate and justify values competently.

Values education as a key element of problem-based learning has played an important role in the National Curricula of Georgia since 2006. In the new National Curriculum (2018–2024) it is stated:

> The National Curriculum is based on the constructivist educational concept and focuses on personal development. (National Curriculum of Georgia, 2018, p. 10)

According to the National Goals of General Education, which was approved in 2004, the general educational system in Georgia today is aimed at creating favourable conditions for the development of national and universal values of free individuals. The educational system promotes the physical and intellectual abilities of youngsters and imparts essential knowledge. In addition, the educational system promotes a healthy lifestyle, fosters civic awareness of the pupils based on liberal and democratic values and helps them to realize their rights and obligations towards family, society, and state (National Goals of General Education in Georgia, 2004, p. 2).

As stated in the National Curriculum of Georgia, which aims to reach the national goals of general education, the following competences and values should be developed: "Problem solving, critical thinking, ability to cooperate, competence to listen and understand others, competence to understand and to value the personal dignity, adherence of ethical norms, feeling of solidarity, empathy, acceptance of variety" (National Curriculum, 2017, p. 10).

The National Curriculum highlights universal values such as tolerance and equality, regardless of the teachers', parents', and pupils' "social, ethnic, religious, linguistic and ideological affiliation" (National Curriculum of Georgia, 2017, pp. 10–11). Among the most prominent values of the curriculum are also, respect of the historical and cultural heritage, and respect and caring attitudes towards the "material or intangible culture (traditions, values, etc.)" (National Curriculum of Georgia, 2017, p. 11).

Values education as an important goal is also emphasized in the Teacher Professional Standard of Georgia, a basic document, which defines "the teacher's professional knowledge and skills, values and obligations". One of the main competences of teachers should be the development of "ethical values among students" for solving conflicts peacefully and leading a healthy lifestyle. (Teacher Professional Standard of Georgia, 2008, p. 3)

In Georgia, all major institutions of higher education, and in particular the five universities which participated in the study to be discussed below, fully realised the importance of values education and included and highlighted the issue in their strategic development plans and mission statements. One of the main missions of Georgian universities is to develop values among students, which is seen as a prerequisite for the level of democracy in the country.

The introduction of values education in schools in Georgia is mainly assisted by civic education as a school subject and as non-formal education. Within the framework of non-formal educational projects in schools, various clubs are set up where students implement different environmental or civic projects (USAID, 2020; CENN, 2020). In these conditions, it is important for future teachers to acquire the necessary competence at universities so that they are able to apply values education in practice. These changes of the education paradigm in Georgia initiated the new vision of universities.

2   CURE and the Georgian Partner Universities

The project "CURE" (Curriculum Reform for Promoting Civic Education and Democratic Principles in Israel and in Georgia) addresses just these issues, emphasizing values education, teaching approaches and the role of universities in these development processes. CURE is a multi-faceted programme for curricular reform that aims to improve the level of curriculum for Civic Education and Principles of Democracy in teacher-training programmes in Israel and in Georgia through developing new courses, faculty training workshops, student leadership training, student activities, establishing civic education clubs/centres at the participating universities, colleges and in schools where students practice teaching. CURE is a bi-regional cooperation project that integrated European innovative pedagogical approaches and expertise in CURE's developed courses (CURE, 2020). VaKE is one of these innovative pedagogical approaches.

Five universities participating in the CURE project were from all parts of Georgia: two in Tbilisi, the Capital city, Eastern Georgia (Ivane Javakhishvili Tbilisi State University – TSU; and Ilia State University – ISU), and three regional universities (Batumi Shota Rustaveli State University – BSU – in the Adjara region, South-West Georgia; Samtskhe-Javakheti State University – SJSU – in Southern Georgia; and Kutaisi University – KU – in the Western Georgia).

The mission statements of Higher Education Institutions (HEIs) reflect institutional diversity of Georgian higher education institutions. Textual analyses of mission statements of the web pages of the CURE partner universities suggest some disparities between the Tbilisi based and the regional universities:
– In case of universities located in the capital city Tbilisi a clear tendency to describe the mission in the broader meaning of the universities' social function can be observed. It is described as "the university's role in encouraging

societal development" (Ilia State University, n.d.), promotion of "intellectual, moral, cultural and socio-economic development of the society" (TSU, 2013), etc.
- In the mission statements of regional universities, the social function of university is highlighted while taking into consideration the local context. The social function of a university located in a region populated by ethnic minorities is described as "support of integration of non-Georgian population into the Georgian society" (Samtskhe-Javakheti State University, 2018).
- The rhetoric around the word "value" is related to academic freedom, analytical abilities, and human rights: "(…) values are based on critical, creative, and progressive thinking, the principles of academic freedom and academic ethics" (TSU, 2013).
- The main values on which the University is based are freedom, national identity, tolerance (TSU, 2013), integration with the European higher education area (Batumi Shota Rustaveli State University, 2020), etc.
- (…) prepare highly qualified and competitive graduates (…) with conscious and effective decision-making skills, with good faith and high civic awareness, national and universal values (Kutaisi University, 2020).

The analysed mission statements emphasize their institutions' roles and reflect the European orientation of the country, as well as the implemented reforms in terms of democratic values and local priorities.

3 History of VaKE in Georgia

In recent decades, international projects with the world's leading countries have played an important role in the development of the educational process in new directions, within the framework of which as a result of experience sharing, many successful models have been launched in the Georgian educational space.

VaKE was developed by a team at the Paris-Lodron University of Salzburg (PLUS) over 20 years ago, which enables the combined application of knowledge, values, and skills in teaching (Patry & Weinberger, 2004; Patry et al., 2013). The concept of VaKE is an innovative approach in Georgian reality. VaKE was introduced to the Georgian universities participating in the CURE project in 2016 by the Salzburg University Group, which was also part of the CURE project.

Within the CURE project, 14 faculty members from the above five Georgian universities participated in the training workshops offered by PLUS on methods, didactics, tools, and practices of values education, with the focus on the didactical approach VaKE (Patry & Weyringer, 2020). The workshop participants were introduced to the VaKE concept. The objectives of these workshops were to let participants experience VaKE themselves by going through all the steps of the VaKE process, learning and practicing specific VaKE tools (role-play, perspective taking, how to conceive a dilemma story, etc.). As a result, the participant faculty members gained the necessary competence to plan, guide and implement VaKE processes in their own institutions. During the past two years VaKE has been piloted in all five universities of Georgia involved in CURE in different formats – as a separate course or integrated in other existing courses.

A manual on VaKE in Georgian language has been developed. And the Georgian university students developed country related dilemma stories on ecology, poverty, migration, and multiculturalism (Shaverdashvili & Mosiashvili, 2018, pp. 101–110).

4 The Study and Its Findings

What are the experiences in working with VaKE in the Georgian Higher Education space? This was studied through an online survey that dealt in particular with the piloting of VaKE and with the analysis of problems/challenges connected with the pilots. Faculty members of the above five Georgian universities, working on the implementation of VaKE in teacher preparation programmes, were invited to participate in the survey. The questionnaire included questions about the programmes in which VaKE was implemented in their institutions, in what form it was applied in these programmes (as a separate course, integrated in the existing courses), and what challenges they faced in the process of applying VaKE in their courses.

The survey was conducted online during January and February 2020, and the questionnaire was sent to all the participants of the five universities (21 faculty members). 19 responses have been received from these universities (BSU: 3; KU: 1; ISU: 6; TSU: 4; SJSU: 5). 10 respondents have over 20 years of working experience. All respondents use VaKE in various programmes.

The questionnaire included questions about (a) the programmes in which VaKE was implemented at their institutions, (b) in what form it was applied in these programmes (as a separate course, integrated in the existing courses), and (c) what challenges they faced in the process of applying VaKE in their courses.

VaKE is used in teacher education programmes (300 ECTS) and in teacher preparation certificate programmes.

(1) VaKE is offered as separate courses with the title "Values and Knowledge Education" (i) at a BA stage for a teacher education minor programme students as an elective course (6 ECTS); (ii) for a teacher preparation certificate programme (60 ECTS), in which clinical practice at schools and practice research are integrated; and (iii) in a primary teacher preparation/education programme (300 ECTS) as an elective course (3 ECTS).

(2) VaKE is embedded in other courses, namely (i) in BA courses (Teaching citizenship at primary, lower and upper secondary schools; Intercultural education – pedagogical approaches; Organizational behaviour; Practical course in English; Stylistics of English language; Career management and leadership; Theory of education and teaching; Methods of civic education; Introduction into economics and business); (ii) in MA courses (Research methods; Foundations in multicultural education; Education in a diverse society; Strategic management; Civic education for sustainability; The English language structure and contemporary methods of teaching; Using multimedia in teaching and learning); (iii) in teacher preparation certificate programme courses (Pedagogical ethics).

In one university, apart from teacher preparation programmes, VaKE was also integrated in the introductory course in business and economics in order to work on various dilemmas and problems.

The respondents encountered some challenges while working with VaKE. Most of the respondents answered that they had no problems applying VaKE: "Students were happily engaged in the process and were rather motivated". One respondent encountered problems when working with VaKE: "The involvement of students at the first stage was low, as it was a new approach and they found it difficult to be involved in the process". According to the respondent, the reason for this may be low motivation related to a non-mandatory subject. If the subject was mandatory, the students would probably be more enthusiastically involved in the working process.

Two respondents think that while working with VaKE, "it takes a lot of time to explain the efficiency of this method" and working with this method is "very time-consuming". One respondent wrote: "The main challenge was that VaKE was added to the course syllabus, which meant that there wasn't enough time to apply VaKE comprehensively. Mostly, it was about introducing this method to future teachers, as one of the practical methods for values education".

Another respondent notes that "there was no serious problem encountered. The only thing I can mention is that students found it difficult to think of subject-specific dilemmas, and it took a lot more time to formulate the dilemma well".

5 Conclusions

Despite the above-mentioned challenges, it can be concluded that it is possible to implement VaKE in Georgian higher education space within diverse courses (such as teaching a foreign language; business administration).

Integrating VaKE in teacher education programmes is highly beneficial, as pre-service teachers, after starting regular teaching in schools, will support pupils in acquiring subject knowledge in combination with developing values.

It must be noted that the students' motivation depends on the application of VaKE, and it influences the learning issues and values development; this model encourages the students' autonomous learning and fosters the development of the values at the same time.

Collecting data on the application of VaKE in Georgian higher education institutions may provide a useful resource for future research. In the future, it is feasible to study VaKE effects in these institutions and in general education schools in terms of students' attitudes, school culture and academic performance.

The introduction of VaKE in teacher training programmes will assist the establishment of values argumentation in students as future teachers, and the development of value education in the schools where they work. All of these foster the formation of values towards democracy in students and the creation of a strong and free society.

Acknowledgement

The programme in this chapter was implemented in an ERASMUS+ Key Action Capacity Building Program for Higher Education: Curriculum Reform for Promoting Civic Education and Democratic Principles in Israel and in Georgia: CURE, Project number: 573322-EPP-1-2016-IL-EPPKA2-CBHE-JP.

Disclaimer: The European Commission's support for the production of this publication does not constitute an endorsement of the contents, which only reflect the views of the authors, and the Commission cannot be held responsible for any use which may be made of the information contained therein.

References

Batumi Shota Rustaveli State University. (2020). *Mission*. Batumi, Georgia: Batumi Shota Rustaveli State University. Retrieved June 5, 2020, from https://www.bsu.edu.ge/main/page/2-1/index.html

CENN. (2020). *Our history*. Tbilisi, Georgia: CENN. Retrieved June 5, 2020, from http://www.cenn.org/who-we-are/our-history/

CURE. (2020). *About the project*. Haifa, Israel: Gordon Academic College of Education. Retrieved June 5, 2020, from https://cure.erasmus-plus.org.il/course/view.php?id=13

Ilia State University. (n.d.). *Mission statement*. Tbilisi, Georgia: Ilia State University. Retrieved June 5, 2020, from https://iliauni.edu.ge/en/iliauni/mission

Kutaisi University. (2020). *Mission*. Kutaisi Georgia: Kutaisi University. Retrieved June 5, 2020, from https://www.unik.edu.ge/Mission

National Goals of General Education. (2004). *Resolution No. 84 of the Government of Georgia*. Retrieved October 18, 2004, from https://matsne.gov.ge/en/document/download/29248/56/en/pdf

Patry, J.-L., & Weinberger, A. (2004). Kombination von konstruktivistischer Werterziehung und Wissenserwerb. *Salzburger Beiträge zur Erziehungswissenschaft, 8*(2), 35–50.

Patry, J.-L., Weinberger, A., Weyringer, S., & Nussbaumer, M. (2013). Combining values and knowledge education. In B. J. Irby, G. Brown, R. Lara-Alecio, & S. Jackson (Eds.) and R. A. Robles-Piña (Sect. Ed.), *The handbook of educational theories* (pp. 565–579). Charlotte, NC: Information Age Publishing.

Patry, J.-L., & Weyringer, S. (2020). Values and Knowledge Education for promoting civic education and democratic principles – University of Salzburg Training Program for the Special Mobility Strand of the CURE project. In R. Sofer & S. Sofer (Eds.), *CURE's Special Mobility Strand faculty training program to promote civic education through innovative pedagogy* (pp. 45–53). Haifa, Israel: Gordon Academic College of Education.

Prokofiev, M. A., Chilikin, M. G., & Tulpanov, S. I. (1961). *Higher education in the USSR*. Paris, France: UNESCO.

Samtskhe-Javakheti State University. (2018). *Mission of LEPL Samtskhe-Javakheti State University*. Akhaltsikhe, Georgia: Samtskhe-Javakheti State University. Retrieved June 5, 2020, from http://www.sjuni.edu.ge/ge/en/mission/

Shapiro, S., Nakata, S., Chakhaia, L., Zhvania, E., Babunashvili, G., Pruidze, N., & Tskhomelidze, M. (2007). *Evaluation of the Ilia Chavchavadze program in reforming and strengthening Georgia's schools*. Tbilisi, Georgia: Padeco.

Shaverdashvili, E., & Mosiashvili, T. (2018). *Values und knowledge education*. Tbilisi, Georgia: Ilia State University.

The Ministry of Education and Science of Georgia. (2007). *National Curriculum Georgia 2007*. Retrieved March 29, 2019, from http://ncp.ge/files/ESG/2010%20wlamde/esg_2007.pdf

The Ministry of Education and Science of Georgia. (2008). *Teacher's professional standard Georgia*. Retrieved March 21, 2008, from http://old.tpdc.ge/index.php?action=page&p_id=101&lang=eng

The Ministry of Education and Science of Georgia. (2011). *National curriculum Georgia 2011–2016*. Retrieved March 11, 2011, from http://ncp.ge/ge/curriculum/satesto-seqtsia/mimdinare-esg-2011-2016

The Ministry of Education and Science of Georgia. (2018). *National curriculum Georgia 2018–2024*. Retrieved May 27, 2020, from http://ncp.ge/ge/curriculum/satesto-seqtsia/akhali-sastsavlo-gegmebi-2018-2024/datskebiti-safekhuri-i-vi-klasebi-damtkitsda-2016-tsels

TSU. (2013). *Mission of the university*. Tbilisi, Georgia: Ivane Javakishvili Tbilisi State University. Retrieved June 5, 2020, from https://www.tsu.ge/en/about/mission_statement/

USAID. (2020). *Georgia – Education*. USAID. Retrieved June 5, 2020, from https://www.usaid.gov/georgia/education

VaKE. (n.d.). *Home*. Salzburg, Austria: VaKE. Retrieved June 5, 2020, from vake.eu

CHAPTER 14

Exploring Diverse Cultural Positions in Multicultural French and American Higher Education Student Groups Using V*a*KE

Grazia Ghellini

1   Aim, Theoretical Framework, and Methodology of the Study

The main aim of this chapter is to share some of the insights I gained from my first implementations of V*a*KE as well as from my subsequent ones using the *Sikh Applicant dilemma*, which might be of some use to teachers who would like to try V*a*KE with international students.[1] Since the use of V*a*KE in the intercultural classroom has already been discussed (Brossard Børhaug & Harnes, 2020; see also Chapter 23 in this handbook), the main points that I will address here are the strengths and limits of the method I perceived in my teaching practice. I will also seek to trace some patterns in the students' reception of V*a*KE that might be related to cultural differences and their different expectations in terms of teaching styles and the students' roles in the classroom and will issue some recommendations for higher education teaching practitioners.

Brassier-Rodrigues (2015) found different and at times contrasting expectations that American, Chinese, and French students tend to have in relation to the teacher in terms of teaching styles, teaching effectiveness, and, indirectly, the students' role in the class. She pointed out, for instance, that French students are used to deductive instructional methods and normally expect teachers to "prepare theoretical classes and present updated material". In contrast, American students who are used to primarily inductive teaching approaches, tend to expect teachers to "relate material discussed in class to the real world" and their instructors to "make the class interesting by involving students in class discussion and making it interactive" (Brassier-Rodrigues, 2015, table 3). Chinese students do not have any expectations in any of these areas but attach instead importance to the teacher's authoritarianism and helpfulness in class.

The present study, which aims at comparing student reactions to V*a*KE in this regard, is based on my observations of my students' reception of V*a*KE looking at implementations in French and American higher education. My conclusions in relation to how cultural differences might impact the students' responses to the method have been partly informed by Brassier-Rodrigues (2015).

More specifically, in order to illustrate the differences and commonalities that I noticed in my students' reactions to VaKE, its assets and drawbacks, and the changes I made subsequently when using it, I will deal with and compare different student responses when using the same dilemma story: those of four large groups of 1st year Bachelor degree students of International Business and Administration at the Montpellier Business School in 2017, and those of two smaller groups of 3rd year visiting American students from the University of Minnesota during the academic years 2018–2019 and 2019–2020 taking an international business course entitled "Global Business: France at the Crossroads".

2 Implementing VaKE with Business Ethics Students at Montpellier Business School

My first implementation of VaKE in my "The Game of Ethics" courses with four mixed groups of 35 to 40 French and international students of International Business Administration (aged 18 to 19) in two units of three hours each was rather challenging. The courses' main aim was to initiate students to business ethics and ethical diversity management practices by getting them to sample a variety of ethical dilemmas and explore different approaches to ethics entertainingly. The courses' teaching objectives included fostering understanding of cultural differences and promoting intercultural dialogue in the classroom and getting students to practice the English language while acquiring the basics of business ethics. My specific teaching objectives with respect to VaKE were to get students to explore the issues of religious discrimination and nepotism in the workplace and help them reflect on how the current French law banning wearing ostentatious religious signs in French administrations, schools, and state-owned companies (Légifrance, 2004) might lead to racial and religious discrimination in hiring when wrongly interpreted, especially in a tensed social climate. In the autumn 2017 France was in the wake of a series of Islamist terror attacks which had left it scarred and swept over by a wave of islamophobia and anti-Islamic feelings. Dealing with delicate issues in a direct way while fostering intercultural dialogue in a mixed classroom comprising Muslim students and students belonging to other religious groups as well as students endorsing radical secular, anti-religious positions would have been extremely perilous, and using a non-dogmatic, dilemma-based approach seemed the best solution.

2.1 *Procedure*
In the *Sikh Applicant dilemma* story, the students are asked to put themselves in the place of the Human Resources director of an international IT company

headquartered in Paris with a branch in London and decide which applicant he should hire between two equally qualified candidates for a position involving developing the company's business in India, France and England: a French applicant or a Sikh Indian candidate wearing a turban. The HR director in the dilemma story sees the Sikh applicant's great potential but is perplexed because of the French law on religious attire, and feels pressured to hire the French applicant, as he has been recommended by the CEO's son.

In each group I first introduced the students to VaKE[2] (step 0), pointing out that they were going to work on an ethical dilemma story using a process which would make them reflect on their core values while acquiring knowledge in relation to some ethical issues. I then introduced the first part of the *Sikh Applicant dilemma* story (step 1) and then went through steps 2 to 4: "What is the story about" (step 2); "What are the values at stake in the dilemma" (step 3); and "Why did you make the choice you made"/"What are your values behind your choice" (step 4). I worked closely with the entire class for 45 minutes to an hour (depending on the group's size and level of responsiveness).

After a class discussion of the issues at stake in the dilemma story and of the values that prompted the students' first vote and reactions to it (steps 2 to 4), I split the participants into groups of 6 and asked them to share the information that prompted their initial decisions (steps 5 to 6). I then beckoned them to gather and share with their team, further pieces of information they deemed necessary to make a well-informed decision (steps 7 and 8), and then continue their research, information, and opinion exchanges at home (following the *VaKE-dis* steps 9 and 10). The students' assignment for the following session was to prepare a creative presentation to sum up and present their group's findings to the rest of the class.

In the second VaKE session, after presenting their group findings, voting again, and reflecting collectively on their new vote (steps 11 to 13), according to their choices, students were given the second part of the dilemma (step 14) and were asked to reconsider the situation, which had complicated further. Students who chose the French applicant were given a version of the second part of the dilemma in which the French CEO is suddenly taken ill, and the HR director must announce his choice to the General Director of the London Branch who is a Sikh. Students who chose the Sikh Applicant were instead given a different version of the second part of the dilemma, in which the Human Resources Manager is faced with the fact that two Muslim employees have decided to come back to work wearing a hijab after the Summer holidays and he fears this, together with hiring a Sikh applicant wearing a turban, might disrupt the company's balance and raise issues concerning opening prayer rooms in the company. After discussing what they would do at this point, the students had to show their position via a role-play (steps 15 and 16) in which one of them played the role of the CEO, and the other that of the HR director who had to justify his decision to his boss, who in case had decided to hire the French candidate, had changed to the Sikh General Director of the British branch of the company. Then, the students were asked to vote again (step 17) and during the debriefing session, they were invited to reflect on why they had maintained or changed their minds (step 18). To finish, they were required to write a brief reflection paper (step 19) including a bibliography/webography of reliable sources supporting their final decisions, to reflect in-depth on the evolution of their thinking and their learnings. To enhance the students' engagement, presentations, role-plays, and reflection papers were marked.

2.2   Assets and Limits of the Method in This Teaching Context

V*a*KE proved to be exactly what my school had asked for: an interactive, student-centred method to promote ethical thinking, non-conflictual intercultural communication, and collaborative group-work in diverse teams. What I appreciated the most was that, thanks to the fact that V*a*KE welcomes all positions as soon as they are expressed respecting those of others, students dealt with the highly controversial issue at the core of the dilemma and shared their values without any hostile reactions troubling the class or small group discussions.

  The method also revealed to be a valuable tool for deepening the students' knowledge in a constructivist way about antidiscrimination laws in France, the UK and India, and French secularism and the French law concerning religious attire in public institutions and state-owned companies. Students also learnt why it was introduced in France, in which cases private companies can ask their personnel not to wear ostentatious religious signs in the workplace and in which cases they cannot and became familiar with other countries' laws in relation to wearing religious signs in the workplace. The reflection papers revealed that even those students who due to their personal or cultural preferences, had not engaged actively in group discussions, in the light of their work and their peers' presentations had acquired deeper levels of knowledge.

  The method also proved highly advantageous in terms of making the students' ethical thinking evolve and take individual responsibility for their choices. Presentations and discussions during the debrief after the final vote, role-plays, and reflection papers (step 19) showed that some students changed their minds following their exchanges with their peers, research findings and presentations.

  A crucial issue was the use of the term "value" all along the V*a*KE process. As experienced by Dorato and Legué (Chapters 22 and 21 in this handbook) as well, using the word "value" to ask students to reflect on what had driven them to make their respective choices, proved challenging. In particular, French students' reactions often revealed that they had not fully grasped the meaning of the word "value", even though they had already worked on this concept and on that of the dilemma (a situation involving a difficult choice involving conflicting values) in previous sessions. Providing concrete examples of "what made me make the choice I made in relation to the dilemma story" (step 4) proved more helpful. Only then, students became more responsive during the class discussion concerning the core values at stake for them and the motives behind their choices.

When students were split into small groups and asked to share their knowledge and then conduct research to deepen their knowledge to be able to justify their decisions in an informed way whatever their choice was, some of them did not really see the relevance of digging deeper. It became necessary to push the individual groups via guiding questions to search further and find reliable pieces of evidence which would fully justify their initial choice, even if they thought they were right. Giving students concrete examples of what was expected of them proved essential: i.e., to look into the English and Indian legislation in relation to religious attire or to conduct research on the various aspects of the particular French law to see whether it is actually an obstacle to wearing a turban, a hijab or a kippah in private companies, or to explore the motives behind the French law banning wearing religious signs in state-owned companies and public administrations.

Furthermore, when asked to prepare a creative presentation to present their findings, some learners did not understand or preferred to ignore the instructions. Again, I had to clarify that giving a creative presentation meant using for example: role-plays, cartoons, songs, or videos. Independently from their nationality, most students were puzzled by the request to present their data in a non-canonical way and resorted to PowerPoint presentations. But some eventually unleashed their creativity and used less conventional and highly creative ways to share their core findings and conclusions such as comic strips, drawings, role-plays, or short movies.

Time constraints, discipline issues regarding the students-centred freedom in the learning process and high noise levels given the large group size were some of the main issues I had to face. More specifically, having been allocated fifteen hours face-to-face in total for a course comprising a variety of teaching objectives and contents, spending two three-hour long sessions implementing VaKE took up a large portion of the few teaching hours I had to teach the wide range of notions included in the syllabus. But most importantly, using a method involving small group discussions and presentations with a large-sized group of rather young, easily distracted students proved challenging. Given the numerous small groups in the classroom from step 5 onwards, keeping the level of noise down and students engaged and collaborating while working in groups was almost impossible.

Also, some students of Asian and African origin had trouble integrating into mixed nationality groups, probably due to the current racial and religious tensions underlying contemporary Western society, and tended to either drift away from the group or work separately within the group with students like them, despite my instructions to work in mixed nationality groups. Occasionally, students got "ejected" from their group or wanted to form separate nationality groups themselves. That meant I could not always meet one of the course's objectives, which was to get diverse students to work and collaborate in teams in a climate respectful of diversity, which ended up posing a dilemma to me as the instructor of this specific course.

2.3 Culture-Related Patterns in the Students' Responses

Using the same dilemma with four groups of students enabled me to see a nationality-related pattern in terms of choice of candidate, and of core values mentioned by the learners. Many French students who had chosen the Sikh applicant mentioned the value of "equality" (not surprisingly, since *égalité* is one of the core values of the French Republic) and the importance of giving candidates equal opportunities. As will be shown below, this was not the case of my American students, for whom "fairness" and "meritocracy" were often behind their justifications.

The students' spontaneous reactions were mostly predictable: They tended to choose the candidate with whom they identified. The degree of familiarity with the French law, which depended on whether they were French or had lived in France for a long time enough to be acquainted with French legislation, also influenced the students' initial choice, but often in a misleading way. Not surprisingly, when asked to justify their choice, many students from France who chose the French candidate when they voted the first time, said that despite its anti-discrimination laws, France is a country where currently there are many tensions concerning wearing headscarves or other visible religious signs, and hiring an applicant with a turban given the French law in question seemed highly problematic to some of them. Some students from France, Italy, Latin America, as well as from African and Arab countries said they had no choice but to hire the French applicant, as he was supported by the CEO's son. International students from Northern European countries or North America, especially those who had recently arrived in France, tended to react in a very different way, and mostly chose to hire the Sikh applicant. Most French students and other ones who identified themselves with the Sikh candidate, as they were Muslim or belonged to other orthodox religious groups attached to wearing visible religious signs, did not hesitate: Not hiring the Sikh applicant seemed both an act of racism and religious discrimination to most of them. As for French students who claimed they would have not hired the Sikh candidate, they often had trouble providing reliable sources to justify their choice.

Using VaKE with a mixed group of French and International Business School students made their different expectations in terms of teaching style emerge. Some French students for instance did not seem to engage much with the small group discussion, information-sharing and searching phase and showed little interest in listening to the other students' presentations. During group discussions they tended to get distracted and engaged in small talk instead of concentrating on the task at hand. I imputed this to the fact that the traditional French education system reflects the French high-power distance acceptance – using Geert Hofstede et al.'s cultural dimensions (2010) – and value teacher's authority and expertise. As already pointed out in the above-mentioned study by Brassier-Rodrigues (2015), teaching in France tends to be teacher-centred and primarily theoretical, and students used to such teaching methods usually value theory more than practical activities.

Chinese students also tended not to participate much in the discussion/comparison of their findings unless exhorted to do so: mostly they duly presented their results but were reluctant to express their opinion in front of the rest of the class, perhaps being used to more top-down, less participative teaching methods based on high-level teacher input and valuing memorisation of information rather than critical thinking.

Nevertheless, they mostly did the required research work in class and at home diligently, possibly due to the importance they tend to attach to discipline, respecting the teacher's authority and obtaining good final marks. My observations are therefore consistent with Brassier-Rodrigues's (2015) findings about the different and at times contrasting expectations that American, Chinese, and French students tend to have in relation to the teacher and their own role in the classroom, teaching styles, teaching effectiveness, and indirectly, the students' role in the class, which can explain my students' different reactions to VaKE.

3 Using the *Sikh Applicant Dilemma* Story and VaKE with American Students in Global Business Courses: Adjustments Made Following the Previous Experience

My experience of implementing VaKE using the *Sikh Applicant dilemma* story with two smaller groups of 3rd year American visiting students taking a "Global Business: France at the Crossroads" course at the University of Minnesota

Abroad Branch in Montpellier in 2019 and in 2020 was rather different from the one I had at the Montpellier Business school.

3.1 Procedure

Following my previous experience with the 2019 group of American students, I devoted only three hours split into two subsequent one-and-a-half hour slots in class and had them work on the first part dilemma story only. I proceeded by working with them on the dilemma story closely in class during steps 1 to 4 only and got them to do the validation check, research work and information sharing, as well as the preparation of their creative group presentations at home, to be given in the next class.

In 2020 I did the same but had to use Zoom due to the coronavirus pandemic. After presenting the dilemma, getting students to vote, brainstorming the values behind the choices using Mentimeter, and holding a virtual class discussion concerning their choice, I told them to conduct independent research and share their individual findings using Flipgrid. I also asked them to prepare creative small group presentations to be posted on Canvas, to peer review another group's presentation and then write a reflection paper.

3.2 Culture-Related Patterns in the Students' Responses

American students seemed to me, to adopt the method more easily than French and most of other international Business school students in my classes, which I impute to the fact that American teaching methods tend to be highly student-centred, generally placing responsibility for learning on the student, and value teacher and interactive teaching methods that keep them engaged (Brassier-Rodrigues, 2015). They also did not seem to have trouble grappling with the concept of values and participated immediately and actively in the class and small group discussions and work.

Interestingly, in both groups the students (with a few exceptions) opted for hiring Mr Singh, the Indian applicant, based on the values of fairness and meritocracy, whatever racial or religious group they identified with. I also noticed less resistance in terms of working in diverse groups.

What I saw as a hindrance in using VaKE with my American Global Business students, was their tendency to make their choice based on a universalistic, Kantian logic ("what is right is always right, and what is wrong is always wrong"); it seemed to me that, once this was established, the dilemma story did not deserve any more thoughts in their eyes. Digging deeper and reflecting on the dilemma on a more personal level was seemingly pointless to some of them: they mostly claimed that discriminating against someone on the basis of their faith and the religious attire they wore would be illegal and considered as highly unfair in the United States, whatever the specific context.

A problem I experienced while guiding these two groups of American students in their research phase was getting students to go beyond the fact that they felt they would have needed more information concerning the applicants' individual profiles in order to give the job to the most deserving one in relation to the position. These students had to be coached in a rather directive way for them to move onwards and focus on the aspects they were supposed to explore.

Eventually, working closely on the dilemma with VaKE enabled them to acquire further knowledge of European, French, English, and Indian antidiscrimination laws and of a wide range of controversial court cases involving wearing religious attire in the company in different countries. But they also explored aspects such as the reasons why French secularism was introduced in France and learnt that the ban on wearing so-called ostentatious religious signs only applies to employees of public administrations, schools, and state-owned companies and to private companies with internal regulations specifying (and able to prove) that this is against the company's interests or endangers the safety or health of its employees.

4 Conclusive Recommendations for Higher Education Teachers

Following these formative experiences, I have made a few adjustments to the way I implement VaKE into my current teaching practice, which I recommend to educators using it for the first time.

Firstly, I am now cautious about implementing the method with students entirely in class, especially with large groups of students. I limit small group discussions in class to shorter periods of times, and usually ask the learners to do their individual/group research, share their findings and prepare their presentation at home to be delivered in class during the next session. Alternatively, I ask them to submit their presentations using Moodle, Canvas, or Flipgrid (when in the form of video or audio presentations) or slideshows with audio to be peer-reviewed. Then, after voting again in class or online and a debriefing session in the virtual or physical class, I ask students to write a reflection paper based on guiding questions.

Furthermore, I avoid transparent voting, which to me is not a reliable way of showing and measuring the real evolution of the participants' thinking during the VaKE process. French or Asian students for instance, tended to apprehend their teacher's and peers' judgment when speaking publicly, and often changed their vote in relation to their decision when observing their reactions. Since such students also avoided expressing their opinions and being singled out in front of the entire class when the topic was particularly controversial, I find it more effective to ask them to vote and share the values at stake for them by

EXPLORING DIVERSE CULTURAL POSITIONS 171

means of anonymous online polling and brainstorming tools like Mentimeter. I then invite those who feel like sharing why they voted in a specific way and have a class discussion.

Concerning the problem of reducing noise levels when working with large groups of students, this can be solved by splitting them into groups working in separate rooms with the help of a teaching assistant or a colleague, or otherwise getting students to go through steps 5 to 11 separately, and then drawing them together again for the final stages of the VaKE process. As far as ensuring diversity within groups, this can be achieved by forcing students to stick to assigned groups using randomised grouping techniques, but this involves taking the risk of having one or more students drift away from the group.

In conclusion, I highly recommend VaKE in international Higher Education settings, as it usually fosters more open-minded and respectful dialogue amongst students of all nationalities about ethical issues and enables them to consider the perspective of the other, while prompting them to take a position aligned with their own values. It also leads them to see how cultural differences can significantly impact their decision in relation to an ethical dilemma, while going beyond cultural relativism, which as Milton Bennett (2016) pointed out, is becoming increasingly important. VaKE makes students experience that type of ethical decision-making that Bennett has defined as grounded in "contextual relativism", which enables one to take a position while being empathetic and respectful of diversity.

> That developmental position demands that we take the perspective of others; it calls for emphatically participating in the others' reality, including taking their ethical position on the conflictual issue. [...] [C]ontextual relativism is based in constructivism, in that it assumes that alternative viable realities exist and that we can empathically have access to them. Then, only after having experienced our opponents' world, can we formulate an ethnorelative action – Commitment in relativism. Such an action [is] respectful of the full humanity of others, including their differing viable values. (Bennett, 2016, penultimate paragraph)

However, I invite teaching professionals working with Higher Education international students to provide extremely clear explanations concerning terminology and what is expected of them when using VaKE, and to anticipate and give full attention to possible culture-related student responses to this method if they wish the class to be successful. Considering effective ways of getting around time constraints, such as using shorter VaKE versions, or strategies for avoiding excessive noise when implementing VaKE with high numbers of students by getting them to do such activities at home or in separate rooms, or yet, helping students whom they think might apprehend losing face when voting or speaking publicly by using brainstorming tools can avoid pitfalls.

Furthermore, even though in this chapter I have been alerting teaching practitioners of possible culture-related student response patterns to VaKE, I would like to finish by recalling that individual responses related to personal preferences may also contradict the patterns described above. As globalisation and the popularity of study abroad programmes, as well as innovative teaching methods are leading students world-wide to become acquainted with a variety of teaching approaches, the culture-related gaps in the different education systems are becoming less prominent.

Notes

1 See also Chapters 21 (Legué) and 22 (Dorato) in this handbook.
2 Although the steps I used in implementing VaKE are similar to the original version (VaKE with 11 steps; Chapter 2 in this handbook), I extended the number of steps involving working with two follow-up stories.

References

Bennett, M. J. (2016). *The value of cultural diversity: Rhetoric and reality. Reflections on the end of relativism.* Intercultural Development Research Institute. Retrieved October 17, 2020, from https://www.idrinstitute.org/resources/value-cultural-diversity-rhetoric-reality/

Brassier-Rodrigues, C. (2015). How do American, Chinese, and French students characterize their teachers' communication? *Journal of Intercultural Communication 38*, 1404–1634. Retrieved October 17, 2020, from https://www.immi.se/intercultural/nr38/brassier.html

Brossard Børhaug, F. (2016). How to challenge a culturalization of human existence? Promoting interculturalism and ethical thinking in education. *FLEKS – Scandinavian Journal of Intercultural Theory and Practice, 3*(1).

Brossard Børhaug, F., & Harnes H. B. (2020). Facilitating intercultural education in majority student groups in higher education, *Intercultural Education, 31*(3), 286–299.

Hofstede, G., Hofstede, G. J., & Minkov, M. (2010). *Cultures and organisations.* Paris, France: Pearson Education.

Légifrance. (2004). *Dossier Législatif: Loi n° 2004-228 du 15 mars 2004 encadrant, en application du principe de laïcité, le port de signes ou de tenues manifestant une appartenance religieuse dans les écoles, collèges et lycées publics.* Retrieved April 22, 2021, from https://www.legifrance.gouv.fr/loda/id/JORFTEXT000000417977/

SECTION 3

VaKE in Nonformal Education

CHAPTER 15

Promoting the Idea of European Citizenship with V*a*KE

Sieglinde Weyringer

1   Introduction

What is the European Union (EU) besides open borders for travelling and economic transfer? Such and similar questions may have been at the origin of the reflection on what can be understood by European citizenship. Since its inception through the Treaty of Maastricht in 1992, the European Union has been endeavouring to raise awareness, to acquire knowledge and to establish a sense of belonging among its citizens, particularly among young adolescents. This chapter aims to discuss how EU awareness and related citizenship behaviour can be promoted with V*a*KE. The research project on the summer camp called *Plato Youth Forum* provides results which indicate that using this approach successfully meets related objectives and expectations. Before this, a brief introduction about the idea of European citizenship and about the motto "United in diversity" will be presented in the first two sections.

2   The Idea of European Citizenship: Basic Information and Criticism on Practice

European citizenship is anchored in several treaties signed by all EU member states. It is given automatically to a person additional to the national citizenship, not replacing it. Therefore, European citizenship can be characterized as supra-national or transnational. It emphasizes the shared aims and values as columns of the constitution: peace, freedom, well-being and equality of its citizens, dignity, solidarity, citizen rights, and justice (European Union, 2016). Starting with a practice similar to making national citizenship visible, several symbols have been implemented, besides others the motto "United in diversity".

However, criticism has been sparked at the lack of substance of the idea compared to national citizenship. The implemented symbols as well as the efforts on mobility and programmes could not attenuate the fact that some

EU citizens remained distant to the EU during the first decade. The lack of dynamic and transformative concepts of citizenship towards citizenship practice was identified as one out of several reasons (Wiener, 2007).

Since 2004, the European Commission has been promoting active European citizenship with the programme "Europe for citizens" (European Commission, 2004, 2020) aiming at bringing the European Union closer to its citizens and at strengthening their sense of belonging to this community. The young generation of European citizens is especially at the heart of the EU initiatives. Many funding programmes and initiatives for formal and nonformal education, training, sport, mobility, and voluntary engagement are aiming to inspire young people to create ideas on how they can manifest the active European citizenship in their daily life (e.g., European Youth portal[1]).

Furthermore, EU initiatives have contributed to the further development of theoretical considerations on concepts of active European citizenship as well as to scientific research on practical implementation (e.g., Dolejsiová & López, 2009; Mindus, 2017; Alt, 2017; Bauböck, 2019; Veugelers, 2019). Since the question "What is active European citizenship?" cannot be answered once and for all, the available theoretical concepts provide fruitful bases for developing further educational concepts. For their practice there is also a need to develop innovative didactical approaches. One among several interesting concepts is V*a*KE. It can contribute to establish a sense of belonging to Europe as a policy beyond and additional to nationality and to develop competences for active citizenship; for this assumption encouraging evidence could be found in the *Plato Youth Forum*, a research project on V*a*KE lasting several years. Before the presentation of this study a brief consideration on the motto "United in diversity" intends to draw the frame for the creation of the practical concept.

3   "United in Diversity" – Considerations on a Practical Implementation

Since 2004, the European Union has been and is still "under construction" as a loose bundle of states neither having a final form nor a final constitution. There are however rather clear ideas about what the EU is *not*, e.g., no United States, no Federal State, no confederation, because there are concrete historical examples for all these models, which would narrow down the free space for innovative formation. The agreed term "Union" opened up the prospect of overcoming national state-thinking without dissolving the nation states. Looking into the past for shared aspects between all European states brings military conflicts as well as ideas of justice and humanity into focus. The national states share the tragedies of two World Wars, but also the development of democratic constitutions and the development of human rights. These common experiences and developments – even if they can be interpreted very controversially and differently – link the EU member states to a common destiny. They serve as a possible link in addition to the joint programmes.

The range of diversity throughout Europe is given in any area of life: cultures, languages, traditions, religions, philosophies, ethnical affinities, and many more on local, regional, and national levels. Diversity as a core characteristic may become a unifying element if one takes into account that opposing views are a reality of life. So, negotiating standpoints, checking facts by evidence, opening the mind for consent are some of the related skills and need to be trained by all citizens.

Moreover, the slogan "United in diversity" is influenced by European philosophers and other communicative concepts, as for instance the postmodern approach of difference (Lyotard, 1983/1988), language games (Wittgenstein, 1953), and discourse ethics and communicative action (Apel, 1980; Habermas, 1984, 1987). Various tools for communication and social interactions have been developed based on these concepts, and their use can serve to fill the slogan with meaning.

Still, concretizing the idea of European citizenship by using terms of values is a challenge. One reason is that for this, the European values for the Union must be made visible and put in relation to experiences in daily life together.

Moreover, this idea cannot be limited to the European Union itself. Investigating *Europe* as an idea in a broader sense, the question can be raised "Which Europe are we talking about?" (Blockmans, 2003). Extending this question towards "What is Europe?" also reveals the vagueness of the concept of European citizenship and the associated ideas, because numerous questions appear addressing areas of diversity, migration movements, and even its borders. Thus, there is no single answer and final determination as to where Europe begins and where it ends, "who is in or who is out". It also applies for answering "Who am I as a European citizen?".

This problem leads to questions of identity formation and the development of the self-concept, which are given a special importance as developmental tasks during adolescence (e.g., Havighurst, 1953). According to Mead (1934/2015), identity is tied to concepts of meaning, cultural values, and the orientation towards the past, present and future within a society. The ego-identity can only develop when a human being is able to consider and to experience him- or herself as an object by mentally and effectively distancing oneself from oneself and observe and evaluate one's own behaviour. In addition, conflict resolution and crisis management are seen as driving forces for ego and identity development (Erikson, 1968; Marcia, 1980). For both challenges related to identity-formation and conflict management, appropriate strategies can be taught, for example, how to take on the other's perspective, how to act from their position, how to discuss problems, how to collaborate, and how to find consent. In that context, the summer camp called *Plato Youth Forum* was created and implemented as an education project as well as a research project.

4 The *Plato Youth Forum*

The research project called *The application of VaKE to gifted young students in an international summer camp* (VaKE-GS) was sponsored by the Anniversary Fund of the Austrian National Bank (Project number 10946; see Patry, 2003). It was run by the Department of Education in the University of Salzburg, Austria, between 2004 and 2008. Although the research project did not aim at European citizenship education *per se*, this issue became important during the first year of implementation.

The idea of the project was to focus on highly gifted young people between 15 and 18; it arose from the current academic interest of the applicants and the assumption that a didactic concept based on constructivism, such as VaKE, would provide appropriate challenges for this group.

The core objectives of the research project were:
– to apply VaKE in an international voluntary setting of non-formal education for young people with high ability needs;
– to apply two types of viability checks (see Chapter 2 in this handbook) within the prototypical VaKE course: the one related to knowledge checks whether and how information and facts used in discussions can strengthen a standpoint sufficiently; the one related to values checks whether and how the preferred orientation of personal values is applicable and practicable in the discussion on problems related to a moral dilemma;
– to gain experience regarding teaching and training in a nonformal educational setting managing multilingual, multicultural groups of young multigifted people;
– to test whether already existing types of instruments for data collection, the WALK – W Assessment of Latent Knowledge and LIM questionnaires – Lesson Interruption Method (see Chapter 31 in the handbook for both), are applicable to young gifted adolescents;
– to test selected effects of VaKE-based interventions in workshops, among others on the participants' self-awareness, using pre-post-follow up questionnaires.

During the project period, the camps were organised annually for one week during the summer vacations. They took place in a youth hostel in a small town located in the lake district near Salzburg (Weyringer & Patry, 2007; Weyringer, 2008). After 2008, the summer camp was continued in Austria by former participants through a private initiative until 2014. In 2015 it took place in Brasov, Romania, also organised by former participants.

The name *Plato Youth Forum* was inspired by the Greek philosopher. Plato founded a school called *The Academy* on his property close to ancient Athens. The teachers in this school posed problems to the students, who had to discuss them using the Socratic method and to find solutions (Dancy, 1991). The learning process did not follow a formal curriculum. The academy was rather like meetings between citizens of Athens instead of a school with a clear distinction between teachers who provide knowledge and students who acquire it.

Giftedness and high ability were operationalized pragmatically. Many theoretical models share intelligence, motivation, task commitment, creativity, multiple factors of abilities, taking into account family background, culture and environment (for an overview see Heller et al., 2000). Due to this wide range of approaches, using testing results or school marks as criteria for giftedness were not considered to be appropriate. Rather, an invitation letter for participation was sent to cooperation partners and to selected schools all over Europe. The call asked for applicants showing interest in European issues presented as very complex problem areas and not very close to their living experiences; they would be confronted with an unfamiliar didactical approach (VaKE), forced to cope with language diversity either using German or English or any other way of communication, and with a very strict schedule for a week with work session until 4 pm in the afternoon followed by daily evening sessions. The assumption underlying this very uncommon announcement was: If an adolescent is challenged by this offer, he or she is assumed to meet most of the criteria for giftedness mentioned above to an acceptable degree. A letter of recommendation from the school was also requested.

When considering the appropriate topics for the target group, the focus was less on curriculum related knowledge. The organisers' claim was to find topics currently discussed in international newspapers. As the young participants would come from different EU countries, the European dimension was prominent in the choice of topics, with a strong orientation towards the values of the European Union from the second year of the project onwards. Given the assumption that in 2005 young people were unfamiliar with both aspects – knowledge of the European Union and its values – the programming was designed to contribute to raising awareness towards the idea of European citizenship. "Raising awareness" was not merely interpreted as "knowing", but to look for meaning, to be sensitive, to search, to select, to think critically, to weigh and assess, to decide and to make judgment, to communicate, to examine the decision, and to act accordingly (Weyringer, 2008).

The overall objective of the summer camps was: Each participant should find and establish their own and personal idea of European citizenship based on the discussions on the presented dilemma stories, on the elaboration of related problem topics and on the experiences from the time spent together.

In more detail, the pillars of the concept are highlighted in a set of oppositions. For each opposition an example for a topic is given together with the year of implementation.

Topics were selected:
- with regards to vagueness: tacit knowledge about a tacit construct (idea of European citizenship) – however explicit knowledge on the diversity of national perspectives on EU related problems (example in 2006: Referendum on the contract of EU constitution – How should the protagonist vote?);
- with regards to citizenship: consciousness of historical problems in the collective memory – however historical distance on the individual level (example in 2005: Is Robespierre guilty for the death of Danton?);
- with regards to the European dimension: presentation of highly complex problems in the European dimension – however working on the problems in the dimension of individual person (example in 2007: Firing orders on the former inner German border between Federal German Republic and the German Democratic Republic – Should the prosecutor, whose father was involved in these orders, roll up the legal process again?);
- with regards to identity: addressing and coping with heterogeneity – however strengthening criteria of personal belonging (example in 2007: Love and marriage between former national enemies or cultural opponents – Should the two young lovers ignore the rejection on the part of their families and flee to another EU country?);
- with regards to the EU slogan: facing the difference – however as an integrating component (example in 2005: My fundamental rights in the EU – Does the protagonist have the freedom or the duty to act?).

Each summer camp lasted for seven days including two days for travelling and offered up to six parallel workshops to groups of 15 persons each as a maximum. From Monday to Friday the workshops started with the plenum meeting in the morning, followed by six working hours per day. Leisure time began around 4 pm. The accommodation and the area of the small city provided many facilities for sport, making music, playing games, or simply relaxing.

On Wednesday afternoon the whole group went on a trip to the city of Salzburg. During the evening the participants learned to dance Viennese waltz and other partner dances in a dancing school. Informal cultural meetings took place during the other evenings, in which the participants presented their own country and its typical food and beverages ("Evening of regions" on Monday), they also organised group activities for all ("Evening of games" on Tuesday and Thursday) and created an "Evening of Europe" on Friday in mixed national teams.

One V*a*KE dilemma story was offered in each workshop. The stories were written by the group moderator, who also provided access to information and material for the investigation and managed all group activities. All the stories were written from the perspective of a young person involved in the addressed issues. The participants had to discuss and find solutions not only according to their individual estimation, but also in the role of a representative of their home country, or in the role of an international or European decision maker. In their roles, they became aware of values driving a decision and experienced the feelings and frames of mind in such deciding situations. To inhibit group tendencies within a workshop like sharing similar arguments and overlooking or neglecting crucial issues, two forums – public presentations of the dilemma story and the state of their discussions – were compulsory: in a midterm forum for the participants of the other workshops, and as a final forum for an invited audience of experts, parents, and other guests. These audiences were asked to further challenge the group by providing critical feedback. Through this the participants should experience the connection to real life and also the fact that dilemmas cannot be settled once and for all but continue to be virulent, in contrast to problems that can be solved with a "right" solution within a scope of conditions.

According to EU rules for communication, the diversity of languages was to be accepted, and understanding to be aimed at despite all barriers, by the support of the whole workshop group. Concerning different standpoints, the participants had to highlight the occurrence of dissent, however they were not forced to find a consent solution.

5   Outputs of the Research Project

During the duration of the research project (2004 to 2007) 180 young people from Andorra, Austria, the Czech Republic, France, Germany, Great Britain, Hungary, Italy, Latvia, Lithuania, Luxemburg, Poland, Portugal, Romania, Slovakia, Spain, and The Netherlands participated in 19 workshops. The hypotheses were as follows: Participants are sensitised for highly complex topics, and they develop awareness for related moral values; they nurture critical thinking skills; the cognitive challenge is adequate; they establish interest and motivation, and they report a positive impact on their self-image and their self-confidence regarding communication, cooperation, and abilities. Special instruments and methods of quantitative and qualitative data collection were developed, e.g., questionnaires, videos, daily reports of moderators, observations, narratives.

The results show that all five objectives mentioned above have been satisfactorily achieved: VaKE provides adequate cognitive challenges for gifted students. They could apply knowledge as well as values-oriented viability checks. They could cope with the multi-diversity of aspects. The existing types of instruments could be tested. The tested effects on aspects of self-awareness are long lasting. The data allow the conclusion that the teaching method (VaKE) is the moderating variable, while the topics have little impact on the attainment of the objectives and the sustainability of the acquired competences. In general, the participants enjoyed the workshops and activities during the whole week (for more details see Weyringer, 2008, 2011; Patry et al., 2010).

Regarding the establishment of a personal idea of European citizenship, no data have been collected during the period of the project due to the scope of the funded research. However, observations and informal talks during the workshops made apparent that dealing with dilemmas from the diverse background of European cultures supported widening the personal horizon towards European citizenship (Brossard Børhaug & Weyringer, 2018). The teamwork provided situations, in which the participants realized the diversity of perspectives and thinking traditions. Furthermore, they identified differences between the collective memory of events told by their native society and the stories about the same events told by the participants from other countries. They also experienced that being exposed to heterogeneity, difference and insecurity can strengthen their personality, independence, and empowerment. A further experience was that a discussion does not necessarily end in a consensus; a dissent or an open end are also possible and acceptable. However, this does not mean that one cannot agree and cooperate on another level. Another experience was that legal regulations can be negotiated and that the adherence to specific ethical values may lead to violations of legal regulations such as in civil disobedience. The participants also realized that a critical assessment of the impact of a decision is needed.

Besides the very satisfying results and pedagogical experiences, it needs to be mentioned that the idea of the *Plato Youth Forum* was influential for some of the participants. During the four-year project one group kept contact across national borders by meeting at festivals. They also established virtual meetings and regular exchange, although current social media platforms like Twitter and Facebook did not exist during the project duration. At the end of the project in 2007, this Plato group came up with the idea to continue the summer camp, and with the concern to take over the roles of moderator, host, and organiser step by step in the following years until 2014. The overall responsibility and the supervision remained with the group of researchers in Salzburg. In advance, the young organisers came to Salzburg for separate VaKE training courses and organizational concerns. They also prolonged their stay after the camp for reflection and preparing the camp for the following year. They also got involved in the promotion of the summer camp in their schools. During these years they started and finished their secondary education and started their studies and careers in universities and companies. Nevertheless, they continued to be part of the Plato group: either they took extra vacations to continue as workshop moderators, or they came in addition for the final presentation, taking the role of an expert or of a critic similar to the advocatus diaboli.

In 2008, the Plato group also applied for the Charlemagne Youth Prize presenting The *Plato Youth Forum* as their initiative for living together in Europe. Even though they did not receive this award, they still took an active interest in ideas on how citizens can live together in Europe.

In Austria the *Plato Youth Forum* finally ended in 2014, while in 2015 Romanian participants took over the idea and organised a course in their home city.

6 Promoting European Citizenship through VaKE: A Brief Conclusion

This chapter claims to present evidence that using VaKE promotes active European citizenship. As this issue was not explicitly in the focus of the presented study, indicators for active citizenship and citizenship education are addressed to justify this claim. The final report for a study on active citizenship by De Weerd et al. (2005) to the European Commission identifies such indicators: Active citizenship refers to behaviour, not to attitudes or knowledge. It becomes visible through participation in associations and networks. Indicators are voluntary work, organising activities for the community, engagement in interest groups and involvement in public debate. Debating and writing skills as content of education are very relevant input indicators, as well as the culture of education including class climate and didactical approach. Indicators for the output of this education are specific citizenship competences, including combining political and civic knowledge, civic skills including organisation, communication, collective decision-making, critical thinking, attitudes including acknowledgement of the rule of law and human rights and values including tolerance and non-violence.

Checking the outputs of the study according to this list shows that most of these input and output indicators can be identified in the follow-up activities of the Plato group. Nurturing related skills and competences characterizes the Plato Youth Forum camps, and they are also immanent of V*a*KE. Furthermore, these activities indicate that the young adolescents additionally could include the European dimension in the elaboration, planning and implementation. These activities show that the young adolescents are able to think and plan beyond their daily life environments. Together they have developed a behaviour that can be evaluated as a practical idea of active European citizenship.

The transformation of this idea into practice will remain the duty of the hour and a special pedagogical challenge. This is due to the difficulty of making the European dimension a visible and tangible issue in more concrete terms. V*a*KE and this chapter may inspire and encourage educators and trainers to pursue further innovative solutions with creative considerations. We believe that the more diverse these innovations are, the more this education meets the essence of the European citizenship: United in diversity.

Note

1   https://europa.eu/youth/home_en

References

Apel, K.-O. (1980). *Toward a transformation of philosophy*. London, UK: Routledge & Kegan Paul.
Alt, D. (Ed.). (2017). *Lifelong citizenship*. Rotterdam, The Netherlands: Brill Sense.
Bauböck, R. (2019). *Debating European citizenship*. Cham, Switzerland: Springer Nature.
Blockmans, W. (2003). Europe? Which Europe? In M.-L. von Plessen (Ed.), *Idee Europa* (pp. 17–22). Berlin, Germany: Henschel.
Brossard Børhaug, F., & Weyringer, S. (2018). Developing critical and empathic capabilities in intercultural education through the V*a*KE approach. *Intercultural Education, 30*(1), 1–14. doi:10.1080/14675986.2018.1534042
Dancy, R. M. (1991). *Two studies in the early academy*. Albany, NY: State University of New York Press.
De Weerd, M., Gemmeke, M., Rigter, J., & Van Rij, C. (2005). *Indicators for monitoring active citizenship and citizenship education*. Amsterdam, The Netherlands: Regioplan Beleidsonderzoek.

Dolejšiová, D., & López, M. Á. G. (Eds.). (2009). *European citizenship – In the process of construction*. Strasbourg, France: Council of Europe Publishing.

Erikson, E. H. (1968). *Identity, youth, and crisis*. New York, NY: Norton.

European Commission. (2004). *Europe for citizens programme. 2004–2006*. Retrieved August 23, 2020, from https://ec.europa.eu/citizenship/europe-for-citizens-programme/programme-2004-2006/index_en.htm

European Commission. (2020). *Europe for citizens programme*. Retrieved August 23, 2020, from https://eacea.ec.europa.eu/europe-for-citizens_en

European Union. (2016). *Consolidated version of the treaty on European Union*. Retrieved August 23, 2020, from https://eur-lex.europa.eu/legal-content/EN/TXT/?uri=CELEX:12016M/TXT

Havighurst, R. J. (1953). *Human development and education*. New York, NY: David McKay.

Habermas, J. (1984). *The theory of communicative action, Vol. 1*. Boston, MA: Beacon Press.

Habermas, J. (1987). *The theory of communicative action, Vol. 2*. Boston, MA: Beacon Press.

Heller, K. A. Mönks, F. J., Sternberg, R. J., & Subotnik, R. F. (Eds.). (2000). *International handbook of giftedness and talent* (2nd ed.). Amsterdam, the Netherlands: Elsevier.

Lyotard, J.-F. (1983/1988). *Le différend*. Paris: Minuit. Minneapolis, MN: University of Minnesota Press.

Marcia, J. E. (1980). Identity in adolescence. *Handbook of Adolescent Psychology, 9*(11), 159–187.

Mead, G. H. (1934/2015). *Mind, self, and society: The definitive edition*. Chicago, IL: University of Chicago Press.

Mindus, P. (2017). *European citizenship after Brexit*. Palgrave Studies in European Union Politics. doi:10.1007/978-3-319-51774-2_7. 103

Patry, J.-L. (2003). *Values and knowledge education for gifted students*. Projektantrag für Jubiläumsfond der Österreichischen Nationalbank. Unpublished project application.

Patry, J.-L., Weyringer, S., & Weinberger, A. (2010). Values and Knowledge Education (VaKE) in European summer camps for gifted students: Native versus non-native speakers. In C. Klaassen & N. Maslovaty (Eds.), *Moral courage and the normative professionalism of teachers* (pp. 133–145). Rotterdam, The Netherlands: Sense Publishers.

Veugelers, W. (Ed.). (2019). *Education for democratic intercultural citizenship*. Leiden, The Netherlands: Brill Sense.

Weyringer, S., & Patry, J.-L. (2007). VaKE and education for leadership and European citizenship. *Faísca, 12*(14), 4–27.

Weyringer, S. (2008). *VaKE in einem internationalen Sommercamp für (hoch)begabte Jugendliche* [Unpublished PhD dissertation]. University of Salzburg, Austria.

Weyringer, S. (2011). Becoming a European citizen: Education to overcome mistrust. In J. Satterthwaite, H. Piper, P. Sikes, & S. Webster (Eds.), *Trust in education: Truths and values* (pp. 87–110). Trentham, UK: Stoke on Trent.

Wiener, A. (2007). *European citizenship practice* [Paper]. European Union Studies Association (EUSA) Tenth Biennial International Conference. Retrieved July 28, 2020, from https://ssrn.com/abstract=1911084

Wittgenstein, L. (1953). *Philosophical investigations*. Oxford, UK: Blackwell.

CHAPTER 16

Training of Integration Competences for Female Asylum Seekers and Refugees with V*a*KE

Sieglinde Weyringer, Jean-Luc Patry and Natascha Diekmann

1   Introduction

In autumn 2015 the European countries were confronted with a novel situation: The violent and long-lasting armed conflicts and economic and social problems in the Middle and the Far East as well as in Africa led to a wave of refugees of previously unknown proportions towards Europe. One of the reactions of the governmental administrations of several receiving countries was to implement extensive measures for refugees to help integrate them into the host society.

In Austria, the Austrian Integration Fund (Österreichischer Integrationsfonds ÖIF[1]), a fund of the Republic of Austria and a partner of the Republic in promoting integration, is responsible for organizing and managing the integration. Among others, it organises language courses and mandatory values courses for asylum seekers. The concept of the values courses is based on the transfer of knowledge of democratic values and their implementation in everyday practices in Austria (Österreichischer Integrationsfonds, 2020). Due to the participants' lack of competences in speaking German, these courses are taught in bilingual settings by a German-speaking teacher and a native-language interpreter, using presentations and lectures as methods.

In contrast, we, the authors, promoted training for refugees using V*a*KE and aiming at the empowerment of the refugees to develop and strengthen competences for integration. A workshop with unaccompanied male minors and a pilot study supported by the ÖIF were carried out. In the present chapter we describe the underlying framework for integration (with a particular focus on women) and present the concept of the studies, the adaptive modification of V*a*KE triggered by the identified needs of the participants, and core results related to the question whether and how the training could support the development and strengthen democratic citizenship competences.

2   Challenges of Unaccompanied Minors and Female Refugees

Being forced to leave one's country because of life-threatening inner conflicts, or for economic reasons is a huge and perilous challenge for the individual which is very difficult to cope with. The nature of the events forcing one to leave the home country, as well as the nature of the motive for the stay in a host country, determine whether the person is referred to as a migrant, refugee, or asylum seeker. The United Nations High Commissioner for Refugees (UNHCR) insists that "refugees are not migrants" (Feller, 2005, p. 27; Sebastien, 2016, p. 32), because they cannot go back to their home country. A further differentiation concerns the status accorded to a refugee by a host country, namely the right to asylum or to subsidiary protection or being a stateless person; for a detailed description see the International Migration Organization (IOM, 2020).

Women and unaccompanied minors belong to the most vulnerable groups on the migratory routes to the host country. Women especially experience violations and discriminations in the origin, in the transit, and in the destination stages (Castellá, 2017). Prompt coordinated and effective protection is required from the moment of entering the respective countries (UNHCR, 2016). Gender-based violence is evident, not only during the migratory movement, but also during the integration process in the host country (Freedman & Jamal, 2008; FitzGerald & Arar, 2018).

In the host country female refugees and asylum seekers are confronted with divergent forms, perceptions, and expectations of how a woman should be and act compared to the home country. This includes the expectations of their families and communities which have a great impact on whether and how the different female roles like care for the children, household, language, and food can be adapted (Sansonetti, 2016, p. 8), but it also includes expectations from the society in the host country. Therefore, integration policies should aim at the empowerment and independence of the target group so that they can cope with the different and often contradictory demands.

Amiot et al. (2007) provide a cognitive-developmental model aiming at the integration of social identities in the self. Social changes like migration initiate intraindividual changes which affect the self-concept. The model describes how multiple social identities develop and become integrated into individuals' self-concept over time. The process passes through four stages. In stage 1 (anticipatory categorization) the person projects his or her own characteristics onto the novel group. He/she imagines him-/herself already before leaving the home country, e.g., how they make contact with the neighbourhood in the host country. In stage 2 (categorization), the migrants have highly differentiated "old" and "new" social identities which are isolated and hardly have any overlap; the first time of living in the host country is dominated by cognitions and awareness of this type. For example, the person realizes that in the host country neighbours do not invite for a coffee spontaneously. In stage 3 (compartmentalization), multiple identification and overlaps between identities are possible and mostly context specific. The person establishes specific attitudes towards the neighbours like making eye contact, smiling, and greeting when passing by. In stage 4 (integration) the recognition of similarities between the different important social identities becomes possible and facilitates simultaneous identification through the creation of higher order categorization. Depending on the conditions and demands of a concrete situation, the person can switch in his or her behaviour between the customs of the host and the home country without disequilibrating the self-concept.

The integration process lacks a definite temporal endpoint. It can extend over several generations, and its progress is independent from the time a person has already been living in the host country. Therefore, in each sequence, depending on the stage, different supportive training programmes for the development of integration competences are needed, aiming at the respective stages of the cognitive-developmental model and to prevent the emergence of parallel societies and a slide into extremism.

We claim that using VaKE as the didactical approach for such competence training supports the adaption of the habits of migrants towards the requirements of integration in a host society. Through the inductive approach (a life-worldly VaKE dilemma story as a starting point), the adaptations of the knowledge base as well as those of behaviours and attitudes, which are absolutely necessary in all stages due to the new social conditions of the living environment, can become individual-specific, i.e., determined by the individual's needs. This approach counteracts the danger of indoctrination of predetermined knowledge and values, and can strengthen a person's maturity, empowerment, resilience, and autonomy. First evidence for this claim has been found in two pilot studies. Their concepts, their realization, especially the adaption of VaKE, and core results will be presented in the next sections.

3 Competence Training for Integration

We define competence as a person's *ability* to act in a specific situation focusing on specific objectives. Whether the competence is turned into action depends on several conditions, among others, (a) the availability of adequate skills, techniques, and knowledge which either have been trained or experienced before or are applied by the principle of trial and error; (b) on the awareness that one is able of doing something and the confidence that one can achieve it (self-efficacy, Bandura, 1977); (c) on knowledge about the situation and related background information; (d) on the degree of socio-emotional and affective excitement and the assessment of the necessity and viability of its activation, and (e) particularly on the person's individual hierarchy of values and – hopefully – their justification (Mischel & Shoda, 1995; Patry, 2019).

The key competences to be addressed have been described by the EU as a combination of knowledge, skills, and attitudes (European Union, 2019), emphasising especially (f) citizenship; (g) multilingualism; (h) personal and (i) social competences; (j) learning to learn; and (k) cultural awareness, each of which needs a specific interpretation when aiming at a satisfying integration process. Dai and Chen (2020) present a model of dimensions and components of cultural integration competence constructed on specific (l) affective; (m) cognitive; and (n) behavioural abilities and (o) desired outcomes, each of them with several sub-categories. We have broadened this concept by adding sub-categories like language competence, moral competence, situation specific behaviour, empowerment, and resilience (Weyringer et al., forthcoming). Given the independence of the different sources, there is much overlap between the categories, and some of them do not represent pure abilities but include other features as well; this does not restrict their usefulness.

We advance the view that the training for integration has to focus on the needs of the refugees, i.e., to elaborate the pillars of established identity, to reflect on them in comparison with the new social reality, and to create visions of a way of living which reduces the subjective gap between the home and the host cultures. The next step of the training provides possibilities for exercising new habits, behaviours, and role models in a protected area, in repeated events, with possibilities for individual reflection and feedback, and guideline transfer, i.e., for implementing the adaptation of behaviour outside the training situation. The trainer, then, is a mentor or facilitator, not a teacher in the classical sense.

4   Two Pilot Projects: "Wahinu" and "Being a Woman in Austria"

In this section, we present two pilot projects, in which first experiences on a competence training for integration could be gathered. The related studies have already been published in detail; therefore, we will concentrate on the normative issues and the educational objectives, on the content-related frameworks, and on the challenges of using VaKE as a didactical approach in the training with a particular group of participants.

4.1   Pilot Project 1: "The People on the Planet Wahinu"

This training course (Patry et al., 2016) was carried out with ten unaccompanied male minors from Afghanistan, Somalia, and Syria in an Austrian refugee home in 2016. All participants had already applied for asylum in Austria. Their German language competences differed – on average, they had participated in language courses for seven months.

The integration competence training aimed at understanding the principles and benefits of democracy involving all citizens of a state in contrast to other political systems like absolute monarchy, tyranny, aristocracy, or oligarchy (normative and content-related framework; for details see, e.g., Encyclopaedia Britannica, 2020). The specific educational objective was the development of maturity. The steps achieved were equivalent to steps 2, 3, 10, 11 of the prototypical VaKE course (see Chapter 2 in this handbook), which means the participants had to make a decision, to find pro and con arguments for the own standpoint, to discuss the different standpoints in a discursive manner following the discussion rules, and finally to accept the vote of the majority – the latter in simulation of a democratic process. The course was limited to three sessions of 2.5 hours each.

The dilemma story described a science fiction situation: 100 people are sent to a fictitious planet called *Wahinu*, to start a new life. All of them are different; they are unfamiliar with the environmental conditions; no rules nor laws exist, which leads to chaos. They want to establish a governmental system. Two options are given: Either one person ("king") sets the rules and laws and decides for all the others about right and wrong; or all do this together based on joint decisions. Which option should the people choose, and why?

The challenges for the application of VaKE were the understanding of the story, the insufficient language competence of the participants, the assumed lack of experience in participating in a discussion, and finally the assumed low ability to empathize with the opposing point of view. For a better understanding, the story was presented using several pictures, and additional didactical settings were implemented: (1) To make sure that the participants understood the story, two circles of chairs were formed, and two people sitting opposite to each other told each other the story, and then one person moved on, and the story telling was repeated between the next pair; (2) to overcome the lack of language skills a participant tried to formulate his argument in the German language; the trainer corrected vocabulary and grammar, and the participant repeated the correct argument; (3) to stimulate the involvement into the discussion, the group was randomly divided into a pro and a contra group; the presentation of arguments for or against an option was done in alternate order with the support of the trainer; to illustrate how speeches go their way and to regulate who is allowed to speak, a string from one speaker to the other was passed on, and showed how a network of arguments is formed; (4) to stimulate empathy the groups had to do a second discussion round promoting the opposing standpoint.

On the third day the participants asked for an extension for another day, which could be organised. The course ended up in a final unrestricted and free discussion, where each participant could vote for his personal point of view and present his personal arguments. They used the facts they had investigated, and they referred to the arguments of the other participants. They all preferred a democratic system on the planet, governed by two or three people with a limited time of rule, sharing of powers, and mutual control. And at the end they even organised an election within the group.

4.2 Pilot Project 2: "Being a Woman in Austria"

This pilot study (see Patry et al., 2019; Weyringer et al., forthcoming) was funded by the Austrian Integration Fund (Österreichischer Integrationsfonds ÖIF) and carried out between 2018 and 2019. The aim was that female refugees with asylum or subsidiary protection status should receive further voluntary integration training based on VaKE, after they had taken part in one of the compulsory state value courses focusing on knowledge related to Austrian culture as well as to living traditions and their legal basics (see above).

96 women from Syria, Afghanistan, Iraq, Somalia, Dagestan, Yemen, and Iran participated in eleven training courses of between 4 and 16 women. Most had Islam as their cultural/religious background. The scope of their school education ranged from illiteracy to a university degree. The field of employment was similarly heterogeneous. Most of the women were married and had children.

The communication in the training was in German, with translation into Arabic and Farsi/Dari, respectively. Each course lasted 12 hours divided into three meetings of four hours each. Between the second and the third meeting a two-week break was inserted, in which the participants were to carry out a self-chosen resolution to change some specific behaviour in everyday life. They created daily records in a predetermined mode. A daily reminder SMS supported them in doing this documentation. In the third meeting the women shared their experiences with the group, reflected on possibilities to overcome experienced problems, and created visions on their further development as being a woman in Austria.

In general, the training was aimed (1) at the adaption of the women's self towards the circumstances of living in Austria and its stable and reliable integration in their identity and (2) at the ability to participate in social coexistence in Austria: The women were to get to know, to understand and to accept fundamental democratic principles, values, and duties as they are practiced in Austria. Summarizing the aims, the normative framework focused on their empowerment, resilience, and autonomy, and on their awareness that democratic governmental systems provide protection and encouragement for active participation in citizenship.

The descriptions of knowledge, skills, and competences on level 1 and 2 of the European Qualification Framework for Lifelong Learning (European Union, 2020) framework for the concretisation of content-related objectives. Three types of knowledge were worked on:

1. Knowledge about myself, concretized in the question "Who am I?": First, the participants talked about what they personally liked/did not like, and what was important for them. In a next step, each woman had to compare between their home country and Austria with respect to positive and negative aspects in general. The third task was to produce a list of characteristics of a typical woman in their home country and a similar one for an Austrian woman.

2. The women discussed the knowledge on law, religion, and traditions of living in Austria compared to the home country by answering the question "What is right, and why it is right?". First, the building blocks of each system were presented as general points for orientation: Law is constructed on rights and obligations, religion provides commandments and prohibitions, living traditions are based on norms, rites, customs, and their opposite. In a next step, the priority of the law over religion and traditions in Austria was addressed. The participants discussed their experiences and attitudes with respect to this hierarchy. The third task was to discuss fictitious dilemma stories, and to find out where to get the relevant information. The VaKE dilemma stories addressed problems and needs from the perspective of a wife, mother, or employee, e.g., a young woman wants to marry a non-Muslim Austrian; a young woman should become the second wife of a Muslim man; a woman's husband is violent against her; the daughter wants to participate in a mixed-sex swimming course; the husband forbids his wife to go out for work; the employer requires that the woman does not wear a headscarf; the woman is offered a job working with men.

3. Knowledge how one can be a woman in Austria, i.e., the response to the question "What can I adapt?": In the second meeting each woman had to reflect on one personal learning outcome as an intent which she wants to and can transfer into her daily routine during the next two weeks (behaviour resolution). She had to document this process in a daily

written report which consisted of predetermined questions. In the third meeting each of the women was asked to share her experience. This evaluation aimed at the conscious self-knowledge that and how she can be successful in a behavioural change.

There were several didactical challenges using VaKE in these eleven groups. For preparation, the establishment of a trustworthy atmosphere was essential. The women were not used to talking about their own concerns. With games as well as with tasks to draw or to talk about, they could be won for a confrontation with themselves. They were also not used to verbalizing their wishes, visions and needs even in their own language. When they were invited to draw these, many of them were reluctant, since in their perception this was a childish activity. When memories of violent experiences suddenly become acute, space had to be given for them. Immediately after the presentation of the story (step 1), the participants started to discuss what the female protagonist should do (step 3). It was neither possible to vote, (step 2) nor to talk about additional options. They enjoyed transforming the discussion into a role-play (step 10); especially the argumentation from different perspectives and arguing in favour of the contrary to their own opinion was experienced as valuable. They also enjoyed including roles for representatives of law, religion, and tradition in their home country or in Austria in the role-plays. The search for information was not only done in connection with the stories (step 4, 5, 6), but also because of their own actual problems. Activities to find reliable information to solve a problem was an unfamiliar experience for some.

The evaluation at the end of the training showed high acceptance. According to their own statements, the participants learned about women's rights, how to make decisions, how to solve problems, about their self-determination and self-care, about Austrian culture, and society, about information search and freedom of expression. Their intentions for transfer into daily behaviour concentrated on learning the language, solving problems, looking for a job, looking for an honorary engagement, looking for evidence of information and strengthening self-determination and self-care.

5   Concluding Remarks

Conclusions can be drawn with respect to two issues: What can be said about VaKE after these experiences, and what can be said about the integration of migrants and refugees?

With respect to VaKE, first, the experience that VaKE can be applied, with adaptations in many different settings, with many different audiences, with many different topics, and focusing on many different objectives – an experience that pervades throughout this handbook – was confirmed once more. The two target groups came from countries in which discursive teaching-learning approaches and open teaching situations have no tradition. Therefore, the participants had to be prepared for that. Once they had recognised the principles and gained both trust and confidence, they were highly motivated, as can be seen by the request of the adolescents of the first pilot study to extend the workshop and by the evaluation results of the women from the second group. Maybe in further research we should address the role of trust and confidence, at least for specific groups. Both trust and confidence were fostered by the open situation and by the discussion rules which exclude feedback on the person: Only statements (arguments) could be discussed. All opinions were accepted and never criticised, and if they were questioned, then only in the form of "Could you give a concrete example for this?" or the like. And that this kind of feedback came from the peers and not from the workshop leaders was also encouraging. The restraint of the workshop leaders to comment on the participants' statements and to express their own point of view prevented them from trying to comply with the formers' presumed opinion. Thus, they felt much freer to open up and express what they really thought and felt compared to a closed teaching-learning situation, as the official values courses they had experienced had been.

A second issue with respect to VaKE is relevant, namely the importance of thinking about the goals one wants to achieve through applying VaKE. In this particular case, the research group had to think very carefully about what the integration of refugees and asylum seekers means, both from the point of view of the refugees themselves as well as from the point of view of the host society. However, the latter is not a homogeneous group, rather there are many different perspectives which need to be measured. Hence, some normative decisions had to be taken. Some of them are presented in the sections 2 and 3 above, others were omitted because of space restrictions but have been addressed elsewhere (Weyringer et al., forthcoming). The particular case of women refugees adds the issue that not only the host society is relevant, but also the traditions and customs within their own actual cultural communities (extended family, local community) on which women are highly dependent even in their interaction with the representatives of the host society (administration, teachers of their children, etc.). And again, in this regard, the experiences of the women were very different – and the recognition that peers living under other circumstances had similar experiences and that they could freely express these experiences was very beneficial for the women.

With respect to the normative decisions to be made ahead of introducing VaKE, we found that the values system underlying VaKE, complies perfectly with our perspective of the integration of refugees. In particular, the emphasis is on Human Rights and respect of human dignity as a primary ethical principle; furthermore, the primacy of law over tradition and religion, and the empowerment of participants not only with respect to their cognitions and potential emotions, but also in their actual behaviour are emphasized.

Indeed, these are high ambitions, and we could not aim at their full achievement in workshops running for only about twelve hours. Nevertheless, despite the shortness of the intervention, it seems that we were able to trigger some experiences and thoughts that might prove beneficial for the further integration process.

Note

1 The support by the ÖIF does not constitute an endorsement of the contents, which reflect the views only of the authors.

References

Amiot, C. E., de la Sablonnière, R., Terry, D. J., & Smith, J. R. (2007). Integration of social identities in the self: Toward a cognitive-developmental model. *Personality and Social Psychology Review, 11*(4), 364–388. Retrieved July 30, 2020, from http://mapageweb.umontreal.ca/delasabr/Eng%20website/publications/Amiot%20et%20al.,%202007.pdf

Bandura, A. (1977). Self-efficacy: Toward a unifying theory of behavioral change. *Psychological Review, 84*, 191–215.

Castellá, H. (2017). *The situation of refugee women in Europe, the Spanish State and Catalonia.* Centre Maurice Coppieters. Retrieved July 30, 2020, from https://www.academia.edu/31176620/The_situation_of_refugee_women_in_Europe

Dai, X.-D., & Chen, G.-M. (2020). Conceptualizing cultural integration competence. *China Media Research, 16*(2), 13–24.

Encyclopaedia Britannica. (2020). *Typologies of government.* Retrieved July 29 2020, from https://www.britannica.com/topic/political-system/Issues-of-classification

European Union. (2019). *Key competences for lifelong learning.* Luxembourg: Publications Office of the European Union.

European Union. (2020). *Europass*. Retrieved July 29, 2020, from https://europa.eu/europass/en

Feller, E. (2005). Refugees are not migrants. *Refugee Survey Quarterly, 24*(4), 27–35. https://doi.org/10.1093/rsq/hdi077

FitzGerald, D. S., & Arar, R. (2018). The sociology of refugee migration. *Annual Review of Sociology, 44*(1), 387–406. https://www.annualreviews.org/doi/full/10.1146/annurev-soc-073117-041204

Freedman, J., & Jamal, B. (2008). *Violence against migrant and refugee women*. Euro-Mediterranean Human Rights Network. Retrieved July 30, 2020, from www.euromedrights.net

IOM. (2020). *Key migration terms*. Retrieved July 26, 2020, from https://www.iom.int/key-migration-terms

Mischel, W., & Shoda, Y. (1995). A cognitive-affective system theory of personality: Reconceptualizing situations, dispositions, dynamics, and invariance in personality structure. *Psychological Review, 102*, 246–268.

Österreichischer Integrationsfonds. (2020). *Mein Leben in Österreich*. Retrieved June 23, 2020, from https://www.integrationsfonds.at/kurse/werte-und-orientierungskurse

Patry, J.-L. (2019). Situation specificity of behavior: The triple relevance in research and practice of education. In R. V. Nata (Ed.), *Progress in education* (Vol. 58, pp. 29–144). Hauppauge, NY: Nova.

Patry, J.-L., Weyringer, S., Aichinger, K., & Weinberger, A. (2016). Integrationsarbeit mit eingewanderten Jugendlichen mit V*a*KE (Values *and* Knowledge Education). *International Dialogues on Education: Past and Present. IDE Online Journal, 3*(3), 123–139. Retrieved July 30, 2020, from http://www.ide-journal.org/article/2016-volume-3-number-3-integrationsarbeit-mit-eingewanderten-jugendlichen-mit-vake-values-and-knowledge-education/

Patry, J.-L., Weyringer, S., & Diekmann, N. (2019). V*a*KE intervention method: Education for democratic citizenship for female refugees. In E. Gutzwiller-Helferfinger, H. J. Abs, & P. Müller (Eds.), *Thematic papers based on the conference migration, social transformation, and education for democratic citizenship* (pp. 191–205). Essen, Germany: University of Duisburg-Essen. Retrieved June 26, 2020, from https://duepublico.uni-duisburg-essen.de/servlets/DocumentServlet?id=47633&lang=de

Sansonetti, S. (2016). *Female refugees and asylum seekers: The issue of integration*. European Parliament. Retrieved July 30, 2020, from http://www.europarl.europa.eu/supporting-analyses

Sebastien, M. (2016). *UNHCR and the migration regime complex in Asia-Pacific*. UNHCR New Issues in Refugee Research, Research Paper No. 283. Retrieved July 30, 2020, from https://www.unhcr.org/5823489e7.pdf

UNHCR. (2016, January 20). Report warns refugee women on the move in Europe are at risk of sexual and gender-based violence [Press release]. Retrieved July 30, 2020, from http://www.unhcr.org/569f99ae60.html

Weyringer, S., Patry, J.-L., & Diekmann, N. (forthcoming). Education for democratic citizenship through V*a*KE in communities with cultural diversity: Fostering migrants' competences for migration and integration. In E. Gutzwiller-Helferfinger, H. J. Abs, & K. Göbel (Eds.), *Migration, social transformation, and education for democratic citizenship – addressing challenges of extremism and radicalisation.*

CHAPTER 17

"Equal Right to Talk"

Fostering Hospitality and Intercultural Dialogue in the University of Sanctuary 'Mellie' Project through VaKE

Julie Daniel and Veronica Crosbie

1   Introduction

This chapter concerns itself with the introduction of Values *and* Knowledge Education (V*a*KE) in a higher education context in Ireland where practitioners work in the field of intercultural education in a University of Sanctuary (UoS), which is part of a movement to create a culture of welcome for refugees and international protection applicants. Dublin City University (DCU), where the study is set, is pioneering in this regard, being the first university in Ireland to receive the UoS designation, based on a commitment to promote the core principles of 'learn', 'embed' and 'share' what it means to be forcibly displaced (Grace & Margolis, 2019, p. 5).

In addition to providing scholarships to access higher education, a number of initiatives is implemented annually to promote integration. In this study, we focus on one project, *Mellie* (Migrant English Language, Literacy, and Intercultural Education), which brings together protection applicants living in reception facilities (Joyce & Quinn, 2014) also known as 'Direct Provision' (DP) centres (Ní Chiosáin, 2018), with volunteer staff and students of DCU to engage in paired reciprocal storytelling, with a view to promoting intercultural dialogue through language and intercultural exchange.

The introduction of the V*a*KE methodology adds a critical layer to the project, in which the participants are invited to discuss a cultural dilemma and exchange ideas and reactions in small group and plenary sessions. The aim is, thus, to deepen the conversations and cross-cultural exchanges by adding reflective, cognitive, and evaluative dimensions. Our research is guided by the following question:

> How and to what extent might V*a*KE act as a catalyst to deepen reciprocal intercultural learning, support integration, and enhance voice and agency in a University of Sanctuary setting?

In the following, we provide a theoretical overview of constructs that inform our study, including integration, hospitality, intercultural dialogue, and epistemic justice. We then outline our methodological approach, which is based on participant observation, textual analysis, and a survey, followed by a presentation and discussion of findings of the VaKE intervention. We conclude with a reflection on the value added through the implementation of *VaKE* in the *Mellie* project.

2   Theoretical Overview

2.1   *Integration*

In our increasingly globalised world, in which forced migration has been identified as a twenty first century global challenge, and, therefore, a "crisis of solidarity" (Ki-Moon, 2016), governments, social organisations and institutions of higher education, *inter alia*, are tasked with the ethical duty of integrating people of refugee background into increasingly multicultural host communities. According to Berry (2019), diversity and equity are the two fundamental constituents of a thriving multicultural society. In the case of the former, this is manifested through the co-existence of differing values, beliefs, and practices, including heritage languages, religious adherences, gender norms and familial duties and responsibilities. The second dimension, equitable participation, is equally important; diversity without equitable participation may lead to identification with distinct cultural groups, which in turn may lead to separation or segregation. Conversely, equitable participation without diversity may lead to assimilation and a denial of heritage culture and identity. The worst-case scenario, the absence of both diversity and equitable participation, may, in turn, lead to marginalisation and exclusion.

Many multicultural societies, for example Canada and the EU, subscribe to a policy of integration that encompasses these two dimensions of diversity and equitable participation. For example, the European Commission's most recent 'Action Plan on Integration and Inclusion' (EC, 2020), foregrounds inclusion for all and itemises targeted funding to support a range of strategies including enhanced migrant participation and long-term integration.

A key aspect of integration is the development of social connection, articulated persuasively in the 'Framework for Integration' developed by Ager and Strang (2008). They recognise social connection as a facilitator of 'two-way' mutual accommodation, with the notion of 'belonging' seen as an important marker of living in an integrated community. Drawing on theories of social capital, they distinguish between three different forms of connection: social bonds, where there is solidarity at family, co-ethnic, or similar, level; social bridges, with other communities; and social links, with the apparatus of the state. For the purpose of this study, we are interested, in particular, in the domain of social bridges, in which 'host' and 'guest' interact, as articulated in the following section.

2.2   Hospitality

The seminal work of Derrida on the concept of hospitality explores the reciprocal nature of the relationship between hosts and guests, inherent in such multicultural contexts, which he sees as dynamic and only substantial when put into practice (Derrida & Dufourmantelle, 2000). Notwithstanding the potential for risk which any act of hospitality inevitably brings, Derrida insists on the need for constant negotiation and dialogue between both parties involved. Reflecting on what it means to live together with others (*vivre ensemble*), Derrida comes to the conclusion that a viable status quo between newcomers and host societies can only be achieved by providing people with enough education and the means to be able to participate in public debate (Derrida, 2013; Schmidtke, 2018; Weber, 2013).

Ultimately, the Derridean philosophy of hospitality reframes integration as a democratic invitation to participate in the public sphere. In this act of hospitality, hosts and guests alike are invited to engage in intercultural dialogue and exercise voice and agency with a view to achieving desired change.

2.3   Intercultural Dialogue

Intercultural dialogue, the concept that is recognised as a means for individuals and groups to make sense of each other and to learn to live well together in diverse, multicultural societies (Council of Europe, 2008), is often seen as an unproblematic panacea of social disharmony, especially in educational pedagogical contexts where it is cast as a skill or competence to acquire (Phipps, 2014; Todd, 2015). Rather, we argue that intercultural dialogue can be viewed as a capability (Nussbaum, 2000; Sen, 1999), and, as such, intrinsically more complex, with all its concomitant dimensions of power, choice, and value attributes (Crosbie, 2014).

In recent times, since the outbreak of Covid-19, intercultural dialogue has been under threat, in particular in the case of minority ethnic groups. In a UNESCO commissioned report, Mansouri (2020) details four key trends in this context, namely: an increase in social inequalities and vulnerabilities; the escalation of xenophobia and ethno-cultural racism; a rise in gender-based violence; and aggravated discrimination against non-citizens. The report calls for enhanced commitment by key stakeholders, including governments and civil society, to "nurture and sustain solidarity with and between disadvantaged communities" (p. 4). In response, a number of new forms of intercultural dialogue and solidarity has emerged on-line, including creative arts-based initiatives, according to Mansouri (ibid.), which reflect the response that the *Mellie* project took when the pandemic interrupted normal practices, as referenced below.

2.4 Epistemic Justice

The acculturative experiences of forced migrants, as a unique cohort, is both complex and dynamic, not easily categorised into binary definitions of 'voluntary–involuntary', 'permanent–temporary', or 'sedentary–migrant'; and cultural contact with the host society is often limited (Donà & Young, 2016). As such, this cohort of refugees and international protection applicants invariably has to battle against epistemic injustice (Fricker, 2007, 2015). In other words, it is denied the opportunity to contribute to debate in the public sphere by sharing information and understanding. Forced migrants are, thus, subject to capability deprivation, especially those, as in the case of this study, who are forced to reside in DP centres that are located in remote areas, rendering them both invisible and voiceless. Fricker (2007) argues that testimonial exchange, involving all parties to a discursive act, speakers, and hearers alike, is influenced by identity power, both of an agentic and structural nature, and, as such, forced migrants face the danger of being marginalised and/or silenced.

We argue that a key role of educators is to challenge such injustices by creating spaces for powerful and equitable social interaction. The concepts of integration, hospitality, intercultural dialogue, and epistemic justice offer individual yet mutually inclusive insights into steps that might be taken to achieve these ends if social agents, including institutes of higher education, are serious about addressing the 'crisis of solidarity' signalled by Ki-Moon (2016).

3 Methodological Factors: The V*a*KE Intervention in Mellie

The *Mellie* project is designed to facilitate cultural and language exchange between volunteers from the university community and people living in Direct Provision. Volunteers of both communities are paired up on campus three hours per week to exchange experiences and life stories and produce collaborative and reciprocal narratives drawn from their encounters. A typical session includes a mutual interview, scaffolded by a set of guided questions articulated around a theme (e.g., hope, hospitality, the self, the land). Artifacts are subsequently produced by the pairs and can take various forms such as, for example, a photovoice production or a story (text). Themes are chosen, sometimes by the participants themselves, to represent and value universal human lived experience.

In 2020 V*a*KE was introduced and adapted to complement the programme and the participants' profile. It was envisaged that the reflection, discussion, and research initiated by the chosen dilemma would deepen the intercultural dialogue, allowing participants to reflect on a real-life situation and to challenge their own points of view while learning about each other's values and, ultimately, coming to a mutual understanding, as per Derrida's notion of 'vivre ensemble'. In the middle of the semester, due to Covid-19 pandemic social restraints, the project was forced to move online, with variable outcomes, both positive and negative.

3.1   Description of the Group

The 2020 *Mellie* group was composed of a total of forty participants with twenty from asylum seeking and refugee backgrounds and twenty from the DCU community, the latter not all native Irish. Levels of literacy across both sets of participants varied from low (young adults with interrupted schooling) to high (PhD). Participants came from Australia, France, Georgia, India, Iraq, Ireland, Italy, Malawi, Nigeria, Pakistan, Romania, Slovakia, Spain, Syria, USA, and Zimbabwe. The ratio of male to female was approximately 40:60 and there was a diverse range of ages, spanning from eighteen to sixty-five.

3.2   V*a*KE for Mellie

The dilemma written by the course leaders for the purpose of the V*a*KE intervention introduces a realistic situation in an Irish context in which a young Syrian teenage girl, Rima, confronts her parents when she asks to be allowed to go to a climate change demonstration with her school friends. The dilemma tackles a range of diverse issues, such as intergenerational dialogue, migration, climate change, activism, integration, education, and political representation and participation of minorities. Given the heterogeneity of the group, it was important that the dilemma did not divide the *Mellie* participants into two groups, with the DP residents on the one side and the DCU volunteers on the other. In order to avoid stereotypes and misrepresentation, the dilemma had been read in advance and approved by a member of the Syrian community and former *Mellie* participant.

The V*a*KE intervention took place in the fourth week of the programme as it was believed that at this stage the group would know each other well enough to feel comfortable in sharing their ideas and expressing their points of view freely. It was agreed that, exceptionally, a second session would be added during the week in order to have two full afternoons dedicated to the workshop and to allow time for further reflection and research to happen. After the V*a*KE method was explained to the group, which on this occasion, comprised thirty-one participants, the dilemma was presented to them to read individually (in English, Arabic and Georgian). After reading the text and clarifying any queries, the following dilemma question was introduced: *"Should Rima go to the demonstration?"*. Individuals were asked to vote, using the digital app Mentimeter, accessed via their smartphones. The results of the vote were: 15: yes; 9: no; 7: I don't know.

Following the vote, the *Mellie* participants were divided into groups for discussion, according to how they voted, following V*a*KE-*dis* (i.e., differentiated, individualized, and specified) steps (Patry et al., 2013; see Chapter 2 in this handbook). As the 'Yes' group was the largest, it was divided into two subgroups. A rapporteur was appointed from each group to present feedback on discussion in plenary, and based on the emergent sub themes presented, new subgroups were formed to work on researching and deepening related thematic knowledge.

The themes, on this occasion, were prompted by the course leaders as some of the participants were not used to this type of independent learning and were somewhat reluctant to come up with their own. Three groups chose to work on the following theme: *"What constitutes good parenting in your country and in Ireland?"*; and another group chose to work on the question: *"Why do youngsters demonstrate for climate change?"*. They were then tasked to come back to the follow-up session having done some preliminary research on their own and to elaborate artifacts and present them to the rest of the group, drawing on their newly acquired knowledge and group discussion. Artifacts presented to the class consisted of a play, representing an interaction between a child and a parent in the context of Nigerian parenting; two sets of PowerPoint presentations, looking at what good parenting is with examples from America, Georgia, Ireland, Syria, and Zimbabwe; and one diagram (Figure 17.1), illustrating the reason behind the engagement of youngsters to raise awareness around climatic issues.

While the activities were carried out according to plan, a number of difficulties was encountered, which made the implementation rather challenging. A key issue was the chaotic nature of working with a group composed of 50% protection applicants and 50% DCU volunteers, including erratic attendance and incomplete or different groups per session. This was compounded by the range of English language levels and the heterogeneity of literacy levels in evidence. Time was also a significant factor as the *Mellie* tutors wished to avail of the expertise of V*a*KE practitioner, Prof. Frédérique Brossard Børhaug, who was visiting DCU from abroad, and the workshops could therefore only happen

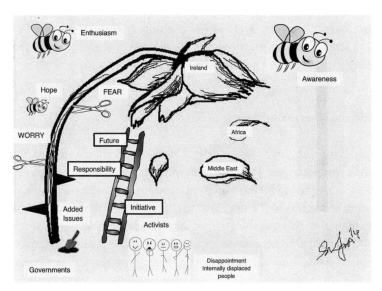

FIGURE 17.1   Artifact from Mellie participant group, illustrating reasons for demonstrating for climate change response

during the fourth week of the project. This necessitated an extra session to which some of the original participants could not attend. As both sessions were scheduled for the same week, there was not enough time to complete the artifacts to a satisfactory level. Finally, there was also a shortage of computers and resources to hand to create larger, more ambitious, and original artifacts. These challenges notwithstanding, the project participants managed to engage in valuable conversations and produce good quality artifacts.

3.3   Methods of Data Collection

At the end of semester, everyone who had participated in the V*a*KE intervention was invited to complete a survey comprising a set of eight questions, some of which were closed, yielding quantitative data, and others more open-ended, which were subsequently coded according to emerging thematic content. The questions attempted to ascertain the participants' reaction to this type of activity; whether they felt comfortable sharing opinions in group format; the extent to which they felt their opinion was valued; if the V*a*KE method helped them to evaluate their own 'taken for granted' assumptions; and whether it presented them with the opportunity to gain new knowledge. As there was a gap of several weeks between the delivery of the V*a*KE intervention and the follow-up survey, the response rate was relatively moderate, with approximately 50% of the cohort, i.e., fifteen respondents, who completed the survey. This was compounded by the fact that *Mellie* had to move online due to the aforementioned Covid-19 restrictions. Additional qualitative data was gathered by the *Mellie* tutors, as participant observers, being in the position to evaluate the level of response to the V*a*KE dilemma by mingling with the different groups while the workshops were in progress and noting their engagement with the process.

4   Results and Discussion

The set of V*a*KE workshops was well received by the participants with 93.3% reporting that the sessions were 'interesting'. From the moment that the method was introduced to the group by the V*a*KE expert tutor, curiosity was sparked across the board, regardless of the profile of the participants. We believed that a thorough explanation of both the method and the chosen themes played a key role in preparing the group how to approach the sessions and to manage expectations, language issues notwithstanding, as for most, including experienced tutors, the approach was new.

4.1   *Enhancing Intercultural Communication*

Although the V*a*KE intervention happened at a stage of the *Mellie* project where the group was just beginning to become well acquainted with each other, working in a larger group setting was reported by many as a welcome change, allowing them to engage in conversations outside of their usual pair. This helped reinforce the atmosphere of confidence and trust in this pedagogical space that the *Mellie* project usually seeks to promote. Indeed, the group discussion allowed for a renewed interactivity and enhanced intercultural dialogue, with participants giving accounts of being able to talk about issues on parenting and climate change in meaningful ways with people from different cultures, backgrounds, and experience. This is captured in the following data extracts from the survey:

> It was very interesting to hear the variety of views across the room in the beginning as a whole group. It was interesting to see what personal views were and what were cultural.

> I thought that it was good to hear multiple voices on sensitive and relevant dilemmas, and it was quite heartening to find out that people from different backgrounds and walks of life had similar concerns and enlightening thought processes.

4.2   *Towards Epistemic Justice: Fostering Reciprocal Learning*

We believe that this enlarged space for discussion gave participants the opportunity to challenge their received opinions with a diversity of views, which contributed to effective collaborative learning. Participants reported learning from each other's points of view as well as being able to examine their own and others' values, as the following quotes from the survey attest:

> It was useful in evaluating values.

> It was engaging and thought provoking.

> The issue of climate is important to be discussed today to hold people responsible and be aware not to abuse the environment. Bringing that issue to *Mellie* and integrating it with migration, values and people was very interesting and interactive.

The opportunity to discuss values in this way allowed participants to conceptualise their initial instinctive reactions and to elaborate on them with the help of the group. Some respondents said that this process prompted them to change their initial vote or intuition after having been challenged by others' points of view, as follows:

> The V*a*KE session helped me in evaluating values to extent that I changed my opinion about Rima's dilemma.

> It encourages us to think more by hearing what others in my group have to say and [challenges our] perspectives by looking at what other groups have come up with.

When asked about knowledge gained, a majority of the participants reported that, more than learning new facts about the chosen topics, they had broadened their understanding of the Other by engaging in dialogue which they had not participated in heretofore. This is exemplified in the following extract:

> I would say that instead of deepening my knowledge on the topic, it made me see better the reasoning behind the yes/no/I don't know choices. Contrasting the three groups' ideas on the whiteboard during the session made me rethink some of the reasons which I thought were rock-solid.

We see this dialogue between contested values as a key feature of the concept of reciprocity as it plays a significant role when it comes to integration of forcibly displaced populations into a host society. Indeed, it gives back a voice to people who have been, in too many ways, deprived of it, thus helping, in a small way, to restore epistemic justice, as evidenced here:

> We are [able to] feel free to give our thoughts and opinion during session. Everybody gives respect, value and listen nicely my point of view. You never feel any member not listening to me or respect me during my conversation. All have equal right to talk in room.

Being in the same group based on voting meant that each member of the group in general agreed on the opinion held towards this dilemma. However, there were differences in reasons behind this choice, based on cultural background, values, history, religion, and personal experiences. Discussing those reasons within the group offered a glimpse into each other's life circumstances, which in the end are what forms one's view on life.

Comments from participants from asylum-seeking backgrounds indicate how they valued the opportunity to be included in social events outside their remote DP centre setting, to be able to participate in intercultural dialogue and engage with cultural norms and values that could assist them and their own children to integrate, as voiced in the following:

> It's very interesting specially people like us living in Direct Provision are isolated from other society. This programme is very helpful to integrate in society. Also, its great experience to make friends and learn knowledge.

> It was an opportunity for some of us parents living in direct provision to know well in advance on how we can handle this if such issue happens in future with our children. Putting into consideration our status and the importance of that demonstration.

The variety and the creativity of the artifacts produced by the participants testify to how the V*a*KE sessions facilitated cooperation among all. We believe that the task of having to work toward a common project, while managing issues of differences in cultures, languages, and values, as well as ensuring equal participation, represents an important step towards a more inclusive and democratic model of a multicultural society.

5 Conclusion

This chapter, which captures the beings and doings of a V*a*KE intervention in the University of Sanctuary *Mellie* integration project, articulates the value added by introducing a dilemma scenario to the habitual storytelling practices that the participants were used to. In so doing, it is argued, it enhanced the act of hospitality, evoked by Derrida and Dufourmantelle (2000), by creating opportunities for dialogue and negotiation, both of content as well as process.

Of particular importance was the evidence that the participants felt that they were engaging in a shared, democratic space, faced with real-world issues such as climate change and intergenerational and cross-cultural dilemmas. Discussing these issues through value perspectives moved the learning from being framed as a set of skills or competences to ones that are capability enhancing, inviting the participants to consider choices that are informed by knowledge and rational consideration.

The capability of 'epistemic contribution' (Fricker, 2015) is equally at play in that participants of refugee backgrounds, with little or no opportunity in the host environment to share information and understandings, were given the opportunity to use their voice and make meaningful contributions. Equally, the university volunteers appreciated the space to listen to other points of view and frames of reference.

This account is a small example of the effort to create a democratic, dialogic space. The next task is to explore how such encounters can be replicated in other contexts: however, intercultural dialogue of this nature takes time to foster, as it rests on generosity, openness, and trust.

References

Ager, A., & Strang, A. (2008). Understanding integration: A conceptual framework. *Journal of Refugee Studies*, 21(2), 166–191.

Berry, J. (2019) *Acculturation: A personal journey across cultures*. Cambridge, UK: Cambridge University Press.

Council of Europe. (2008). *"Living together as equals in dignity": White paper on intercultural dialogue*. Strasbourg, France: Council of Europe. Retrieved April 22, 2021, from https://www.coe.int/t/dg4/intercultural/source/white%20paper_final_revised_en.pdf

Crosbie V. (2014). Capabilities for intercultural dialogue. *Language and Intercultural Communication*, 14(1), 91–107.

Derrida, J. (2013). Avowing – the Impossible: "Returns", repentance, and reconciliation. In E. Weber (Ed.), *Living together: Jacques Derrida's communities of violence and peace* (pp. 18–41). New York, NY: Fordham University Press.

Derrida, J., & Dufourmantelle, A. (2000). *Of hospitality*. Stanford, CA: Stanford University Press.

Donà, G., & Young, M. (2016). Refugees and forced migrants. In D. D. Sam & J. Berry (Eds.), *The Cambridge handbook of acculturation psychology* (pp 153–172). Cambridge, UK: Cambridge University Press.

European Commission. (2020). *The EC reveals its new EU action plan on integration and inclusion (2021–2027)*. Brussels, Belgium: EC: Comm (2020) 758. Retrieved April 22, 2021, from https://ec.europa.eu/migrant-integration/news/the-ec-presents-its-eu-action-plan-on-integration-and-inclusion-2021-2027

Fricker, M. (2007). *Epistemic injustice: Power and the ethics of knowing*. Oxford, UK: Oxford University Press.

Fricker, M. (2015). Epistemic contribution as a central human capability. In G. Hull (Ed.), *The equal society: Essays on equality in theory and practice* (pp. 73–90). Lanham, MD: Lexington Books.

Grace, A., & Margolis, B. (2019). *Universities of Sanctuary resource pack* (2nd ed.). UK: City of Sanctuary. Retrieved April 23, 2021, from https://universities.cityofsanctuary.org/resources

Joyce, C., & Quinn, E, (2014). *The organisation of reception facilities for asylum seekers in Ireland*. Dublin, Ireland: The Economic and Social Research Institute. Retrieved April 22, 2021, from https://www.esri.ie/publications/the-organisation-of-reception-facilities-for-asylum-seekers-in-ireland

Ki-Moon, B. (2016). *Remarks on forced displacement: A global challenge*. UN Secretary General website. Retrieved April 22, 2021, from https://www.un.org/sg/en/content/sg/speeches/2016-04-15/remarks-forced-displacement-global-challenge

Mansouri, F. (2020). *The socio-cultural impact of COVID-19: Exploring the role of intercultural dialogue in emerging responses*. UNESCO report. Retrieved April 27, 2021, from https://unesdoc.unesco.org/ark:/48223/pf0000374186

Ní Chiosáin, B. (2018). Dispersal and direct provision: A case study. *Studies in Arts and Humanities, 4*(2), 33–50. Retrieved May 1, 2021, from http://sahjournal.com/index.php/sah/article/view/140

Nussbaum, M. (2000). *Women and human development*. Cambridge, UK: Cambridge University Press.

Patry, J.-L., Weinberger, A. Weyringer, S., & Nussbaumer, M. (2013). Combining values and knowledge education. In B. Irby, G. Brown, R. Lara-Alecio, & S. Jackson (Eds.). and R. A. Robles-Piña (Sect. Ed.), *The handbook of educational theories* (pp. 565–579). Charlotte, NC: Information Age Publishing.

Phipps, A. (2014). 'They are bombing now': 'Intercultural dialogue' in times of conflict. *Language and Intercultural Communication, 14*(1), 108–124.

Schmidtke, O. (2018). The civil society dynamic of including and empowering refugees in Canada's urban centres. *Social Inclusion, 6*(1), 147–156.

Sen, A. (1999). *Development as freedom*. Oxford, UK: Oxford University Press.

Todd, S. (2015). Creating transformative spaces in education: Facing humanity, facing violence. *Philosophical Inquiry in Education, 23*(1), 53–61.

Weber, E. (Ed.). (2013). *Living together: Jacques Derrida's communities of violence and peace*. New York, NY: Fordham University Press.

CHAPTER 18

The Values *and* Knowledge Education in Transformative Learning

Dimitris Pnevmatikos and Jean-Luc Patry

1   Introduction

In this chapter, we will show that V*a*KE is also an appropriate instructional approach for lifelong learning and particularly for transformative learning. The Transformative Learning Theory (TLT) was developed over the last quarter of the 20th century by Mezirow and his associates (Mezirow, 1985, 1997, 2003; Mezirow et al., 2010). It provides a framework for how learners deconstruct and give new meaning to their experiences.

Previous theories for adult learning were based on the presupposition that adults as learners are engaged in learning activities because they enjoy learning and that the education practices are always successful in meeting the needs of the learners (Brookfield, 1995; Pnevmatikos et al., 2016). These presuppositions were based on the assumption that the adults are engaged in learning activities in their leisure time, and, from a broad spectrum of activities, they choose those activities that meet their basic psychological needs as described by the self-determination theory (Deci & Ryan, 2002). However, regardless of the increase of the time that adults have available for the free time activities (OECD Social indicators, 2009), to maximize their work opportunities and efficiency, adults invest more time in their professional development (Jarvis, 2012).

Thus, lifelong learning has two critical dimensions that adults are interested in combining (Thoidis & Pnevmatikos, 2014). One is the dimension of lifelong learning as a part of their leisure time, and the other is their need to be engaged in learning activities that are related with their work, either as learning at work or as learning for work (Desjardins et al., 2006; Nahrstedt et al., 2002). In other words, the theoretical tools for approaching lifelong learning only as leisure or free time activities do not meet the needs of the current society.

The TLT changed the priorities of lifelong learning. Mezirow introduced the term "transformative learning" to stress the need to formulate educational practices aiming to foster the development of socially responsible individuals that will align their actions for the improvement of society. Whenever adults engage in learning processes, they have their meaning perspectives, assumptions, and habits that facilitate or constrain the ways of thinking, feeling, and acting. Their meaning perspectives serve as fixed assumptions or expectations. Thus, TLT is a theory about how adults learn by making meaning of their experiences. This chapter discusses how VaKE can be a didactical approach that is in alignment with the three basic ideas that operationalize transformative learning, namely the frames of reference, the critical reflection, and the action.

2   The Frames of Reference

Mezirow (1994, 2000) calls the structures of assumptions through which adult learners understand their experiences as *frames of reference*. The frames of reference are coherent structures that include habitual ways of thinking, feeling, and acting (habits of mind). Adults structure these frames of reference in a particular cultural and social environment, and these are expressed as particular points of view, as a set of "beliefs, value judgment, attitudes and feelings that shape a particular interpretation" (Mezirow, 1997, p. 6). Transformative Learning (TL) is the learning that facilitates the transformation of the coherent fixed frames of reference, making them "more inclusive, discriminating, open, reflective, and emotionally able to change" (Mezirow, 2003, p. 58; see also 1998, p. 188). In other words, TL helps the learners to construe their new experiences by changing their frame of reference and revising the way they interpret their experiences (Mezirow, 1998).

The frames of reference involve cultural and social aspects that are expressed as points of view. The moral aspect is at the core of the frames of reference and one of those most involved in transformations. Moral developmental theories help to conceptualize the transformations that one could experience as a result of transformation learning.

Kohlberg (1969) presumed that, in making moral judgments, individuals consciously apply *a priori* principles that constitute the domain of justice and harm, which involve the values of equality, fairness, and rights. In his stage theory, Kohlberg described moral development in terms of changes in the justifications of what is right, reasons for doing right, and in consideration of the social perspective of these values. The change of the frame of reference consists of a shift from the well-established ideas and beliefs to a more open and better-justified frame of reference. In terms of Kohlberg's theory, TL can help the individuals to shift in the openness of the justifications; they will shift their justifications from the selfish and egocentric to prioritizing the common over the personal good. There is evidence showing that VaKE courses facilitate such shifts in moral judgments, and adults change their justifications to higher levels of social perspective (see Pnevmatikos & Christodoulou, 2018; Pnevmatikos et al., 2016). These shifts are vital for citizens for functioning in a democracy by making responsible moral decisions.

A more recent view of moral psychology suggested that moral judgments can pertain to domains other than justice and harm. For instance, Haidt and colleagues (e.g., Graham et al., 2009; Haidt & Graham, 2007; Haidt & Joseph, 2004) described at least five such domains: harm/care, fairness/reciprocity, ingroup/loyalty, authority/respect, and purity/sanctity. These domains are considered fundamental elements of moral judgment, and they involve discrete sets of interrelated principles, rules, and values. Moral domains relate to moral judgments as the actions are judged morally virtuous if perceived to be in alignment with these values and rules. These domains are present in virtually all cultures. Nevertheless, there are also cultural variations in how each culture prioritizes the relative importance of each domain (e.g., Haidt et al., 1993; Rozin et al., 1999; Shweder et al., 1997; Vasquez et al., 2001). Evidence demonstrates that in making moral judgments, individuals first activate intuitions, i.e., automatic fast emotional reactions as the hunch of right and wrong (Greene & Haidt, 2002; Haidt, 2001, 2007). When individuals make moral judgments, distinct emotions for each moral domain are activated (Horberg et al., 2009).

In the lenses of the TLT, intuitions are tacit forms of judgments occurring without recourse to reasoning (Mezirow, 1998) and can be seen as habits of mind that are involved in moral judgments. Moreover, the cultural variation in the moral domains constitutes a challenge for transformative learning. Changes in the frame of reference might reflect changes in the values that are prioritized given the circumstances. One could shift the interpretation and the suggested action in a dilemma from one solution that is supported by the authority/respect to another solution that is supported by fairness/reciprocity. Indeed, when they experience a VaKE course, adults often change their interpretation in the circumstances invoking different moral domains.

For instance, in teacher training about dealing with disruptive pupil behaviour, pre-service teachers participating in a VaKE course changed from direct intervention concepts (their interpretation of the circumstances: I have to tell the pupils how to behave) to discursive behaviour (interpretation: Let us look together for a solution of the problem), whereas pre-service teachers just being told about discursive behaviour did not change (Pnevmatikos et al., 2016; Weinberger et al., 2016). In other words, they experienced the transformation of their prior interpretations and justifications that were no longer functional compared to the newly revised interpretations. At the same time, through the reflections, they became more appreciative of the frames of reference of others, as exemplified with the discursive teacher behaviour in the example above.

Furthermore, VaKE facilitates the adults to construct new knowledge, enabling them to change their frame of reference. Pre-service teachers learned about new theories and how to apply them in real situations affecting their actions substantially (Pnevmatikos et al., 2019). Moreover, adults acquire new knowledge of a higher level in the taxonomy of Bloom et al. (1956) than traditional methods: analysis, synthesis, and, particularly, evaluation (e.g., Pnevmatikos et al., 2016; Weinberger, 2006). A critical dimension is that the evaluation of the new frame of reference is done through viability checks (Glasersfeld, 1980; Patry, 2014). The knowledge is not considered as true or false but as viable (or not) to satisfy a specific set of criteria. This helps the adults to be more conscious and rational about the use of knowledge in practical action (Pnevmatikos et al., 2016).

3 Critical Reflection

Critical reflection is a crucial component of the TL that can challenge the established frames of reference. Transformation theory maintains that to understand the meaning of what is communicative, it is necessary to critically reflect the assumptions one has (Mezirow, 1998, p. 188). The critical reflection might refer to our assumptions (self-reflection) or the assumptions of the others. The importance of critical reflection is that it helps individuals to find solutions that might work better because they are more functional (viable) in the specific context and time. The critical reflection might focus on the objective or on the subjective reframing, or both.

The critical reflection as an aim in the objective reframing helps the adults to acknowledge the viability of the concept and of the premises that constitute the problem. In VaKE dilemmas, one can use invalid concepts or assumptions that can probably bias the decision of the protagonist. A critical reflection on the content of the dilemma then is necessary to acknowledge the epistemic difference between beliefs and evidence. In a dilemma that has been addressed in pre-service teachers, one of the experts in a committee suggested an action that he (falsely) justified on Maslow's theory (see Pnevmatikos et al., 2019). The pre-service teachers did not initially realize this, and no-one suggested them to examine the viability of this premise. At the end of the course, the pre-service teachers reflected critically on their initial interpretation, and they were convinced about the need for reflecting critically on the content and the premises that support their own or others' inferences. Having this experience, they realized the need for a transformative redefinition of the problem in a form that is a valid expression of the theory of reference (in this particular case, Maslow, 1943). This example shows that VaKE can serve the objective reframing by improving performance and pertains to the instrumental learning that aims to make meaning through problem-solving.

In the long term, the learners establish a disposition to seek for viability or truth (in traditional non-constructivist terminology), which is an essential aspect of critical thinking (Facione, 1990). Moreover, they can decide about the theories they want to use and, due, among others, to the generality-concreteness antinomy (Herrmann, 1979, p. 160ff.; Gastager et al., 2017) – theories cannot prescribe the action in the circumstances in detail – the learners have a degree of freedom for how to transfer the theories into the action (Patry, 2018; applied to VaKE by Linortner & Patry, in press).

Critical reflection also aims to subjective reframing through a critical self-reflection on the adults' assumptions about the appropriate thinking, feeling, and acting. In VaKE-dis (differentiated, individualized, specified), a more elaborate form of VaKE, additional steps are integrated that focus explicitly on self-reflection (see also Chapter 2 in this handbook). In a VaKE course, it is usual for the learners to change their standpoints. Then, they are asked to reflect and give the reasons that forced them to change their standpoints. This critical reflection on their assumptions leads them (a) to realize the connection between their standpoints and the values that support them (i.e., variations in the standpoints are supported by different values), and (b) to understand the role of the cultural systems (economic, religious, political, bureaucratic, educational, linguistic, etc.) in forming their assumptions for the social roles, relationships, and the current status quo in general. Additionally, self-reflection helped the learners to be aware of the role of their emotions to take particular standpoints.

In many VaKE courses, for instance, workers in the health care professions realized that their first standpoint was guided by their emotions and not from a rational deliberation of the evidence they had. Their reflection helped them to change their habits of mind and to consider inhibiting their first emotional reaction and taking a standpoint based on the available evidence before deciding on their reaction – and if necessary, to look for additional evidence (Pnevmatikos et al., 2016).

VaKE dilemma stories are structured to support two standpoints. Learners expressing their standpoints use different discourses and justifications to support them. The critical reflection leads them to realize that although they have the same standpoint with respect to the protagonist's decision, they start from different starting points. Thus, they become more conscious of their own assumptions and interpretations and more open to new ideas and transformations.

4   Practice: Reflection on Action

Action is the third component of the TL and indispensable. Humans act based on the beliefs they have for a situation (Gastager et al., 2017, 2018). The TL aims not only to changes in the existing frames of reference, but it is expected that individuals act upon the newly acquired frames of reference. Although Mezirow (1989, p. 174) assumes that transformative learning will lead to action, he does not expect that the transformative learning experiences will always lead to collective or radical actions. Teachers who engaged in a critical reflection on a VaKE course about a common problem, back in their classes, act based on their new frames of reference. This is an action for transformative learning but is not a collective action in terms of other theoretical frameworks.

Notably, for Mezirow (1989), the responsibility for the action is always on the part of the learners (not the educators/teachers). When the educator perceives that the action is acceptable, then he or she should help the learner to elaborate on the idea and develop the skills that are necessary to overcome possible constraints. VaKE fosters the learners' decision to act based on what they have learned. For instance, in a course for female refugees from Muslim countries, the participants were asked to make a resolution about action and to document whether they acted accordingly in a diary – it turned out that the majority followed their resolutions quite reliably (Weyringer et al., in press; see also Chapters 16 and 28 in this handbook).

A particular issue of the connection between transformative learning and action emerges in the area of professional development (Pnevmatikos et al., 2016). We have already addressed the problem of multiple available theories and of transferring theories into action (Part 2). Further, in research and theory formulation, the scientists follow a coherent framework of principles, but in the action, one has multiple goals and uses more than one theory simultaneously (Patry, 2018). Finally, acting is always a dynamic process with the others in the environment and the action is situation-specific (ibid.). For instance, in the health care professions, the reactions of the patients cannot be predicted precisely, but they will affect the reactions of the professionals. In this case, a variation of VaKE, the VaKE-Tact (Linortner & Patry, in press), is more suitable. This variation enables the learners to acquire the necessary skills and competencies and to establish a protocol of reactions in new circumstances. An example is a study by Weinberger et al. (2016) discussed above: Discursive behaviour as fostered by VaKE is flexible in that it permits to approach each pupil – whether disruptive or not – in a way that suits him or her best and that is likely to yield a positive problem-solving approach on which all stakeholders agree.

5 Conclusion

Transformative Learning Theory (TLT) stresses the need for transformative learning in adult education, which means changes in the frames of reference which had been established through the exposure in the cultural systems. We argued here that VaKE is an instructional approach that could support the aims of the TLT. In particular, we showed that VaKE courses offer to adult learners the framework to resolve authentic dilemma stories. The dilemma stories have two standpoints in a competition that are supported by different frames of reference. Through critical reflections, the learners are prompted to approach the circumstances not only instrumentally but in a communicative way, that is involving feelings of oneself and others, and considering social aspects.

So far, we implemented VaKE in many lifelong learning programmes. We are aware that most adults who experienced VaKE transformed their previous meanings for the topics discussed and usually were moved away from their previous fixed assumptions or expectations that they had constructed in the past. They acquired new knowledge and skills while with the critical reflection on the dilemma arguments, they acknowledged the role of the values in their arguments, and they abandoned their previous egocentric perspective, adopting more open, socio-centric justifications and interpretations. In other words, experiencing VaKE, adults facilitated transforming their frames of reference and undertook initiatives to act based on the new interpretations.

References

Bloom, B. S., Englehart, M. B., Furst, E. J., Hill, W. H., & Krathwohl, D. R. (1956). *Taxonomy of educational objectives. The classification of educational goals. Handbook I: Cognitive domain.* New York, NY: Longmans Green.

Brookfield, S. (1995). Adult learning: An overview. In A. Tuinjman (Ed.), *International encyclopedia of education* (pp. 1–16). Oxford, UK: Pergamon Press.

Deci, E. L., & Ryan, R. M. (2002). *Handbook of self-determination research.* Rochester, NY: University Rochester Press.

Desjardins, R., Rubenson, K., & Milana, M. (2006). *Unequal chances to participate in adult learning: International perspectives.* Paris, France: UNESCO.

Facione, P. A. (1990). *Critical thinking: A statement of expert consensus for purposes of educational instruction.* Millbrae, CA: Academic Press.

Gastager, A., Bock, A., Patry, J.-L., Präauer, V., & Fageth, B. (2017). Pedagogical tact in mentoring of professional school internships. *Global Education Review, 4*(4), 20–38.

Gastager, A., Bock, A., Präauer, V., Resch, B., & Patry, J.-L. (2018) Der pädagogische Takt bei Mentorinnen und Mentoren und ihren Lehramtsstudierenden: Erste Ergebnisse einer empirischen Untersuchung. In A. Gastager & J.-L. Patry (Eds.), *Pädagogischer Takt: Analysen zu Theorie und Praxis* (Studienreihe der Pädagogischen Hochschule Steiermark, Band 11) (pp. 175–195). Graz, Austria: Leykam.

Glasersfeld, E. von. (1980). Viability and the concept of selection. *American Psychologist, 35*, 970–974.

Graham, J., Haidt, J., & Nosek, B. A. (2009). Liberals and conservatives rely on different sets of moral foundations. *Journal of Personality and Social Psychology, 96*, 1029–1046.

Greene, J., & Haidt, J. (2002). How (and where) does moral judgment work? *Trends in Cognitive Sciences, 6*, 517–523.

Haidt, J. (2001). The emotional dog and its rational tail: A social intuitionist approach to moral judgment. *Psychological Review, 108*, 814–834.

Haidt, J. (2007, May 18). The new synthesis in moral psychology. *Science, 316*, 998–1002.

Haidt, J., & Graham, J. (2007). When morality opposes justice: Conservatives have moral intuitions that liberals may not recognize. *Social Justice Research, 20*, 98–116.

Haidt, J., & Joseph, C. (2004). Intuitive ethics. *Dædalus, 133*, 55–66.

Haidt, J., Koller, S. H., & Dias, M. G. (1993). Affect, culture, and morality, or is it wrong to eat your dog? *Journal of Personality and Social Psychology, 65*, 613–628.

Herrmann, T. (1979). *Psychologie as Problem*. Stuttgart, Germany: Klett.

Horberg, E. J., Oveis, C., Keltner, D., & Cohen, A. B. (2009). Disgust and the moralization of purity. *Journal of Personality and Social Psychology, 97*(6), 963.

Jarvis, P. (2012). *The sociology of adult and continuing education*. New York, NY: Routledge.

Kohlberg, L. (1969). Stage and sequence: The cognitive-developmental approach to socialization. In D. A. Goslin (Ed.), *Handbook of socialization theory and research* (pp. 347–480). Chicago, IL: Rand McNally.

Linortner, L., & Patry, J.-L. (in press). VaKE: Training Manual for MIT. VaKE within SDT and implementation plan. In R. DeGroote (Ed.), *Proteach*. Tel Aviv, Israel: Mofet.

Maslow, A. H. (1943). A theory of human motivation. *Psychological Review, 50*, 370–396. Retrieved April 20, 2021, from http://psychclassics.yorku.ca/Maslow/motivation.htm

Mezirow, J. (1985). A critical theory of self-directed learning. *New Directions for Adult and Continuing Education, 25*, 17–30.

Mezirow, J. (1989). Transformation theory and social action: A response to Collard and Law. *Adult Education Quarterly, 39*, 169–175.

Mezirow, J. (1994). Understanding transformation theory. *Adult Education Quarterly, 44*, 222–232.

Mezirow, J. (1997). Transformative learning: Theory to practice. *New Directions for Adult and Continuing Education, 74*, 5–12.

Mezirow, J. (1998). On critical reflection. *Adult Education Quarterly, 48*, 185–198.
Mezirow, J. (2000). *Learning as transformation: Critical perspectives on a theory in progress. The Jossey-Bass Higher and Adult Education Series.* San Francisco, CA: Jossey-Bass Publishers.
Mezirow, J. (2003). Transformative learning as discourse. *Journal of Transformative Education, 1*(1), 58–63.
Mezirow, J. et al. (2010). *Learning as transformation: Critical perspectives on a theory in progress.* San Francisco, CA: Jossey-Bass, Wiley.
Nahrstedt, W., Brinkmann, D., Theile, H., & Röcken, G. (Eds.). (2002). *Lernort Erlebniswelt. Neue Formen informeller Bildung in der Wissensgesellschaft. Endbericht des Forschungsprojektes: Erlebnisorientierte Lernorte der Wissensgesellschaft Gefördert vom Bundesministerium für Bildung und Forschung (bmb+f).* Bielefeld, Germany: Institut für Freizeitwissenschaft und Kulturarbeit.
OECD Social Indicators. (2009). *Society at a glance. Special focus: Measuring leisure in OECD countries.* OECD. Retrieved April 20, 2021, from www.oecd.org/berlin/42675407.pdf
Patry, J.-L. (2014). Die Viabilität und der Viabilitäts-Check von Antworten. In C. Giordano & J.-L. Patry (Eds.), *Fragen! Antworten? Interdisziplinäre Perspektiven. Freiburger Sozialanthropologische Studien* (pp. 11–35). Vienna, Austria: Lit.
Patry, J.-L. (2018). Theorie-Praxis-Transfer: Hindernisse und Probleme. In A. Gastager & J.-L. Patry (Eds.), *Pädagogischer Takt: Analysen zu Theorie und Praxis* (Studienreihe der Pädagogischen Hochschule Steiermark, Band 11) (pp. 17–42). Graz, Austria: Leykam.
Pnevmatikos, D., & Christodoulou, P. (2018). Promoting conceptual change through Values *and* Knowledge Education (V*a*KE). In A. Weinberger, H. Biedermann, J.-L. Patry, & S. Weyringer (Eds.), *Professionals' ethos and education for responsibility* (pp. 63–74). Leiden, The Netherlands: Brill/Sense.
Pnevmatikos, D., Christodoulou, P., & Georgiadou, T. (2019). Promoting critical thinking in higher education through Values *and* Knowledge Education (V*a*KE) method. *Studies in Higher Education, 44*, 892–901.
Pnevmatikos, D., Patry, J.-L., Weinberger, A., Linortner, L., Weyringer, S., Maron, R., & Gordon-Shaag, A. (2016). Combining values and knowledge education for lifelong transformative learning. In E. Panitsides & J. Talbot (Eds.), *Lifelong learning. Concepts, benefits, and challenges* (pp. 109–134). New York, NY: Nova Science.
Rozin, P., Lowery, L., Imada, S., & Haidt, J. (1999). The CAD triad hypothesis: A mapping between three moral emotions (contempt, anger, disgust) and three moral codes (community, autonomy, divinity). *Journal of Personality and Social Psychology, 76*(4), 574.
Shweder, R. A., Much, N. C., Mahapatra, M., & Park, L. (1997). The "big three" of morality (autonomy, community, divinity) and the "big three" explanations of suffering. *Morality and Health, 119*, 119–169.

Thoidis, I., & Pnevmatikos, D. (2014). Non-formal education in free time: Leisure or work orientated activity? *International Journal of Lifelong Education, 33*(5), 657–673.

Vasquez, K., Keltner, D., Ebenbach, D. H., & Banaszynski, T. L. (2001). Cultural variation and similarity in moral rhetorics: Voices from the Philippines and the United States. *Journal of Cross-Cultural Psychology, 32*, 93–120.

Weinberger, A. (2006). *Kombination von Werterziehung und Wissenserwerb. Evaluation des konstruktivistischen Unterrichtsmodells VaKE (Values and Knowledge Education) in der Sekundarstufe I*. Hamburg, Germany: Kovac.

Weinberger, A., Patry, J.-L., & Weyringer, S. (2016). Improving professional practice through practice-based research: VaKE (Values *and* Knowledge Education) in university-based teacher education. *Vocations and Learning, 9*, 63–84. Retrieved April 20, 2021, from http://link.springer.com/article/10.1007/s12186-015-9141-4?email.event.1.SEM.ArticleAuthorContributingOnlineFirst

Weyringer, S., Patry, J.-L., Diekmann, N., Linortner, L., & Furlan, N. (in press). VaKE as education for democratic citizenship for female refugees. In InZentIM (Eds.), *Migration, social transformation, and education for democratic citizenship – Addressing challenges of extremism and radicalization*.

PART 4

VaKE for Specific Topics

∴

CHAPTER 19

Improving Language Skills in EFL Classes through VaKE

Mariam Kilanava

1   Introduction

Generally, teaching methods in TEFL (Teaching English as a Foreign Language) are dictated by the learners themselves and their common requirements. Currently, the most popular reason for learning a new foreign language is to communicate with native/non-native speakers who do not share the same first language. Accordingly, the teaching approaches have been modified compared to the previous, grammar-translation oriented concepts. In the present chapter, it is argued that VaKE is an appropriate method in this regard.

While a decade ago it was popular to use a grammar-translation method, today it is successfully replaced with the direct or communicative teaching methods. The grammar-translation method tended to teach the material with translation and gave priority to grammar competences as the basis of language proficiency (Richards, 2006), and the target language did not use to be dominant during the teaching process. Accordingly, the frequency of a code-mixing (Crystal, 2008) used to occur during a teaching and learning process.

Meanwhile, the communicative language teaching methods are exclusively oriented on improving the learners' communicative competences in a target language. However, improving these competences is not only dependent on classroom activities as it is best to learn a language when using, rather through studying how language works and practicing rules (Richards, 2006). Practicing a target language speaking competence is complicated if some elements of motivation are not found in it. EFL students mostly struggle with the productive skills, as they accumulate the knowledge and do not show it off in productive competences; this can be linked to some factors of lack of intrinsic or extrinsic motivation, that somehow reflect on success or failure in learning activities (Deci & Ryan, 2001). According to Uznadze's theory of attitude (2018), an attitude is crucial as it appears to be a milestone in a successful learning process. Motivation and attitude are mostly associated with the topics to be worked on in the TEFL sphere, since they encourage learners be more or less engaged in classroom activities; accordingly, VaKE with its unique characteristics can be a good method to implement as it covers some tangible thought-provoking moments with the form of dilemma stories and open-ended questions expanding and shaping in arguments which appear to be challenging and engaging moments for the EFL learners. Sometimes, the learners are unable to realize that they already possess some knowledge and that they can easily build on using it (Reza, 2016). The teachers as facilitators are in the position to motivate and help the learners to express themselves and to reveal the knowledge in the target language with the help of properly chosen teaching methods.

Generally, an EFL classwork is intended to be full of interactive learning activities; their implementation depends on the teaching methods and the students' willingness to be actively involved in the working process. However, activities that are only class-based cannot provide a successful teaching process in the target language. Although the methodologists focus on the kinds of classroom activities that could be used to implement group work, task work, and information-gap activities (Richards, 2006), active learning still remains complex.

VaKE differs from other teaching methods with its specific features integrating the values and knowledge education with the dilemma-based learning style (Patry et al., 2007). VaKE also provides the learners with the aspects of reflecting on values and their implementation diversity in specific situations, critical thinking, the possibilities to work in groups as well as autonomously, the questions to discuss and the possibility to get the knowledge relevant to the topic (Kilanava, 2019).

2   Four Basic EFL Skills

The wide variety of teaching methods sometimes leads to some confusion even among EFL teachers, and it is not evident whether the chosen one can successfully cope with the target points set in advance or not (Richards & Rodgers, 2001). Not all the methods cover more than two skills to be improved at the same time in the TEFL field; though, the teaching methods used in EFL classes, generally, should be intended to combine linguistic and intercultural aspects.

The four basic language skills listening, reading, speaking, and writing, in combination with the vocabulary and grammar components are successfully taught when they are well balanced and combined. Accordingly, the integrating styles are more fruitful in EFL classes than those oriented only on one specific skill (Oxford, 2001).

The two passive language skills, reading and listening, create a fundament for the successful production of speaking and writing, the productive ones.

Listening – EFL learners mostly listen to the model, mocked dialogues/monologues from Podcasts or CDs of the textbook material, which are of little interest for the learners, whereas listening to the peers speaking in a target language can be more engaging. However, some risks arise in this case: The learners are listening to the peers, who are not proficient enough in EFL to be duplicated or to learn from. If the listening topic is motivating for the learners, they listen to it not just because they are required to do so or for answering the questions, but they try to decode the meaning and grab the information from the narrative they are listening to.

Reading – Generally, reading is considered to be the process of decoding the text written by an author. Reading in the target language can be seen as the source not only for getting new information but for remembering the new lexis and ready-made sentence structures too, which helps learners to acquire the foreign language more naturally and with interest, particularly when they have focused questions.

Speaking – Using the speaking activities in EFL classes can be seen as the primary source for revealing all the knowledge acquired previously by the learners. As Hymes (1972) mentions in the theory of communicative competences, the grammar aspects, integrated with the psycholinguistic and sociolinguistic ones, make up successful communication. Hence the combination of these aspects brings a desirable result in teaching speaking skills in EFL.

Writing – as the form of self-expressing is the process of shaping the thoughts and arguments into tangible forms. The process of writing covers the moments of exposing the information in a written form and a means for improving the self-evaluation and self-reflection skills among the learners with writing portfolios (Wolf & Dietz, 1998) or reflective notes. The aspects of teaching writing skills are considered to be the most complex in TEFL, since for writing activities in the target language, it is essential to have some background skills of writing at least in the mother tongue.

The VaKE experience in using foreign/native language is discussed by Patry, Weyringer, and Weinberger (2010) where the main accents are on speaking competences and their influence on cognitive, social, emotional, and moral aspects of the VaKE process. A successful combination of teaching language skills is realistic within VaKE steps and activities, which are presented below.

3 VaKE and EFL Skills

It is assumed that VaKE complies with some teaching peculiarities of foreign language teaching. VaKE with its steps can be considered as an integrative teaching approach since it is flexible for teaching the four basic language skills together with the moral connected and dilemma-based aspects.

As already mentioned above, the four basic language skills of listening, speaking, reading, and writing are taught with different methods in the TEFL sphere and not always practiced simultaneously during classroom activities. Methods which could unite important elements of these skills under one umbrella are rare. VaKE as one of them can be fit in EFL class activities with its steps to improve the four skills under just one roof. Each VaKE step can be devoted to improving at least one of the four skills as they consist of elements of reading, writing, listening, and speaking.

According to Weyringer Patry and Weinberger (2012), a prototypical VaKE unit consists of 11 or 16 steps, out of which the vast majority covers aspects of improving the language skills as follows:

0. Preparation: Clarification; the teacher explains the VaKE details, and the learners *listen* to it.
1. Presentation of the dilemma: Brainstorming on knowledge and values (the teacher introduces the dilemma story; first exchange of opinion between the students); the learners *listen* to the teacher speaking in a target language and *speak* in the target language.
2. Reflection/Proflection: The learners think about their first associations with the dilemma; they think in the native and target languages and *write* their associations.
3. First decision: The class is divided into two groups (pros and cons); the learners start creating (*writing*) the portfolios if the teacher asks for it.
4. First dilemma discussion: The learners discuss the dilemma; they try to support their arguments in a target language (*speaking* and *listening*) and fill in the portfolios with the necessary information (*writing*).
5. Reflection/proflection: The learners revise their arguments and think of the questions that arose; they discuss (*speaking* and *listening*) within their groups and *write* down all the possible questions for the further discussion.
6. Exchange about experiences and need for information: The learners sort out strong and weak arguments and ask questions; they discuss in a target language (*speaking* and *listening*) and start to *read* the relevant information for further discussion.
7. Looking for information: The learners search for the required information; they *read* the relevant information in a target language and *write down* all the required information.
8. Exchange of information: The learners make presentations in a target language, discuss the information they obtained, and plan the future steps; they *speak* and *listen* in the target language.

9. Synthesis of information: The learners make presentations in a target language (*speaking*).
10. Reflection/proflection: The learners rethink about their opinions; they *write* down the plans for the future discussion in the native or target language.
11. Second decision: The learners stay in or change the groups; they *write* notes in their portfolios.
12. Second dilemma discussion: The learners discuss the dilemma; they try to support their arguments in a target language (*speaking* and *listening*).
13. Repetition of steps 5 to 12.
14. Reflection/proflection: The learners rethink about their opinions in their native or a target language, *write* down the future steps.
15. General synthesis: The learners sum up the VaKE process; they present in a target language (*speak*ing) and *write* some final notes.
16. Generalization and transfer: Joint work on a new topic; the learners and the teacher discuss a similar topic (*speaking, listening*).

This shows VaKE's flexibility to combine and connect the four basic skills with one chain, though speaking as a communicative skill is in a vast majority in this case. The VaKE steps can be seen as the provoking factors for the students to confront the opponents with new arguments and use the target language in real communicative situations.

According to the list, EFL learners may face some informational gaps within VaKE when they do not have sufficient knowledge and information to argue on a high level and start looking for further information (Weyringer et al., 2012). The process of searching for the applicable information requires the reading skills: scanning or skimming on the target language as this is the language of the sources, and therefore the reading skills are also covered. The learners have to note the arguments for further discussion, which is a meaningful way to develop skills in writing too. Although the experience of writing a portfolio in VaKE is not usual, it can be seen as the fruitful addition in the TEFL context.

4   One Example of a Case Study

The case study (Kilanava, 2019) carried out in 2019 at the European University in Tbilisi, was oriented on exploring the beneficial factors of implementing VaKE in the intermediate and upper-intermediate level EFL groups. The study was carried out by the EFL lecturer, who introduced VaKE to the students and implemented the method in the teaching process. The lecturer provided the students with the relevant reading material and facilitated them throughout the study process. The data were collected through non-participant observation as well as with open-question interviews and questionnaires. The dilemma topics were selected both by the teacher and the students. The purpose of the study was to investigate the possibilities for integrating VaKE in an EFL class. After summing up the students' answers and the teacher observations the study results could illustrate the benefits of VaKE in EFL context.

5   VaKE and Distance TEFL

Due to the Corona pandemic, face to face teaching had to be transformed into virtual form, which challenged some teaching methods requiring the learners' physical attendance in classes. It is obvious that the current teaching methods have to adapt to a new educational reality and adjust to the situation. Among other teaching methods, VaKE had to meet the necessity to adapt to a new reality and be transformed into a virtual version of functioning.

The process of VaKE virtualization is not trivial, but not a difficult one as the modern online platforms widely offer virtual rooms to work in for individual, peer, or group work (such as zoom.us breakout rooms). VaKE steps can be modified in their virtual version and the main idea of working on dilemmas in EFL context is thought-provoking for the further theoretical and practical extension.

6   Conclusion

VaKE is suitable for EFL context as it successfully unites the aspects of teaching the four basic language skills. VaKE is generally seen as the mean for moral judgement and dilemma discussion in a class, though according to its characteristics and depended on the list, it is adjustable for the TEFL sphere too. VaKE's flexibility of being able to be implemented in different teaching fields and even in distance learning conditions makes it distinguished.

References

Crystal, D. (1995). *English as a global language* (2nd ed.). Cambridge, UK: Cambridge University Press.
Deci, E. L., & Ryan, R. M. (2001). Extrinsic rewards and intrinsic motivation in education. *Review of Educational Research Sprint,* 71(1), 1–27.

Hymes, D. H. (1972). On communicative competence. In J. B. Pride & J. Holmes (Eds.), *Sociolinguistics. Selected readings* (pp. 169–193). Harmondsworth, UK: Penguin.

Kilanava, M. (2019, May 3–4). Teaching speaking skills with real-life aspects in EFL classes. The 9th International research conference on education, language, and literature. In *Proceedings book* (pp. 260–270). Tbilisi, Georgia.

Oxford, R. (2001). *Integrated skills in the ESL/EFL classroom*. Retrieved June 15, 2020, from https://files.eric.ed.gov/fulltext/ED456670.pdf

Patry, J.-L., Weyringer, S., & Weinberger, A. (2007). Combining values and knowledge education. In D. N. Aspin & J. D. Chapman (Eds.), *Values education and lifelong learning* (pp. 160–179). Dordrecht, The Netherlands: Springer.

Patry, J.-L., Weyringer, S., & Weinberger, A. (2010). Values *and* Knowledge Education (V*a*KE) in European summer camps for gifted students: Native versus non-native speakers. In C. Klaassen & N. Maslovaty (Eds.), *Moral courage and the normative professionalism of teachers* (pp. 133–145). Rotterdam, The Netherlands: Sense.

Raza, M. (2016). *Teaching listening to EFL students* (Version 2). Figshare. https://doi.org/10.6084/m9.figshare.11640267.v2

Richards, J. (2006). *Communicative language teaching today*. Cambridge, UK: Cambridge University Press.

Richards, J., & Rodgers. T. (2001). *Approaches and methods in language teaching* (2nd ed.). Cambridge, UK: Cambridge University Press.

Uznadze, D. (2018). *The psychology of attitude* [Gantskobis teoria]. Tbilisi, Georgia: Sakartvelos Matsne.

Weyringer, S., Patry, J.-L., & Weinberger, A. (2012). Values and knowledge education. Experiences with teacher trainings. In D. Alt & R. Reingold (Eds.), *Changes in teachers' moral role. From passive observers to moral and democratic leaders* (pp. 165–179). Rotterdam, The Netherlands: Sense. Retrieved June 15, 2020, from https://brill.com/view/book/edcoll/9789460918377/BP000015.xml

Wolf, K., & Dietz, M. (1998). Teaching portfolios: Purposes and possibilities. *Teacher Education Quarterly, 25*(1), 9–22.

CHAPTER 20

V*a*KE in Teaching the Hearing-Impaired

Lydia Linortner

1   Introduction

V*a*KE is very much based on communication, with usually most of it being oral. Hence, to practice V*a*KE with hearing-impaired students, specific adaptations need to be made, on one hand to ascertain communication, on the other to counteract some major life-long problems of this minority, such as opinion enforcement. Since current principles of education of the deaf focus on character building, V*a*KE offers a conjunction of these overlapping goals.

The following research questions will be discussed in this chapter: Can V*a*KE be used in the education of hearing-impaired children? Is the increase of knowledge higher or the same as in traditional education forms? What adaptations of V*a*KE are necessary for teaching hard of hearing children?

2   Theory

The hearing-impaired and deaf people are a minority (one of 1000 Austrian residents have a hearing-impairment). They communicate with sign language, which has been officially recognised in the Austrian constitution as a language in its own right as of September 1, 2005 (Austrian sign language, Krausenecker, 2006); hence, sign language is considered as a national language. It includes separate vocalized dialects such as in Vienna and Tyrol. In contrast to spoken language using oral communication, sign language uses hand and body gestures as the means of communication; facial expression, gaze, the upper body and especially the form of the mouth, the hand shape, its relative position, and movement as well as hand position produce a limited linguistic code. Sign language has its own grammar and a complex structure that can be analysed (Braem Boyes, 1995, p. 35).

Two of the main components of V*a*KE – the constructivist theory of cognition development following Piaget (1985) and the values education following Blatt and Kohlberg (1975) – are based on communication and hence jeopardized by the restricted communication process of deaf people (e.g., Hampf & Szagan, 2000) in a culture that is dominated and controlled by hearing people. Moreover, given the usual lack of offered information in the hearing-impaired culture, specific information providing techniques need to be established to satisfy the requirement for new knowledge in VaKE. The deaf children scientist Jann warmly recommends the use of interactional-communicative teaching techniques in practice (Jann, 1979, p. 83f); this is another huge advantage of VaKE in contrast to other teaching techniques. It is of great importance to enable independent access to information and media to hearing-impaired students and to have them attain the ability for critical reading in the sense of interactional text comprehension (cf. Jussen, 1987, p. 212f).

The typical faults of the communication processes between hearing and hearing-impaired youth people have been analysed in studies in American and Anglo-Saxon areas (cf. Galic, 2006, p. 245 ff). These show:
– the hearing people practice dominance and control of the interaction and a behaviour-controlling, patronizing and overprotective interaction style;
– there are disparities with respect to the relationship and content level;
– the language interaction style is limited to simplified and short utterances;
– the interaction style is situationally based and causes limited opportunities to access information and experiences conveyed by language.

An interview by the author with faculty members of the school in which the investigation (see below) took place, showed the same results as the research by Hampf and Szagun (2000):
– The teachers complained about the very striking experience of students asking the teachers to provide them with values. The hearing-impaired students are used to getting any ready-made information.
– They are very surprised to be asked about their own opinion followed by "to be heard", which seems to be breath taking to them.
– Due to that, learning basic knowledge, such as writing and reading properly, more time is needed than with hearing students, opinion formation is mostly forgotten.

VaKE is an appropriate method to work with hearing-impaired students: As previous research results show, VaKE is highly applicable in very heterogeneous classrooms (Weinberger, 2006). Speakers who are non-native in the language spoken in the VaKE process have more interest in social/affective contexts (Patry et al., 2010), but there are no differences in morality or critical thinking due to language. Furthermore, while using basic knowledge, participants in VaKE focus on the formation of opinions. And finally, the movement away from polarization between hearing and hearing-impaired participants can be established through the use of dilemma stories because there is no right or wrong opinion or decision, only more or less appropriate or justified arguments, and it plays no role in who is uttering them.

3 Hypotheses

In the study (see Linortner, 2014, for details), the research questions were: Do deaf/hearing–impaired children benefit from the characteristics of a V*a*KE lesson, which foster development on multiple levels? Is the knowledge requirement in a V*a*KE-process with deaf/hearing-impaired children equal or higher than in traditional school lessons?

The corresponding hypotheses were: (1) The knowledge acquisition of students taught using V*a*KE is equal or even higher than when taught with traditional instruction. (2) The knowledge acquisition of hearing-impaired children through V*a*KE lessons that are adapted to their needs is as high as for hearing children. (3) The knowledge acquisition of hearing-impaired students through V*a*KE lessons that are adapted to their needs is equal or even higher than that of the hearing-impaired students in traditional school lessons.

While the first hypothesis is independent of whether the students are hearing-impaired or not and corresponds to the hypothesis tested in many previous studies (e.g., Weinberger, 2006), the latter two address specifically the hearing-impaired and refer to whether V*a*KE is appropriate for them.

4 Method

The knowledge was assessed with WALK (see Chapter 31 in this handbook), an assessment tool in which students are confronted with pictures and required to ask questions; this has the advantage for hearing-impaired students that no oral language is required. The coding plan followed the rules of Zlöbl's (2008) Environmental WALK Test (EWT; see also Patry, Zlöbl, & Felber, 2009). By using the cross-over-design (see Chapter 32 in the handbook), the teaching methods and the respective groups of participants are compared, with a distinction of the hearing and the hearing-impaired students.

Two elementary school classes participated; the group of hearing-impaired students (N = 18) consisted of wearers of CI (Cochlea-Amplifier-Implanted) and APD (Auditory Processing Disorder) as well as hearing-impaired, hard of hearing, and deaf students, the other group consisted of hearing students (N = 12). They were randomly split into the two experimental groups with equal numbers through matching with respect to three variables: male and female; the degree of the hearing disorder; and age (third vs. fourth grade).

The V*a*KE process was adapted to the needs of the hearing-impaired students as follows: The adapted V*a*KE was dominated by visual support in several stages, like in the beginning of the process by showing the dilemma story within a self-created comic. The students' presentation of their findings as well as the synthesis was partly done visually. The more explicit structure of VaKE was seen constantly on a board in the classroom so everybody could see at which steps the process was and what task would come next. The use of a bilingual language – spoken, accompanied by sign language, that all participants were requested to use – made all "spoken" information accessible to everyone. A specific questionnaire for the information research that was improved during the process gave a framework to students who needed a bit more guidance. Finally, a role-play (see Chapter 5 in this handbook) was chosen to allow the students to change their perspective in order to open up their spectrum of values.

According to the cross-over design, each group received both treatments in succession, once with VaKE, once in the traditional way. Two topics were addressed: energy and food. These were aligned with the curriculum and yielded similar interest for the students.

5   Results

The results confirm the assumption that VaKE teaching can be adapted to the particular needs of specific groups of people. Furthermore, equivalent knowledge gains for groups of people with different characteristics have been found.

In the comparison of traditional teaching methods with VaKE, knowledge gains have been confirmed as equal: The hypothesis 1 concerning a general increase in knowledge could be confirmed: When hearing and hearing-impaired students are instructed according to the VaKE concept, the increase in knowledge is the same as with traditional instruction.

Hypothesis 2 concerning hearing and hearing-impaired children in VaKE lessons can be accepted: It was shown that for VaKE lessons, the increase of knowledge was equal for both hearing and non-hearing students.

The hypothesis 3 comparing hearing-impaired students can also be accepted: The knowledge increase for VaKE was higher than the increase using traditional school instruction in one group, while in the other both groups had the same increase.

6   Discussion

VaKE instruction can be well adapted to meet the needs of deaf and hearing-impaired children. Education for the hearing-impaired calls for exactly those character-building components addressed by VaKE (cf. Kerschbausteiner,

2010). According to Paul and Quigley (1993), students taking part in bilingual instruction show considerably better school performance than the national norm. The present analysis based on VaKE, confirms this theory. According to Paul (1991), it is recommended that teachers make use of role models as examples of how to infer conclusions, find answers to questions, and when to use other strategies with the purpose of helping students learn how to apply what they know in areas they have no knowledge of. Based on the positive results of this analysis, proposals that correspond to VaKE's educational goals can be strongly recommended.

The adaptation of VaKE for deaf, hearing-impaired and hearing students included the following elements: visual support in several stages; more explicit structure of the VaKE process; visible for everyone, the current step of VaKE was shown the whole time of durance on the board, moreover work sheets precisely described the actual task; bilingual language (spoken accompanied by sign language); assignment support; a specific questionnaire especially for the information research that was improved during the process; support by a wireless microphone technology; and finally, a role-play. In further VaKE classes, it is recommended to have smaller groups for more individual activation, even clearer instructions, equality of the decision opportunities, even more explanations of the terms used, and more time in the steps of the knowledge acquisition.

References

Blatt, M. M., & Kohlberg, L. (1975). The effects of classroom moral discussion upon children's level of moral judgment. *Journal of Moral Education, 4*(2), 129–161.

Braem Boyes, P. (1995). *Einführung in die Gebärdensprache und ihre Erforschung. Internationale Arbeiten zur Gebärdensprache und Kommunikation Gehörloser* (3rd ed.). Hamburg, Germany: Signum.

Galic, B. (2006). "Was du nicht willst das man dir tu' ..." Gedanken zur Erziehung hörgeschädigter Kinder aus einer ethischen Perspektive. In M. Hintermaier (Ed.), *Ethik und Hörschädigung. Reflexion über das Gelingen von Leben unter erschwerten Bedingungen in unsicheren Zeiten* (pp. 399–425). Heidelberg, Germany: Median.

Hampf, T., & Szagun, G. (2000). Normal hörende Kinder und Kinder mit Cochlea-Implantat: Der Dialog zwischen Mutter und Kind im frühen Sprachalter. *Sprach-Stimme-Gehör, 24*, 164–168.

Jann, P. (1979). *Kommunikative Kompetenz für Gehörlose. Theoretische Begründungen eines inter – aktional – kommunikativen Sprachaufbaus*. Rheinstetten, Germany: Schindele.

Jussen, H. (1987). Möglichkeiten und Grenzen der gemeinsamen Unterrichtung behinderter und nichtbehinderter Kinder und Jugendlicher unter besonderer Berücksichtigung der Hörgeschädigten. *Sonderpädagogik, 17*(4), 158–169.

Kerschbaumsteiner, A. (2010). *anGEHÖRt. Kulturkonforme Soziale Arbeit mit Gehörlosen* [Unveröffentlichte Diplomarbeit]. Universität für sozialwissenschaftliche Berufe Linz.

Krausenecker, V. (2006). *Taubstumm bis gebärdensprachig. Die Österreichische Gebärdensprachgemeinschaft aus soziolinguistischer Perspektive*. Klagenfurt, Austria: Drava.

Linortner, L. (2014). *"Gehört sich das?" Adaption von VaKE für die Gehörlosenbildung* [Unpublished master's thesis]. University of Salzburg.

Patry, J.-L., Weyringer, S., & Weinberger, A. (2010). Values and Knowledge Education (VaKE) in European summer Camps for gifted students: Native versus non-native speakers. In C. Klaassen & N. Maslovaty, N. (Eds.), *Moral courage and the normative professionalism of teachers. Moral development and citizenship education* (pp. 133–148). Rotterdam, The Netherlands: Sense.

Patry, J.-L., Zlöbl, S., & Felber, M. (2009, March 21–25). *Der WALK-Test zur Erhebung des Umweltbewusstseins (Environmental WALK Test EWT): Konstruktion und erste Ergebnisse*. [Paper]. The DGfE Sektionstagung Empirische Bildungsforschung, Landau.

Paul, P. V., & Quigley, S. (1993). Theoretical and empirical perspectives. In P. V. Paul (Ed.), *American annals of the deaf, 138*(2), 72–75. Boston, MA: Allyn & Bacon.

Paul, V. P. (1991). Hörschädigung und schulische Leistung. In H. Jussen & H. Claußen (Eds.), *Chancen für Hörgeschädigte. Hilfen aus internationaler Perspektive* (pp. 125–131). München, Germany: Ernst Reinhard Verlag.

Piaget, J. (1985). *The equilibration of cognitive structures: The central problem of intellectual development*. Chicago, IL: University of Chicago Press.

Weinberger, A. (2006). *Kombination von Werterziehung und Wissenserwerb. Evaluation des konstruktivistischen Unterrichtsmodells VaKE (Values and Knowledge Education) in der Sekundarstufe 1*. Hamburg, Germany: Kovac.

Zlöbl, S. (2008). *Nationalparkunterricht in Osttirol – Eine Vergleichsstudie unter Anwendung des Umwelt-Walks zur Untersuchung der Wirksamkeit des vierjährigen Nationalparkprojekts auf das Umweltbewusstsein von Kindern der vierten Klasse Grundschule* [Unveröffentlichte Masterarbeit]. Paris Lodron Universität Salzburg.

CHAPTER 21

When Value and Moral Are Problematic Concepts

Using VaKE in an Intercultural Management Context

Bénédicte Legué

1 Introduction

The author implemented V*a*KE (11 steps) in 2018, at ESAIP, an engineering school located in Angers (West of France). The dilemma was about religion at work, more specifically, hiring or not a Sikh candidate wearing a turban in a French company.[1]

The first part of this chapter describes the implementation of the *Sikh dilemma story* and the reactions of French students. The second part puts the use of the concepts of values and moral (*morale* in French), into perspective through axiological sociology, according to a theoretical approach of values registers (Heinich, 2017a). However, the discussion about the terms value, moral and morality is a broad and complex discussion which this chapter cannot deal fully within the limited space.

2 Implementation of the *Sikh Dilemma Story*

In the specific context of the author's course in International Intercultural Management, the use of the *Sikh dilemma story* had three aims: to make the frameworks for applying secularism in France; to promote student awareness of their possible cultural bias when recruiting a person with visible religious signs; and to integrate the constraints of international recruitment. My observations concern 6 students, including 2 females, 20 to 43 years old, enrolled in a BA's degree in digital engineering at the engineering school. Although of religious obedience, this Higher Education School is labelled Private Establishment of General Interest according to a public education agreement with the State.

The short version of the *Sikh dilemma story*, which was included in a training course of three widely spaced one-day sessions, was carried out in three stages: (1) raising student awareness of religion at work, cultural bias and knowledge of the subjects (secularism and Sikhism); (2) a home essay about different information sources (political, Indian, history, etc.) in order to increase knowledge of Sikhism; (3) an oral presentation where the participants used knowledge-based arguments and values followed by a second pooling.

The implementation of the dilemma took place in a specific societal context. In 2010, French law (L. n°2010-1192[2]) had prohibited the complete concealment of the face in public. Then in 2017, the debate surrounding the wearing of visible religious signs, linked to the prohibition of any proselytizing by agents working in French institutions, was a lively one. The 2004 law (L. n° 2004-228) reinforced by the circular of 2011 (JORF n° 52) requires that all ostentatious religious signs be prohibited for adults or pupils engaged in any activity related to public secondary schools. The numerous reactions heated debates on *values* in French society. Regarding Higher Education's public service missions, it aims at preserving the general interest through the neutrality of the nation on religious, political, and philosophical convictions. The State enforces common teaching for all, irrespective of their beliefs. It is the corollary of the students' *freedom of conscience*. In V*a*KE (11 steps), the *Sikh dilemma story* thus triggered sensitive questions and represented the first challenge in a debated context (steps 1 and 2).

Regarding knowledge acquisition, each student was asked to adjust his or her position (steps 3 to 5). The small size of the group and the disparities in age and professional backgrounds enriched the knowledge and led to different recruitment perceptions. The implementation of secularism in France became more concrete. The discovery of Sikhism, little known to all, led the participants' focus on the historical development and the ensuing difficulties of workers wishing to retain visible signs of belonging to their religion (steps 6 and 7). While the Sikh turban has undeniable religious value, students discovered that its use was changing in space and time in different parts of the world.

The involvement of everyone in the individual and collective discussion strengthened the cohesion of the group. Through V*a*KE, the values of the dilemma were unbundled and debated (steps 8 and 10). Also, beyond the legal framework and acquired knowledge, the awakening of consciences on the anchors of "the Other" has given way to an applied humanity, taking into account the recurring setbacks in the protagonist's professional daily life. Between the problematic of French secularism and the complexities of globalization, V*a*KE's critical model gave the participants a perspective on their own position (where I speak from), while considering the *local/global* asymmetries of the strategies in management (step 11). In the course, larger topics about hypermodernity and *complex thinking*[3] were discussed. The dilemma focused on the management of companies, which in turn impacts the daily lives of workers (visible signs of religion, laws on secularism, geographical boundaries,

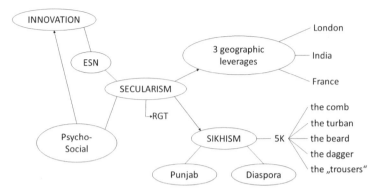

FIGURE 21.1 Sikh dilemma and retroactions in RH recruitment (© B. Legué, 2018, with kind permission of the student)

psychosocial realities, digital services (ESN), and innovation). Figure 21.1 summarizes this *complex thinking*, a sign of hypermodernity.

3 Value Registers: Another Understanding of Social Practices

A second challenge was about moral education as such. The aim of VaKE is to articulate moral development and the acquisition of knowledge. Nonetheless, during the introduction to the method, this explicit formulation provoked adverse non-verbal and verbal reactions from the French students, requiring a sensitive, reflexive approach about how to understand *morality* and *values*. VaKE proved to be very useful and structuring in dealing with sensitivity towards the use of religion. We could have stopped there on the discussion of values and used arguments "for" or "against". However, the students had also revealed an evident mistrust of the use of the terms *value* and *morality* as such.

Intercultural anthroposociology[4] states that any individual or collective discomfort calls into question the social practices. More than education in values, the latent questioning of students on what is *the Value of values* has become the main focus of research for me, the teacher. This student trouble, which I shared, forced me to reconsider methodically the notion of *Value* in intercultural teaching.

Based on the axiological sociology of Heinich (2017a), human relations are examined according to four functions of values: normalization (doing or not doing), socialization (sharing of values), distinction (tastes and lifestyle) and identity formation (individual or collective).

Heinich (2017a) analyses the stated value judgements, i.e., the relationship of a thing to its ideal. She postulates that it is desirable to go beyond what is conditioned, i.e., to go beyond the mere enunciation of what individuals already know. Benevolent exchanges alone will not be able to resolve value antagonisms. Also, to understand the dispute, the sociologist develops the notion of *values registers*. She does not hierarchize the concrete values but rather analyses how people attribute values. When antagonistic values emerge (e.g., economic domains vs. the ethical domains of managers, or private domains vs. political domains), one cannot stop at a simple observation of opposition. If we all have more or less the same repertoire of values: honesty, profit, pleasure, responsibility, etc. […], we do not mobilize them in the same way according to objects and contexts, said Heinich (2017b) to the journalist of the French newspaper *Libération*. Working with value registers adjusts as closely as possible to the feeling, which in relation to the contexts brings out the underlying values. Possible areas of agreement are revealed without any frontal opposition: It is no longer one *or* the other, but an inferior or superior register that specifies the values at stake. In that way, it avoids the risk of simplification in order to comply with prescribed values.

The didactic approach of V*a*KE provides the opportunity to study how people evaluate, refute, or approve: that precise moment when a person attributes value to what surrounds him or her by "the price, the judgment or the attachment" (Heinich, 2017a, p. 18; author's translation). V*a*KE also promotes Heinich's idea of avoiding the usual trap of neutrality mistaken for objectivity (pp. 344, 379). By ceasing to reduce the *value* to a single reason, a single and precise cause, one appreciates the rationality of its sociological anchoring in contexts (philosophical, religious, historical, economic, etc.), thus, to perceive its temporal and situational variations or transformations. In fact, in the course of their research, the V*a*KE students reconsidered the obligations of wearing religious signs according to various registers. While the participants found that some young Sikhs from Punjab currently reject wearing the turban, they noted that it is claimed by the 2nd or 3rd generation Sikhs living in England. Without over-interpreting, the registers of autonomy, identity, or even politics or others could be considered as objects of new questioning.

If, as Max Weber (2003) states, in *comprehensive sociology,* any prescriptive hierarchy of values is prohibited,[5] how under the sole term *Value* can one approach without antagonizing, the beliefs, reasons, and principles which mark out this study? In the example of our dilemma, rather than postulating *The Value*, we can update our understanding by discerning *registers* like religious belief (wearing a turban), economic reason (preservation of the market), and legal constraints (principle of neutrality of the State). This subtlety of analysis allows considering that by increasing the value of *laïcité* (laicism) in the French Constitution as a foundation (*principial value*), the term predicates *a right* – that of the citizen to any *private belief* – prohibiting anyone from imposing a change of religion. Also, in a democratic context, the notable difference of this method by the *register of values* permits not to seek to reify the compromise as a new value but, following the example of VaKE, to elaborate "the agreement of thoughts which will *ipso facto* determine that of common wills" (Jankélévitch, 1957, p. 184, author's translation).

4 Morality: An Updated French Antivalue

Today the explanation of *values* is based either on the transcendence of philosophical and theological traditions or *rational beliefs*;[6] however, nothing is set in stone. *Values* are constantly changing and are reconceptualized. They can even be transformed into an *antivalue*, i.e., a value position opposite to its original definition. For instance, in France the use of moral has changed from being a positive asset to a negative understanding where *morale* (in French) is seen as a controlling pattern (often mentioned as *moralité*): For French students, this feeling could roughly be interpreted as follows: What is this didactical tool that combines in the dilemma, secularism with the terms *value* and *morality*? Does it seek to inculcate a new moralizing code, a particular political vision? These are in total contradiction with the obligation of *neutrality* of teaching by an institution approved for its state mission.

In France, the age-old tradition of the obligations and prohibitions of the divine refers back to predominant, even traumatic models of education. The term *morality* was at the heart of the practices: For some, it recalls the historical stakes of the struggles of the State's institutional powers against the rights that the Church had arrogated to itself over the education system; for others, it evokes an authoritarian model of civic education until the 1960s. Since 1905, the State, more or less secular, has preserved a national education system in which free and compulsory education for all up to the age of 16 years, that is the pillar for the application of the principles of *neutrality* of teaching and *freedom of thought*. Nevertheless, it was only after 1968 that the transcendental *values* and the *moral* were generally ignored in order to avoid any model of prescription by teachers (L'Heureux, 2012, p. 10). Using the approach developed by Heinich (2017a) and her argument about the different *value registers*, it becomes possible to see and analyse the temporal evolution of the French terms *morale* and *moralité* and the values connotated with these terms.

Students reacted to the use of moral as they understood it as morality. As such, the underlying values questioned by the students were the value of *neutrality*, the *free choice of the individual* and his or her *private life*. Through VaKE, the students touched a foundational issue, namely, to deal with the registers of values. With this tool, it becomes more possible to highlight and unravel the interpretative subtleties of the emotional, contextual, and historical sources that determine resistance and to deepen the approach to values.

5   Conclusion

Sociologists know how demanding it is to attempt to explain ordinary life, the difficulty of which lies in actualizing the objective tensions between several frames of representation, which nevertheless seem to belong to a common culture, i.e., to collective axiological equipment. The representations we have deciphered here demonstrate two positions. The first, that only "the collective and social dimension of experience gives a form of rationality to the values and not the other way round" (Heinich, 2017a, pp. 299–300; author's translation). The second, that the term *Value* has neither neutrality nor universal interpretation, despite a trend in Western companies to use values in that way. And one must not forget that in a competitive globalized context, the use of *values* invokes the power struggles at stake.

The concept of *registers of values* makes it possible to set out the structures of *values* to mitigate open disagreements. Inserted into the courses, it neutralizes the risk of creating indefinitely interchangeable "recipes for all" where, from the point of view of the bearer, *value* remains a hyper-rational concept or an immutable postulate. In this management context, the discursive and didactic reflexive tool VaKE has made it possible to confront local societal logics with international managerial logics. Furthermore, by developing knowledge on *values* and the *Value of values*, it allows individuals and groups to make the "world after" evolve together.

Acknowledgment

I would like to thank Frédérique Brossard Børhaug for her very valuable support during the writing of this chapter.

Notes

1   The *Sikh dilemma* is a creation by Grazia Ghellini, Jimena Andino Dorato and Bénédicte Legué (2018) and is also addressed in Chapters 14 and 22 in this handbook.
2   The principle of secularism dates to the French Revolution of 1789. Public education has been secular since the Third Republic (1882). The principle of secularism was included in the preamble of the Constitution in 1958.

3 In 1982, Edgar Morin conceptualized *complex thinking*, the relationship between the whole and the parts that develop the ability to link: "It is not a question of finding a unitary principle of all knowledge, but of indicating the emergence of complex thinking that is neither reduced to science nor philosophy, but allows for intercommunication" (p. 24; author's translation).
4 Based on a socio-anthropological approach to the intercultural notion, the project of Intercultural Management at Paris Dauphine University is to take the human being and his or her feelings as a basis for work. "In seeking cross-study of practices, values, and behaviors, it studies the different ways that each finds to accommodate cultural differences" (Legué, 2012, p. 8; author's translation).
5 This sociology is a point of reference used in intercultural management. Patry (2006), although agreeing with Max Weber's concept of *non-hierarchical values*, goes further and rejects a total abstention from value decision especially in educational context.
6 In a social context of industrialization, Weber (1923) saw Western values as a specific type of rational belief, *rational ethos* [internalized value system], which would not appear anywhere else, and embodied in the organization of work.

References

Heinich, N. (2017a). *Des valeurs. Une approche sociologique.* Paris, France: Éditions Gallimard.

Heinich, N. (2017b). Les valeurs, un objet absolu très relatif. *Libération*, Retrieved June 20, 2020, from https://www.liberation.fr/debats/2017/03/08/nathalie-heinich-les-valeurs-un-objet-absolu-tres-relatif_1554294

Jankélévitch, V. (1957). *Le Je-ne-sais-quoi et le presque-rien.* Paris, France: Éditions Presses Universitaires de France.

L'Heureux, G. (2012). *Le problème de l'Éducation morale en France au XXe siècle dans l'enseignement élémentaire* [Doctorate thesis]. University of Rennes 2, France.

Legué, B. (2012). *Google: Un modèle de gestion interculturelle des ressources humaines?* [Master thesis, Master 2 de Management Interculturel]. Université PSL-Paris-Dauphine, France.

Morin, E. (1990). *Science avec conscience.* Paris, France: Éditions Point-Seuil.

Patry, J.-L. (2006). Die Werturteilsproblematik in der Erziehungswissenschaft. In G. Zecha (Ed.), *Werte in den Wissenschaften* (pp. 279–302). Tübingen, Germany: Mohr Siebeck.

Weber, M. (1921/1923). *La domination légale à direction administrative bureaucratique.* Retrieved June 15, 2020, from http://classiques.uqac.ca/classiques/Weber/domination_legale_direction/domination_legale_direction.pdf

Weber, M. (1959/2003). *Le savant et le politique* (C. Colliot-Thélène, Trans.). Paris, France: Éditions La Découverte, Poche.

CHAPTER 22

Bridging Teaching, Coaching and Interculturalism through V*a*KE

Jimena Andino Dorato

1   Introduction

My goal in this chapter is to share my experience in using V*a*KE in two French Undergraduate contexts where I combined interculturalism, coaching, and V*a*KE in the context of ISIT (*Intercultural School*) and ICP (*Institut Catholique de Paris*). This experience is the combination of individual and collective work. I aimed to teach intercultural communication in a way that students would be faced with a reflection process that allowed an experiential development of their capacity to better understand their own cultural perspectives and interact with people with different ones. My choice was then to teach through a coaching approach which implied encouraging students to find answers within themselves and develop strategies to challenge their actual thinking and feeling to make accountable changes for the future. V*a*KE proved to be a powerful pedagogical tool to attain this goal.

More specifically, following Milton Bennett's ideas, I aimed for students to acquire general and transferable intercultural competence, to embody and enact the ability to "discriminate cultural differences and to experience those differences in communication across cultures" (2013, p. 12). My goal was to make learning experiential. For that, I assumed the role of a professor-coach more than a lecturer. Coaching as a profession is a relatively new phenomenon in organizations and even newer in education. A professor-coach acts as a facilitator moving from a top-down approach "delivering knowledge to 'inexperienced' students", to a multifaceted teacher facilitating the emergence of what students already know or what they discover by themselves in the learning process. As Rosinski clearly states, coaches "assume [that] people have more potential than they are currently able to use [and] help clients to unleash this potential, just like good sports coaches enable athletes to access the champions within" (Rosinski, 2003, p. XVII). This need to move from a traditional role in teaching when using V*a*KE was already studied in the V*a*KE literature (Weyringer et al., 2012; see also Chapter 6 in this handbook).

A key concern for me as a professor-coach was increasing students' cultural self-awareness. Self-awareness was already outlined by Gallwey, one of the founders of modern coaching (1974). The notion of self-awareness in coaching is linked to diming the focus on the external world and recognizing and knowing what is present, the ability to understand inner strengths and weaknesses, beliefs and values and their impact. This approach to focusing on self-awareness is less common in French higher education as the teaching is carried out in a more traditional top-down approach for often large student groups.

At ISIT and ICP, the two institutions where I implemented VaKE, the heart of the programmes was to teach intercultural communication, and the study was aimed to promote a learning experience that itself was based on a different cultural approach of teaching: a professor-coach. The assumption was also that students experiencing a different pedagogical methodology and a different relationship with the professor would be part of the intercultural learning of the course. For my purpose, I combined this idea of self-awareness with Bennett's ideas of intercultural sensitivity, competence, and learning (2003, p. 12) and I used cultural awareness in the sense of the capacity to engage in learning one's own culture or patterns of behaviour, to then better communicate through cultures other than their own.

2   Combining VaKE with Cultural Values and Intercultural Awareness in Teaching Practice

The objective of my teaching thus was combining VaKE with cultural values and intercultural awareness at ISIT in the Lawyer-Linguist Program (three courses) and at ICP in the Language Department (five courses).

In the first context, students were enrolled in a double major in Law (at two of the most renowned Law Schools in Paris) and in the jurist-linguistics programme at ISIT where they studied Law notions in two second languages. My courses were on Intercultural Communication in Law (in English) and Legal News (in Spanish).

At ICP, advanced second language proficiency students from social disciplines (Law, Communication, History and Geography, Political Science or Theology) had the opportunity to choose different subjects of their interest in second languages. My courses were on intercultural communication (in English and in Spanish). In both contexts, the majority of the students were French native speakers who had been educated in the French education system. Also, the courses were new to the curricula, and, at its core, classes were meant for the students to learn Intercultural Communication in a second language (English or Spanish) either in general or with a special purpose: Law. Furthermore, all groups had students with an average age of 20 years. In total, during the 2017–2018 and 2018–2019 academic years, I used VaKE as a pedagogical tool with different dilemmas with three groups at ISIT and five groups at ICP. Despite some interesting challenges that emerged from these different experiences, I will focus in the chapter on commonalities experienced in applying VaKE, in general, through a coaching approach to teach intercultural communication and, in particular, using one dilemma: the *Sikh dilemma story*.

Using VaKE in my teaching was also part of a collective work as both the creation of dilemmas and the choices on best practices to implement VaKE in teaching intercultural communication were a team effort with two other teachers, Grazia Ghellini and Bénédicte Legué. We created a dilemma about religious attire in a French professional context, that we called the *Sikh dilemma*. This dilemma presents students with a pertinent theme in Social Science both in general and in Law and treated a subject recurrently portrayed in the news as to attract their interest. In preparing the dilemma to increase its credibility and impact, we interviewed a couple of Human Resources Directors who shared their biggest concerns on the place of religion in the workplace in France adjusting original versions of the dilemma to get the final one that we used. We also carried out meticulous research on *laïcité* in France and secularism in the Anglo-Saxon world in order to be up to date and have possible sources to offer students if blocked during their research work. In my case, this did not become necessary, and the different groups of students managed well their collection of information. As for the details of its implementation, each of us introduced the dilemma in different academic contexts, with different aims and foci (see Chapters 14 and 21 in this handbook).

More specifically, I used the *Sikh dilemma story* in two out of the total three courses at ISIT, both in English, with a total of 8 teaching hours and a small group (less than 15 students each). As for ICP, I used it in two out of the five courses, one in Spanish and one in English, both with a total of 24 teaching hours and in larger groups (around 20 students in Spanish and around 50 students in English). As mentioned before, intercultural communication was the key subject in both schools as well as teaching through a coaching approach.

I started the course about interculturalism at ICP with a more traditional top-down approach of sharing theories and discussing materials on some interculturalist authors (Hall & Reed Hall, 1990; Hofstede, 2010). At ISIT I also added some authors focusing on Law and Culture in particular (Eberhard, 2001).

I then conceived a portion of the teaching programme focused on accompanying students in developing cultural self-awareness with a coaching approach. For this part, I was guided by Bennett's constructive approach to develop intercultural competence (2013) where a key aim is to outline the importance of identifying not only a particular other culture but one's own cultural premises and biases. To structure my teaching programme, I followed what he calls a set of five "culture-general frames" (p. 61) that operate "as an observational strategy and as a learning-to-learn technique (…) since they call attention to the areas of difference that are most important to consider when first encountering another culture" (p. 62). My goal was to apply this framework to develop the students' cultural self-awareness in the sense of the ability to recognise the impact of their cultural group(s) in their beliefs, values, and behaviours. When preparing the teaching experiment, it was quite easy to find activities in my training toolbox for the first four frames developed by Bennett (2013). Here are some short examples of those activities.

The 1st frame, *language use*, is the one that identifies differences in the social contexting of language – and not the use of different languages (p. 62). Watching and discussions on short videos showing different verbal greeting or leave-taking rituals was a good first activity for students to gain trust in the group and start exploring how they personally related to this framework.

The 2nd frame, *nonverbal communication behaviour*, "represents phenomena by creating contexts that can be experienced directly" (p. 64–65). Playing in pairs on voice tone, body language or eye contact was a first step to move from the first more passive video debate activities to embody different nonverbal behaviour.

In the 3rd frame, *communication style*, different styles in the way we may communicate are described; it addresses continuums such as high-low context – considering how much meaning is derived from the surrounding situation or what is said explicitly – or linear-circular –considering that, if linear, the message marches from a to b and, if circular, a context, or story is necessary to deliver the message (pp. 69–73). This was an excellent opportunity to activate role-playing exercises where students were assigned a particular communication style and had to interact with others whose assigned style was unknown for them.

The 4th frame, *perceptual style*, "contrasts 'patterns of thinking'" where the basic continuum runs from concrete – description and physical metaphor – to abstract – theory and explanation (p. 73). It provided the opportunity to have a meta-discussion on what they had experienced in the former exercises for the first three frameworks where the approach for learning was more experiential or concrete; then they did a review on intercultural, revisiting the readings shared at the beginning of the course in a more top-down posture (abstract in the continuum).

The 5th frame is *cultural assumptions and values*. To develop Bennett's understanding of intercultural competence, it was important to introduce an activity that prevented or limited the risk of leading to value judgment and moral standards that could promote biases and stereotyped thinking. Thus, the key aim was to include pedagogical activities that truly offer perspective-taking and dialog. The challenge in my teaching was to focus on the verb "to value" and not base it on the static noun "value"[1] (p. 79). Searching for an activity that would activate students to reflect on "to value", I chose the VaKE methodology to address this 5th frame, e.g., how to relate to cultural values interculturally.

The different VaKE steps proved to be an excellent approach to be true to Bennett's idea on his 5th frame, cultural assumptions, and values. The different individual and group tasks had the benefit to put students into an action mood and avoid the risk of reifying cultural values, what might have been a risk only working on a list of values or examples coming from outside. By using the *Sikh dilemma story*, the idea was to put the students in the shoes of a Human Resources (HR) Director having to decide what candidate to choose paying attention to what they culturally valued.

3 Implementation of the VaKE Steps and Learning Experiences

VaKE was adapted, and 11 steps were used: (1) introduce the dilemma; (2) 1st vote; (3) 1st discussion; (4) looking for missing information (asking questions); (5) looking for evidence (possible answers to questions); (6) information exchange; (7) 2nd vote; (8) 2nd discussion; (9) synthesis of results; (10) general synthesis; (11) generalization.

After the first vote and working through steps 3 to 6, students were moved away from an exercise of ranking values and towards realizing their own role in creating them. This part of the exercise allowed them to perceive how the way they voted had been influenced by the cultural assumptions and values of the cultural group they were part of as young French students, and how to start approaching the cultural assumptions and values of others. This was an important first step in increasing student cultural self-awareness.

In order to make the students' experience more vivid and to further develop their reflection, I chose to suppress the option "I don't know" in the 2nd vote. Impersonating the role of a hiring HR Director, I challenged the students to make a decision and choose the candidate with all the gathered information. The goal was to make them more conscious of the consequences when making the decision. I dedicated little time to the second discussion (step 8) as this would have led to deepen how to better debate with others and it would have needed more focus in developing other competencies covered by Emotional Intelligence studies such as self-management, social awareness, and relationship management (Goleman et al., 2017). Instead, the focus should be primarily on self-awareness and anchoring learning. With this in mind, more time was assigned for synthesis of results (step 9) and to present conclusions by a creative presentation (step 10).

These creative presentations took the form of drawings created by the students, press conferences, role-playing and theatre plays. Students moved beyond speech and traditional PowerPoint presentations to experience their ideas; they abandoned a more abstract rational-logical approach (particularly dear to French culture) to reach an embodied approach as it became more tangible and experiential and they had to enact at least through role-playing their learning. Eventually, I used the last step of generalization (step 11) to anchor the students' individual cultural self-awareness and asked them for an individual report on what they had learnt about themselves from the exercises. Many of them shared how surprised they were to discover new ideas and assumptions, for instance that French *laïcité* as a foundational value for the French Republic and a specific mode of organizing the society could be perceived by strangers as intolerant. They also shared how hard it was to listen to other perspectives and be open and flexible to change, particularly during group discussions pointing out how focused on the individual candidate they were, not considering the firm's best interest and how hard it was to accept to debate on this with those who put the subject on the table.

4 Using Coaching in V*a*KE, a Useful Bridge in Teaching Practice

In the aftermath of implementing the dilemma, I realized that coaching ideas and skills were not only present when conceiving the teaching programme to develop the students' cultural self-awareness; rather, coaching also influenced the way I facilitated the implementation of V*a*KE. As facilitating seems to me a crucial part of the V*a*KE methodology, I argue that coaching competencies may be a useful guide in facilitating the learning activity. To build this guide in the implementation of the V*a*KE methodology, I use eight core coach competencies updated in 2019 by ICF (*International Coaching Association*), which is one of the largest international coaching associations, advocating the professionalization of the profession. Based on the eight competencies I suggest that the V*a*KE teacher should pay attention to the following competences, which also seem inherent in V*a*KE:

– *Competence #1. Demonstrate Ethical Practice:* When creating, choosing, and proposing the dilemma, believe in it! Do not use it to give a moral right answer!
– *Competence #2. Embody a Coaching Mindset:* Be open, curious, flexible, and centred towards the students, meet the students where they are in their

development process. Acknowledge that students are responsible for their own choices.
- *Competence #3. Establish and Maintain Agreements:* Do not rush into the dilemma, spend time in explaining the methodology and what is expected from the exercise.
- *Competence #4. Cultivate Trust and Safety:* Be sure to gain trust among the student group, possibly use a confidentiality agreement to freely discuss. It is important to acknowledge and respect the students' unique talents, insights, and work in the process.
- *Competence #5. Maintain Presence:* Be ready to have very different experiences using the same dilemma with different groups. It is important to be comfortable working in a space of not knowing and to create or allow space for silence, pause or reflection.
- *Competence #6. Listen Actively:* Engage the full group respecting their communication styles and personal behaviour preferences, for instance from introverts to extroverts.
- *Competence #7. Evoke Awareness*: Share your own observations without attachment to them and promote in students the creation of sustainable insights coming from their discoveries. Always leave enough time for the last steps of synthesis of results, general synthesis, and generalization. Not doing this is not an option as it may increase stereotypes and beliefs instead of transformation and learning.
- *Competence #8. Facilitate Growth*: Always leave enough time for step 11: application to other fields.

Using these skills helped me to put in practice some of the actions and attitudes that also are suggested by Weyringer et al. (2012) in another teaching context. For instance, do not express the teacher's own point of view and refrain from intervening (p. 169); this can be linked to competence #2. And even if intervening, always explain that it is a proposition and students are free to take it or not (pp. 170–171; see competences #4 and #5) Another important skill outlined by those authors is the acceptance of possible moments of silence (competence #5) and the adoption of ideas opposite to the teacher's where the lack of attachment to one's own ideas of competence #6 can be very useful. Several other chapters in the handbook discusses the teacher roles.

5   Conclusion

My expectations when conceiving the teaching programme were attained. Using Bennett's five frameworks to increase the students' cultural self-awareness provided a structure for the programme to include enough experiential activities to boost what they knew and anchor insights from the experience. V*a*KE was a powerful tool to address cultural assumptions and values as Bennett's 5th frame putting students in "verb" or action mode rather than a "noun" understood here as static or passive learning. In facilitating the activities, my coaching skills helped me move from a traditional teaching approach to one that allowed fostering student autonomy.

Acknowledgments

I thank Adelina Escamilla-Sánchez from ICP and Agata de Laforcade from ISIT for allowing me to experiment new pedagogical approaches and all their support. I thank the colleagues I worked with in my V*a*KE journey: Bénédicte Legué, Grazia Ghellini and François Brossard for all the discoveries and learning opportunities and in particular Frédérique Brossard Børhaug for her generous sharing, meticulous reading and rich exchanges.

Note

1   See also Chapter 21 in this handbook (Legué) for similar discussion about different meanings and uses of the concept of *value*.

References

Bennett, M. J. (2013). *Basic concepts of intercultural communication* (2nd ed.). New York, NY: Intercultural Press N. Brealey Publishing.

Eberhard, C. (2001). Towards an intercultural legal theory: The dialogical challenge. *Social & Legal Studies*, *10*, 171.

Gallwey, T. (1974). *The inner game books series*. Retrieved April 26, 2021, from https://theinnergame.com/inner-game-books/

Goleman, D., Boyatzis, R., Davidson, R. J., Druskat, V., & Kohlrieser, G. (2017). *Building blocks of emotional intelligence*. Florence, MA: More than Sound Key Step Media.

Hall, E. T., & Reed Hall, M. (1990). *Understanding cultural differences*. Boston, MA: Intercultural Press.

Hofstede, G., Hofstede, G. J., & Minkov, M. (2010). *Cultures and organizations* (3rd ed.). New York, NY: McGraw Hill Education.

International Coach Federation. (2019). *Core competencies. Updated model.* Retrieved April 26, 2021, from https://coachfederation.org/core-competencies

Rosinski, P. (2003). *Coaching across cultures.* London, UK: Nicholas Brealey Publishing.

Weyringer S., Patry, J.-L., & Weinberger, A. (2012). Values *and* Knowledge Education: Experiences with teacher trainings. In D. Alt & R. Reingold (Eds.), *Changes in teachers' moral role. From passive observers to moral and democratic leaders* (pp. 165–179). Rotterdam, The Netherlands: Sense.

CHAPTER 23

Creating Moral Dilemma Stories for Intercultural Education

Frédérique Brossard Børhaug and Helga Bjørke Harnes

1   Introduction and Aims of the Project

Norway is a multicultural society, and intercultural education (IE) is a national priority. In 2016, 15% of the pupils had a non-Norwegian ethnic background (Utdanningsdirektoratet, 2018); however, in 2018, only 5% of students in teacher education had immigrant background (SSB, 2019). Thus, although pre-service teacher education facilitates intercultural learning, the structural pattern of the students' cultural majority background may make intercultural teaching and learning difficult.

Through a self-study project, the authors have used VaKE-*dis* to shed critical light on their own intercultural teaching practices and learning outcomes in student groups with mainly majority cultural background, at NLA University College in Bergen, Norway.[1] Our aim was to renew our teaching by enhancing complex understanding and enabling our students' critical systemic examination of educational structures that often privilege majority interests (NOU, 2010).

In this chapter, we discuss the challenges we experienced in constructing and implementing moral dilemma stories in higher education that aimed at achieving our pedagogical intentions of complex and critical intercultural reflection.

Our project is a qualitative self-study, a methodology that empirically examines the researchers' own practices (Ham & Kane, 2004; LaBoskey, 2004). Our data includes our VaKE preparation forms, one individual interview with each teacher, two focus-group interviews with the teachers and two mentors, three sets of students' texts (n = 16, 18, and 13), and four observations of teaching. In all, our data provides a rich understanding of the process of using VaKE didactics in intercultural educational (IE) settings. Our project was approved by the Norwegian Centre for Research Data, all participants gave informed consent and confidentiality is secured (Brossard Børhaug & Harnes, 2018, 2020). In the analysis for this chapter, we focused particularly on the students' responses to, and our reflections on the dilemmas we created. We first go on to present key pedagogical aims before we present and discuss our two VaKE dilemma stories and the learning outcomes of the process. Towards the end, we discuss our experiences when using these dilemma stories in intercultural teaching.

2 Combining Pedagogical Aims in IE and VaKE

One central pedagogical aim in IE is complexity in the learning process. Intercultural education "requires retaining complexities, accepting multiple voices, openness and the questioning of fixed truths" (Lanas, 2014, p. 174). Complexity may prevent some of the pitfalls of education in a multicultural society, for instance racialisation of minority pupils (Brossard Børhaug, 2016) and cultural relativism (Ouellet, 2008), or to limit cultural issues to folklore, food, and national costumes (Gorski, 2008; Øzerk, 2008). Complex thinking, openness and questioning presumably fixed truths are also key aims in VaKE (Patry et al., 2007, p. 171; see also Chapter 30 in this handbook).

IE emphasises the importance of critically examining values and their basis for people's choices and attitudes. It grapples with partly contradicting values, for instance, acceptance for cultural diversity vs. shared collective belonging and social cohesion or equality vs. equity education (Brossard Børhaug, 2013; Ouellet, 2008, p. 4). In intercultural teaching, a critical awareness of and reflection on these inherent value contradictions and their consequences in educational structures and practices are thus essential (Brossard Børhaug & Weyringer, 2018). Otherwise, we are in danger of reinforcing social and political hierarchies rather than undermining them, despite good intentions (Gorski, 2008, p. 516).

To achieve this, we need dilemma stories that future pedagogues may encounter in diverse multicultural teaching settings (Baloche, 2014). According to VaKE, a dilemma should "be authentic and have a relationship to real-world environments" (Patry et al., 2007, p. 172; see also Chapter 4 in this handbook).

3 Our Two Dilemma Stories

Two dilemmas were used. The first dilemma was used with one student group in teacher education and was created to cover geography learning outcomes in the curriculum. It is inspired by an authentic British school project (Mohamud & Whitburn, 2014). We asked the students the question in italics:

> Emilie (…) teaches 18 year 7 pupils at a small, rural school. Most of them have lived their whole lives in the small town where the school is, four

have moved from other places in the country. One of them is Saida, born in Somalia and brought up in Bergen, Norway. She has been in the class for two years, does well at school and speaks Norwegian. Emilie is about to plan the next month's teaching in the social sciences and wants to cover the learning aims: the use of maps, to understand the interrelatedness of natural resources and ways of life, comparison between countries in Europe and countries on other continents, and migration.

She has an idea for a project that will fulfil many of the competence aims: What if she asks the pupils to compare Norway and Somalia?

The next day, Emilie mentions the project to Saida, and Saida spontaneously answers: "Do we have to?" Emilie replies, "Well, we don't have to, why?" "There is so much about war and piracy and starvation when they talk about Somalia in the media. I want the others to think I am from Norway".

Should Emilie go through with a project of comparison that emphasizes Saida's Somali background?

The second dilemma story was used with one student group in teacher education, and one in intercultural education. It was constructed to cover curricular learning aims related to language and IE, and is inspired by an authentic educational situation:

Kari Monsen is a teacher in a Norwegian school in Bergen. She is highly qualified and has a long experience of being a teacher in lower secondary school. Especially important for her is the principle of adapted education. Although the principle is difficult to realize in practice, she is a fervent supporter of the ideology that every pupil should get the education adapted to his/her needs, skills, abilities, and context. Many of the pupils have a minority background, and Kari likes to work with this kind of multicultural class! Still, she is very preoccupied with Ahmed's schooling. Ahmed is having a lot of trouble in Norwegian and in the other subjects of mathematics, history, and biology. Because Kari is the main teacher for the class A 5 which Ahmed is part of, she contacts the teachers of the three subjects to talk about Ahmed's academic progression. They all confirm that Ahmed is having a difficult time coping with the abstract concepts.

What can she do to help him? Some years ago, she attended a lecture about intercultural education. She remembers vaguely that the lecturer was arguing for mother-tongue teaching besides learning the Norwegian language. She knows Ahmed speaks Turkish at home.

Should Ahmed be given mother-tongue teaching for a while? Yes, no, I don't know.

4 Complexity, Critical Reflection, and Intercultural Dilemmas

To what extent did we manage to reach the pedagogical aims of enhancing complex and critical understanding in our student groups and to construct expedient moral dilemma stories in our intercultural learning settings?

4.1 Raising Awareness for Complex Thinking and Developing Critical Systemic Reflection

When it comes to complexity, our dilemmas were successful, as a great majority of our students appreciated the dilemmas as complex (Brossard Børhaug & Harnes, 2020) and we can see from their knowledge and values that many topics have been mentioned. At the same time, the complexity was not necessarily related to intercultural questions, rather it dealt with general aspects of education (adapted education, care, the pupil's interests, etc.). V*a*KE is an open teaching approach. We chose the topic and wording in the dilemma stories, but we could not decide how the students would approach and discuss the dilemmas. Thus, V*a*KE as a student-centred method became a challenge to us, aiming at reaching intercultural goals and at the same time encountering the students' rather monocultural worldviews.

More specifically, did our dilemmas enhance critical reflection towards a school system that still reproduces inequalities and lower school results for and within minority pupil groups (Bakken & Hyggen, 2018; Steinkellner, 2017)? We argue that intercultural teaching implies a critical systemic reflection towards majority privileges that deconstructs power distribution in multicultural schools (Brossard Børhaug & Harnes, 2020). The students' discussions on values revealed a worthwhile sense of care and respect for the individual in the school context, and the pupils' right to participation is judged as important, as the following quote reveals:

> A multicultural person enriches the classroom, but it is important to ask whether it is okay with that person and whether you can use the cultural knowledge of that pupil. Also, one has to consider whether it will have [negative] consequences for the pupil, socially in class.

Participation is fundamental indeed. However, we find that the students focused on the individual and how to make the situation better for 'the other' and thus, they did not need to reconsider their own place and participation opportunities in unequal educational structures. The following quote also shows an understanding that the problem is *not* the Norwegian school system, but how imagined students may react individually: "Not all students with a multicultural background are comfortable with all topics that come up in the

Norwegian school system". The beliefs underlying such quotes are problematic when it comes to promoting equity and critical, transformative school practices (Gorski & Dalton, 2019).

In addition, many values expressed in class were abstract and did not question the prevalent problematic understanding of equality as sameness (Gullestad, 2002). According to this understanding, minority members should assimilate into the society and not question dominant power structures embedded in Norwegian curricula, for instance limited opportunities for minorities to use their first language (Brossard Børhaug, 2013). Consequently, the learning outcomes were limited as the students did not sufficiently reflect on differences between formal and real equality in educational practices and the need for social reconstruction (Gorski, 2008). In sum, we experienced that our dilemmas did not sufficiently trigger critical, intercultural learning that could sustain transformative action (Gorski & Dalton, 2019), and we will go on to discuss our dilemmas in light of intercultural teaching.

4.2 *Making Moral Dilemmas Relevant for Intercultural Teaching*

Initially, we wanted to single out some characteristics of intercultural moral dilemmas, but during the research process, this proved difficult. Our position at the end of the project is that there is no definite difference between an intercultural and a general moral dilemma, and whether one perceives a dilemma to be intercultural or not has most of all to do with "the glasses one wears, and how one solves it [the dilemma]". However, we argue that there are aspects that are important to bear in mind when constructing dilemmas for relatively homogenous student groups.

The teacher needs to carefully consider the wording in the dilemma, keeping in mind the majority background of the students. If the dilemma is not explicitly about different cultures or groups, the opportunity of intercultural reflection might be lost:

> If the topic is not explicit, then it depends more on your view of the world in a way, your interpretation (…) if you want people for the first time to think about intercultural issues, maybe you have to be more explicit than you are later on.

There were examples that students interpreted the dilemma about Saida, which in our view explicitly invites students to intercultural discussions, *solely* as a general issue of class management, and not in the light of intercultural questions.

On the other hand, explicit focus on intercultural issues may also reinforce and/or create stereotyped or problem-focused thinking. After the V*a*KE session, one of the students wrote, "the multicultural classroom has even deeper and more difficult challenges then I was aware of". Thus, we do need explicit intercultural dilemmas but at the same time, we do not want to set 'a trap' so that the discussions enforce resistance or create stereotypes. We find that some students partly exotified 'the other' through their thoughts about what it is to be Norwegian and who belongs in a Norwegian classroom:

> What can be difficult in a multicultural classroom might be who feels Norwegian and who has close contact with their home culture.

> One might think that all are proud of their 'home country', since we are, that is not necessarily the case.

We therefore find that there are real risks in intercultural teaching using moral dilemmas: On the one hand, the participants tend to avoid intercultural questions altogether, and on the other, V*a*KE discussions might enhance stereotypical thinking.

5   Conclusion

We experienced that our V*a*KE dilemma stories were fruitful in many ways; they offered good discussions and started or continued an intercultural reflection in our higher educational context. However, they neither fully questioned prevalent Norwegian ideals nor achieved a challenging and powerful discussion of a critical systemic view on education. Although our students evaluated the V*a*KE process as a learning situation that provided rich knowledge and value reflection, it contained pitfalls for us teachers that need to be investigated further. One of them is the partly contradictory situation to lead an open-ended, student-centred learning-process towards a teacher-determined goal, here exemplified by the delicate path between the students' majority cultural opinions and the teachers' intercultural aims.

Another pitfall is the challenging process of creating good intercultural dilemma stories. The dilemmas must avoid both the possibility of leaving the intercultural perspective out completely and the danger of creating or reinforcing stereotypes and must encourage students to delve into the important but often messy work of critical, social reconstruction. We do not believe there exist blueprint solutions to solve these pitfalls, but that continuous reflection about teaching practices is crucial. This project has been an eye-opener for us, and we encourage teachers at different educational levels to initiate collaborative self-study projects in order to improve their intercultural teaching practices.

Note

1   Our research project has resulted in two former publications with different theoretical and empirical scope (Brossard Børhaug & Harnes, 2018, 2020). The Norwegian Directorate for Education and Training has contributed to the funding of this project.

References

Bakken, A., & Hyggen, C. (2018). *Store karakterforskjeller mellom elever med ulik innvandrerbakgrunn*. Retrieved May 20, 2020, from https://www.oslomet.no/forskning/forskningsnyheter/store-karakterforskjeller-elever-ulik-innvandrerbakgrunn

Baloche, L. (2014). Everybody has a story: Storytelling as a community building exploration of equity and access. *Intercultural Education, 25*(3), 206–215.

Brossard Børhaug, F. (2013). Conflicting anti-racist values in Norwegian and French civic education: To what extent can the curriculum discourses empower minority youth? In G. Gestur, D. J. Beach, & V. Vestel (Eds.), *Youth and marginalisation: Young people from immigrant families in Scandinavia* (pp. 105–131). London, UK: Tufnell Press.

Brossard Børhaug, F. (2016). How to challenge a culturalization of human existence? Promoting interculturalism and ethical thinking in education. *FLEKS – Scandinavian Journal of Intercultural Theory and Practice, 3*(1).

Brossard Børhaug, F., & Harnes, H. B. (2018). Verdirefleksjon i pedagogisk arbeid mot frykt i et samfunn preget av kulturelt og religiøst mangfold. In E. Schjetne & T.-A. Skrefsrud (Eds.), *Å være lærer i en mangfoldig skole: Kulturelt og religiøst mangfold, profesjonsverdier og verdigrunnlag* (pp. 158–173). Oslo, Norway: Gyldendal Akademisk.

Brossard Børhaug, F., & Harnes, H. B. (2020). Facilitating intercultural education in majority student groups in higher education. *Intercultural Education, 31*(3), 286–299.

Brossard Børhaug, F., & Weyringer, S. (2018). Developing critical and empathic capabilities in intercultural education through the VaKE approach. *Intercultural Education, 30*(1), 1–14.

Gorski, P. C. (2008). Good intentions are not enough: A decolonizing intercultural education. *Intercultural Education, 19*(6), 515–525.

Gorski, P. C., & Dalton, K. (2019). Striving for critical reflection in multicultural and social justice teacher education: Introducing a typology of reflection approaches. *Journal of Teacher Education, 71*(3), 357–368.

Gullestad, M. (2002). Invisible fences: Egalitarianism, nationalism, and racism. *Royal Anthropological Institute, 8*(1), 45–63.

Ham, V., & Kane, R. (2004). Finding a way through the swamp: A case for self-study as research. In J. J. Loughran, M. L. Hamilton, V. K. LaBoskey, & T. L. Russell (Eds.),

International handbook of self-study of teaching and teacher education practices (pp. 103–150). Dordrecht, The Netherlands: Springer.

LaBoskey, V. K. (2004). The methodology of self-study and its theoretical underpinnings. In J. J. Loughran, M. L. Hamilton, V. K. LaBoskey, & T. L. Russell (Eds.), *International handbook of self-study of teaching and teacher education practices* (pp. 817–869). Dordrecht, The Netherlands: Springer.

Lanas, M. (2014). Failing intercultural education? 'Thoughtfulness' in intercultural education for student teachers. *European Journal of Teacher Education, 37*(2), 171–182.

Mohamud, A., & Whitburn, R. (2014). Unpacking the suitcase and finding history: Doing justice to the teaching of diverse histories in the classroom. *Teaching History, 154*(3), 40–46.

NOU. (2010). Mangfold og mestring Flerspråklige barn, unge og voksne i opplæringssystemet. *Norges offentlige utredninger 2010: 7*. Retrieved May 20, 2020 from https://www.regjeringen.no/contentassets/4009862aba8641f2ba6c410a93446d29/no/pdfs/nou201020100007000dddpdfs.pdf

Ouellet, F. (2008, September 29–October 1). *Pédagogie de l'interculturel: Mettre en oeuvre une pédagogie de la citoyenneté* [Paper]. Conference "Culture, cultures: À l'épreuve de l'altérité, quelle(s) pédagogie(s) de l'interculturel?", Marly-Le-Roi, France.

Øzerk, K. (2008). Interkulturell danning i en flerkulturell skole: Dens vilkår, forutsetninger og funksjoner. In P. Arneberg & L. G. Briseid (Eds.), *Fag og danning – mellom individ og fellesskap* (pp. 209–228). Bergen, Norway: Fagbokforlaget.

Patry, J.-L., Weyringer, S., & Weinberger, A. (2007). Combining values and knowledge education. In D. N. Aspin & J. D. Chapman (Eds.), *Values education and lifelong learning* (pp. 160–179). New York, NY: Springer Press.

SSB. (2019). *Students in selected programmes*. Retrieved May 20, 2020, from https://www.ssb.no/en/utdanning/statistikker/utuvh

Steinkellner, A. (2017). *Ulike perspektiver på skoleresultatene til barn og unge med innvandringsbakgrunn*. Retrieved May 20, 2020, from https://www.ssb.no/utdanning/artikler-og-publikasjoner/hvordan-gar-det-med-innvandrere-og-deres-barn-i-skolen

Utdanningsdirektoratet. (2018). *Utdanningsspeilet 2017*. Retrieved May 20, 2020, from http://utdanningsspeilet.udir.no/2017/

CHAPTER 24

VaKE in Healthcare

Using VaKE in Different Healthcare Settings

Lydia Linortner, Jean-Luc Patry, Dimitris Pnevmatikos, Rachel Eichler and Mirjam Tonheim Augestad

1   Introduction

Healthcare professionals (nursing, medical treatment, paramedical interventions) are strongly involved with values as they have to make difficult decisions relating with health and sometimes relating with life and death. All these ethical decisions are linked with factual knowledge, as the physical and psychic situation of the patient, the factual diagnosis, the intervention possibilities, the social and societal contexts both of the patient and of the Healthcare team and institution, and many more issues need to be taken into account. Furthermore, many of these decisions are genuine dilemmas as the values involved may be antagonistic, i.e., depending on the decision taken some values are followed but others are broken. Hence, education for healthcare professions is predestined for using VaKE to foster the professional's disposition for responsible decision-making.

In the present chapter, four studies are presented from different countries and different fields in which VaKE was implemented for healthcare professionals, either in training or in-service. They studies are examples for the utility of VaKE in the field of healthcare in four countries.

2   Healthcare Professionals in Greece

Twenty-five care professionals – doctors, nurses, and administrative staff in hospitals at Thessaloniki, Greece – attending a Master's programme (90 ECTS) participated in a VaKE unit. A structured VaKE dilemma story about a doctor who had to decide between cheating (communicating the personal medical data of a patient) to protect his wife from unemployment and not cheating (being righteous by following the deontology) which would reduce the chances of his wife getting a job. Most participants' quick first reaction was emotional – compassion for the doctor's wife – and guided by his desire to protect and care for her. The discussion and the reflection on the two alternatives helped them to understand the role of emotions when they make decisions under the pressure of the time. At the same time, their profession demands fairness, justice, and trustworthiness.

After the critical reflection (see Chapter 17 in this handbook), they realized the need to search for a psychological theory that would help them to understand their own behaviour. They agreed that two theories could be useful to explain it.

First, the Moral Foundation Theory (MFT; Haidt & Joseph, 2004) could be a solid ground to capture the moral intuitions that guided their standpoints. The MFT proposes that humans' unique evolutionary history provides the neonate humans with a universal first draft of the moral mind, the moral foundations, that allows them to learn values, norms, and behaviours permitting them to deal with a wide set of recurrent everyday social problems. The MFT comprises six foundations that are activated when we are confronted with a moral problem: care vs. harm; fairness vs. cheating; loyalty vs. betrayal; authority vs. subversion; sanctity vs. degradation; and liberty vs. oppression (Haidt, 2012). According to the MFT these foundations are not finished structures; instead, each society can prioritize a different combination of them, producing thus a pluralism in moral standpoints. Even within a society, one could find different combinations of moral intuitions.

Second, the Dual-Process Theory of thought suggested by Evans and Stanovich (2013) could explain the characteristics of the participants' first spontaneous reaction, as opposed to the second, more elaborated standpoint. The Dual-Process Theory describes two systems or types of thought: The System or Type I is fast, emotional, based on impulses, beliefs, and habits. The System or Type II is slow, effortful, following rules of logic to solve problems, demanding high cognitive load for planning and reflection. Familiarity with the Dual-Process Theory led care professionals to suggest two alternative processes for their reaction: They realized the benefits of each of the processes and the ways they might react in their everyday professional practice.

Based on their experience with the VaKE dilemma, the students helped to write VaKE dilemma stories dealing with a problem they are confronted with in their everyday practice. Then, they presented their VaKE dilemma to ten colleagues in their sector. They collected the responses and commented across two axes.

First, using the MFT, they identified the intuitions in their colleagues' responses. They captured responses that were supported by intuitions such as the care/harm (The law often does not defend the weak and vulnerable; The doctor must do the best for the health and safety of the patient), loyalty/betrayal (The doctor must do his or her duty), fairness/cheating (What if I were in the position of the patient?), the authority/subversion (Medicine is an act of power; I am the doctor, he or she is the patient), or liberty/oppression (The law is not necessarily a good advisor. For me the most important thing is the freedom of the patient). They did not capture standpoints that could be supported by foundations such as the sanctity/degradation.

Second, based on the Dual-Process Theory, they examined whether the responses could be an output from the Type I or Type II thought. To their surprise, care professionals often suggested standpoints in the dilemma stories that were classified as Type I thoughts: Fast, emotional reactions ignoring the (sometimes hidden) information the participants had for the circumstances that were crucial to resolving the dilemma. Most of these reactions were triggered by the participants' interest in caring to protect the patients or themselves, depending on the dilemma. However, many standpoints expressed Type II thoughts. These were slow and after consideration of the variables of the problem, and they were always theoretically and logically justified.

VaKE dilemma stories were used with care professionals to fulfil two crucial goals for their professional development: first, to increase their knowledge about the theoretical interpretation of their own behaviour in important situations, and second, as a tool to familiarize with others' standpoints in the same situation and to reflect on them critically. In the end, they changed the way they approached the problems by realizing how dangerous it is to react emotionally and intuitively. They concluded that they should think rationally and construct some heuristics for which they would be trained to use in the circumstances under pressure from time and emotions.

3   Nursing Students in Norway

Dealing with ethical issues is both a priority and a challenge in nursing education. However, students find it hard to identify and reflect on ethical dilemmas from clinical practice (Dahl & Alvsvåg, 2013). Also, teachers at VID Specialized University find it challenging to get students involved in ethical reflections. They use the SME model,[1] but some still find that the discussion remains on a superficial theoretical level.

To help students develop their reflection skills, and to support them in better handling ethical challenges in nursing practice, VaKE was introduced into ethical reflection groups during clinical practice in the hospital, in the second year of the bachelor study programme.

The five teachers all started VaKE processes[2] with their students using the same dilemma (step 1) highlighting the complex issue of assisting patients in the hospital. The reflection process was carried out systematically by using the

VaKE steps (steps 2 to 12). The structure had been made even more detailed beforehand by setting the time for the various steps, to help teachers, stay on schedule. Students used their mobile phones to search for information (step 7), and after the second dilemma discussion (step 12) most sessions were finalized (steps 15 and 16).

A brief questionnaire was given to the teachers asking the following questions: What did you experience as positive about VaKE?; Did you experience something challenging about the method?; How and to what extent did the method contribute to the reflection about values?; Why or why should we not implement this method in our teaching?

According to the teachers, the implementation of VaKE highlighted values more clearly than in previous reflection groups discussing similar dilemmas. The teachers claimed that voting and reasoning aloud facilitated the reflection and awareness of questions like "What is a value?" and "What values are important to me?"

Active and engaged participants were mentioned as particularly positive. VaKE's framework and structure were seen as crucial in creating lively student involvement. Students were strongly encouraged to vote and to reason their choice in front of the others (steps 3 and 4). Also, making the voting results visible on the blackboard and discussing the values and knowledge seemed to increase students' activity compared to previous reflection groups.

Each student's development through the visualization of the different perspectives, and towards a new decision (step 11) was seen as important for the respective group's awareness, and something that they could continue to develop. The students were exploring the dilemma *together,* which also made the session seem productive and less threatening.

The dilemma itself was highlighted as important. Creating a realistic case story with a clear dilemma was challenging and time-consuming, and correction and support were provided by the teachers and also by a supervisor familiar with the method. All teachers appreciated having the dilemma story available beforehand as this helped them prepare for the coming session.

The teachers' role could be challenging. Some felt stressed if the first decision (step 3) ended up with all students voting for the same alternative. Others mentioned it as slightly challenging, having to improvise when students wanted more in-depth knowledge about the situation than was included (steps 4, 6, 8). The teachers all agreed that practice was necessary. Even from the first to the second session they felt more confident in their role. However, they questioned how deep into the dilemma they should progress or delve (steps 4, 6), how much they should participate in the group discussions or how passively they should behave to give the students space (steps 4, 6 and 8).

All the teachers experienced VaKE as a valuable and helpful method to help students reflect upon ethical dilemmas. Exciting discussions about value issues were considered to be highly rewarding, and the structure was a considerable support in planning and organizing the group sessions. The mentoring from one person familiar with the method was appreciated. VaKE may lead to better student involvement into ethic reflection and be in line with the education purpose that is educating critically reflected and value-conscious professionals (Programme Description for Bachelor of Nursing, VID scientific college, 2019–2020) who can reflect on and deal with ethical issues (Regulation on National guidelines, 2020).

4   The Theory-Practice Transfer with VaKE: The Case of Prospective Optometrists in Germany and Israel

In this section, we aim at providing some concrete examples of the use of VaKE in adult learning settings.[3] So far, the studies on VaKE have mainly been done with children and adolescents, on one hand, and in teacher training on the other. Also, we have begun a new approach with VaKE addressing a professional practice of college students, particularly prospective optometrists. Reflection about concrete actions during the internship (practicum) of prospective professionals (teachers and optometrists) is fostered through VaKE by having the participants address dilemmas that they have encountered themselves during the internship in VaKE processes.

The new methodology of teaching, VaKE-Tact, focuses on the diminution of the theory-practice gap that students leaving university are confronted with when they have to translate professional knowledge and theories into daily practice. VaKE-Tact is a combination of VaKE, and the construct of the pedagogic tact first defined by Herbart (1802). The theory-practice transfer, among others, is jeopardized by problems like the generality-concreteness antinomy (theoretical statements are general, but abstract, whereas practice needs specific concrete recommendations), multiplism of goals (practitioners usually aim at several goals simultaneously), theory pluralism (they use several theories simultaneously), situation specificity (they adapt their behaviour to the situational requirements), etc. (Patry, 2018). Tact is the person's individual and situation-specific translation of his or her subjective theories (which is influenced by scientific theories, e.g., those learnt in college) into decision-making and action. With VaKE-Tact, these problems are considered by stimulating tact awareness. For this, the prototypical VaKE process of eleven steps was adapted to figure out one's own tact by becoming aware of the six issues mentioned above specifying the theory-practice gap in one's own practice following the theory by Schön (1983) of the reflective practitioner.

4.1 The Pilot Study in Germany

The pilot study took place at the Hochschule für Optometrie in Aalen. In VaKE-Tact, first a dilemma is presented, addressing a prototypical practical situation for optometrists. During the first four steps, the key features of tact were explained and a printed form addressing them was filled out. In the following practical investigation, the students had to (re-)act in a role-play of a practical dilemma situation (initiated by the graduate students). The students then completed the form again and described real dilemmas with the tact features. In the second unit, the dilemma situations were presented in a number of role-plays, mainly to stimulate empathy (Selman, 1984) and to expose the students to experiencing more than one practical dilemma situation.

At the general synthesis step (step 10) the students figured out that in the optometric profession, even if different dilemmas arise, the main objectives, values, subjective theories, and theories used in decision-making are similar. Thinking of all these factors can provide more situation security, one of the main characteristics of tact according to Muth (1962). Feedback on one's own reaction in the dilemma situation by the plenum provides information about the appropriateness of one's attitude; this enables one to act with more self-confidence in further situations.

At the end, a feedback questionnaire was provided to the students evaluating the whole VaKE process; it turned out that the tact features were not well understood. In the future, there should be more detailed explanations or improved communication of the tact features before the practical experience and the self-reflection steps begin. The other feedback factors such as lack of a solution, few proposals and less professional knowledge of the teacher show that the constructivist didactic is misunderstood or needs more time to be appreciated. Some students would like to reduce the length of the discussions.

The positive feedback clearly demonstrates the constructive aspects of the VaKE process, particularly about the practical relevance and new ideas concerning behaviour in various practical dilemma situations; additionally, positive effects of teamwork, role-plays and discussions about professional topics including an ethical issue. The motivational and interactive characteristics of the VaKE process were positively marked.

These results were basic for a modification of the initial VaKE-Tact process in three main steps: (1) Familiarising with VaKE: It is advisable to provide the possibility for participants to become familiar with the constructivist process of VaKE, especially if there is further complex input like the tact elements.

Thus, steps one to seven deal with a prototypical pro-contra story that emphasizes the tact features. (2) Preparation: Additional steps are included, addressing personal hypotheses about one's practice in a practical dilemma situation, with a special focus on the previously discussed tact elements. (3) Addressing one's own concept about the theory-practice transfer: The participants are called upon to become aware of and improve their own tact. Common problems and obstacles, as well as solutions proposed by the whole group, are important means of support for the next dilemma situation in practice.

The changes of the V*a*KE process in the three main steps were done with the primary aim to make the key features of tact more evident. The first step refers to V*a*KE and the tact elements, the second one is used to permit the participants to translate the general tact elements into their own applied field, and the third one is the direct implementation of the insights into practice.

4.2 The Study in Israel

Students at the end of their second year of optometry school have acquired a lot of theoretical and practical optometric knowledge. However, have we, as educators, done all we can to prepare them for formally seeing patients at the start of their third year?

In the course "Introduction to Patient Care", the college teacher tries to bridge between acquiring optometric knowledge and starting clinical work with patients, using constructivist teaching methods. Constructivism encourages students to be critical thinkers, involves students in the learning process and requires students to apply knowledge to new situations. Through the use of Case Based Learning (CBL), Evidence Based Learning (EBL) and Team Based Learning (TBL) the course helps to prepare the students for patient care in the upcoming year and throughout their life.

V*a*KE-Tact was used to complement this already highly original and exciting course as it fit very well with the goals of the course. The students were introduced to V*a*KE through a presentation where the goals, participation requirements and the term dilemma were clarified. A standard procedure for V*a*KE consisting of eleven steps (Patry et al., 2013) was described in detail in the presentation with its special adaptation to optometric education. The students were given a "V*a*KE student packet" which they brought to class for the three weeks of V*a*KE participation. They were asked to reflect on their reasons for studying and wanting to become optometrists as well as what qualities they thought were required to be a "good" optometrist.

Throughout the three weeks the students were able to explore their subjective theories, present opinions about the dilemma, debate, collaborate and search for and present acquired knowledge about the subject. At each stage, the students reflected on their experience of V*a*KE in the form of an assessment questionnaire in the V*a*KE student packet. It consisted of 5-point Likert scales where the students were asked to quantify their responses to the V*a*KE process.

The use of role-plays was central to the implementation of V*a*KE. The students role-played the dilemma as well as the many responses to it. This helped them to prepare for the many patient encounters they will experience as optometrists. At the conclusion of the three weeks the students had to create their own optometric dilemmas and present them to the class. In addition, they were asked to reflect on the list of the qualities required to be a good optometrist they had written prior to V*a*KE and add to it after their experience with V*a*KE.

The 62 students that participated in V*a*KE were very positive about their experience with it. The majority were very animated and involved in their learning process. They spoke about it after class and involved many others (family, friends, professionals) in the dilemma and its different facets.

As a veteran educator yet new mediator to her students in V*a*KE, the teacher had mentoring for V*a*KE-Tact by Linortner and Patry (2015). The mentor was present in some of the classes where V*a*KE-Tact was practiced so the teacher was able to have real time mentoring. This absolutely enhanced her confidence and enjoyment of employing this innovative technique.

The course "Introduction to Patient Care" is valuable in helping the students develop their professional identities. Through using CBL, the students gain experience that will help them when confronting patients. The process of seeking the information needed through EBL trains the students to become lifelong learners. Working in pairs and groups and having the "audience" critique and provide a viability check, adds a lot to the students' perception and interpretation of the case at hand. Inserting a V*a*KE-Tact module into the course helped the students develop self-awareness and the ability to reflect upon crucial decisions that they will be required to make in their professional career. This course will produce optometrists who can maintain their competency and at the same time be self-aware and empathic throughout their patient interactions.

5   Discussion

V*a*KE in the biomedical field showed that it was necessary to find a psychological reasoning on how important decisions are made and how it is necessary to take a moment before acting. V*a*KE was used to obtain a metatheoretical view on decision-making.

For nursing students, too, the deepness of involvement within the dilemma experience is a crucial factor; this confirms the utility of VaKE in the field of healthcare.

The VaKE-Tact process as a new tool found its usefulness in fostering the theory-practice transfer for optometry students. In preparation for the daily work, students are also confronted with an overall reflection about why they become professionals and what makes a person highly professional, which deepens their knowledge and personality within their profession.

Overall, one can see that VaKE is flexible, so it is particularly appropriate in the field of healthcare where people decide about patients' life and health. It is a very important tool to bring decisions to a higher level in several dimensions, knowledge, and reflection wise and with respect to values.

Notes

1. The model (SME), developed at the Center for Medical Ethics at the University of Oslo, centers on the following questions: What is the ethical problem? What are the facts of the case? Who is involved, and what are their views? What values, laws and guidelines are relevant? What are the alternative courses of action (Lillemoen & Pedersen, 2015)?
2. Based on the 16 steps of VaKE-*dis* (Weyringer et al., 2012; see Chapter 2 in this handbook).
3. This study was supported by the European Union through the TEMPUS IV program (project Life-Long Learning in Applied Fields, LLAF 543894 TEMPUS; see https://www.erasmusplus.org.il/llaf). The European Commission's support for the production of this publication does not constitute an endorsement of the contents, which reflect only the views of the authors, and the Commission cannot be held responsible for any use which may be made of the information contained therein.

References

Dahl, H., & Alvsvåg, H. (2013). Å fremme studenters evn til refleksjon – en pedagogisk utfordring. *Uniped, 36*(22724), 32–45.

Evans, J. S. B., & Stanovich, K. E. (2013). Dual-process theories of higher cognition: Advancing the debate. *Perspectives on Psychological Science, 8*(3), 223–241.

Haidt, J. (2012). *The righteous mind: Why good people are divided by politics and religion.* New York, NY: Vintage.

Haidt, J., & Joseph, C. (2004). Intuitive ethics. *Dædalus, 133*, 55–66.

Lillemoen, L., & Pedersen, R. (2015). Ethics reflection groups in community health services: An evaluation study. *BMC Medical Ethics, 16*, 25.

Linortner, L., & Patry, J.-L. (2015). *Teaching manual, module 1: VaKE-Tact – Values and Knowledge Educationand Agogical Tact.* Unpublished paper, Life-Long Learning in Applied Fields (LLAF), Project 543894 – TEMPUS-1-2013-1-IL-TEMPUS-JPHES, Group 4: Learning to Be. Salzburg, Austria.

Patry, J.-L. (2018). Theorie-Praxis-Transfer: Hindernisse und Probleme. In A. Gastager & J.-L. Patry (Eds.), *Pädagogischer Takt: Analysen zu Theorie und Praxis.* (pp. 17–42). Graz, Austria: Leykam.

Patry, J.-L., Weinberger, A., Weyringer, S., & Nussbaumer, M. (2013). Combining values and knowledge education. In B. J. Irby, G. Brown, R. Lara-Alecio, & S. Jackson (Eds.) and R. A. Robles-Piña (Sect. Ed.), *The handbook of educational theories* (pp. 565–579). Charlotte, NC: Information Age Publishing.

Programme Description for Bachelor of Nursing, Faculty of Health Studies, VID Scientific College. (2019–2020). Retrieved May 17, 2020, from https://www.vid.no/site/assets/files/17586/fagplan-bachelor-i-sykepleie-vid-bergen-2019-2020-vid-1.pdf?nc=1561119595

Regulation on National Guidelines for nursing education. (2020). Retrieved May 17, 2020, from https://lovdata.no/dokument/SF/forskrift/2019-03-15-412

Weyringer, S., Patry, J.-L., & Weinberger, A. (2012). Values and knowledge education. Experiences with teacher trainings. In D. Alt & R. Reingold (Eds.), *Changes in teachers' moral role. From passive observers to moral and democratic leaders* (pp. 165–197). Rotterdam, The Netherlands: Sense.

PART 5

Practical Extensions of VaKE

CHAPTER 25

Meaningful Teaching Using Moral Dilemmas
From VaKE to DBM

Roxana G. Reichman

1   Introduction

There is a consensus that in the 21st century it is very difficult to predict what knowledge and skills graduates will need to function in a society characterized by rapid changes. Therefore, it is crucial to teach students how to learn and to help them develop critical and creative skills and help them build a moral foundation that will allow them to live a meaningful life. In addition to that, it is important to motivate them to learn, to encourage their curiosity and to teach them how to build knowledge in a constructive way. One of the ways of achieving this goal is by exposing students to moral dilemmas to prepare them for real life situations that they will face by themselves or in groups (Shapira-Lischshinsky & Orland-Barak, 2009).

Teachers are used to focusing on teaching content, and many teachers have hesitated to deal with moral values in their classes because they fear creating conflict between the students and conflict between themselves and parents. In addition to that, many teachers as well as university professors admit that they are specialists in a specific field but are not sure how to teach values (Patry, Reichman, & Linortner, 2017). During the last decade, several models have been developed to help educators deal with moral issues in classrooms. No single model is suitable for all, and sometimes a variation of a model, or a combination of models may be the best option.

This chapter is divided into two parts. In the first part, three models, the VaKE model, the Dilemma Based Model (DBM) developed by Reichman (2017a), and the Reflective Cycle Model developed by Gibbs (1988) will be exposed to offer several options for using moral dilemmas while not giving up knowledge. The second part will present a study based on a moral dilemma which combines DBM and the Gibbs model.

2 Three Models Combining Moral Dilemmas with Teaching Content: VaKE, the Dilemma Based Model (DBM), and the Reflective Cycle Model

The VaKE model and its diverse variations are presented in detail in Chapter 2 in this handbook, therefore we concentrate on the two other models and the links between all three.

2.1 VaKE model

The very complex VaKE model stresses the fact that by using all the steps the educators achieve a double goal: dealing with moral issues while making sure that this does not come only at the expense of knowledge, but also that fact learning becomes deeper and more meaningful. Unfortunately, some teachers and teacher educators believe that although the results of research on the implementation of VaKE in formal education (see Part 3, Sections 1 and 2 in this handbook) provides evidence for meeting its educational aims, and that therefore its principles are very much to be supported, the whole VaKE course with its eleven or more steps is too time consuming and therefore difficult to implement (Reichman, 2017a).

The following Dilemma Based Model offers the opportunity to achieve similar results by using a shorter way that is therefore easier to implement. After the presentation of the model, an example will be provided based on the combination of the two models.

2.2 Dilemma Based Model (DBM)

The Dilemma Based Model (DBM) has been found to be appropriate in several Israeli institutions of teacher education as well as in some short-term programmes for in-service teachers who have been exposed to it as part of their professional development. The DBM model (Reichman, 2017a) was initially developed as a variation of VaKE, and it agrees with the main principle, which is to combine knowledge and moral values. Today DBM has been implemented in various ways, but it is always based on six steps:

Step 1: The educator (teacher or faculty member) presents a short story that contains a moral dilemma in which at least two conflicting values are presented. It is recommended to read the vignette at least twice and then each student writes his or her first reaction, without sharing the information with his or her colleagues. This detail is very important because it allows the discussion to be based on the facts presented and not on personal issues.

Step 2: The educator randomly divides the class into five groups. Then one of the two values is chosen randomly, and the educator gives each group a role without taking into consideration the personal opinions of the students (which in fact remain secret). The first group is asked to look only for *facts*, and the second group must look only for the *advantages* of acting according to the chosen value. The third group must find the *disadvantages* of this type of action. The fourth group focuses on the *emotional aspects* of all those involved, and the last group looks for *creative ways* of dealing with this issue. If there is a lack of time or if the group is small, the educators can choose only the first four options when dividing the students into groups.

Step 3: The students look for the information they need. During this step, which needs the most time and mentoring, the educator's role is to be a facilitator who helps them look for relevant and reliable information. This task is performed both in class and at home as an assignment.

Step 4: Once every group has acquired the necessary information, the whole class prepares for the discussion. For this, the students are not divided according to their opinions (for, against etc). They are given roles by the instructor, which they have to "play": you will be in favour of this idea, you will be against. So, they represent a role, not their real thoughts. They get time to prepare these roles and get ready to present the results to the entire class. Since each student/group of students has been assigned a role, conflicts are avoided, because it is not a personal opinion, but rather a task they had to perform.

Step 5: The students present the results/arguments of their group to the whole class. This can be done using short lectures, role-play, artistic work, or any other technique that the groups may choose. Once the information is shared and all the students reach a similar level of knowledge, this information becomes the basis of a new group discussion.

Step 6: The students assess their own work (self-evaluation) as well as the work of their colleagues (peer evaluation), and they reflect on ways to apply their solutions to similar moral conflicts they might face. The professor evaluates the work of each group and of every student in the group (top-down evaluation) according to criteria presented to the students in advance.

Although the last step of DBM offers students the opportunity to reflect on their own work as well as the work performed by their peers, this is not the main purpose of the model. The main goal is to offer students meaningful learning which prepares them for life and not for a specific test. Reflection is a very important part of the learning process because it improves academic skills by identifying strengths and weaknesses, thus enabling the learners to improve their performance in the future.

2.3 *The Reflective Cycle Model*

The American psychologist and sociologist Gibbs (1988) has developed a six-step reflective model which allows the participants to reflect in depth about a certain experience or action, to become aware of the reasons behind their behaviour and to allow them to act in a better way in the future. We think that this model can be easily combined with DBM. Also, the reflective cycle model uses short dilemma stories as starting points.

Step 1: Description of the situation: What has happened in the story which was presented? This step allows the participant to build a subjective view of what has happened, of the time and space, of the involved persons, etc.

Step 2: Feelings and thoughts: What did you (the student) think and feel? The students stop their actions to become aware of the way they feel about a certain situation and their own behaviour regarding what has happened. For example: How did I feel when I was asked to play a role entirely different from my point of view? How did I feel when I was asked to be in a group with students I like or not, know or not?

Step 3: Evaluation: What was good and bad? The students think about their experience of working alone or in groups (in order to find information), about the way in which their opinions were important to the group, etc.

Step 4: Analysis: What sense do you make of the evaluation? The students reflect on the reasons why their point of view was or was not accepted by the group, etc.

Step 5: Conclusion: What else could you have done? The students reflect on what worked well both from the point of view of content and of the process.

Step 6: Action plan: What would you do in a similar situation? After having learned more about themselves and about their way of working in groups, the students can make better decisions about the way they should react in the future when they face another moral dilemma.

After having presented three models that were taken into consideration for the purpose of this study, in the second part of this chapter, the study will be described.

3   A Moral Dilemma as a Basis for Teaching Values in High School

As it was previously explained, the purpose of this study is to allow high school students to learn by using moral dilemmas that will invite them to build their own code of behaviour while also developing critical skills, creative skills, and the ability to work in heterogeneous groups.

The research question is: What are the attitudes of high school students regarding learning through moral dilemmas? The study was conducted using qualitative methodology based on the analysis of documents (reflective journals). Josselson, Lieblich, and McAdams (2003) claim that it is very important to listen to the voices of the participants, to their narratives, and to make sense of the ways in which they perceive different situations. High school students are not often asked what their opinion is about the way in which they are taught and are seldom asked to reflect on the way in which they work with others. This type of study allows them to reflect on their learning style, on the way in which they work with others, while also allowing them to gain new knowledge and to deal with moral dilemmas.

The participants were 25 Israeli high school students who study in the same class. They were exposed to a moral dilemma as well as to a combination of the two models presented above: Dilemma Based Model (DBM) and the Reflective Cycle Model. The researcher is a faculty member in an Academic Teacher College in Northern Israel, and a high school teacher helped with the data collection. The school principal was aware of the fact that this research was taking place and the teacher was interested to try this innovative type of teaching as part of her professional development. For ethical reasons, the anonymity of the participants has been preserved and the researcher did not meet the students at any point.

The high school students, 13 males and 12 females, aged 17–18, were presented with the following short story:

> Adam is a young Jewish religious man who has dreamt all his life of studying Law at the famous University of Oxford. He was very excited when he was among the few lucky ones accepted at the prestigious university. In addition to that, he was awarded a merit scholarship, which meant that he would receive a tuition waiver. He was thrilled with his new life and was an excellent student appreciated by his professors and colleagues. At the end of the first semester, he saw the list of exams and he could not believe his eyes. The most important exam was scheduled for Yom Kippur. As a religious Jew, Adam knew that not only he would have to fast that day, but that he is not allowed to travel, nor to write anything on that specific holy day. He also knew that not taking this exam will mean failing the entire course and risking losing his scholarship.
> What should Adam do? Why? Please explain!

Finch (1987) showed that short stories are one of the best methods of eliciting sincere responses regarding values and beliefs. According to the DBM model, it is very important to use third person question because this way the participant does not feel that it is a personal question and answers truly. Research shows that in fact, people give their personal opinion when asked about the actions a third person should perform (Finch, 1987).

Then, according to the same model, the teacher divided the students into five groups and assigned them random roles, similar to five out of the six thinking hats of De Bono (1988). In the original model of De Bono (1988), the class is divided into six groups: one is in charge of discussing the advantages of a certain argument, another group focuses on the disadvantages; a third group discusses the facts, and the fourth group thinks of creative solutions to the problem; the fifth group focuses on the feelings and the last group (the blue hat) oversees the process. In the DBM model, the instructor is in charge, and "wears the blue hat" while the students are only divided in the other five groups. At every step, the students also had to write according to the Reflective Cycle Model of Gibbs (1988). The teacher gave each student a booklet, in which they were supposed to write in class their reflections regarding their experience after each step of the DBM model. These reflections were based on specific questions asked by the teacher according to Gibbs' model. After each meeting, the teacher took all the booklets and returned them the following lesson without any grade or comments in order not to influence the students' reactions. At the end of the process, after five 90-minute lessons, the students handed in the booklets and the researcher collected the booklets and used them for the purpose of this study.

It is important to stress the fact that this dilemma was presented to high school students who study in a non-religious school in Israel. All the students are secular Jews, but none of them came from a religious family. At the beginning, the students read the short story and wrote in the journal their opinions about the way in which Adam should act. Then, the teacher who took part in this study wrote on two pieces of paper, the two main possible choices Adam faces: to take the exam in spite of his strong religious beliefs or not to take it knowing that it would mean failing the entire course and losing the scholarship. She folded the two pieces of paper, put them in a can and asked a volunteer to come and pick out one of the choices. Reichman (2017b) believes that it is important to act in such a way so that the students cannot know what is the teacher's position regarding this dilemma. Then, the teacher showed them the text, read aloud what was written on it, and declared: Adam decided to follow the requirements of his faith and not to take the exam.

From this point on, the students had to examine Adam's action according to the roles they have been given. Some looked for *facts* about the requirements and regulations in such situations, legal precedents, others discussed *advantages* of respecting religious beliefs, another group found *disadvantages* of failing the course and risking losing a very prestigious scholarship, others thought of the *feelings* of everyone involved: Adam himself, his parents, his professors, etc. and finally *creative* solutions to this dilemma. Then, the students wrote about their own thoughts and feelings regarding the process: some were assigned a role that fit their own opinion, while others were forced to find ideas that were not necessarily compatible with their own. Some had to work in a group with friends while others had to work with colleagues with whom they normally have little to no interaction. In addition, they had to persuade their colleagues that the materials they found were relevant and important and they had to listen to their comments. This experience was new to them, and they were not used to working in this manner. The teacher was impressed by the fact that all the students thought and wrote their reflections, including those who normally do not like to participate in class and those who do not always do their homework. The fact that they were given time to perform this task in class, forced them to complete it and to hand in the reflective journal to the teacher. This was done to prevent the loss of the booklets or the possibility of not doing homework.

According to the fourth step of the DBM model, the students had to summarize the materials they read, and each group had to think of interesting ways in which to present it to the entire class. After doing that, they also had to write in their reflective journal how they reached this decision, whether the group dynamics worked in their favour or not and why. Then the group presented the work they have done to the entire class.

The group that had to look for facts presented the rules and regulations at Oxford University, the rules followed by Orthodox Jews on Yom Kippur. They did that using Kahoot, which means they prepared a multiple-choice test that contained the information in a very interesting manner which involved the entire class. The group that had to present the advantages did so by using Kahoot while the students from the other groups had to solve the game and find the advantages themselves. Once again, all the other students were actively trying to find the information. The group that had to focus on the disadvantages prepared a ten-minute TED[1]-like lecture.

The group that had to focus on feelings, did so through a role-play presenting Adam's feelings, the feelings of his parents and of his professors. The creative group offered three solutions, two of which can be implemented and one which seemed more like science fiction since it involved travelling in time and quantum theory. As a result of this activity, the students had to collaborate with their peers in finding information, analyzing the materials they found and, in the decision-making process of looking for intelligent ways to present it to their colleagues. They were exposed to different sets of values that needed to be considered, learned to work together, and presented their peers the material in innovative ways, thus involving the entire class.

After the teacher finished this unit, the researcher analysed the reflective journals using the content analysis technique, which allows to find patterns

in the written texts of the participants (Holsti, 1968). After having read each booklet several times, coding was done in a consistent manner: first by looking for the main themes in each booklet (vertical coding) and then by comparing the coding of all the booklets (horizontal coding). This coding pattern is unobtrusive since the researcher is invisible and therefore cannot influence the participants' views and it is reliable because other researchers can analyse the same data. As a result of the coding process, eight main categories were found:
1. Getting out of the comfort zone
2. Thoughts about the group work
3. Feelings regarding the group work
4. Dilemmas versus problems
5. Time management
6. Truth and fake information
7. The role of a team leader
8. Sources of support

After a careful division of categories and subcategories, four main themes emerged:
1. The students' attitudes regarding dilemmas in general and the specific dilemma in particular
2. Coping with the group work
3. Self-reflection
4. Plans for future actions

Some of the participants initially expressed negative feelings toward dilemmas in general: "I prefer to be given a situation with one correct answer. I was not comfortable with a situation in which there are two options with both advantages and disadvantages" and "I expected the teacher to give us the solution, but I was frustrated because she kept on saying that we should look for information in order to make up our minds". Others were actually relieved to know that there is more than one solution to a dilemma: "At the beginning I didn't understand what the problem was. I thought that Adam should take the exam regardless of his religious beliefs. Then I understood his point of view although I disagree with him. I understand that for him there was no easy answer".

Some students liked working in groups ("It was real fun working with them, I got to know them better"), but for others this task proved to be quite difficult: "I would have liked to choose my group partners. I think things would have moved more swiftly".

Self-reflection was something new to many of the participants. "I understood what motivates me and what annoys me, and I learned how to get motivated and how to use time more wisely. I never thought of this aspect before". Another student wrote: "At the beginning I didn't understand why it was not enough to look for material and prepare the final product. Why do I need to write about the process? Now I can see that I learned a lot about myself and about how I can get others to agree to my point of view".

One of the most interesting themes had to do with the students' plan for future action, not only for class assignments, but also for real life situations: "I understand that life is not black and white… that there is more than one way of looking at the same information. I understand that not only I can consult with my friends and family, but also, I can find the fors and againsts of many issues. For example, this year I will vote for the first time in my life. I have always been certain about who to vote for. Now I am thinking that maybe I should read more and talk to more people to see if I can convince them or if their arguments can convince me. I understand it is not a matter of who has the right solution, but maybe some issues are more complex and should be looked at from more than one point of view".

4   Discussion and Conclusion

The findings show that the students dealt in a very serious manner with moral dilemmas and with the sometimes-difficult process of self-reflection, which provided them with a mirror in which to look in, to learn more about themselves and about the ways in which they enjoy learning alone and with others. They also learned that to change one's opinion is not a sign of weakness, but rather a sign of maturity when confronted with new information. In dealing with dilemmas, the students learned not to see life in terms of black and white; they had to face the challenge of finding the strengths of a different point of view. As for the instructor, the main challenge was not to express his or her point of view, but rather to take the students on a learning journey which would allow them to have a meaningful and eye-opening experience.

As the VaKE principles taught us, one of the purposes of education is to prepare students to become moral, critical thinkers who are able to work with people from different backgrounds and with different opinions, educators should be ready to take upon themselves the challenging task of teaching knowledge as well as values. The VaKE model allows them to work in depth and simultaneously with content and values. If, however, an educator feels that time is limited, the choice should not be to give up teaching values altogether, but rather to use a different model which allows to reach the same goal by using different means. They can choose to do so by using a specific model, variations of a model, combinations of more than one model, or to work in teams to develop a new model that better serves their students' needs. The most important thing is to be bold enough to do it because the reward is worth taking up this challenge.

Note

1   TED: Technology, Entertainment, Design; a non-profit organisation for sharing innovative ideas in talks of max. 18 minutes (see www.ted.com).

References

De Bono, E. (1988). *Six thinking hats*. Boston, MA: Back Bay Books.
Finch, J. (1987). The vignette technique in survey research. *Sociology, 21*, 105–111.
Gibbs, G. (1988). *Learning by doing: A guide to teaching and learning methods*. London, UK: Further education.
Holsti, O. R. (1968). Content Analysis. In G. Linzey & E. Aronson (Eds.), *The handbook of social psychology, Vol. 2, Research methods* (pp. 595–692). New York, NY: Addison-Westey.
Josselson, R., McAdams, D. P., Lieblich, A., & McAdams, D. P. (Eds.). (2003). *Up close and personal: The teaching and learning of narrative research*. Washington, DC: American Psychological Association Press.
Patry, J.-L., Reichman, G. R., & Linortner, L. (2017). Values and Knowledge Education (VaKE) for lifelong learning in applied fields: Principles and general issues. In H. E. Vidergor & O. Sela (Eds.), *Innovative teaching strategies and methods promoting lifelong learning in higher education: From theory to practice* (pp. 187–214). Hauppauge, NY: Nova Science Publishers.
Patry, J.-L., Weinberger, A., Weyringer, S., & Nussbaumer, M. (2013). Combining values and knowledge education. In B. J. Irby, G. Brown, R. Lara-Alecio, S. Jackson, & R. A. Robles-Piña (Eds.), *The handbook of educational theories* (pp. 565–579). Charlotte, NC: Information Age Publishing.
Reichman, R. G. (2017a). *Dilemma-Based Model (DBM): Effective teacher and learning in higher education* [Paper]. The Conference on Higher Education Pedagogy, Blacksburg, VA.
Reichman, R. G. (2017b). Methods for effectively teaching large classes. In *Innovative teaching practice* (pp. 37–53). Hauppauge, NY: Nova Science Publishers.
Shapira-Lischshinsky, O., & Orland-Barak, L. (2009). Ethical dilemmas in teaching: The Israeli case. *Education and Society, 27*(3), 27–45.

CHAPTER 26

The V*a*KE Model through the Lens of a Computer-Supported Collaborative Learning Environment

Tamar Meirovitz and Liat Eyal

1   Introduction

Use of authentic dilemmas during academic studies of novice teachers is an excellent way to develop critical thinking and enhance ethical perspective and professional identity. In 21st Century Learning, where principles of collaborative learning are brought to the forefront, ethical dilemmas can be taught in a way that is tailored to the learning challenges of our technology-intensive realities. The present chapter presents a dilemma-based learning framework based on the V*a*KE model, which incorporates pedagogical principles of collaborative learning and technology-supported learning with an emphasis on applications that promote classroom active learning, thereby demonstrating how technology can support educators to manage and enhance collaborative activities in professional dilemmas. Considering recent world events, when distance learning has become the order of the day, we can integrate new digital tools within the V*a*KE model and demonstrate how new technologies actually enhance pedagogy.

2   Combining V*a*KE with Computer-Supported Collaborative Learning (CSCL)

To tackle constant societal and technological changes, it is evident that there is a need to develop a sustainable conceptual framework for future learning and teaching. To this end, the OECD has advanced the 'Learning Compass 2030' which "defines the knowledge, skills, attitudes and values that learners need to fulfil their potential and contribute to the well-being of their communities and the planet" (OECD, 2019). The Learning Framework 2030 presents a clear vision and a set of goals which promote innovative learning environments. These focus on student development and empowerment while taking into consideration the changes in education systems both locally and in the wider ecosystem. The core competencies needed are global competencies, digital literacy, collaboration, critical thinking creativity and empathy (OECD, 2019). In our chapter, we discuss the significant contribution of Computer Supported Collaborative Learning (CSCL) in enhancing the application of the *VaKE* model to answer the challenges presented in the Learning Framework 2030.

Recent research on CSCL documents its rising contribution to active learning. Collaborative and argumentative practices which combine the principles of inquiry-based learning and technology-enhanced environments contribute to student learning and effective use of technology affordances (Song & Looi, 2012). Scholars note a further benefit in learning gains and preparation for adult life at the workplace (Wise & Schwarz, 2017). However, these scholars note that ethical dimensions, mainly dialogic and democratic, have not been sufficiently brought to the forefront (ibid.). A major challenge of any CSCL environment which views learning from a sociocultural perspective is the understanding of the cultures at play, the ethical dimensions involved and how the intended outcomes can be supported (Hod & Sagy, 2019). That is to say that there is a need to further look into *how to design* authentic learning of disciplinary knowledge and values education in computer-supported collaborative learning environments.

One of the options that promotes this goal is designing up-to-date digital learning environments with authentic learning activities. Authentic learning encourages learners to explore, discover, and discuss problems in which they are interested and that happen in real life. According to Bozalek et al. (2013) authentic learning places an emphasis on the students' proactive learning and calls for learners to immerse themselves in the problem-solving process. Namely, learners are problem solvers who construct meaning through problem situations that are very close to those which exist in the real world or real situations. Hence, learning is supported by being situated in an environment that aligns learning objectives with real-world tasks, content, and context. In this reading, authentic learning is based on a constructivist view in which students create their own understandings of new concepts and practices by integrating their previous experience, the resources they have, their own research and their current experience.

In up-to-date digital learning environments with authentic learning activities, teachers can be introduced with professional dilemmas and a range of diverse opinions. The *VaKE* model (Patry, Weyringer, & Weinberger, 2007; Weinberger, Patry, & Weyringer, 2016) is a didactical method that engages learners in authentic learning activities using a dilemma as a starting point. It is a collaborative pedagogical tool and therefore when implemented in a digital environment should be taught using collaborative digital tools.

It is suggested that integration of technological applications serves to advance active learning, to further learner engagement and to foster knowledge construction (Seifert, 2012, 2016). The VaKE model, which is underpinned by constructivist learning frameworks, inherently harbors knowledge construction processes and as such promotes critical thinking. Meirovitz and Aran (2020, p. 12) have noted "the added value of digital instruction to dramatically expand access to knowledge, the capacity to read critically, and contribute to the collaborative co-creation of knowledge". Hence, incorporating Computer-Supported Collaborative Learning (CSCL) in VaKE considerably upgrades the learning experience, enabling (and enforcing) active involvement of *all* enrolled students in instilling values of equality, fairness, tolerance, and inclusion.

The conceptual framework on collaboration in collaborative E-learning environments presents a taxonomy of the various levels of collaboration (Salmons, 2006). This taxonomy contains three elements: the levels of collaboration, learning activities and trust continuum. The five levels of collaboration are: (1) dialogue – learners exchange ideas in discussion or shared event; (2) peer review – learners exchange work for mutual critique through peer review and incorporate others' comments. At this level, learners create individual outcomes based on peer input, or the process moves to another level of collaboration; (3) parallel – learners each complete a component of an assignment or project. Thereafter, elements are combined into a collective final product, or the process moves to another level of collaboration; (4) sequential – learners build on each other's contribution; all are combined into a collective final product, or the process moves to another level of collaboration; and (5) synergic collaboration – learners collaborate fully at all phases in creation of an original product that meshes contributions into a collective outcome. In this chapter, each VaKE stage will include its level of collaboration. The benefit of using such a taxonomy is that it enables participants to gain skills needed to lead, organise, and participate in collaborative projects, skills which are significant for innovative and collaborative digital work online.

3 VaKE Steps, Collaboration Levels, CSCL Tools and Core OECD Competencies

In the following section we present our proven experiences together with a pedagogical rationale in combining the VaKE model (see also Chapter 2 in this handbook) with levels of collaboration described by Salmons (2006), and pertinent relevant CSCL tools that support the activity at hand. Core competencies of the OECD 2019 learning framework form an integral part of each of the steps of the VaKE model: cooperation, collaboration, equality, and critical thinking. These are inherent to the essence of the model and therefore appear in each of its steps. Other important core competencies are not directly connected to the model's intrinsic essence but are dependent on specific content of individual dilemmas and decisions of course instructors. These, therefore, are not mentioned in this chapter.

The free of charge collaborative tools that have been chosen for each of the VaKE stages are a proposal; clearly, they may be exchanged for other tools. However, they do illustrate the need for digital tools that support the learning process. There is a need for instructors to consider what tools to use if the course is face-to-face or online. It may transpire that the face-to-face tools are used to document the process and then to share it, while CSCL also serves as a thinking tool and a platform for joint construction of knowledge.

Our considerations in the choice of the digital tools presented are that the tools are simple and easy to learn and use, and no less importantly, they are free of charge. Undoubtedly, there are other tools possessing a similar functionality. These might be occasionally employed. For the past four years, we have implemented the tools presented here in our academic courses in teacher training programmes at academic colleges in Israel. They are based on the VaKE model with CSCL (Eyal, 2012, 2018; Eyal et al., 2018). It is important to note that the use of digital tools enables the integration of several VaKE stages together and this is its added value. We propose two options: (1) to use a precise digital tool (or a similar one with the same function) for each stage, (2) to join several steps of VaKE together in the same tool.

VaKE steps 0 & 1: Preparation, Clarification, and Introduction of the Specific Dilemma

The focus during these VaKE steps is on understanding the dilemma and interpreting the values that are involved, and on the clarification of the content and the questions involved. The level of collaboration is the dialogue. The class takes part in a brainstorming activity about the possible values that arise from the dilemma using a pedagogical digital tool which allows the group in one glance to see the interpretations that arise from all the participants. The CSCL application which may be used at this stage is online mapping tools for brainstorming that visually create and share the concepts and values that are involved in the dilemma, e.g., Mindmeister, Cacoo, Mind42. This step, similar to the next steps enhances core competencies like digital literacy and critical thinking.

VaKE steps 2 & 3: First Reflection & First Decision
Again, the level of collaboration is dialogue. Learners will individually work on their associations with the dilemma. Each student will find out his/her opinion and what values are at stake. Thereafter, students will make their first opening decisions. Personal decisions are required of students; therefore, digital voting tools are selected by the instructor. These enable anonymity and neutralization of social pressure. Digital voting tools allow participants to see the results of the group's election results in graphs or percentages at the end of the vote. The CSCL tools are cooperative decision-making platform apps, for example: Mentimeter, Answergarden, Socrative, Google Forms, Kahoot. The participants take part in a shared event; therefore, the CSCL tools are at the *dialogue* level.

VaKE step 4: First Dilemma Discussion
Collaboration takes place on the level of peer reviews. Learners might participate in small groups or as a whole class. Each participant raises arguments for or against the various solutions offered within the dilemma. Participants find out on which points they agree and on which they do not. At this stage, it is important that each participant explains his/her choice without any peer pressure. Thereafter, in the interest of transparency, we recommend participants to be exposed to the diverse arguments presented by all participants. The CSCL-tool can be a Google Form which has at least two questions: (1) What is your decision? (This is a closed question), and (2) What are your arguments? After each participant completes the form, the facilitator can present the figure with the distribution of the decisions made by all participants and in addition the accumulated arguments appear on the main screen for all to see. No one person can take over the discussion thereby imposing their point of view on all present.

For example, the obligatory course "School as an Organizational System" has been taught for the last four years at Levinsky College of Education in Israel. The course is designed for in-service teachers studying for the M. ED degree. Its purpose is to understand the complexity of dilemmas in the context of the educational system by presenting a problem situation, discussing which issues of right and wrong are at stake and arriving at complex decisions regarding which course of action to take. In one unit, student-teachers were presented with a dilemma in the context of employing teachers in their school. The teachers were asked to work in four teams, with each team writing a claim from a different perspective: the claim of the school principal, the claim of teacher A, the claim of teacher B and the claim of the Ministry of Education. Each claim was made on a slide in a collaborative presentation. Afterwards, a representative from each group presented the group's claim for six minutes, in front of the plenum. After the four arguments (or claims) were presented, each participant in the plenum voted through a survey on the Google Form and justified his/her position. The class results could then be presented to the plenum and discussed.

Another option is to use the To-Be Education tool. To-Be Education is an online role play game that engages learners in solving dilemmas. Participants are assigned several roles throughout the game and requested to argue different viewpoints of the characters; these differ from their personal point of view. Thereafter, a lively discussion takes place in which all sides present their stand points. Following the discussion, students have a chance to vote on the issues according to their own opinions. A control panel enables the instructor to view discussions, comment, collect feedback for the class discussion, and hand out badges. Finally, a post-game discussion can take place with interesting points to cover. The benefit of taking part in a digital role play activity is that digital roleplaying forms neutral entities. Taking the roles of different digital characters does not convey the same negative associations which often lead to unwanted heated arguments which sometimes accompany traditional classroom teaching.

These two choices illustrate how incorporating the VaKE pedagogical model in the CSCL environment enhances and develops competencies like collaboration – by enabling the active involvement of all participants and empathy – by instilling values of equality, fairness, tolerance, and inclusion.

VaKE step 5: Reflection
Once more, the participants collaborate on the level of dialogue. Participants individually reflect on how she or he thinks now about the problem following the discussion in the previous stage and what questions and quandaries have come up as a result of critical thinking, verification and change of standpoint. Following this stage, reflections are posted on a Google Doc for all to see. This step enhances core competencies like digital literacy and critical thinking.

Steps 2–5 can be carried out using the Tricider app in which learners engage with a social brainstorming, argumentation and voting tool. The instructor or learners write a description of a dilemma in which there is a specific question. The participants are presented with the dilemma and each one of them is asked to submit (before a specific due date), a proposal to solve the dilemma in the left column "IDEAS". The participants are requested not to repeat proposals that have already been suggested. In the next stage, each participant is requested to add arguments to the other participants' answers/ideas and indicate whether they are in favour of, or against the views presented (under the columns + or –). Finally, after reviewing the limitations and opportunities raised by the group members for each proposal, each participant should vote for the solution that he or she thinks may best suit the dilemma presented. There are some advanced features that enable students to add links to express the ideas and set a deadline for voting. This digital platform could also take the dilemma discussions to a wider level. For instance, you can think about making a parallel survey at city/national/global levels.

Another alternative is when learners do not present their personal viewpoints but take part in role playing a specific character's standpoints. In stage 2 in the IDEA column, participants can suggest characters related to the dilemma and then each one should write from the character's point of view, the character's position – within the same column, as an addition (parent, teacher, child, principal etc.). Thereafter, they are asked to support their position towards the dilemma (using the column of + or –).

VaKE steps 6–8: Experiences Exchange & Looking for and Sharing Information
The work in these steps is organised as a parallel collaboration. It is constructive to discuss the alternative solutions that were offered in the previous stage to solve the dilemma and collaboratively, to work out which are the strongest arguments presented so far. Thus, the group conducts a discussion in which important information is missing and presents an in-depth discussion on the dilemma. The CSCL tools can be Padlet, Google Forms or other tools for collecting notes and sharing tools. These digital collaborative tools allow learners to visually post and share arguments and attach links to resources with additional information. Once again, the open discussion conducted in a collaborative computer-supported environment enhances and develops competencies of collaboration and empathy.

VaKE steps 9–10: Synthesis of Information & Reflection
The work is organised as a sequential collaboration. At this stage, group members are requested to look at the new facts presented on the digital apps and to reflect on whether the new information presented is productive. In traditional frontal teaching, this VaKE stage requires the instructor to inform the group of new facts. However, in the CSCL learning environment, stages 9–10 are conducted collaboratively and are accessible and transparent to all. Learners build on each other's contribution, all are combined into a collective final product. The CSCL tools can be digital poster presentation tools like Padlet, Genial.ly, Crello. RealtimeBoard, miro, flinga, canva. An innovative CSCL environment succeeds to enhance core competencies like digital literacy, collaboration, and critical thinking.

VaKE steps 11 & 12: Second Decision & Second Dilemma Discussion
Once again, dialogue is in the center of collaboration. *Repeating* stages 3 & 4 the participants take part in a shared event.

VaKE step 13
Repeating steps 5 through 12 the change of perspective is useful.

VaKE step 14: Reflection
Collaboration is based on dialogue – equivalent to stage 5 – although the work is done individually. Each participant reflects on how he or she now considers the problem and which questions come up. Subsequently, these reflections can be posted on a Google Doc for all to see.

VaKE steps 15 & 16: General Synthesis & Generalization & Transfer
These steps are characterized by synergistic collaboration. The last stage finalizes the learning process and products of the whole session and is followed by a discussion on similar dilemmas and problems. This is the highest level of collaboration. It includes a general synthesis and considerations on how a transfer of the learning outcome to other issues is possible. The CSCL tools could be digital poster presentations: Padlet, Linoit, Canva, Vengage, Postermywall, Ripl. Learners collaborate fully at all phases in the creation of an original and innovative product that meshes contribution into a collective outcome that may be transferred to other similar dilemmas. The entire process may be organised and monitored by a digital platform that is used in the institution (e.g., Moodle, Blackboard) or a blog: Cooperative Digital Platforms: Doingtext, Blog app. At this final stage, important core competencies such as digital literacy collaboration and critical thinking come to the forefront of CSCL instruction.

4 Discussion

Our chapter shows how Computer Supported Collaborative Learning (CSCL) can enhance the application of the VaKE model to answer the Learning Framework 2030 challenges. We argue that incorporating digital collaborative environments when teaching educational dilemmas using the VaKE model enhances competencies like digital literacy, collaboration, critical thinking, and empathy. Our view of the suggested model is that when the process is collaborative, we build collaborative values, precisely in the digital global age, to find together what we have in common, without impairing the differences and subtleties of the individuals in the group. The latter can be expressed within the group sharing during the deliberations that take place in the process. At the end of the process, a collaborative group/community with shared values is established and therefore both the process and the digital tools have to be collaborative.

Notably, there are significant implications for teacher training. Researchers claim that the importance of developing ethical aspects in the teacher development process cannot be underestimated (Patry et al., 2013). The V*a*KE model enhances the professional identity of beginning teachers as leaders of change, developing critical thinking and an ethical perspective/identity. Teaching V*a*KE in the CSCL environment has an important added value: in collaborative digital learning, situations are created in which particular forms of interactions among learners are expected to occur, leading to collective productive learning experiences. Course facilitators in a teacher education framework can collect and document the metacognitive process collaboratively, in a spiral manner, via the digital platform that is in use at any specific institution.

Moreover, beyond the added value of documenting the process, which allows us to monitor, analyse and research the process (the obvious benefits) in the V*a*KE model using CSCL, we can promote democratic values of transparency, dialogue, supportive environment, and a sense of empowerment. When each participant presents an argument, it gives her or him responsibility and ownership of the process, thereby increasing engagement collaboration and cooperation. In a multicultural group (Alt & Raichel, 2018) this didactic tool can overcome psychological and cultural barriers that often prevent learners from understanding different values as well as cultural and ethical norms.

On the one hand, the collaborative applications offered in this chapter are specific and allow immediate and precise implementation of each of the V*a*KE stages; however, on the other hand, our presentation could inspire other pedagogical ideas in accordance with the model. We recommend that educators explore and experiment with further ways of implementing CSCL in a V*a*KE model that may be suitable for diverse needs of different communities and cultures.

There might be some limitations when incorporating digital collaborative activities (CSCL) in teaching educational dilemmas using the V*a*KE model. First, facilitators should be wary of allowing the technology itself to hog the limelight. It is easy and unproductive to be carried away by technology; in our case this would come at the expense of the very discussion we are trying to get under way.

Then, digital collaboration allows for documentation of the entire process (this does not happen in V*a*KE face-to-face instruction). Documentation, however, is dispersed and not organised in one digital tool, this at times might cause confusion. Nevertheless, one must remember that documentation is not at all possible in traditional VaKE instruction. In CSCL instruction of VaKE model learners have no option but to collaborate and connect in dilemma instruction which prepares our next generation to become good citizens of the world.

One solution can be blended or a hybrid instruction, which combines digital educational materials and opportunities for interaction online with traditional in class teaching methods. It requires the physical presence of both teacher and student, with some elements of student control over time, place, path, or pace. In our opinion, this solution may be the most effective one when teaching VaKE using digital tools.

References

Alt, D., & Raichel, N. (2018). *Different pedagogy – lifelong learning and higher education*. Tel-Aviv, Israel: Resling.

Bozalek, V., Gachago, D., Alexander, L., Watters, K., Wood, D., Ivala, E., & Herrington, J. (2013). The use of emerging technologies for authentic learning: A South African study in higher education. *British Journal of Educational Technology, 44*, 629–638.

Eyal, L. (2012). Digital assessment literacy – The core role of the teacher in a digital environment. *Journal of Educational Technology & Society, 15*(2), 37–49.

Eyal, L., Klavir, R., & Magid, N. (2018). The forum of excellent students: A model for cooperative learning in a multicultural environment. In M. Shonfeld & D. Gibson (Eds.), *Collaborative learning in a global world* (pp. 211–231). Charlotte, NC: Information Age Publishing.

Eyal, L. (2018, July 2–4). *Dilemma based learning integrated collaborative technologies: Teacher education course model* [Paper]. EDULEARNN 2018 Palma, 10th International Conference on education and new learning technologies.

Hod, Y., & Sagy, O. (2019). Conceptualizing the designs of authentic computer-supported collaborative learning environments in schools. *International Journal of Computer-Supported Collaborative Learning, 14*(2), 143–164. doi:10.1007/s11412-019-09300-7

Meirovitz, T., & Aran, S. (2020). An investigation of digital thinking skills in EFL digital instruction. *Interdisciplinary Journal of e-Skills and Lifelong Learning, 16*, 19–41. https://doi.org/10.28945/4610

OECD. (2019). *The OECD learning compass 2030*. Retrieved September 9, 2020, from http://www.oecd.org/education/2030-project/teaching-and-learning/learning/

Patry, J. L., Weyringer, S., & Weinberger, A. (2007). Combining values and knowledge education. In D. N. Aspin & J. D. Chapman (Eds.), Values *education and lifelong learning* (pp. 160–179). Dordrecht, The Netherlands: Springer.

Patry, J.-L., Weinberger, A., Weyringer, S., & Nussbaumer, M. (2013). Combining values and knowledge education. In B. J. Irby, G. Brown, R. Lara-Alecio, & S. Jackson (Eds.) and R. Robles-Piña (Sect. Ed.), *The handbook of educational theories* (pp. 565–580). Charlotte, NC: Information Age Publishing.

Pnevmatikos, D., Patry, J. L., Weinberger, A., Linortner, L., Weyringer, S., Maron, R., & Gordon-Shaag, A. (2016). Combining values and knowledge education for lifelong transformative learning. In E. Panitsides & J. Talbot (Eds.), *Lifelong learning: Concepts, benefits, and challenges* (pp. 109–134). New York, NY: Nova Science Publishers.

Salmons, J. E. (2006). *An overview of the taxonomy of collaborative e-Learning*. Boulder, CO: Vision2Lead.

Seifert, T. (2012). Social media and web 2.0 tools–modeling practices and online pedagogy. In *Proceedings Society for Information Technology & Teacher Education international conference* (pp. 4303–4308). Association for the Advancement of Computing in Education (AACE).

Seifert, T. (2016). Involvement, collaboration, and engagement: Social networks through a pedagogical lens. *Journal of Learning Design, 9*(2), 31–45.

Song, Y., & Looi, C. K. (2012). Linking teacher beliefs, practices, and student inquiry-based learning in a CSCL environment: A tale of two teachers. *International Journal of Computer-Supported Collaborative Learning, 7*(1), 129–159.

Weinberger, A., Patry, J.-L., & Weyringer, S. (2016). Improving professional practice through practice-based research: V*a*KE (Values *and* Knowledge Education) in university-based teacher education. *Vocations and Learning, 9*(1), 63–84.

Wise, A., & Schwarz, B. (2017). Visions of CSCL: Eight provocations for the future of the field. *International Journal of Computer-Supported Collaborative Learning,* 423–467. doi:10.1007/s11412-017-9267-5

CHAPTER 27

Civic Media as a Multicultural Dialogue

The Dilemma of Arab and Jewish Students via Documentary Filmmaking in Israel

Evanna Ratner

1 Introduction

In the 2018 Israeli election, the right-wing parties came into power, challenging coexistent dialogue and creating a dilemmatic situation for Cinema, Communication, and Civics students of Arab and Jewish origin. They met for a series of seminars that aimed to break down the wall of hostility and create a dialogue about the "elephant in the room" – the Jewish-Arab conflict. They knew they were not going to bring peace on Earth; all wanted to get to know the other's culture. They met together in the seminars but as teenagers, they were full of stereotypes and negative feelings and were very certain about their own righteousness. The meetings were very emotional and when raising the nationality dilemma, there were mixed feelings to deal with. What is "The nationality dilemma"? questioning Israel as a Jewish state. And denying the right of Arabs on it. We thought that these judicial racist events would ruin what we had just started to build in the seminars. However, the conflicts only strengthened the connection between the two groups, keeping them on an island of sanity in the sea of hatred. It was understood that this project of "Civic Media" (Heffner & Zuckerman, 2007) is a tool for bridging this gap by simply meeting, talking, getting to know each other, and reaching a solution by questioning and creating a mutual story. Inspired by that first experience with teachers, for more than ten years, Arab and Jewish students come together to create collaborative videos. Our studies illustrated how these encounters have an effect on the students' empathy and their ability to acknowledge each other's narrative (Friesem, 2015; Ratner, 2015).

Media has the power of telling stories to help us identify with characters and to affect viewers. Cinema has the power to foster empathy towards the others' narrative, because it tells personal stories that are more difficult to argue with. Creating a collaborative and yet personal video allows for a place where both Arab and Jewish stories can be told. The equality that does not exist in reality has a place in the movies.

Learning cinema allows students the ability and skill of media literacy that includes inspiring and creative viewing. This skill is a significant skill of the adult character as seen in the basic skills of the OECD (2017). Similar to Freire's process of teaching literacy skills to liberate students from oppression, media literacy education aims to enhance the students' competencies in access, analysis, creation, reflection, and action (Hobbs, 2010). Media literacy is defined as the ability to locate, analyse, evaluate, and create media messages using a wide range of technological tools that characterize the information age and can be used for shared life. (Salomon, 2006; Jenkins, 2007)

There is no doubt that the students' dialogical encounter, despite being hostile and including distrust, is intended to try to bridge a contrasting reality and allow for a co-creation as in the contact hypostasis (Petigrew, 2008; Allport, 1954).

The 20% Arab minority in Israel is mainly Muslim, but also contains Christians and Druze. Their cultural heritage and identity are challenged daily as they represent an Arabic speaking minority in a country with a significant Hebrew speaking Jewish majority (Bar-Tal, Rozen, & Nets-Zehngut, 2009). This case study provides an insight into challenges and dilemmas as well as affordances of media literacy as an approach to civic education in conflict areas such as Israel. Based on our own observations and the participants' reflection, we demonstrate how the process of learning to produce a documentary as a form of deliberation, had potential to promote deep and challenging dialogue between the Arab and Jewish students. The language gap however prevented the dialogue but increased the need of working together in film. Each participant represented her/his cultural heritage by producing a personal narrative and celebrating media as a language.

This study examines collaborative documentary filmmaking within the framework of the bi-national programme "Dialogue through Cinema". As part of a national programme in the film classes from 2016 to 2018, students of civic education Film and Communication studies created documentaries as a way to have a cultural dialogue for the purpose of peace education. The structure of the meetings was based on the model of collaborative film making of dialog through media (Ratner, 2015) and media for empathy (Friesem, 2017), while practicing media literacy to analyse, create, and reflect on each other's personal narratives (Hobbs, 2010; Shalita, Friedman, & Harten, 2011). Producing collaborative films allows Jewish and Arab students to tell their personal narratives as well as stories of their communities and nations through symbols that include sound, movement, and other tools of cinematic emotional manipulation that a written story cannot generate (Bar On & Adwan, 2006). Creating a movie is an artistic subjective expression of thoughts, emotions, motivations, and fears that affect and give a voice.

To underline the development and the outcome of this project, an example is presented.

2   Naama & Riham Learning to Produce a Documentary

In one of the intercultural exchanges, Naama (pseudonym), a Jewish student, talked about her trauma of living near an Arab village and experiencing the workers come into her settlement for work. She always remembers her grandmother's stories from Iraq where she experienced the Farhood (Arab rioters). When reflecting on Naama's comment, Riham (pseudonym) a shy Arab student, shared her experience as the granddaughter of a Palestinian descendent of the village of Safury. This village is a symbol since a Jewish settlement called Zipory was built on the ground of Safury.

This revelation was a defining moment as each of them was telling their story. In a shy voice, Riham explained how being a Palestinian refugee in your own country is devastating, and not having it recognised by the government is really hard. Everybody was curious and asked questions about the situation. Naama was stunned and sat quietly. In her interview, she reflected on how she was looking at Riham at that moment and felt empathy for her story. It took Naama and Riham two meetings of collaborative exercises and hesitations until they decided to work together. Facilitators acknowledged that it is important that the goal of the mutual creation comes from participants themselves. They did not force them to choose a more difficult path. At some point, one of the facilitators even suggested to both of them to produce different movies with other participants because he thought that the conflict was too painful: "It's like a victim meeting his aggressor and being asked to understand him". And yet, both Naama and Riham decided to make a documentary together, visiting each other's home, and village.

Naama decided to visit Safury, Riham's grandparents' village. This visit was especially emotional, considering that Riham told her story in the Palestinian cemetery that is in the middle of the settlement and Naama listened to her story closely. Then they went together to Riham's village and that was the first time Naama visited an Arab village in person. When both of them came back with the footage and screened it in class, all the other participants were moved by the student's collaboration of the two. Naama shared the experience of visiting the ancient Arab village which is now a Jewish settlement, and you can only imagine how it was, and of course her visit to Riham's home. "It does not look like anything that we know. I've never ever visited Arabs and I discovered welcoming pleasant and generous people. However, most Israeli Jews, don't have Arab friends and don't visit Arab villages".

3 How Do the Principles of the V*a*KE Approach Engage in Civic Media?

Riham and Naama's experience is a great background story for questions and dilemmas as part of an active process: the new information is checked for its viability. Naama hasn't been to an Arab village, Riham has never heard of life stories of Jews in Arab countries, both were learning and creating an individual reality. The learning person is constructing his/her knowledge according to his/her experience, each one has her personal narrative, learning is not a striving for objective knowledge and a finding of the ontological reality; it is the construction of a personal and individual world. Civic media is a method for learning and creates conflict situations, where people are confronted with problems, which they cannot solve with the knowledge they have.

The learning process happens when the subject has a close relationship with the learner. So, the answer to the question "For what reason do I learn?" has an enormous effect on learning: the quality of the learning process depends on the extent to meet this target. (Patry et al., 2007) Teachers have to create learning situations, which provoke cognitive conflicts for the students. The role of the teacher is to accompany the students in their very personal process of knowledge acquisition followed by the viability-check of the knowledge.

The highlight of the collaborative documentary was when Riham told her family's story and Naama told her family's story. It increased empathy and encouraged both of them to acknowledge and celebrate each other's cultural heritage. As we saw in Ratner's (2015) research, making videos with a personal or communal narrative enhances the connection between young filmmakers and increases the viewers' empathy toward the characters' narrative. Riham's story in the cemetery (the most holy place), created a moment of empathy. This moment of viewing together generated empathic reactions also among the participants' families who saw the film for the first time. These viewers did not know Naama and Riham. Interestingly enough, Naama and Riham's movie became politically relevant. In a time when politicians are fighting over settlements and the rights of return for Palestinian, their movie was able to bring Jewish viewers a little bit closer to the issue and generate understanding and recognition of the legitimacy of each other's narrative.

4 Conclusion

Discussions about ethics and values mostly take place in special lessons. Media literacy and film studies are some of these lessons. The main emphasis is put on teaching knowledge by enquiry and film. In school the students learn facts, in the sense that knowledge might be useful for life. But the importance of special knowledge is exposed to the process of cultural development and to the personal decision of getting involved in this change. Education in school has not only to provide knowledge, but also to stimulate reflective thinking about the viability of this knowledge when sharing responsibility in a future social community.

So, the role of values within the decision-making process has to be brought into the awareness of any individual person. Therefore, school education has not only the responsibility for teaching but also for the debate on active participation in social development.

The programme fostered coexistence and provided practical tools for peace education between Arabs and Jews in Israel. The yearlong collaboration between two students who participated in the programme, produced a joint documentary, reduced hostility, adverse emotions, and stereotypes while at the same time creating a will for recognition, contact, and legitimacy of each other's narrative (Jewish and Arab). As we re-evaluate existing paradigms for teaching and learning about the impact and potential of media for democratic processes and civic engagement, this case study showcases a successful practice for fostering a cultural dialogue. In his article, Lan (2013) suggested a framework of democratic media literacy to include deliberative, pluralistic, and participatory practices. The story of Naama and Riham is an example of how civic media can reduce stereotypes, foster empathy, and offer a path to overcome conflict. Making a collaborative documentary is a participatory action that includes a deliberate approach to acknowledge and be sensitive to the other's narrative that leads to empathy and recognition of the legitimacy of each other's narrative. The students practiced empathy and a deliberate democratic and civic action as part of producing a documentary. This case study offers a practice where media literacy education can advance civic engagement and be a model for professional development of students in conflict areas.

References

Allport, G. (1954). *The nature of prejudice*. Cambridge, MA: Addison-Wesley.
Bar-On, A. S. (2006). The psychology for a better Dialogue. In R. Rotberg (Ed.), *Israeli and Palestinian narratives of conflict: History's double helix,* Bloomington, IN: Indiana University Press.
Bar-Tal, D., Rozen, Y., & Nets-Zehngut, R. (2009). Peace education in societies involved in intractable conflicts: Goals, conditions, and directions. In G. Salomon & E. Cairns (Eds.), *Handbook of peace education.* New York, NY: Psychology press.

Friesem, Y. (2015). Empathy for the digital age: Using video production to enhance social, emotional, and cognitive skills. In S. Tettegah, & D. Espelage (Eds.), *Emotions, technology, and behaviors* (pp. 21–45). San Diego, CA: Academic Press. doi:10.1016/B978-0-12-801873-6.00002-9

Friesem, Y. (2017). The media production hive: Using media education for differentiated instruction. *Media Education – Studies, Research, Best Practice, 8*(1), 123–140. doi:10.14605/MED811708

Heffner, A. (Interviewer) & Zuckerman, E. (Interviewer). (2017, September 7). Defining civic media. *PBS' The Open Mind* [TV program]. Retrieved August 10, 2020, from https://www.thirteen.org/openmind/media/defining-civic-media/5792/

Hobbs, R. (2010). *Digital and media literacy: A plan of action* [White Paper]. Washington, DC: The Aspen Institute. Retrieved September 9, 2020, from http://www.knightcomm.org/wp-content/uploads/2010/11/Digital_and_Media_Literacy_A_Plan_of_Action.pdf

Hobbs, R., Donnelly, K., Friesem, J., & Moen, M. (2013). Learning to engage: How positive attitudes about the news, media literacy, and video production contribute to adolescent civic engagement. *Educational Media International, 50*(4), 231–246. doi:10.1080/09523987.2013.862364

Jenkins, H. (2007, October 3). *What is civic media?* Confessions of an ACA-fan: The official weblog of Henry Jenkins. Retrieved June 3, 2017, from http://henryjenkins.org/2007/10/what_is_civic_media_1.html

Lan, C. (2013). Democratic education in the new media era: Toward a framework of democratic media literacy. *The Ohio Social Studies Review, 50*(1), 52–62.

Minister of Education. (2009). *Report of the Public Committee to formulate national policies regarding shared life education between Jews and Arabs in Israel.* Jerusalem, Israel: Salomon & Essawi. [in Hebrew with executive summary in English]

Patry, J.-L., Weyringer, S., & Weinberger, A. (2007). Combining values and knowledge education. In D. Aspin & J. Chapman (Eds.), *Values education and lifelong learning* (pp. 160–179). New York, NY: Springer Press.

Pettigrew, T. F. (2008). Future directions for intergroup contact theory and research. *International Journal of Intercultural Relations, 32,* 187–199.

Ratner, E. (2015). *Dialogue through cinema: The contribution of film-production in a bi-national framework to coexistence and peace education* [Unpublished doctoral dissertation]. University of Haifa, Israel.

Salomon, G. (2006). Does peace education really make a difference? Peace and Conflict. *Journal of Peace Psychology, 12*(1), 37–48.

Shalita, R., Friedman, A., & Harten, R. (2011). *Visual literacy in action: Education in the visual era.* Tel Aviv, Israel: Mofet.

CHAPTER 28

MAaKE – Moral Action *and* Knowledge Education
Considerations on a Practical Model for Moral Action Based on VaKE

Sieglinde Weyringer

1   Introduction

"This is immoral". This sentence is often heard as a commentary on an observed or narrated everyday action. But when you react with the question "Why?" and ask for a rationale for this assessment, you get answers that very often suggest that the justification stands on swampy ground, i.e., that it follows a feeling rather than factual logic. This vagueness, in turn, makes it difficult to plan an action with the claim to be a moral one.

In various scientific disciplines (e.g., philosophy, sociology, psychology, pedagogy, economics, ecology, political science), a huge variety of theoretical and practical models of action have been developed. Each of these disciplines has a different focus, e.g., questions on epistemology, logical argumentation and ethics in philosophical models, the aspects of culture, environment and belonging in sociological models, the acquisition of knowledge and skills in models of learning and training, their transfer and realization in models of process management, morality in politics or the effects of a concrete project on the environment in ecological models.

Many philosophical arguments are psychological in essence, although they are based on philosophical accounts, particularly Aristotle's virtue ethics. There is a hot debate among philosophers – the situationism debate – whether the virtues issue is appropriate, with reference to the situativity of moral behaviour (e.g., empirical studies by Hartshorne & May, 1928; Milgram, 1974; Latané & Darley, 1970; etc.).

There are also a variety of theoretical approaches to moral action, which focus on selected characteristics of action and their interaction with regard to the claim of wanting to perform an action as a moral one.

The aim of this chapter is *not* to provide an analytical overview of the practicability of all these approaches in order to answer the question "Why?" on a more stable foundation than the affective one. The idea for this chapter is rather to elaborate a practice model for the use in daily life, how it is possible "to walk the talk". This means: to provide a frame within which diverse components are suggested as potential indicators for the assessment of an action as "moral", to use a process model of action for identifying milestones of a respective formative evaluation of the implementation, and finally to create a training model aiming at the establishment of a moral habitus as a core characteristic of a person's behaviour. This idea builds on V*a*KE as a precondition for the further nurture of attitudes and dispositions developed through repeated participation in V*a*KE courses. The assumption is that a person first needs to establish knowledge and a subjective understanding of an issue at stake – this could happen through a preliminary V*a*KE course. Linking the "talk" (moral judgement) with the "walk" (acting morally) could be organised by addressing explicit knowledge on the components of an action and their modulation when ethical principles are respected. This knowledge provides the base to plan and perform an action which could be assessed as moral. A first draft of an appropriate training concept will be presented. It is called MA*a*KE (Moral Action *and* Knowledge Education) since it is in line with V*a*KE and based on this approach. Additionally, it takes into account characteristics elaborated by scientific disciplines as relevant for action. The reader is cordially invited to contribute to the further development with critical feedback and remarks.

Aiming at this, several questions arise: (1) What is a moral action? or What are the components and criteria for describing a line of action as moral? (2) How can the process of a supposedly moral action be described? or Which steps within the line of an action need ethical considerations? (3) Which competences nurture an action based on ethical thinking? Or how can a person trained with V*a*KE transfer ethical thinking into a moral action? (4) Based on the elaboration of these questions, the practice model MA*a*KE will be presented.

2 Moral Action – An Approximation to the Concept

As mentioned earlier, reflections on the question "When does an action deserve the attribution of being a moral one?" can look back on a long and varied research tradition. Referring to the studies of Hartshorne and May (1928), moral action can be defined as "conformity to a social norm of honesty" (Mosher et al., 1999, p. XXII). Moral actions involve an internal component, a moral cognition (Blasi, 1980) or moral judgement, and they have a moral emotion component (Kohlberg, 1984, p. 500). Moral worth is characterized by the agent's motives and aspects of character. Further, internal circumstances like the agent's intellectual and emotional condition as well as external ones like characteristics of the social milieu in which a person lives, enfold their impact on the judgement whether an action is morally good or morally right

(Spielthenner, 2005). Other concepts highlight the thinking actor and his or her thoughtfulness as categories for defining an action as moral: the thoughtful dimension is given the defining form, through which mere behaviour turns into a moral act. This dimension opens possibilities to handle the distinction between choice and voluntary action which is estimated central in the moral discourse (Sokolowski, 2017).

2.1   The Field of Action Components and Criteria

Scientific debates contribute fundamentally to finding answers for questions like "Why and when can an action justifiably be called moral?" However, from the point of view of practical everyday routines and related decisions, the following very simple and unsophisticated question is more appropriate for finding answers, or better: for initiating the search for answers: "How many components of an action must be ethical to qualify the action as moral?" The wording chosen raises the question of whether, in addition to qualitative criteria (ethical or other values?) quantitative criteria (how many components?) should additionally be used for an evaluation. Such questions also play a role in the day-to-day evaluation process.

Figure 28.1 brings together a number of potential components that may play a role in the evaluation. The compilation was carried out by the author in the form of a brainstorming after an extensive review of existing scientific literature and theoretical concepts on the diverse components constituting an action. It does not claim to cover all the relevant components, therefore, it includes the component "Other issues". All components can be analysed in terms of either ethical-moral criteria or other qualitative, e.g., economic, ecological, aesthetic, democratic, political, cultural, religious, etc. criteria. Although all these qualitative criteria have different meanings concerning the types of components, in daily life this distinction is not in the foreground when the respective term is used together with the criteria.

Figure 28.1 presents the field of potential components of action. The main constitutional components are:
– the *agent*, this is the person who is doing something;
– the *values*, these are the criteria for the decision, why the person should do something;
– the *matter*, this is the issue to be solved;
– the *process* in its timeline of activities with a start and an end;
– the *consequences* of the action, these are the outcomes together with real or possible side effects and their impact on further actions.

Each of these components is constituted by a bundle of further elements, e.g., maturity of the agent and within this component for example courage, which

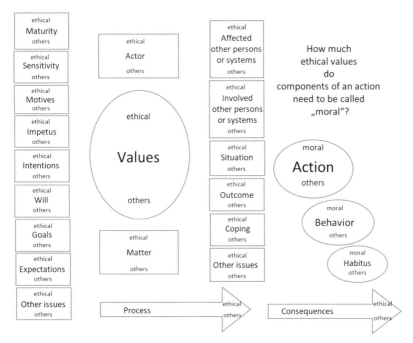

FIGURE 28.1 Field of potential components of action

can be attributed either to ethical or other criteria, e.g., economic, aesthetical, ecological, political, legal, ecological, sociological, religious, cultural, traditional, etc. The figure avoids presenting links, relationships, interference or interactions between the presented components and elements. It aims at opening the floor for specific questions of the type "What is needed to be qualified as 'moral'"?

Five components highlight the related difficulties with possible answers; only several examples are provided here:

- *Agent:* Does the agent need to have ethical maturity? If we consider ethical maturity based on the theoretical traditions following Jean Piaget and Lawrence Kohlberg (high stage of moral judgment), any action of a child will miss this qualification.
- *Values:* Can an action be called "moral" if it involves financial gain, such as when a politician gives the contract for ordering means necessary for the containment of the Corona pandemic to a contractor with close relationship to the politician and without competitive bidding because that company can deliver the means quickly?
- *Matter:* Is it a moral action, if a criminal syndicate gives facilities of health care to families aiming to increase its own influence and power on a neighbourhood?
- *Process:* Can an action become morally justified, if during the activity ethical principles and human rights are neglected, e.g., if a volunteer on a rescue

vessel for illegal migrants in distress at sea fights with a frontier solder and throws him into the sea?
– *Consequences:* Can an action be qualified as moral, if the outcome and impact of the activity hurts ethical principles, e.g., when a person founds orphanages in Africa and thereby destroys existing family structures?

Other questions concern the classification of the act: Is it a conscious individual action, is it a more unconscious behaviour, or is it a habit and characteristic of a person?

A brief insight in related concepts provide the theoretical base for anchoring the practical model MA*a*KE.

2.2 The Act: Behaviour, Action or Habitus?

This section brings together selected topics and theories from which a sum of anchor points can be derived providing a base for qualifying an action as moral and for the base of a respective training concept.

The three terms *behaviour, action, and habitus* have been quite important in the scientific debates about moral action. The aim and the scope of this chapter limits the considerations only to the main lines of these debates. In psychological approaches *behaviour* first of all is linked to a mechanism of overt reactions on one or more stimuli. Within this scientific discipline further theoretical developments include cognitive processes such as thinking, perception, and consciousness as well as emotional and affective processes regarding concepts of human behaviour. Reward and reinforcement as well as their opposite hold a corresponding learning, training, or appropriation process in progress. The complexity of this expanded concept of human behaviour makes it possible to distinguish it from the concept of human action: In sociological approaches the term behaviour is used in a more comprehensive and general understanding in contrast to the term «action».

Action can be described as the summing up of all activities which are ultimately based on the same idea of an objective (Heckhausen, 1991, p. 13). It derives from behaviour in the sense of stimulus – response interaction, and it is rather related to concrete situations and activities (independent whether visible or invisible). Furthermore, action is especially linked to one or more people as doing or not-doing something, and who associate a subjective sense – understood as meaning and understanding – with it (Weber, 1922/1978, p. 1). If this subjective sense is oriented towards the behaviour of another person or people, it is called "social action". Picking up this description for the concern of this chapter, an action can be called moral, if this subjective sense is orientated towards the agent's moral values and towards those of the people involved.

Weber (1922/1978, p. 12f.) distinguishes four types of social action: goal rational social action, value rational social action, affective social action, and traditional social action. For the idea of MAaKE, priority is given at this place to the first two types (goal and value rationality) for clarification over the other two types (affective and traditional). Furthermore, the term action is used without the attribute social because this change opens the possibility to include the moral aspect into the further considerations.

Goal-rational (or rational-purposeful) actions refer to a means-end relation. A person acts rationally and expediently when, throughout the process of drawing up and implementing an action plan, she or he keeps an eye on the objective (or objectives), the means and the presumed consequences, and constantly weighs the means against the ends and the ends against the expected consequences rationally.

Value-rational actions are guided by a person's conviction and self-commitment that he or she must act in accordance with certain transferred or self-imposed claims. Such claims may be based on different values, e.g., duty, guilt, human dignity, aesthetics, the importance of a matter, religious values, etc. – not just moral values.

These descriptions highlight that the weighing of objectives and their consequences as well as their qualitative assessment in the sense of right/wrong or good/bad should accompany the entire course of an action as a core activity. Ethical principles but also other ones are possible to serve as criteria for this. Following Weber (1926/2015, p. 81), every ethically oriented action can be based on an "ethics of moral convictions" that does not contemplate the consequences of the actions but only the underlying principles, or based on "ethics of responsibility", in which consequences for the ordered actions are anticipated and full responsibility is taken. The two ethics are not mutually exclusive. According to Weber (1919/1994), they are complementary to one another, and only in combination can they unfold their power in social actions. This effect is assumed to be also valid for an action with the claim to be moral. This contrasting interweaving of the two ethics unfolds its power in different phases of an action, e.g., a person plans an action based on his or her own convictions of goals and values, however during the implementation the person changes goals and values towards demands of responsibility towards others. For the intention and claim to plan an action not only as a social but also as a moral one is a situation considered as an additional challenge. This challenge needs to be particularly in the focus of the development of a training concept for MAaKE, because it requires reliable mental tools such as sensitivity, awareness and knowledge about ethics and moral values to be able to make appropriate corrections and to justify them.

Every action is embedded in social systems – this tenet receives a specific relevance when linked to moral action. The theory on the structure of social action (Parsons, 1937) offers to explore the interlinkage between ends, means and the interdependence between four subsystems: organism, defined as the person's bio-physical system; personality, defined as the individual's orientation system for actions; culture, defined as the person's values; norms shared with a social group; and the social system, defined as a system of different roles which a person can take in interpersonal relationships and interactions. These subsystems with their structures and interrelationships unfold a huge variety of influences on the evaluation of whether an action can be qualified as moral.

Systems theory raises social fields into the horizon of perception, which would not be considered directly for a current action. For example, the Ecological Systems Theory (Bronfenbrenner, 2009) lends itself to identifying five different layers of social systems and exploring how their structures interact between and within them. Following this approach, the range of layers include the microsystem represented by the individual person, the mesosystem represented by the group to which the person belongs (e.g., the friends), the exosystem represented by a group category to which the person does not belong (e.g., migrants), the macrosystem (e.g., Austrians as a specific society), and the chronosystem representing the dimension of time. This model can be broadened by including the layer of the natural environment system, because climate and biodiversity of the location where the activity is hosted, are also justified to be respected (Jonas, 1984). Questions about the influence of position, equipment and rewards of these social systems arise in terms of cohesion, consistency, stability, and orientation dynamics. Corresponding answers affect whether an action can be described as moral.

To establish an understanding of a moral act requires negotiation processes between agents and stakeholders and interactions with these social systems. It is not enough for individuals to build up their own catalogue of criteria. Language and communication are the core tools and acts for this purpose. Following Habermas (1984, 1987), speech acts are related to three different areas of reality – the objective, the social, and the subjective world – and they shape personality, culture, and social systems. The overall ethical principle claims four rules for validity: truth, correctness, truthfulness (in the sense of sincerity) and comprehensibility. This applies to all communicative actions and is not limited to speaking, as these aim at understanding. They combine teleological, normative, and dramaturgical actions and provide reflexive and reflected relations between the three different areas of reality. Understanding can be linked to the subjective sense of Weber (see above). It requires active participation in communication processes, especially when norms and values are in the focus of agreement.

Communicative actions are not limited to speech acts. They require the perception of, and the exchange with the person I. The principles of recognition, e.g., showing visible gestures of love, esteem, respect, and friendship (e.g., Honneth, 1992) are recommended to accompany social actions. They serve as an instrument of navigation within this wide field of components and interdependencies not only for social actions but also for creating an action as moral.

Habitus – this term is associated with habits of thinking, feeling, and acting a person or a social entity develops over time and applies them in various situations. It is a system of dispositions (Elias, 1994; Bourdieu, 1977). They include all expressions of personality or corporate identity like habits of thinking, feeling, and acting, lifestyle, language, dressing, taste, etc. Furthermore, they are indicators for the social status of a person within a social class or system. In contrast to behaviour (based on stimulus-response reactions) habitus develops by actively creating strategies and forms of practice in a social context.

The idea of MA*a*KE and the intention to create the respective training concept is guided by the objective that acting morally should become part of habitus – its performance should not remain reduced to a concrete situation; it should become part of personality as a generalizing quality of thinking, feeling, and acting across similar situations. This claim leads the considerations towards the *agent* and towards the *process* of an action. With reference to the extensive research on moral character (e.g., Rest, 1986), the following focus is not on personality factors of the agent, but on the process of an action and its consequences. Rather, the focus is on identifying ways to build the MA*a*KE training concept on V*a*KE, with the aim of using the skills and competences acquired there to qualify an action as moral. Aspects such as the consistency of behaviour, the control of action in all its particular sequences, and evaluation and retrospective are also of interest when establishing a transsituational habitus.

Before the presentation of a first draft for a MA*a*KE training concept, however, the next section contains a list of different anchor points for assessing an action as "moral", which are derived from the above.

2.3   *Anchors for Qualifying an Action as Moral*

The following list contains eleven anchor points which should provide a stable frame for the training concept of MA*a*KE. In each anchor the core aspect is highlighted in italics. These anchors can also be used as inspiration for other pedagogical activities beside MA*a*KE. This list does not claim to be complete. It claims validity for the training concept of MA*a*KE due to the interest of the author.

- Anchor 1 is related to *behaviour*: Acting morally *includes unconscious as well conscious aspects*. It is influenced by emotions and affective processes, and it needs reward and reinforcement – either on the level of personal self or from others.
- Anchor 2 is related to *action*: Acting morally is *orientated towards oneself as well as toward others* – people as well a nature – by taking into account the values orientations as well as the needs of both the agent and the others regarding the chosen goals and their consequences.
- Anchor 3 is based on *Weber*: Acting morally demands *weighing means, ends and consequences* for the involved parties.
- Anchor 4 is based on *Weber*: Acting morally is *sensitive to the two opposing ethica maxims* – moral conviction and responsibility – and finds ways to combine them appropriately.
- Anchor 5 is based on *Parsons, Bronfenbrenner, and Jonas*: Acting morally is *embedded in more than one social system*.
- Anchor 6 is based on *Habermas*: Acting morally *follows rules of communication* like truth, correctness, truthfulness, and comprehensibility.
- Anchor 7 is based on *Habermas*: Acting morally *respects and accepts different areas of reality* (objective, social, and subjective).
- Anchor 8 is based on *Honneth*: Acting morally *applies visible gestures* of love, esteem, respect, friendship.
- Anchor 9 is related to *habitus*: Acting morally *aims to develop a routine* by establishing transsituational consistency and controlled ethical behaviour.
- Anchor 10 is related to *agent*: Acting morally needs *permanent critical self-reflection on the development of personality factors*.
- Anchor 11 is related to *process and consequences*: Acting morally needs *permanent evaluation of ethical orientation* throughout the process and including the consequences.

For learning to act morally, each anchor can be considered as an educational objective in a training course or can serve as a criterion for formative and summative evaluation throughout the training course.

3   The Model MA*a*KE Moral Action *and* Knowledge Education

This section concentrates on establishing a model for a training course, in which competences related to discussion (see Chapter 3 in this handbook) diverse thinking styles and collaboration (see Chapter 30 in this handbook) trained in a V*a*KE course are applied on the concrete performance in a process of action. This model is called MAaKE (Moral Action *and* Knowledge Education), highlighting its foundations in VaKE and *making* as action. The Rubicon model developed by Heckhausen and Gollwitzer (1987) is used to demonstrate the process of action prototypically. This model continues to gain recognition and interest from researchers, particularly in the context of changing behaviour patterns (e.g., Keller et al., 2020).

3.1 The Base: Rubicon Model and VaKE Competences

The Rubicon model (Heckhausen & Gollwitzer, 1987; Heckhausen, 1991) consists of the following phases: (1) predecisional motivation in which selected motives unfold their power to nurture the intention to act (e.g., Cesar's intention to cross the Rubicon); (2) pre-actional volition in which the possibilities of action execution are considered (called fiat tendency) and which is concluded by the decision for a certain execution; (3) actional volition in which the intention is realized and which is concluded by the deactivation of the intention (e.g., to calm down emotionally); (4) post-actional motivation in which the action is evaluated and further steps are considered. In each phase, a certain activity is predominant: (1) choose, (2) plan, (3) act, (4) evaluate. The parameters, expectations, incentives (meaning the impact of a promised reward on the motivation to act), situations, consequences and attributions have an intensifying or inhibiting effect on the course of action.

When aiming at changing behaviour towards a habitus of morally acting ethical considerations need to be included in this list of parameters, because they unfold their influence in any phase of the course. Additionally, the detailed contemplation of possible consequences (e.g., Colby & Kohlberg, 1987) and the impact on social realities beyond the scope and time horizon of the action have to be considered. Within the scope of this chapter, it is not possible to go into particular approaches of consequentialism (e.g., Darwall, 2003); however, one can keep in mind questions on the relation to utilitarianism and further on types of consequences of what and for whom.

The various activities in VaKE courses strengthen competences that enable a person to recognise the ethical and moral dimension of problems and to take this into account when making the decisions for action. Core competences trained with VaKE are related to awareness and consciousness of one's own value preferences, sensitivity for values involved in problems, realization and coping with diverse views on problems and diverse realities, culture of communication, following discussion rules, decision making combined with justification and argumentation, collaboration within a group, critical reflexion, and anticipation. These competencies can also be used in the concrete implementation of the action plan.

The use of these competences is assumed to contribute to acting morally or to be able to judge an action as moral.

3.2 The MAaKE Course

Table 28.1 presents the proposal for a prototypical course of MAaKE based on the Rubicon model and VaKE-*dis* (see Chapter 2 in this handbook). It needs the participation in VaKE courses as preparation (Step 0), and it proceeds in 20 steps.

The MAaKE course aims at the development of a habitus which includes taking ethical criteria into consideration in all components of an action. The identified anchors serve as frame for educational objectives and for possibilities to set priorities for pedagogical interventions. The overall aim is to develop a routine of acting morally in the sense of habitus. Therefore, particular importance is attached to repeated participation in the course because a change in behaviour and the establishment of a routine does not happen after a single action (e.g., Oser & Schläfli, 1985).

A core difference between VaKE and MAaKE is related to the decision: in MAaKE all involved parties have to pull together, this means the total agreement of all involved parties on the plan and the proceeding of the action is fundamental (discursive ethics, see Oser et al., 1991). Therefore, discussions must continue until the strong arguments for one option prevail and the counterarguments remain weak. In this context the knowledge aspect in MAaKE is given a similar core position than it has in VaKE. The same importance is given to knowledge in the phases of planning and implementing the action.

In the prototypical MAaKE course (Table 28.1) all activities in steps 1 to 20 are accompanied by a formative evaluation bringing ethical concerns into focus explicitly. It is assumed that this permanent evaluation together with discussions and reflections strengthen competences to act morally in daily routine.

4 Concluding and Opening Remarks

The aim of this chapter was to stimulate reflection on how in everyday life the assessment is made that an action is moral. Through a brainstorming based on the reading of scientific papers on the subject of moral action, different determinants of an action were highlighted and linked to the question "How many components of an action must be ethical to qualify the action as moral?" This question may be practical in daily life reflections. However, if the claim to become more aware of the weight of values on daily decisions increasingly

TABLE 28.1   Prototypical course of MAaKE based on Rubicon model and VaKE-dis

MAaKE course Ethical criteria of components considered in each step	VaKE trained competences – applied	Anchor points	Rubicon model
Step 0: VaKE course **Pre-decision phase**	Preparation		
Steps 1 and 2: to elaborate a concrete vision of an action that can be called "moral" and to assess it as an improvement *with explicit emphasis on ethical criteria*	Sensitization: Raising awareness for values Critical reflection and anticipation	Anchor 1 Anchor 2 Anchor 3 Anchor 4 Anchor 5 Anchor 7	Choosing: Motivation pre-decisional
Steps 3, 4 and 5: to specify the difference between vision and current situation and to collect possibilities *with explicit emphasis on ethical criteria*	Discussion: Following discussion rules, coping with different perspectives, with diverse realities, considering consequences	Anchor 1 Anchor 2 Anchor 4 Anchor 5 Anchor 6 Anchor 7 Anchor 8	Choosing: Motivation pre-decisional
			Intention formation
Step 6: to decide *with explicit focus on ethical criteria*	Decision: with agreement on realization	Anchor 1 Anchor 2 Anchor 3 Anchor 4 Anchor 7	
Post-decision phase			
Step 7 and 8: to specify the intention in a plan and to elaborate it *with explicit emphasis on ethical criteria*	Collaboration: communication and search for information	Anchor 1 to Anchor 8	Planning: Volitional pre-actional (fiat tendency)

(cont.)

TABLE 28.1 Prototypical course of MAaKE based on Rubicon model and VaKE-dis (cont.)

MAaKE course Ethical criteria of components considered in each step	VaKE trained competences – applied	Anchor points	Rubicon model
Step 9, 10 and 11: to establish control, monitoring and gratification tools, criteria for success *with explicit emphasis on ethical criteria*	Collaboration: communication and democratic agreement	Anchor 1 Anchor 2 Anchor 6 Anchor 7 Anchor 8	Planning: Volitional pre-actional (fiat tendency)
Step 12: to decide doing the plan and to fix it by contract *including ethical criteria explicitly*	Democratic agreement:	Anchor 1 Anchor 2 Anchor 6 Anchor 7 Anchor 8	Planning: Volitional pre-actional (fiat tendency)
Action phase: Intention initiation			
Steps 13, 14 and 15: to realize the plan, the control and formative evaluation *with explicit emphasis on ethical criteria* and to finish it	Communication and collaboration, democratic agreement: coping with diverse realities, coping with different perspectives	Anchor 1 to Anchor 8	Acting: Intention implementation Volitional actional
Post-action phase: Intention deactivation			
Steps 16 and 17: to evaluate summative and to gain gratification *with explicit focus on ethical criteria*	Critical reflection Critical anticipation	Anchor 1 Anchor 2 Anchor 3 Anchor 5 Anchor 7	Evaluating: Motivation post-actional
Steps 18, 19, 20: to repeat, to transfer, to establish a routine of acting morally	Habitualization establishing routine by repeating the course	Anchor 9 Anchor 10 Anchor 11	Choosing: Motivation pre-decisional

Note: *Italics*: reference to moral action

arises followed by the commitment to establish an awareness and sensitivity for ethical principles, the need for a training concept comes into focus aiming at the establishment of acting morally as a habitus of a person. Inspired by the experienced effects and impact of VaKE on personal development, the idea was to extend this approach towards MAaKE (Moral Action *and* Knowledge Education). The presented training concept is currently an idea, i.e., its feasibility has to be investigated in more details. Preliminary steps in this regard have been done in several studies: monitoring self-willful intent by female migrants (see Chapter 16 in this handbook); analysing one's teaching through teacher training (Weinberger et al., 2016); learning tactful behaviour with VaKE (see Chapter 20 in this handbook); action following VaKE, like becoming a workshop leader (see Chapter 15 in this handbook). Nevertheless, it is a proposal "to walk the talk", this means to continue VaKE courses in the direction of implementing its outcomes into concrete actions in daily life.

The central mechanism for this transformation is formative evaluation. It is an accompanying process, which means that the evaluation of whether the action can be called moral should take place not only after completion of an action, but during the entire action decision and execution process. This requires time to pause and check whether the set requirements are met or whether the subjective evaluation criteria should be adapted to arrive at the desired assessment – the action can be considered to be moral – in the end.

Models and practices for this transformative process can be borrowed from the field of process management (e.g., Haugan, 2010). In those models, the entire plot is divided into sequences. Through the so-called milestones and the associated deliverables, there is an accompanying control of the target alignment. The pre-set claims of alignment with ethical principles could be part of this control, carried out not in the form of a deliverable, but in the form of an individual critical review and a discursive exchange about it with other people.

The presented model MAaKE is a draft for a training course on how to learn the successful transfer of ethical thinking into actions which could be qualified as «moral». The critics invited in the introduction of this chapter may contribute to its improvement.

References

Blasi, A. (1980). Bridging moral cognition and moral action: A critical review of the literature. *Psychological Bulletin, 88*(1), 1–45. doi:10.1037/0033-2909.88.1.1

Bourdieu, P. (1977). *Outline of a theory of practice.* Cambridge, MA: Cambridge University Press.

Bronfenbrenner, U. (2009). *The ecology of human development: Experiments by nature and design*. Cambridge, MA: Harvard University Press.

Colby, A., & Kohlberg, L. (Eds.). (1987). *The measurement of moral judgment* (Vol. 1–2). New York, NY: Cambridge University Press.

Darwall, S. (Ed.). (2003). *Consequentialism*. Oxford, UK: Blackwell.

Elias, N. (1994). *The civilizing process*. Oxford, UK: Blackwell.

Habermas, J. (1984). *Theory of communicative action, Vol. 1: Reason and the rationalization of society*. Boston, MA: Beacon Press.

Habermas, J. (1987). *Theory of communicative action, Vol. 2: Lifeworld and system: A critique of functionalist reason*. Boston, MA: Beacon Press.

Hartshorne, H., & May, M. A. (1928). *Studies in the nature of character: Vol. 1. Studies in deceit*. New York, NY: Macmillan.

Haugan, G. T. (2010). *Project management fundamentals. Key concepts and methodology* (2nd ed.). Vienna, Austria: Management Concepts.

Heckhausen, H. (1991). *Motivation and action*. New York, NY: Springer.

Heckhausen, H., & Gollwitzer, P. M. (1987). Thought contents and cognitive functioning in motivational vs. volitional states of mind. *Motivation & Emotion, 11*(2), 101–120. doi:10.1007/BF00992338

Honneth, A. (1992). *The struggle for recognition: The moral grammar of social conflicts*. Cambridge, MA: MIT Press.

Jonas, H. (1984), *The imperative of responsibility: In search of an ethics for the technological age*. Chicago, IL: The University of Chicago Press.

Keller, L., Gollwitzer, P., & Sheeran, P. (2020). Changing behavior using the model of action phases. In M. Hagger, L. Cameron, K. Hamilton, N. Hankonen, & T. Lintunen (Eds.), *The handbook of behavior change* (pp. 77–88). Cambridge, MA: Cambridge University Press. doi:10.1017/9781108677318.006

Kohlberg, L. (1984). *Essays on moral development, Vol. 2: The psychology of moral development*. San Francisco, CA: Harper & Row.

Latané, B., & Darley, J. M. (1970). *The unresponsive bystander: Why doesn't he help?* New York, NY: Appleton-Century Crofts.

Milgram, S. (1974). *Obedience to authority: An experimental view*. New York, NY: Harper and Row.

Mosher, R. L., Connor, D., Kalliel, K. M., Day, J. M., Yokota, N., Porter, M. R., Whitely, & J. M. (1999). *Moral actions in young adulthood*. Columbia, SC: University of South Carolina. Retrieved August 8, 2020, from https://files.eric.ed.gov/fulltext/ED559000.pdf

Oser, F. K., Patry, J.-L., Zutavern, M., Reichenbach, R., Klaghofer, R., Althof, W., & Rothbucher, H. (1991). *Der Prozess der Verantwortung – Berufsethische Entscheidung von Lehrerinnen und Lehrern*. Bericht zum Forschungsprojekt 1.188-0.85 und 11.25470.88/2 des Schweizerischen Nationalfonds zur Förderung der wissenschaftlichen Forschung. Freiburg, Switzerland: Pädagogisches Institut der Universität.

Oser, F. K., & Schläfli, A. (1985). But it does move: The difficulty of gradual change in moral development. In M. W. Berkowitz & F. K. Oser (Eds.), *Moral education: Theory and application* (pp. 269–296). Hillsdale, NJ: Lawrence Erlbaum.

Parsons, T. (1937). *The structure of social action*. New York, NY: Free Press.

Rest, J. (1986). *Moral development: Advances in research and theory*. New York, NY: Praeger.

Sokolowski, R. (2017). *Moral action: A phenomenological study*. Washington, DC: The Catholic University of America Press.

Spielthenner, G. (2005). What makes actions morally good? *Etica & Politica, 1*. Retrieved August 23, 2020, from http://www.units.it/etica/2005_1/SPIELTHENNER.htm

Weber, M. (1919/1994). *Weber: Political writings* (P. Lassman, Ed.; R. Speirs, Trans.). Cambridge, UK: Cambridge University Press.

Weber, M. (1922/1978). *Economy and society: An outline of interpretative sociology* (2 Vols.). Berkeley, CA: University of California Press.

Weber, M. (1926/2015). *Weber's rationalism and modern society*. New York, NY: Palgrave Macmillan.

Weinberger, A., Patry, J.-L., & Weyringer, S. (2016). Improving professional practice through practice-based research: V*a*KE (Values *and* Knowledge Education) in university-based teacher education. *Vocations and Learning, 9*, 63–84. doi:10.1007/s12186-015-9141-4

PART 6

Research Principles and Prospects for VaKE

CHAPTER 29

The Justification of the Double Assignment

Jean-Luc Patry and Alfred Weinberger

1   Introduction

The most important challenge of humanity throughout its history has been how to get people to act ethically. The world has always been full of ethical challenges or "predicaments of mankind" (e.g., Club of Rome: Meadows et al., 1972). To face them, in many situations, people need to act morally, i.e., in favour of a "common good" ("that which benefits society as a whole, in contrast to the private good of individuals and sections of society", Lee, 2016, p. 1), and possibly to the detriment of selfishness: They need to take responsibility. And for education, this means the need to foster responsibility. Responsible action in concrete situations refers not only to normative systems but also to the specific circumstances and other issues. For instance, ethical decisions related to climate change require recognition of scientific facts (e.g., knowing about the greenhouse effect and the consequences of burning fossil fuels) as well as of the consequences of one's behaviour in this regard. Hence education for both values and knowledge in relation to each other is necessary. This has been called the double assignment of education (e.g., Gustafsson, 2008; Tapola & Fritzén, 2010; Weinberger et al., 2016; Weinberger, 2018). In the present chapter, the question will be elaborated on how the double assignment can be justified. The claim that Values *and* Knowledge Education (V*a*KE) is one possibility among others to practice the double assignment is addressed in detail in the other chapters of this handbook.

In the second section, some basic concepts will be presented that will be discussed later on. The third section deals with the main arguments for the justification of the double assignment. The fourth section will present some models of double assignments and is followed by a short discussion.

2   Basic Concepts

In the present section, concepts that will be used in the course of the chapter will be addressed. We cannot go into the details but present just the issues that will be important later on.

(A) *Responsibility* means that someone judges his or her action with respect to some normative framework (Oser & Patry, 1994). The normative framework can be (1) either a person or group of people with direct or indirect sanctioning power (authority: e.g., administration, parents, religion) who are entitled to prescribe to act in a certain way: "I am responsible to do my job correctly, as judged by the superior", or the like. (2) Or it is the protagonist's personal ethical convictions. The latter can overrule the former, which means that the protagonist follows his or her ethical conviction, even if this means acting against the requirements of the sanctioning authority according to the first normative framework (1); this would then mean civic disobedience (Arendt, 1986).

(B) *Personal ethical standpoint and situation specific responsibility*. The ethical challenges have changed in history. For centuries, the predicaments for mankind were mainly social and societal, with different issues at stake (warfare, slavery, poverty, exploitation, health, and many more); since the 1960ies, the predicaments have been extended, to include the environment (e.g., Club of Rome: Meadows et al., 1972). And other ethical issues can arise at any moment – one example is the Corona crisis that broke out in Winter 2019/2020. Further, the challenges may differ from situation to situation. Given the variability of the challenges and conditions, to act responsibly requires to respond flexibly to the particular circumstances. Ethical imperatives by philosophers and other well-intentioned people provide general rules. These cannot be applied literally in concrete situations because they do not address the specific concrete conditions as would be necessary to guide action (generality-concreteness antinomy, see Herrmann, 1979, pp. 160ff.: The more general a statement is, the less concrete can it be; this applies particularly in the social domain, Patry, 2018, p. 29). Instead of providing compulsory general yet inapplicable rules, in moral education, we should empower people to develop their own personal ethical standpoints, which they justify, and on which they can base their decisions on how to act responsibly in the respective situations.

(C) The *Is-Ought distinction*. Justifying the double assignment is a normative issue. In order to be able to discuss this, we need to clarify our meta-ethical position, i.e., our stance with regard to how such justifications can be. We embrace the position that prescriptive claims cannot rely uniquely on observations (translated into one's thoughts about facts): That something is the case (descriptive) is not sufficient to say that it is (morally) required; such a presumed "deduction" is sometimes called "naturalistic fallacy" and must be avoided (e.g., Morscher, 2018; see also Chapters 2 and 33 in this handbook). In contrast to this, however, descriptions of someone's values system or moral competence are descriptive: This is what someone thinks etc. But from this, one cannot deduce what he or she *should* think or do.

(D) *Superordinate and subordinate norms.* Under this perspective, prescriptive statements – what someone should think or do – can only be justified by basing it on superordinate prescriptive statements and possibly some descriptive conditions to which these apply (principles of the practical syllogism). With very few exceptions, the justification of subordinate norms requires, in addition to using superordinate norms, reference to facts, or descriptive statements, which must relate appropriately to the norm to permit a logically correct argument (see Chapter 33 for a more detailed account). For the double assignment to be discussed in this chapter, the top superordinate norm has been stipulated at the beginning of the chapter: We must increase responsible behaviour. The relationship between descriptive and prescriptive statements, then, must refer to behaviour.

(E) Our approach to relate descriptive statements to the norm is: *Values without knowledge is blind; knowledge without values is irresponsible.* This means:

- People who defend values without appropriate knowledge are considered to be blind because an individual may have the best of intentions (values) but will fail to achieve them because of insufficient knowledge of how to translate them into action given the particular context, conditions and opportunities to put them into effect, and how to deal with contradicting values related with different action options, etc. A teacher, for instance, may have the best intentions (values) to support his or her students, but if he or she does not know how one can handle the varying conditions and antinomies of educational situations (see, for instance, Patry, 2018), he or she will not succeed in the endeavour.
- Knowledge without values is irresponsible because the same knowledge can be used for good or bad purposes; the latter can only be avoided if individuals relate their knowledge with values. More explicitly, (1) according to Francis Bacon (1597, quoted from Baggaley et al., 2013), "knowledge is power"; (2) power can be (and indeed has been) abused for selfish purposes at the detriment of others – which is a predicament to mankind; (3) hence, power needs to be used responsibly, whereby (4) responsibility is values guided and requires that the values are justified appropriately (see above, A). For instance, a teacher who masters the techniques of behaviour modification but who does not acknowledge the human dignity of the students will fail because he or she might get discipline in the classroom but will not establish a relationship of mutual trust and not lead the students to become responsible people themselves.

Responsible education in general, and responsible teaching in particular, are asked to take these issues seriously and hence to practice the double assignment. This will be justified more specifically in the following section.

3   Justification of the Double Assignment

In the history of educational research, the double assignment has been justified repeatedly. We will give some examples from different standpoints showing the relationship between descriptive and normative issues.

(A) From the standpoint of *pedagogy*: Johann Friedrich Herbart (1776–1841), one of the co-founders of pedagogy as an academic discipline, coined in his famous book "Allgemeine Pädagogik" (1806) the concept of "erziehender Unterricht" as general norm; this became a central topic in his theory of education. According to Herbart, "Unterricht" (education in the sense of teaching) is not only a necessary means for "Erziehung" (education in the sense of moral development), but also an essential requirement for "Erziehung". "Unterricht" is the only means of "Erziehung" which makes the success of "Erziehung" predictable. "Erziehender Unterricht" is a form of teaching, which relates factual knowledge with moral questions (Rekus, 2010; Hilgenheger, 1999). Consequently, Herbart sees the foundation of educational theory in two disciplines: psychology (for the descriptive part) and ethics (for the normative part).

(B) From the standpoint of *educational practice*: Teachers and other educators are constantly confronted with antinomies, i.e., with situations in which two or more actions are required, but the two actions are incompatible, i.e., cannot be achieved simultaneously (Winkel, 1988; Seichter, 2013). Antinomies are characterized by descriptive and ethical issues: The situations at stake are described in non-normative terms, and it is the protagonist who identifies the ethical issues which are at stake, from his or her perspective; different people might attribute different norms to the different actions. Many studies have discussed teachers' moral conflicts (e.g., Oser et al., 1991; Tirri, 1999; Millwater et al., 2004; McNally et al., 2005; Stoughton, 2007; Campbell, 2008; Weinberger et al., 2016).

Students are very well aware of many of the antinomies teachers are faced with, and they are sensitive to the way their teacher deals with them. Students regard issues like justice, care, or truthfulness as very important because they are directly concerned by the teacher's decision and concrete actions.

(C) From the standpoint of *curriculum*: For teaching, the curriculum can be considered to be a general norm. Curricula are values-laden per se through the choice of the topics to be addressed, etc. (e.g., Brossard Børhaug, 2013), and how the teachers deal with them is values-laden as well (Hodson, 2003; Patry, 2006a). Furthermore, the curriculum permits some leeway: The curriculum does not prescribe in every detail what to teach, rather it provides in many regards a general framework that can be shaped according to the teacher's preference. In some disciplines, there is more freedom (e.g., literature), in others less (e.g., mathematics). In addition, most curricula state that values education (normative issue) is needed and legally required within subject teaching (descriptive issue) (e.g., Tomlinson & Quinton, 1986; see also Chapters 12 and 13 in this handbook for two examples). In the same vein, societal relations of the contents are called for (ibid; Hofstein et al., 2011). It is the statutory duty of teachers to do values education next to knowledge education. These statements are usually located in the preambles and introductions of curricula which apply to all teachers. "(S)chools have had a substantive moral mission since their inception, and (...) the public has largely supported that mission" (Sanger & Osguthorpe, 2011, p. 570).

Most teachers are aware of that and also would like to values education (Gruber, 2009; see Weinberger, 2018, for a literature review), but often refrain from explicit values education for a series of reasons, in particular content-related curricular pressure, missing competences, and fear of getting in conflict with the values systems of relevant stakeholders (Thornberg, 2008; Gruber, 2009). In contrast, Hodson (2003, p. 655), for instance, advocates a curricular approach to science that has four levels of sophistication, which all include values:

– Level 1: Appreciating the societal impact of scientific and technological change, and recognizing that science and technology are, to some extent, culturally determined.
– Level 2: Recognizing that decisions about scientific and technological development are taken in pursuit of particular interests, and that benefits accruing to some may be at the expense of others. Recognizing that scientific and technological development are inextricably linked with the distribution of wealth and power.
– Level 3: Developing one's own views and establishing one's own underlying value positions.
– Level 4: Preparing for and taking action.

(D) From the standpoint of *society*: Scientific claims, technological innovations, economic concepts, etc., have consequences for society, which may result in some of the many huge social and societal challenges with which our contemporary world is confronted, such as unequal distribution of goods and services across the world, violence, and disrespect for human dignity, egotism on all levels, etc. "Current reform efforts in science education research recommend that science classrooms should allow a place for reflection on the social and cultural implications of scientific claims and innovations" (Cook, 2015, p. 583). Such societal issues cannot be dealt with appropriately if the normative issues are not addressed explicitly. For instance, any attempts to deal with – or to negate – the global environmental challenges, such as climate change, food crisis, shortages of water or various infectious diseases concern human beings and hence moral problems (prescriptive issue), and this must be addressed in education (Tapola & Fritzen, 2010). To be able to act responsibly (normative issue), citizens need to understand the underlying facts (descriptive issue). Thus, it is important that education relates aspects of morality with the subject matter.

(E) From the standpoint of *subject matter*: All school topics in all school disciplines include values and cannot be taught in a neutral values-free way. This is obvious in many topics, for example in language (e.g., literature often includes valuations), history (e.g., the holocaust cannot be taught without valuation), or geography (migration, climate change, etc., are values-laden), etc. Even the STEM disciplines (science, technology, engineering, mathematics) are not values-free (Kincaid, Dupré, & Wylie, 2007), like physics (e.g., nuclear physics – nuclear energy; thermodynamics – burning fossil fuels), biology (e.g., abortion, genetic technology, factory farming, intensive agriculture), etc. In any case, scientific research is values laden (Patry & Patry, 2003; Patry, 2006b), and this transfers to teaching in school. Further, the choice of the specific topic and how it is addressed depend on values choices and convey related values directly or indirectly to the students. One superordinate norm might be the practical relevance of a topic, another the personal interest and competence of the teacher which might lead him or her to prefer one topic over another (see below, F).

(F) From the standpoint of *interaction*. In interactions, we necessarily send not only content related information but also values. For instance, according to Schulz von Thun (2009), one can distinguish four types of messages in an utterance (which includes the verbal, paraverbal and non-verbal components): the state of affairs (content as such), a self-disclosure, a plea, and an expression of the relationship. While the state of affairs is values-laden in the senses discussed above, the latter three are values-laden from a personal point of view. Furthermore, the teacher will necessarily have his or her own ethical standpoint in general and with regard to school topics (superordinate norm); for instance, teachers like some topics and dislike others, i.e., they attribute more or less value to topics, and in their teaching, they convey these values to the students (e.g., Parrisius et al., 2020). In this context, even indifference ("I don't care about the topic" or "I don't care about you") conveys a value judgment.

(G) From the standpoint of the *organization*: Each system has an underlying values system, which is not always made explicit. The representatives of the system act in such a way that certain values are enforced or at least reinforced. This is what has been called "hidden curriculum" (Snyder, 1971). The hidden curriculum refers to the unwritten, unofficial, and often unintended, values and perspectives that students learn in school.

Teachers take normative decisions and relate them with knowledge on all the levels mentioned above, whether consciously or unknowingly. Normative abstention is not possible; rather, teachers practice knowledge-related values education anyway, if not explicitly, then implicitly. Since teaching is a rational endeavour – the attempt to have a positive impact on the students' dispositions (see the definition by Brezinka, 1981, p. 95) – it is important that education addresses this relationship between knowledge and values transparently and explicitly and that it follows certain principles, instead of being haphazard.

4 Models of Double Assignments

To describe possibilities of double assignments, the structural models of synthesis between effectiveness and responsibility (Oser, Dick, & Patry, 1992) can be used. Based on this theoretical approach values education and knowledge education can be integrated in four different ways. The four models represent a series in which the "higher" models represent a more intensive integration of values education and knowledge education in the classroom.

(A) The *interpretative synthesis model*: In this model, whenever one of the two teaching aims is addressed, the other is implicitly addressed as well. Knowledge education inevitably includes values education in that the choice of subject matter, the didactic concept, the materials used, and the social forms or the instructions are not arbitrary but are based on considerations of what may be of value to the learners in the future. Representatives of this model think that values education is always part of the knowledge acquisition process and does not need to be addressed specifically. However, there is a danger with this model in the individual interpretation of what can be considered "valuable" on the one hand and in the "hidden curriculum" on the other.

(B) The *additive synthesis model*: In the second model, the connection between values education and knowledge education is more evident. However, values education and knowledge education are seen as two separate worlds. In ethics or religious education, for example, moral discussions take place, while in the other subjects only knowledge acquisition takes place. The advantage over the first model is that values education is explicit and no longer left to chance. The disadvantage is that values education has little influence on the knowledge acquisition of the other subjects, and vice versa.

(C) The *complementary synthesis model*: The link between values education and knowledge education is more pronounced in the complementary model.

Here, values education is integrated into subject teaching, both refer to each other, but this is not done systematically. This would allow teachers to spontaneously conduct moral discussions on current teaching content.

(D) The *regulative synthesis model*: The connection between values education and knowledge education is practiced rationally and systematically: One side always automatically influences the other in a planned way. It complies with the premise "Values without knowledge is blind, knowledge without values is irresponsible".

In our view, the fourth model (D) is the only one that can be considered responsible because it does not leave the values acquisition of the students to happenstance (model A) or separate (model B), and in contrast to model C it is systematic. In VaKE, the link between values education and knowledge acquisition is based on the fourth model. The solution of the moral question requires knowledge, and knowledge in turn requires an examination of moral aspects in order to find the most appropriate solution to the dilemma.

5 Discussion

One can question whether there is sufficient autonomy for the individual citizens with respect to everyday values decisions. We have distinguished two types of responsibility (1A): one relating to an authority, and one based on one's own value system. Systems that prescribe ethical norms refer to the first type of responsibility, whereas autonomy addresses the second type. The former depends on superordinate norms for which there is no common agreement anymore since the decline of the importance of religious value systems, which has not been replaced. And even those that are accepted individually are not flexible as required in 2 (B). In contrast, one can agree on the superordinate norm *autonomy* addressed amongst others by Kohlberg (1971), because from an anthropological point of view, humans are characterized by their ability and search to decide autonomously, and it complies with the top superordinate norm (1D): increasing responsible behaviour, which is only possible if the person acts autonomously.

But is the double assignment itself realistic? From the teacher's point of view implementing the double assignment following the regulative model (3D) requires more effort than values education and knowledge education separately (additive model, 3B) or unsystematically (complementary model, 3C) because values and knowledge have to be related to each other (section 3; see also other chapters in this handbook).

Based on the justification of the double assignment which emphasises responsibility and autonomy, values, and knowledge education in the sense of conveying specific values and knowledge is inappropriate. Instead, the justification of value decisions is in the focus. This is the approach developed in the Kohlberg tradition, and this is what is favoured in VaKE; this is accounted for in detail in Chapter 2 of the present handbook. Overall, VaKE is a possible response to all issues discussed above: It combines values education and knowledge acquisition, with a strong relation between the descriptive (knowledge) and the normative (values) statements, it focuses on justification of values instead of promoting specific values, it leaves open which general norm the individual wants to favourite, it permits to change the justification framework in the discussion in the group, and it fosters the development of the justification frameworks.

References

Arendt, H. (1986). Ziviler Ungehorsam. In M. L. Knott (Ed.), *Zur Zeit: Politische Essays* (pp. 119–159). Berlin, Germany: Rotbuch.

Baggaley, R., Garcia Calleja, J. M., Marum, L., & Marum, E. (2013). Knowledge is power; information is liberation. *Bulletin of the World Health Organization, 91*, 898.

Brezinka, W. (1981). *Grundbegriffe der Erziehungswissenschaft* (4th ed.). München, Germany: Reinhardt.

Brossard Børhaug, F. (2013). Conflicting anti-racist values in Norwegian and French civic education: To what extent can the curriculum discourses empower minority youth? In G. Gudmundsson, D. Beach Jr., & V. Viggo (Eds.), *Youth and marginalisation: Young people from immigrant families in Scandinavia* (pp. 105–131). London, UK: Tufnell Press.

Campbell, E. (2010). Ethical knowledge in teaching. A moral imperative of professionalism. *Education Canada, 46*(4), 32–35. Retrieved April 15, 2015, from http://www.cea-ace.ca

Cook, K. (2015). Grappling with wicked problems: Exploring photovoice as a decolonizing methodology in science education. *Cultural Studies of Science Education, 10*(3), 581–592.

Gruber, M. (2009). Barriers to value education in schools – what teachers think. *Newsletter from EARLI SIG 13 Moral and Democratic Education, 5*, 23–30.

Gustafsson, B. (2008, June). *Dealing with the democratic aspects in science education.* Paper read at the 9th Nordic Research Symposium on Science Education, 11–15 June 2008 in Reykjavik, Island. Retrieved January 31, 2020, from http://lnu.diva-portal.org/smash/record.jsf?pid=diva2%3A203471&dswid=9574

Herrmann, T. (1979). *Psychologie als Problem*. Stuttgart, Germany: Klett.

Hilgenheger, N. (1999). "Sittenlehre" oder "erziehender Unterricht"? Zum problematischen Verhältnis von kognitiver, affektiver und handlungsorientierter moralischer Erziehung bei J. F. Herbart. In V. Ladentin & R. Schilmöller (Eds.), *Ethik als pädagogisches Projekt: Grundfragen schulischer Werteerziehung* (pp. 119–140). Opladen, Germany: Leske und Budrich.

Hodson, D. (2003). Time for action: Science education for an alternative future. *International Journal of Science Education, 25*(6), 645–670.

Hofstein, A., Eilks, I., & Bybee, R. (2011). Societal issues and their importance for contemporary science education – A pedagogical justification and the state-of-the-art in Israel, Germany, and the USA. *International Journal of Science and Mathematics Education, 9*(6), 1459–1483.

Kincaid, H., Dupré, J., & Wylie, A. (2007). *Value-free science: Ideals and illusions?* Oxford, UK: Oxford University Press.

Kohlberg, L. (1971). From is to ought: How to commit the naturalistic fallacy and get away with it in the study of moral development. In T. Mischel (Ed.), *Cognitive development and epistemology* (pp. 151–235). New York, NY: Academic Press.

Lee, S. (2016). Common good. *Encyclopaedia Britannica*. Retrieved May 18, 2020, from https://www.britannica.com/topic/common-good

McNally, J., I'Anson, J., Whewell, C., & Wilson, G. (2005). "They think that swearing is okay": First lessons in behaviour management. *Journal of Education for Teaching, 31*(3), 169–185.

Meadows, D. H., Meadows, D. L., Ramders, K., & Behrens, W. W. III (1972). *The limits of growth. A report for the Club of Rome's project on the predicament of mankind*. New York, NY: Universe Books. Retrieved May 18, 2020, from http://www.donellameadows.org/wp-content/userfiles/Limits-to-Growth-digital-scan-version.pdf

Millwater, J., Ehrich, L. C., & Cranston, N. (2004). Preservice teachers' dilemmas: Ethical or not? *International Journal of Practical Experiences in Professional Education, 8*(2), 48–58.

Morscher, E. (2018). Metaethics and moral education. In A. Weinberger, H. Biedermann, J.-L. Patry, & S. Weyringer (Eds.), *Professionals' ethos and education for responsibility* (pp. 17–27). Leiden, The Netherlands: Brill.

Oser, F., Dick, A., & Patry, J.-L. (1992). Responsibility, effectiveness, and the domains of educational research. In F. Oser, A. Dick, & J.-L Patry (Eds.), *Effective and responsible teaching: The new synthesis* (pp. 3–13). San Francisco, CA: Jossey-Bass.

Oser, F. K., & Patry, J. L. (1995). Teacher responsibility. In L. W. Anderson (Eds.), *International encyclopedia of teaching and teacher education* (pp. 35–41). New York, NY: Pergamon.

Oser, F., Patry, J.-L., Zutavern, M., Reichenbach, R., Klaghofer, R., Althof, W., & Rothbucher, H. (1991). *Der Prozess der Verantwortung – Berufsethische Entscheidung von Lehrerinnen und Lehrern*. Bericht zum Forschungsprojekt 1.188-0.85 und 11.25470.88/2 des Schweizerischen Nationalfonds zur Förderung der wissenschaftlichen Forschung. Freiburg, Switzerland: Pädagogisches Institut der Universität.

Parrisius, C., Gaspard, H., Trautwein, U., & Nagengast, B. (2020). The transmission of values from math teachers to their ninth-grade students: Different mechanisms for different value dimensions? *Contemporary Educational Psychology, 62*, Article 101891.

Patry, J.-L. (2006a). Science is not values-free – neither in research, nor in school. In R. H. M. Cheng, J. C. K. Lee, & L. N. K. Lo (Eds.), *Values education for citizens in the new century* (pp. 217–232). Hong Kong, Hong Kong: The Chinese University Press.

Patry, J.-L. (2006b). Die Werturteilsproblematik in der Erziehungswissenschaft. In G. Zecha (Ed.), *Werte in den Wissenschaften* (pp. 279–302). Tübingen, Germany: Mohr Siebeck.

Patry, J.-L. (2018). Theorie-Praxis-Transfer: Hindernisse und Probleme. In A. Gastager & J.-L. Patry (Eds.), *Pädagogischer Takt: Analysen zu Theorie und Praxis* (Studienreihe der Pädagogischen Hochschule Steiermark, Band 11) (pp. 17–42). Graz, Austria: Leykam.

Patry, J.-L., & Patry, P. (2003). Werte und Normen in den Sozialwissenschaften. In A. Hiecke & O. Neumaier (Eds.), *Philosophie im Geiste Bolzanos anläßlich des 222. Geburtstages von Bernard Bolzano, Edgar Morscher gewidmet* (pp. 199–222). Sankt Augustin, Germany: Academia.

Rekus, J. (2010). Erziehender Unterricht. In K. Zierer (Ed.), *Schulische Werteerziehung* (pp. 168–177). Hohengehren, Germany: Schneider.

Sanger, M., & Osguthorpe, R. D. (2011). Teacher education, pre-service teacher beliefs and the moral work of teaching. *Teaching and Teacher Education, 27*(3), 569–578.

Schulz von Thun, F. (2009). *Miteinander Reden 1: Störungen und Klärungen. Allgemeine Psychologie der Kommunikation* (46th ed.). Hamburg, Germany: rororo.

Seichter, S. (2013). Über die antinomische Struktur pädagogischen Denkens und Handelns. *Rassegna di Pedagogia, 3–4*, 211–219.

Snyder, B. R. (1971). *The hidden curriculum*. New York, NY: Alfred A. Knopf.

Stoughton, E. H. (2007). "How will I get them to behave?" Pre-service teachers reflect on classroom management. *Teaching and Teacher Education, 23*, 1024–1037.

Tapola, A., & Fritzén, L. (2010). On the integration of moral and democratic education and subject matter instruction. In C. Klaassen & N. Maslovaty (Eds.), *Moral courage and the normative professionalism of teachers* (pp. 149–174). Rotterdam, The Netherlands: Sense Publishers.

Thornberg, R. (2008). The lack of professional knowledge in values education. *Teaching and Teacher Education, 24*(7), 1791–1798.

Tirri, K. (1999). Teachers' perceptions of moral dilemmas at school. *Journal of Moral Education, 28*(1), 31–47.

Tomlinson, P., & Quinton, M. (Eds.). (1986). *Values across the curriculum*. London, UK: Falmer.

Weinberger, A. (2018). The moral dimension of teaching as a precondition for the double assignment. Literature review. *Menon. Online Journal of Educational Research, 3rd Thematic Issue*, 8–29. Retrieved May 18, 2020, from http://www.edu.uowm.gr/site/system/files/menon_issue_3rd_special_112018.pdf

Weinberger, A., Patry, J.-L., & Weyringer, S. (2016). Improving professional moral practice through practitioner research. VaKE (Values *and* Knowledge Education) in university-based teacher education. *Vocations and Learning, 9*(1), 63–84. Retrieved May 18, 2020, from http://link.springer.com/article/10.1007/s12186-015-9141-4?email.event.1.SEM.ArticleAuthorContributingOnlineFirst

Winkel, R. (1988). *Antinomische Pädagogik und Kommunikative Didaktik. Studien zu den Widersprüchen und Spannungen in Erziehung und Schule* (2nd ed.). Düsseldorf, Germany: Schwann.

CHAPTER 30

RAC3 Thinking

Selected Thinking Styles Nurtured with VaKE

Sieglinde Weyringer and Dimitris Pnevmatikos

1   Introduction

Finding solutions to problems and considering the best practicable option is a complex process, especially when these problems are linked to a dilemma. The most important distinguishing feature between a dilemma and a problem is the possibility to find a viable solution: for a dilemma, there is only a temporary way out, whereas, for a problem, a final solution can be found. To handle corresponding challenges, it is advisable to make greater use of rational considerations and not only affective and emotional reactions. In the course of many years of VaKE practice, five thinking styles have been crystallised: *reflective, anticipatory, critical, creative, and collaborative thinking*. Initial studies show some evidence that these thinking styles are central to the completion of tasks in the course and that being exposed to these tasks can increase abilities to perform these thinking styles.

This chapter analyses reflective, anticipatory, critical, creative, and also collaborative thinking on the basis of selected characteristics that allow a link between them. Furthermore, their relevance for ethical thinking and, in particular, for VaKE is examined. Finally, their importance in future-oriented educational concepts is presented briefly.

2   Distinguishing and Connecting Characteristics

Extensive scientific and historically grown schools of thought have researched the five thinking styles (reflective, anticipatory, critical, creative, and collaborative thinking). In the context of this chapter, however, the reference to the respective discourse is limited to a selection that opens connections between these thinking styles and their applicability in ethical discourses and particularly on VaKE.

2.1 Reflective Thinking

The description and exploration of reflective thinking are very prominently linked to the research of John Dewey. In his work "How we think", he defines reflective thinking as "an active, persistent, and careful consideration of any belief or supposed form of knowledge in the light of the grounds that support it and the further conclusions to which it tends" (Dewey, 1933, p. 118). In an in-depth analysis, Rodgers (2002, p. 845) distils the following four criteria from several of Dewey's writings: (1) Reflection is a meaning-making process based on experiences. The possible learning effect develops not only on adding experiences but also in establishing a deeper understanding of their relationships within and with ideas gathered from others. (2) The process follows a systematic structure similar to scientific inquiry. (3) Therefore, this thinking needs the interaction with a community and the agreement that (4) it nurtures personal growth.

Indeed, these four criteria of reflection contain components of thinking essential for human existence and its social inclusion in general: Thinking is a structured, interactive process that can contribute to personal development. A person develops by reflecting on experiences made and trying to link them into a balancing whole; as a result, he or she may establish knowledge and insights that increasingly equip him or her with mental and emotional stability to be able to contribute to a good life in community and appreciative interactions with others. Reflective thinking is a process that requires a certain amount of time to carry out; it is not just a minute-long event. Reflection includes considering past experiences, which must become conscious and as concretely retrievable as possible – only then the past experiences can become actively used for learning and development.

Reflection can lead to uncovering the unconscious, vague and incomplete knowledge about oneself and the world. In addition to personal development, reflection can contribute to building trust in reliable (scientific) concepts and making statements about their viability and, in the best case, their justified enforceability in the sense of Dewey.

As a result, new views, assessments, and ultimately values may arise. We claim that the establishment of reflective thinking as an attitude requires specific conditions, such as time, motivation to do it, possibilities for practice, freedom from sanctioning evaluations (such as grades), role models for practice, guidelines, supervision, feedback (or viability checks in the sense of VaKE) and exchange of experience.

2.2 Anticipatory Thinking

Anticipatory thinking means dealing with the future. When we think, our thoughts do not only revolve around the past. Thinking can also have a future-oriented aspect: Thinking about future events as well as preparing for vague and unclear challenges create assumptions, ideas, plans, visions, indications of actions and reactions and their consequences. In terms of thinking about educational concepts, it is necessary to distinguish foresight from retrospective thinking. Anticipatory thinking is described as "a metacognitive capability (...) to identify future issues and proactively take actions to manage their risks" (Amos-Binks & Dannenhauer, 2019, p. 1), and as a "deliberate, divergent exploration and analysis of relevant futures to avoid surprise" (Geden et al., 2018, p. 1). It refers to expectancies including behaviour-outcome and stimulus outcome expectancies (Mischel, 1973, pp. 269–272), one of the cognitive-affective units that constitute the Cognitive-Affective Personality System (Mischel & Shoda, 1995). This theoretical framework permits us to account for much of human behaviour.

The focus is on the ability to develop assumptions about consequences as well as about unforeseeable future events and influences. In addition, it is essential to realize that expectations and anticipations always have to do with probabilities, which can be heavily biased, for example, depending on the wording of the statement (Tversky & Kahneman, 1973). When these skills contribute to viable problem solving, it promotes stability of personal ego and thus positively impacts the long-term success of social interactions.

Therefore, although it is necessary to differentiate thinking about the past and the future, we should use both ways of thinking in combination. This combination is one way of recognising that, on the one hand, *prior experience does not necessarily determine future events* but that, on the other hand, *the future and the past are interrelated*. This interrelationship is not limited to actions but also includes the assessment of actions and their justification.

2.3   *Critical Thinking*

When talking about critical thinking, mainly the aspect of knowledge is in the focus of scientific considerations (e.g., Lai, 2011). Definitions of critical thinking refer to abilities, skills, dispositions, and attitudes of a person also similar to habitus or a way of being (e.g., Moon, 2007; Lai, 2011), affective states and virtues (e.g., Ballin & Battersby, 2016; Siegel, 2013), or (meta-)cognitive processes (e.g., Magno, 2010) and mental procedures (e.g., Paul & Elder, 2004). In other words, critical thinking is not restricted to the cognitive elements of the individual, but it refers as well to the whole person and the habits of the individual's mind (Facione, 1990; Halonen, 1995). As such, critical thinking, along with critical action and critical doing, displays the need for consistency between thinking and doing and, hence, has an ethical dimension (Davies & Barnett, 2015).

Critical thinking is a complex construct that goes beyond the sum of specific skills. The crucial in critical thinking is how these specific skills interact and align with the various dispositions, creating a unique blend and orientation that allows specific judgements and problem-solving (Elen et al., 2019). Critical thinking demands an introspection proceeding as an inner dialogue between the two parts of the self – this is "I" and "me" *sensu* G. H. Mead (1913), followed by comparisons of its outputs with the surrounding reality. In permanent feedback loops, the results of the considerations are revised. Cognitive skills or strategies are used "that increase the probability of a desirable outcome" (Halpern, 2014, p. 8). This process can remain within the self; however, it can also be transferred into interactions with other people. Although other complex mental activities such as problem solving or creative thinking recruit some specific skills and dispositions, they cannot be identical to critical thinking.

In their effort to assess and promote critical thinking, some scholars describe a series of critical thinking skills and dispositions. This trend entails the danger of reducing critical thinking skills to a collection of skills or dispositions – and having a specific skill and disposition does not mean that one activates it in every situation. On the other hand, they offer a precise description of what an intervention programme oriented to promote critical thinking should include. One can find many collections of skills and dispositions that are important for critical thinking. For instance, Facione (1990) described six skills (i.e., interpretation, analysis, inference, evaluation, explanation, and self-evaluation) and seven dispositions (i.e., truth-seeking, open-mindless, analyticity, systematicity, self-confidence, inquisitiveness, and cognitive maturity) as integral parts of critical thinking.

2.4   *Creative Thinking*

Scientific approaches on creative thinking are mostly linked to the works of J. P. Guilford, E. P. Torrance, M. A. Runco, E. De Bono, A. F. Osborne, M. A. Wallach, and N. Kogan, A. J. Cropley, T. Amabile, and R. Sternberg. As these researchers worked on issues related to creativity during their lifespan, we abstain from giving selected references. All these scientists have developed their own definitions, which were dependent on whether their research concentrated on the *person* who creates, the *process,* or the *result* of thinking. Concepts, tests, and techniques of creative thinking are primarily based on the contrasting concepts of divergent versus convergent thinking developed by Guilford (1967). Divergent thinking is non-linear thinking stimulated by a question and aiming at finding as many different answers as possible, whereas convergent thinking is vertical, critical analytical thinking based on collecting facts to find one single best answer.

Creative thinking skills and techniques can be applied to any challenge and in any situation in life. It is not restricted to artistic disciplines like art, music, dance, or literature. It is unique to every person and every issue. The importance of creative cognitive processes is particularly apparent in the epistemological paradigm of constructivism *sensu* E. von Glasersfeld, H. von Foerster, and P. Watzlawick: The environment as we perceive it is our invention. In a similar vein, for Piaget (1954), every real learning process entails a creative process: the restoration of the inner – that is, the cognitive and affective – balance (equilibration) through assimilation or accommodation is an individual, self-directed, and creative achievement.

Creativity can be described as the thinking skill to find relationships between ideas, thoughts, and experiences that one has not recognised before and are therefore new for the person. These relationships lead to the creation of new or differently structured thought patterns that show up as new knowledge, as new ideas, or as new products of any kind. According to Landau (1990, p. 239), creative thinking is a bipolar activity that balances imagination and logic. This can be seen in brainstorming (Osborn, 1953), where the processes of creating ideas (imagination) and evaluating them (logic) are separated.

Creative thinking (related to divergent thinking) and critical thinking (related to convergent thinking) are identified as transparent, distinct processes (Guilford, 1967). However, both need the communicative exchange of the person with other people and the interaction with a group, without which they would lose potential and quality, as many training techniques for these two thinking styles and the corresponding actions show: A debate with pro and contra arguments needs more than one-person (Gokhale, 1995); and also generating ideas (e.g., with brainstorming: Osborn, 1953) benefits from the cooperation of at least two people (Pun, 2012).

Combining reflective, critical, and creative thinking has the power to predict academic achievement (Akpur, 2020). Based on this evidence and anticipatory thinking, we claim that the combination of these four thinking styles enables a human individual to clarify the diverse relationships between their individual cognitive and affective constitution and the environment of living and, therefore, to develop a suitable self-concept.

2.5 *Collaborative Thinking*
As the four thinking styles (reflective, anticipatory, critical, creative) concentrate on the question "What is my relation towards the world around me?", we can give them the term "egocentric thinking", expressed in the acronym RACC. However, this orientation is one-sided. It must be complemented with prosperous social interactions between humans and with nature and the environment,

as already alluded to in some of them (e.g., creative thinking). Besides the orientation towards the introspection of the *ego,* we place the alignment with *others* in the sense of Mead (1913). We see collaborative thinking as a possible complementary style of thinking.

Collaborative thinking is described as thinking that builds "on anyone else's ideas, listening, and thinking seriously about what the others are saying" (Gini-Newman & Case, 2015, p. 7). The goals of collaborative thinking are to understand and to share multiple perspectives and to be open to others. This means to change one's mind in the face of new ideas and evidence and to find the most sensible position for the person addressed by the problem (ibid.)

René Descartes' (1596–1650) famous statement "cogito, ergo sum" (I think; therefore, I am) is not sufficient to gain insights into human cognition, especially when social issues are at stake. Cognition needs interpersonal exchange. Knowledge is socially constructed – many researchers from different disciplines share this insight, and many studies support them (e.g., Dewey, 1897, 2009; Bloom, 1956; Berger & Luckman, 1966; Vygotsky, 1980). In recent decades, cooperation (how people work and live together) and cooperative learning (how students learn together) have attracted increased research interest (e.g., Razzouk & Johnson, 2012). However, both aspects do not necessarily include collaboration as described above: while for cooperation and cooperative learning, it is sufficient if the participant has his or her *own* progress and the *own* contribution to a project in focus, in collaboration, the person considers the thoughts of *all* those involved in a project and integrates them into their *own* thinking intending to create something new through a permanent exchange with others to achieve a common goal.

In modern societies, people who think differently meet and come together in a community of inquiry or work (McArthur & Markova, 2015; Garrison, 2016). Aiming at overcoming the limitation of the individual cognitive potential, of the problem areas of cooperation (e.g., taking unjustified advantage) and of cooperative learning (e.g., egoistic take-up of group work), collaborative thinking is estimated to be the educational challenge not only for modern universities (Corrigan, 2012) but for any level of education.

3   RAC3 Thinking – The Bundle of the Five Thinking Styles and Their Application to Ethical Thinking

We have introduced the acronym "RAC3" – Reflective, Anticipatory, Critical, Creative, and Collaborative – for merging the five styles of thinking into a bundle. In this bundle, the respective styles of thought remain genuinely independent and separated from each other and do not intermingle in their application. However, they are activated in combination and temporal proximity to each other.

How the five styles of thinking were presented, already aimed at making relationships and lines of linkages between them visible. To facilitate understanding, we will use a metaphor and borrow the god Janus from Roman mythology: Janus has two faces, one looking into the past and one into the future. He symbolizes the duality of given entities and the impossibility to judge them according to the criteria of right-wrong or good-bad. Reflective (R) and anticipatory (A) thinking each corresponds to one face. Similarly, this metaphor applies to critical (C) and creative (C) thinking, as well as to collaborative thinking (the third C) and egocentric thinking as we called the first four thinking styles together (RACC).

Overall, the five thinking styles complement one another, they can only unfold their full potential as a bundle. To investigate the linking lines is increasingly in the focus of scientific research, as for instance, Garrison (2016, p. VII) states: "Collaborative thinking and learning is inevitably associated with critical and creative thought processes". Furthermore, C3-thinking – the term introduced by Gini-Newman and Case (2015) – has been seen as an interdependent relationship between critical, creative, and collaborative thinking, and how to learn it is assessed as a core challenge for current educational efforts.

Critical, creative, and collaborative thinking can be described in three dimensions: attitudes, processes, and competences. The developments of the respective dimension aim at the generation of different outputs and therefore need different procedures:

- The *attitude,* which is a unique entity formed by knowledge, skills, value orientations, and emotions, addresses the question of the person: "What is essential for me?", and hence the development needs to be individually specified.
- The *process* focuses on producing a result within a framework and with specific criteria for assessment; it is illustrated by the question, "What is the best procedure within the framing environmental and social system to achieve one's goal?" System specificity is the leading parameter for development. By system specificity, we mean the social dimension of development in the sense of Bronfenbrenner (2009).
- Aiming at the development of *competences*, the specific situation of application must be considered. The related questions are: "What ability do I need in a given situation?" and "How can I apply my established attitude in a specific situation?" The competence is situation independent; in contrast, for the application, situation specificity and the transfer to new situations are the core principles (e.g., Patry, 2019).

For practitioners, trainers, and developers of didactical approaches to achieve the respective educational objectives, the distinction between these three specificities, person, system, and situation, is essential. Looking for viable answers to these three questions needs the inclusion of prior experiences and the anticipation of possible future situations which may appear as the consequence of a particular answer. Within educational interventions, the values issue comes into the focus of further considerations. Assessing whether the respective results of each thinking style are considered right/wrong or good/bad should, therefore, consider the attitudes developed by the person, the possibilities offered by the system, and the competences required by the situation.

A snapshot of theoretical and practical approaches on criteria of ethical thinking reveals that reflective, as well as critical thinking, are given fundamental importance for the argumentation and the justification of decisions on the question "What is morally good and right?" However, in multicultural and multi-dynamic societies, critical reasoning that is restricted to a particular ethical tradition is not sufficient anymore because there does not exist any agreement on a single universally accepted framework (Reiss, 2010). Besides the possibility to consider the approaches of consensus or of discourse ethics, Reiss (2010, p. 5) suggests orienting one's considerations towards intrinsic principles of rights and wrongs, the most important criteria being autonomy and justice. Furthermore, he promotes virtue ethics focusing on the moral characteristics of good people and providing role models. It is also recommended for widening the moral community from personal to global perspective-taking and developing egocentric considerations towards following reasoned universal principles (Reiss, 2010, p. 7) – following the tradition of Lawrence Kohlberg to deal with intergenerational and interspecific issues, especially with biotechnology and ecological questions.[1]

The concept of Reiss on ethical thinking is one out of many similar and viable concepts. We choose this concept due to the shared theoretical foundation on Kohlberg and because it provides suggestions on how to learn and practice ethical thinking. To include ethical considerations when making decisions should become a principle of conduct- this is the overall aim of using VaKE for educational efforts. Although more theoretical work has to be done, we state that in these suggestions, possibilities for a linkage between VaKE and the presented five types of thinking can be found: reflection on the personal experience and the perception of the personal self, the anticipation of situations in the future, critical analysis of the situation at stake and the possibilities for improvement, creative considerations on more than one possible decision and its respective consequences, finding a viable solution by taking into account the well-being of others, meaning people as well as the environment and nature.

4   RAC3 Thinking in V*a*KE Courses

Within a V*a*KE course, the training of the five types of thinking in the manner of RAC3 thinking can be realised for both the knowledge and the values domains. Especially after the presentation of the dilemma story, reflective thinking is in the foreground to determine whether the single learner has any memories about or experiences with comparable situations and events and which attitude and assessment he or she may hold towards the issues. Critical thinking is required not only when it comes to evaluating one's *own* memories and experiences but also when it comes to the attitude towards the statements of the other discussants during the debate. Evidence has been found for the successful promotion of critical thinking when the V*a*KE method is combined with a systematic reflection (Pnevmatikos, Christodoulou, & Georgiadou, 2019). A critical stance is also necessary with respect to the information one has gathered, as there is the possibility of fake news and biased information, e.g., on homepages of the promoters of certain issues, (e.g., of lobbying organizations or of companies that sell products or provide services linked with one option in the dilemma).

Collaborative thinking unfolds its advantages when it comes to listening to others and looking at the problem from their perspective, but also when new and additional knowledge for a more in-depth examination of the problem has to be sought, and when this research work should be organised as teamwork. This search for viable new information and the reliability of information sources also need to be critically examined. Anticipatory thinking supports the discussant to prepare for the next round of dilemma discussion by the assumption on the course of the debate, and also by the vision of viable answers to the question "What should the protagonist do?" and their short and long-term consequences. Already creating respective visions needs creative thinking, but also to find an agreement on how to finalise the course. The end product of the V*a*KE process should reflect the discursivity of the course and should also show the results for which consensus is not necessarily sought – even dissent can remain at the end of a course.

5   RAC3 Thinking in Future-Orientated Educational Concepts

Globally operating institutions and organizations like UNO, UNESCO, World Bank, OECD, or the European Union attribute great importance to the promotion of reflective, anticipatory, critical, creative, and collaborative thinking in order to cope with future societal challenges (see for example the Faure Report, 1972; the Delors Report, 1996; the United Nations Millennium Development

Goals, 2000; UNESCO, 2015). Specific thinking skills are just as necessary as the acquisition of knowledge content, the learning of artistic techniques, and many other skills and competences. Reflectiveness is seen as the heart of key competences (OECD, 2005, p. 8), furthermore critical thinking, teamwork, intercultural skills, problem-solving, creativity and the ability to plan and manage processes (European Commission, 2018, p. 39). The educational programmes of these organizations aim at strengthening these skills. They are crucial for how an individual can deal with the world and its problems in the present and the future using creative, constructive, critical, and social processes. Also, the scope of the validity of a solution should be considered, specifically to which time continuum (e.g., only current or future), to which group (e.g., only humans or including the whole of nature or even the universe), to which regions (e.g., only Europe or Western Civilizations, other world regions as well) it may apply.

6   Conclusion

The current educational systems have been moved from their efforts to construct declarative knowledge to helping students to acquire crucial procedural knowledge that will help them to cope with the challenges of the new era. Additionally,– and in our view more importantly, newly acquired knowledge, skills, and competences should enable learners to shape and to mould the future in a more positive way than traditionally according to the normative requests, to take responsibility even if against the mainstream, to practice civil disobedience if necessary.

A set of competencies such as reflective, anticipatory, critical, creative, and collaborative thinking are among the most important competencies that people of the 21st century need to be able to cope with the new emerging challenges. Aiming at this, further thinking styles appear within the scope of scientific and practical considerations, e.g., systemic thinking.

In this chapter, we discussed the main characteristics of RAC3, the bundle of five thinking styles, and we claimed that they are practiced in V*a*KE courses and that V*a*KE could facilitate learners to activate, practice, and promote this bundle of attitudes, processes, and competencies.

Note

1   Reiss refers also to other concepts which seem at least questionable.

References

Akpur, U. (2020). Critical, reflective, creative thinking and their reflections on academic achievement. *Thinking Skills and Creativity, 37*, 1–8.

Amos-Binks, A., & Dannenhauer, D. (2019). *Anticipatory thinking: A metacognitive capability.* New York, NY: Cornell University.

Bailin, S., & Battersby, M. (2016). *Reason in the balance: An inquiry approach to critical thinking.* Indianapolis, IN: Hackett Publishing.

Berger, P. L., & Luckman, T. (1966). *The social construction of reality.* New York, NY: Doubleday/Anchor.

Bloom, B. S. (Ed.). (1956). *Taxonomy of educational objectives.* Handbook 1: Cognitive domain. White Plains, NY: Longman.

Bronfenbrenner, U. (2009). *The ecology of human development: Experiments by nature and design.* Cambridge, MA: Harvard University Press.

Corrigan, K. (2012). Collaborative thinking: The challenge of the modern university. *Arts and Humanities in Higher Education, 11*(3), 262–272.

Davies, M., & Barnett, R. (Eds.). (2015). *The Palgrave handbook of critical thinking in higher education.* New York, NY: Palgrave Macmillan.

Delors, J. (1996). *Learning: The treasure within.* Report to UNESCO of the International Commission on Education for the 21st Century. Paris: UNESCO.

Dewey, J. (1897). *My pedagogic creed.* Retrieved July 10, 2020, from http://en.wikisource.org/wiki/My_Pedagogic_Creed

Dewey, J. (1933). *How we think: A restatement of the relation of reflective thinking to the educative process.* Boston, MA: Heath.

Dewey, J. (2009). *Democracy and education: An introduction to the philosophy of education.* New York, NY: Cosimo Classics.

Dominguez, C., & Payan-Carreira, R. (Eds.). (2019). *Promoting critical thinking in European higher education institutions: towards an educational protocol.* Vila Real, Spain: UTAD. Retrieved July 10, 2020, from https://www.researchgate.net/publication/332556274_Promoting_Critical_Thinking_in_European_Higher_Education_Institutions_towards_an_educational_protocol

Elen, J., Jiang, L., Huyghe, S., Evers, M., Verburgh, A., ... Palaigeorgiou, G. (2019). *Promoting critical thinking in European higher education institutions: Towards an educational protocol.* C. Dominguez & R. Payan-Carreira (Eds.), Vila Real: UTAD. Retrieved July 31, 2020, from https://www.researchgate.net/publication/33255627

European Commission. (2018). *Proposal for a council recommendation on key compteneces for lifelong learning.* Retrieved July 10, 2020, from https://eur-lex.europa.eu/legal-content/EN/TXT/PDF/?uri=CELEX:32018H0604(01)&from=LT

Facione, P. A. (1990). *Critical thinking: A statement of expert consensus for purposes of educational assessment and instruction: The Delphi report.* Millbrae, CA: Academic Press.

Faure, E., Herrera, F., Kaddoura, A. R., Lopes, H., Petrovski, A., Rahnema, M., & Ward, F. C. (1972). *Learning to be.* Retrieved July 10, 2020, from https://unesdoc.unesco.org/ark:/48223/pf0000001801

Garrison, D. R. (2016). *Thinking collaboratively. Learning in a community of inquiry.* New York, NY: Routledge.

Geden, M., Smith, A., Campbell, J., Amos-Binks, A., Mott, B., Feng, J., & Lester, J. (2018). Towards adaptive support for anticipatory thinking. In *Proceedings of the Technology, Mind, and Society (TechMindSociety '18).* Association for Computing Machinery, New York, NY, USA, Article 11, 1.

Gini-Newman, G., & Case, R. (2015). Critical, creative, and collaborative dimensions of thinking. In G. Gini-Newman & R. Case (Eds), *Creating thinking classrooms: Leading educational change for a 21st century world* (pp. 45–60). Vancouver, Canada: The Critical Thinking Consortium.

Gokhale, A. A. (1995). Collaborative learning enhances critical thinking. *Journal of Technology Education, 7*(1).

Guilford, J. P. (1967). *The nature of human intelligence.* New York, NY: McGraw-Hill.

Halonen, J. S. (1995). Demystifying critical thinking, *Teaching of Psychology, 22*(1), 75–81. doi:10.1207/s15328023top2201_23

Halpern, D. F. (2013). *Thought and Knowledge. An introduction to critical thinking* (5th ed.). New York, NY/London, UK: Taylor & Francis, Psychology Press.

Lai, E. R. (2011). *Critical thinking: A literature review.* Retrieved June 7, 2020, from http://images.pearsonassessments.com/images/tmrs/CriticalThinkingReviewFINAL.pdf

Landau, E. (1990). *The courage to be gifted.* New York, NY: Trillium Press.

Magno, C. (2010). The role of metacognitive skills in developing critical thinking. *Metacognition and Learning, 5*(2), 137–156.

McArthur, A., & Markova, D. (2015). *Collaborative intelligence. Thinking with people who think differently.* New York, NY: Random House.

Mead, G. H. (1913). The social self. *Journal of Philosophy, Psychology and Scientific Methods, 10,* 374–380.

Mischel, W. (1973). Toward a cognitive social learning reconceptualization of personality. *Psychological Review, 80,* 252–283.

Mischel, W., & Shoda, Y. (1995). A cognitive-affective system theory of personality: Reconceptualizing situations, dispositions, dynamics, and invariance in personality structure. *Psychological Review, 102,* 246–268.

Moon, J. (2007). *Critical thinking.* Taylor and Francis e-Library. Retrieved May 13, 2020, from https://dl.uswr.ac.ir/bitstream/Hannan/130848/1/Jennifer_Moon-Critical_Thinking__An_Exploration_of_Theory_and_Practice%282007%29.pdf

OECD. (2005). *Definition and selection of key competencies: Executive summary.* Retrieved May 13, 2020, from https://www.oecd.org/pisa/35070367.pdf

Osborn, A. F. (1953). *Applied imagination: principles and procedures of creative problem-solving.* New York, NY: Scribners.

Patry, J.-L. (2019). Situation specificity of behavior: The triple relevance in research and practice of education. In R. V. Nata (Ed.), *Progress in education* (Volume 58, pp. 29–144). Hauppauge, NY: Nova.

Paul, R., & Elder, L. (2004). *The nature and functions of critical and creating thinking.* Dillon Beach, CA: The Foundation for Critical Thinking.

Piaget, J. (1954). *The construction of reality in the child.* New York, NY: Basic Books.

Pnevmatikos, D., Christodoulou, P., & Georgiadou, T. (2019). Promoting critical thinking in higher education through the Values *and* Knowledge Education (V*a*KE) method. *Studies in Higher Education, 44*(5), 892–901.

Pun, S. (2012). Collaborative learning: a means to creative thinking in design. *International Journal of Education and Information Technologies, 6*(1), 33–43.

Razzouk, R., & Johnson, T. E. (2012). Cooperative learning. In N. M. Seel (Ed.), *Encyclopedia of the sciences of learning.* Boston, MA: Springer.

Reiss, M. J. (2010). Ethical thinking. In A. Jones, A. McKim, & M. J. Reiss (Eds.), *Ethics in the science and technology classroom: A new approach to teaching and learning* (pp. 7–17). Rotterdam, The Netherlands: Sense.

Rodgers, C. (2002). Defining Reflection: Another look at John Dewey and reflective thinking. *Teachers College Record, 104*(4), 842–866.

Siegel, H. (2013). Educating reason. Routledge. *Teachers College Record, 104*(4), 842–866.

Tversky, A., & Kahneman, D. (1974). Judgment under uncertainty heuristics and biases. *Science, 185,* 1124–1131.

UNESCO. (2015). *Rethinking education. Towards a global common good?* Retrieved May 13, 2020, from http://www.unesco.org/new/fileadmin/MULTIMEDIA/FIELD/Cairo/images/RethinkingEducation.pdf

United Nations. (2000). *Millenium goals.* Retrieved May 13, 2020, from https://www.un.org/millenniumgoals/

Vygotsky, L. S. (1980). *Mind in society. The development of higher psychological processes.* Cambridge, MA: Harvard University Press.

CHAPTER 31

Assessment in VaKE Studies

Jean-Luc Patry and Alfred Weinberger

1   Introduction

Compared to most intervention methods that are evaluated, VaKE has some peculiarities which have an impact on assessments. Two issues require particular attention: (1) The implementation of VaKE is not trivial, hence we need to assess whether the process of VaKE is appropriate. And (2) the assessment of the outcomes of VaKE processes requires particular precautions for reasons which will be elaborated below. We will address three issues: process analyses, assessments of knowledge acquisition, and assessments of moral competence.

2   Process Assessments

VaKE is a complex process that consists of several steps which we have framed as "prototypical" because of the necessity to adapt the VaKE process depending on the specific audience, on specific procedural hypotheses such as the introduction of particular techniques (Chapters 5 and 8 in this handbook) or in order to analyse relationships between variables (e.g., Patry & Schaber, 2010; Ebner, 2011). This means that the suggested steps provide a practical framework that can be changed in accordance with the underlying theory (Chapter 2). For evaluation purposes then, it is necessary to assess the procedure to check whether (1) it follows the theoretical principles and (2) it varies what is supposed to be varied. This is a contribution to checking the treatment construct validity (i.e., the response to the question "Does the treatment represent the intended construct?", Patry, 1989) or treatment adherence (Schoenwald & Garland, 2013).

One instrument to assess the presumed VaKE processes is the Lesson Interruption Method (LIM; Patry, 1997). This instrument enables the assessment of situation specific characteristics of the teaching and the students. For this, several copies of a one- or two-page questionnaire with items concerning the constructs of the VaKE process of interest (or other issues one is interested in) are assembled in a booklet; examples of items are given in Table 31.1. At predetermined times during the lesson, the teacher interrupts the lesson and asks

TABLE 31.1 Prototypical items for a Lesson-Interruption Method questionnaire

1	In this unit, we	worked individually.	1 2 3 4 5	cooperated with each other.
2	The topics addressed in this unit are	useless for me.	1 2 3 4 5	useful for me.
3	The unit was	boring.	1 2 3 4 5	interesting.

the students to respond to the questionnaire items, which takes a half minute or so; the teacher then continues with the lesson. Constructs (features) to be assessed can be chosen depending on one's research question and hypotheses; to operationalize them, several items need to be used to increase reliability. With this method, the teaching-learning situations are captured from the perspective of the most important stakeholders in the process: the students.

The items have a specific format which departs from the traditional items of the type "agree – disagree". The latter are ambiguous, as it is not clear what it means to respond, "I disagree", for instance, to the item "The unit was interesting": Does it mean that it did not hook me, or that it was bluntly boring? In the present format (item 3), this is clear.

According to our experiences (for example Patry, 2000; Weyringer, 2008), once the students become accustomed to this tool, the disturbance in the classroom will be minimal if the students are fairly disciplined. This method enables the assessment of very subtle differences between situations (in this case, units) in class through repeated measures, using time series.

In the LIM assessments, one can distinguish two types of constructs: On one hand, there are descriptions of the situation from the perspective of the students (e.g., how much guidance is exerted by the teacher), on the other, there are characteristics of the person[1] that apply for this specific situation (e.g., how much self-efficacy the student senses in this situation). These two types of constructs must be dealt with differently (Patry, 2019):

– For the description of the situation (like in item 1 in Table 31.1), the students are interpreted as observers *of the situation*. To estimate the reliability then, it is appropriate to use measures of inter-rater reliability, such as Krippendorff's Alpha (Krippendorff, 2011). In such approaches, variations between observers (students) are seen as *inhibiting* reliability.
– For the student characteristics (like items 2 and 3 in Table 31.1), the students are interpreted as observers of *themselves*, of their inner processes or states, or of their behaviour in the situation. To estimate the reliability, it is then appropriate to measure the internal consistency (Cronbach's alpha). In this

kind of approach, variations between people (students) are a *prerequisite*; if there is no variation, there can be no reliability.

Furthermore, if several successive assessments are made (time series), there is the problem of serial dependency (Patry, 2019, section 4.1): The phenomenon under investigation at time t_n may have an influence on the phenomenon on time t_{n+1}. For instance, if a student is not feeling well, one cannot expect that he or she will be feeling well immediately afterwards. Such serial effects can be assessed using autocorrelations (Dumas, 1986). In none of our studies using the LIM, however, were serial effects found (Patry, 2019). This means: The time lag between the assessment situations was always so long that there was no influence from the situation at t_n on the one at t_{n+1} with respect to the phenomenon, or the impact of the actual situation was more important than the influence from the phenomenon in the previous situation.

The LIM assessments can be used for different purposes. The first is to check whether the implementation of the treatment was successful (treatment validity). For instance, one could use the questions like those formulated by Alt (2014, table 2, pp. 14f.), adapted to the specific phase, to assess whether the teaching of the group with VaKE is indeed more constructivist than the one with more traditional teaching methods, and use other variables for which no difference is expected between the experimental and the control groups (e.g., discipline, anxiety) as control variable (for an example, see Patry et al., 2000).

One can also use the LIM approach to assess other research questions. Patry and Schaber (2010; this study was replicated by Ebner, 2011, with similar results), for instance, analysed to what degree the participants in VaKE workshops were focusing on *justice* and on *care* and whether this depended on the participants *concernedness* (situation specific student characteristics); these three variables were assessed through the LIM at the end of each of the five workshop days (five workshops with different topics). The correlations between concernedness and care were positive (from, r = .32 to r = .70 for different days), and there were no sex differences. This example demonstrates how the LIM can be used to address specific hypotheses that are more or less closely linked to VaKE. In this particular case, the study showed (1) that in VaKE processes, care as well as justice issues are addressed – this is important as the literature on dilemma discussions focus mainly on justice, in the tradition of Kohlberg (e.g., Lind, 2016); (2) that the choice of the type of morality (justice vs. care) depends to some degree on how much the participant feels personally concerned by the issues at stake; and (3) that the idea that care is female and justice is male is inappropriate, thus confirming the results of studies using completely different approaches (e.g., Döbert & Nunner-Winkler, 1983).

3   Product Assessments: Knowledge

When introducing a new method like VaKE, it is essential to show that it is at least as good as the traditional approaches. In school, knowledge acquisition has priority over any other goal, as documented in the curricula. Thus, if VaKE leads to less knowledge acquisition, it will not be regarded as valuable for school, no matter what other advantages it may have. With this presupposition in mind, in the first studies with VaKE (e.g., Peticzka et al., 1998; Verwanger, 1998; Weinberger, 2001), we tested the hypothesis that VaKE leads to as much knowledge as traditional teaching. However, VaKE is an open teaching method. This means that the participants decide what they will learn; hence, the researchers cannot fully anticipate what will be learnt. In traditional evaluations of interventions, one would use a knowledge questionnaire before and after the treatment; if no such test is available, a teacher-made test would be a possibility. This can be done with VaKE as well, but if the issues addressed in the VaKE process do not fit exactly those assessed with the questionnaire, one might miss crucial learning experiences. Therefore, we need instruments that are flexible and enable the assessment of issues that were not anticipated.

A second problem is that we claim that VaKE has not only an impact on the lower levels of cognitive processing according to the taxonomies of Bloom et al. (1956) and Anderson and Krathwohl (2001), namely remember, understand, and apply, but also on the higher levels: analyse, evaluate, and create (in the terminology of Anderson & Krathwohl). However, most assessment tools address the lower levels, using questions to which the answer is already known by the teacher (e.g., Stiggins, Griswold, & Wikelund, 1985), which is much easier to assess than the higher levels.

Finally, besides knowledge on the different levels, other issues can be important. VaKE deals with values, and hence we also need to carry out assessments for these. Again, this is not trivial. Similarly, hypotheses about behaviour need to be tested.

An instrument that can satisfy most of these conditions is called WALK (Patry & Weinberger, 2017). The name is an acronym for "W Assessment of Latent Knowledge".[2] "W refers to the six w-questions: What, why, when, how, where, who. In this assessment, the subjects are confronted with pictures and (1) asked to formulate problems or questions specific to the subject matter, with the instruction to formulate them according to specific criteria (like "as complex as possible", "including as many different domains within the discipline as possible", and the like[3]). The latter criteria are also used for grading the student responses. (2) Furthermore, the students are required to answer the questions themselves. This way, the subjects are free to choose themselves the specific topic to address. Depending on the conditions, the researcher can restrict the time for working on the pictures (speeding condition).

The first WALK to assess knowledge in a VaKE study was used by Weinberger (2001, 2006). Some simple pictures[4] were presented, and the students were asked (1) to formulate problems related to the picture; (2) to formulate as many concrete questions as they possibly could; and then (3) to answer the questions. In accordance with constructivist principles, the first and the third steps were performed in groups, whereas the second step was done individually so that the individual learning success could be assessed. That some steps could be done in groups shows how flexibly – and in accordance with the underlying theory – the WALK can be used. For the analysis, only the second step was considered. First, the number of questions was counted. Second, the type of knowledge to be applied was judged: Can the question be answered with elementary knowledge, or is additional knowledge needed (not learnt until now according to the curriculum)? In all regards, the results of VaKE+ were higher than those of VaKE (Weinberger, 2006; see also Chapter 8 in this handbook).

In a more elaborate framework, following a procedure proposed by Zlöbl (2014) to assess environmental awareness, Pnevmatikos and Patry (2012) used a WALK on biodiesel: They presented one exercise picture and three test pictures to the subjects and asked them to respond to the questionnaires presented in Figure 31.1. Five domains are addressed: (1) knowledge; (2) element/function; (3) element/damage; (4) element/action; (5) element/values.

The analysis is focused on hypothesis testing and follows the principles of content analyses, based on a detailed handbook that cannot be presented here. We emphasize that the handbook must be conceived such that interrater reliability and validity are ensured; validity should refer to the constructs addressed in the hypotheses. Furthermore, since several pictures are used, one can conceive the internal consistency (Cronbach's alpha) across pictures.

This instrument can be used for any topic. The sensitive issues are (1) the choice of the pictures, (2) the exact instruction and how the answers are collected, and (3) the analysis. All these issues have to be dealt with in accordance with the hypothesis under consideration. The advantage of the general approach is that the role of the language is much less important than in the traditional assessments with questionnaires. For instance, Zlöbl (2014) was able to compare samples from Vietnam and Indonesia with samples from Austria.

4 Product Assessments: Moral Competence

The second main aim of VaKE besides knowledge education is facilitating the development of moral judgment through dilemma discussion in the

1. What do you see on this picture? Write five different elements.		2. What *functions* do the elements on the picture have?	
		Element (the same or different from the previous)	Function
1		1	
2		2	
3		3	
4		4	
5		5	

3. In what regard can elements be *damaged* or provoke damage?		4. What *actions* we caried out relevant to the elements you see on the picture?	
Element (the same or different from the previous)	Damage	Element (the same or different from the previous)	Action
1		1	
2		2	
3		3	
4		4	
5		5	

5. What *values* are relevant in the elements you see on the picture?	
Element (the same or different from the previous)	Value
1	
2	
3	
4	
5	

FIGURE 31.1
The five pages of the WALK questionnaire used by Pnevmatikos and Patry (2012)

Kohlbergian tradition. According to Kohlberg (1969, 1984) the development of moral judgment with the focus on justice proceeds in several stages in an upward, predictable sequence culminating in principled moral reasoning. Development occurs gradually, and it is assumed that when a person acquires a new stage, he or she adopts the new stage widely and consistently across different problems and contents. The core assumptions of Kohlberg's theory of moral judgment are (1) that not the value itself is at stake, but the way (pattern) the person justifies it (judgment); (2) the judgment is a cognitive act;

(3) they are personal constructions based on epistemological categories (e.g., "rights", "justice"); (4) development is a cognitive "advance" in which "higher is better" in a philosophical normative-ethical sense, that moves from personal interest over conventional to postconventional moral thinking; and (5) moral judgment is a competence, which means that at a given stage of moral judgment, the person is able to use the corresponding argumentation pattern, but does not necessarily apply it in every situation – but he or she is also able to understand, to some degree, the argumentation from the stage above.

To assess moral judgment – and hence to test whether a V*a*KE process has yielded an improvement in moral competence – requires reliable and valid instruments. Since Kohlberg's theory evolved in the last decades, the current instruments draw on evolutions of the original theory of Kohlberg. We will present two instruments and the respective underlying theoretical backgrounds.

4.1   *The Moral Competence Test (MCT)*

The Moral Competence Test (MCT) was developed by Georg Lind and colleagues from the University of Konstanz, Germany, in the 1970s (Lind, 1978). The MCT, which formerly was called the Moral Judgment Test (MJT), is frequently used for cross-cultural studies, and is translated in more than 30 languages. It is a reliable and valid instrument (Biggs & Colesante, 2015; Lerkiatbundit, Utaipan, Laohawiriyanon, & Teo, 2006).

The MCT is grounded in the two-aspect theory of morality (Lind, 1992) that roots in the work of Kohlberg: The *cognitive* aspect refers to moral judgement and the *affective* aspect relates to moral orientations. Both aspects are measured simultaneously in the MCT. The first aspect, moral judgement, is understood as "the capacity to make decisions and judgments which are moral (i.e., based on internal principles)" (Kohlberg, 1964, p. 425). People with a high moral capacity for judgement also deal with the moral quality of counterarguments. The second aspect, moral orientations, refers to the six stages of Kohlberg's model and characterize the moral quality of an argument: (a) orientation towards physical and material consequences (stage 1), (b) orientation towards reciprocity (stage 2), (c) orientation towards the reference group (stage 3), (d) orientation towards law and order (stage 4), (e) orientation towards rights (stage 5) and (f) orientation towards universalizable moral principles (stage 6). According to Lind, moral competence is shown in the ability to *consistently* reject or acknowledge moral arguments on the basis of their moral quality, regardless of whether these arguments correspond to or contradict one's own opinion (Lind, 2008).

The MCT consists of two dilemmas, and for each dilemma, a proposed action to solve the dilemma and six arguments in favour and six arguments against the proposed action; the arguments (justifications) correspond to the six moral orientations according to Kohlberg. The interviewee's task is, for each of the two dilemmas, to assess the appropriateness of the behaviour towards the proposed solution of the dilemma on a 7-point rating scale from "–3" ("rather wrong") to "+3" ("rather right") and to rate the 12 arguments on a 9-point rating scale from "+4" ("completely agree") to "–4" ("completely disagree"). The first dilemma is about two workers who break into their company's management office to take tape recordings proving that they had been taped. The second dilemma is about a doctor who gives a woman who is suffering pain from incurable cancer an overdose of morphine after he was asked by the woman to do so.

The MCT is a repeated measure assessment with three factors (two dilemmas by two opinions – pro vs. con – by six moral orientations according to the stages). By means of multivariate variance decomposition, the C-score ("C" for "competence") is calculated which provides information about the extent to which the respondent is likely to orientate him- or herself towards his or her own opinion or moral quality when evaluating the arguments. The higher the C-score, the higher is the coherence of the person's judgment with respect to the stage of moral judgment, irrespective of whether the respective argument is in favour, or against the chosen behaviour option to solve the dilemma. The C-score can reach values between 1 and 100, whereby moral competence can be pronounced as very low (1–9), low (10–19), medium (20–29), high (30–39), very high (40–49) and exceptionally high (over 50) (Lind, 2008). The C-score is calculated in several steps which cannot be explained here (see Lind, 2016, chapter 4). The MCT can be used with participants from the age of 8 and upwards if the participant has average reading and comprehension abilities. Lind provides the MCT upon request.

The MCT was used in a study on VaKE in teacher education (Weinberger, 2016). The results were that the students who learnt with VaKE significantly increased their moral competence ($C_{pretest}$ = 18.5, SD = 14.0; $C_{posttest}$ = 35.7, SD = 27.1; N = 32), whereas the students who learnt with a traditional case-based setting without systematic combination of values and knowledge education had little improvement ($C_{pretest}$ = 24.8; SD = 14.2; $C_{posttest}$ = 27.4, SD = 15.0; N = 26); the variance accounted for by the interaction treatment (VaKE vs. control) by time (pre vs. posttest) was eta^2 = .17.

4.2 *Defining Issues Test (DIT)*

The most common instrument to assess moral judgement used mainly in the USA is the Defining Issues Test (DIT) which was created in the early 1970s (Rest et al., 1974). It can be used for adolescents from the age of 12 and upwards and adult populations. The DIT is a reliable and valid instrument (Rest et al., 2000).

The current version, the DIT-2, is based on the schema theory of moral judgment which is a further development of Kohlberg's original stage theory (Rest et al., 1999). Based on factor analyses of data from large samples who accomplished the DIT and theoretical assumptions based on critics of Kohlberg's theory, a Neo-Kohlbergian approach of moral development was developed called the schema theory. It differs in several aspects from the original theory of Kohlberg: (1) Development is considered as shifting distributions ("soft" stages) rather than as a staircase ("hard" stages) characterized in changes in the frequency of usage, moving from the less to the more complex. (2) Schemas instead of stages are more specific and concrete and represent conceptions of institutions and role-systems in society, whereas Kohlberg regards social institutions as "content". (3) Schemas do not directly assess cognitive operations (e.g., "justice operations") and do not purge content from structure as in Kohlberg's concept. (4) Morality is considered as social construction ("common morality"), evolving from the community's experience rather than universality. (5) Tacit knowledge (multiple choice task) instead of self-reported explanations is assumed to provide reliable information about the inner processes that underlie moral behaviour.

The Neo-Kohlbergian approach to moral development postulates three structures (schemas) in moral thinking development (Rest et al., 2000). The first schema, Personal Interest, develops in childhood until the age of about 12. It does not entail a socio-centric perspective as described by Kohlbergian stage 1, rather it includes individual prudential concerns and concerns for those whom one has an affectionate relationship. The Personal Interest Schema has elements described by Kohlbergian Stages 2 and 3. It reflects micro morality which concerns the particular face-to-face relations that people have in everyday life. The additional schemas reflect macro morality which concerns the formal structure of society as defined by institutions, rules, and roles. The second schema, Maintaining Norms, includes a socio-centric perspective in that the individual perceives (a) the need for generally accepted norms (e.g., laws), (b) the necessity that the norms apply to all people in society, (c) the need for the norms to be clear, uniform and categorical, (d) the norms are seen as establishing reciprocity (each person obeys the law, expecting that others will also obey), and (e) the establishment of hierarchical role structures. The Maintaining Norms Schema represents conventional thinking and is derived from Kohlberg's definition of stage 4. The third schema, Postconventional, is characterized by (a) the primacy of moral criteria, (b) an appeal to an ideal, (c) shareable ideals, and (d) full reciprocity. It is drawn from Kohlberg's stages 5 and 6.

The DIT is an instrument for activating moral schemas. When confronted with a DIT item that makes sense to the respondent and activates a preferred schema, he or she will give a high rating and rank it as being of high importance.

The DIT-2 consists of five dilemmas (one of them is a doctor's dilemma similar to the one in the MCT). For each dilemma, a proposed solution is offered, which the respondent confirms, rejects, or classifies as undecidable. Twelve items follow, each of which concerns a moral aspect of the dilemma in such a way that it corresponds to a moral schema. The person's task is to rate the twelve items according to their importance on a five-point scale (from 'great importance' to 'no importance'). Finally, the person is asked to rank all twelve items in the order of importance. This process is repeated for all dilemma stories. Several indices can be calculated from the respondents' answers. The most common values scored are the N2-score, the P-score, and the schema scores. The N2-score is the primary index of the DIT-2 and represents the degree to which Postconventional items are prioritized, plus the degree to which personal interest items receive lower ratings than the Postconventional items. It is derived from the four items ranked as most important. This score is adjusted to have the same mean and standard deviation as the P score to allow for comparisons. The P-score represents the proportion of items selected that represent considerations from stage 5 (focus on appealing to majority while maintaining minority rights) and stage 6 (focus on appealing to intuitive moral principles or ideals). The Personal Interest Schema score represents the proportion of items selected that represent considerations from stage 2 (focus on the personal interest of the person making the moral decisions) and stage 3 (focus on maintaining friendships, good relationships, and approval). The Maintaining Norms Schema score represents the proportion of items selected that represent considerations from stage 4 (focus on maintaining the existing legal system, roles, and formal organizational structure).

The DIT-2 is provided as an online or a paper-and-pencil test by the University of Alabama, Center for the Study of Ethical Development.

4.3   *Assessment of Moral Competence: Discussion*

The MCT and the DIT-2 are the most important instruments to assess the development of moral judgment and can be used in VaKE to test the effectivity of values education. However, both instruments are not without their critics. As for the MCT, the main critique concerns the C-score which is based on the consistency of preferring a particular stage reasoning. People with high C-scores can either prefer higher stage arguments or lower stage arguments (Biggs & Colesante, 2015). According to the MCT both groups are considered to be high in their moral competence. The question remains whether moral competence is to be defined independently from an individual's stage of moral development? As for the DIT-2, research showed that political ideology systematically influences the outcome, and the scores can be faked upward (Fisher & Sweeney, 2015; Emler, Renwick, & Malone, 1983).

5   Conclusions

As shown at the end of the section on LIM, VaKE addresses not only justice, but also care as crucial moral categories (Patry & Schaber, 2010; see also Chapter 33 on trans-domain approaches in this handbook). Nevertheless, so far, our studies on the impact or VaKE on morality have focused on assessment of moral competence with respect to justice, as discussed above in section 3, whereas the issues of ethics of care have not been addressed. This is due to the fact, firstly, that the principles of dilemma discussions which are at the origin of VaKE are rooted in the Kohlbergian tradition of ethics of justice. Furthermore, research on care morality is much less well developed than the one on justice. We would not go so far as to say that ethics of care "is dying as a moral psychology but prospering as an ethical theory" (Govrin, 2014, p. 1) – Döbert and Nunner-Winkler (1983) and Oser et al. (1991) are examples of a moral psychology of care – but it is obvious that compared to the moral psychology of justice there is a deficit in the one of care. According to Govrin, the lack of moral psychology of ethics of care is due, at least to a substantial degree, to the importance of emotion within it, in contrast to the domination of rationality in the Kantian concept of justice in Kohlberg. Such a perspective is supported by the insight that a focus on care is closely related to the level of concern, as seen in the study by Patry and Schaber (2010) discussed above (see also Döbert & Nunner-Winkler, 1983), as concern may trigger emotions. Maybe for this reason, ethics of care cannot be conceived as a competence the same way as ethics of justice can be, as addressed in section 3 above, which renders assessment much more difficult. Nevertheless, assessing whether there is an improvement in the morality of care in participants in VaKE is a desideratum for future research. But for this we would need an assessment tool comparable to the moral competence assessment tools, which is not available. Maybe the values part of the WALK (Figure 31.1, domain 5) can be adapted to assess issues of care.

Evaluating VaKE is a challenge due to its peculiarities. Given the trans-domain characteristics of the whole framework (see Chapter 33 in this handbook), there are many issues to be addressed. The most important are the product knowledge and moral competence – these two were discussed in the above chapter. It does not mean that the tools proposed are the only ones, quite the opposite: particularly with respect to knowledge, traditional tools can be used as well, especially when the achievement of well-defined curricular goals are in the focus so that pre- and post-tests can be made. Other tools like writing essays with subsequent content analyses (Weinberger, 2006) can also be used. And of course, process analyses can be applied to test specific hypotheses with respect to the implementation of the treatment and to test particular hypotheses. Obviously, this cannot be achieved in single studies; therefore, we reiterate the claim that the research must be done in the form of research programmes and not only single studies – and the aim of the present handbook is to render such programmes possible.

Notes

1 In the literature, these would be referred to as *traits* or maybe *states*; however, *trait* has the connotation of being a disposition that is stable over time and across situation; in the case of LIM, however, this stability is under investigation, therefore we avoid the term. *State* may be more situation specific but still insinuates some stability. One can also assess the (self-reported) behaviour in the situation.
2 Another reason for the name is that the method builds on a walk in the sense of going around; the so-called "math walk" (Dinauer, 2001) is at the origin of the procedure.
3 This refers to the "maximum performance" in contrast to the "typical performance" (Cronbach, 1970, p. 35). The relevance of this distinction for assessment is discussed in Patry (2019, section 3.3).
4 The pictures cannot be depicted here because of copyright restrictions.

References

Alt, D. (2014). The construction and validation of a new scale for measuring features of constructivist learning environments in higher education. *Frontline Learning Research, 5*, 1–28.

Anderson, L. W., & Krathwohl, D. R. (2001). *A taxonomy for learning, teaching, and assessing: A revision of Bloom's taxonomy of educational objectives.* New York, NY: Longman.

Biggs, D. A., & Colesante, R. J. (2015). The Moral Competence Test: An examination of validity for samples in the United States. *Journal of Moral Education, 44*(4), 497–515.

Bloom, B. S., Engelhart, M. D., Furst, E. J., Hill, W. H., & Krathwohl, D. R. (Eds.). (1956). *Taxonomy of educational objectives – the classification of educational goals – Handbook 1: Cognitive domain.* London, WI: Longmans, Green & Co.

Cronbach, L. J. (1970). *Essentials of psychological testing* (3rd ed.). New York, NY: Harper & Row.

Dinauer, G. (2001). Math Walk. Ein Beitrag zur Realistischen Mathematik. In H. Schwetz, M. Zeyringer, & A. Reiter (Eds.), *Konstruktives Lernen mit neuen Medien. Beiträge zu einer konstruktivistischen Mediendidaktik* (pp. 184–195). Innsbruck, Austria: StudienVerlag.

Döbert, R., & Nunner-Winkler, G. (1986). Wertewandel und Moral. In H. Bertram (Ed.), *Gesellschaftlicher Zwang und moralische Autonomie* (pp. 289–321). Frankfurt am Main, Germany: Suhrkamp.

Dumas, J. (1986). Controlling for autocorrelation in social interaction analysis. *Psychological Bulletin, 100*, 125–127.

Ebner, M. (2011). *Inwieweit beeinflusst die persönliche Betroffenheit (von Jungen und Mädchen) die Argumentation nach Fürsorge-, bzw. Gerechtigkeitsaspekten in Wertekonflikten. Untersuchung von Schüler/Innen einer 3. Klasse HS mit dem Schwerpunkt VaKE (Values and Knowledge Education)* [Bacherlor's thesis]. Paris Lodron University Salzburg.

Emler, N. P., Renwick, S., & Malone, B. (1983). The relationship between moral reasoning and political orientation. *Journal of Personality and Social Psychology, 45*(5), 1072–1080.

Fisher, D. G., & Sweeney, J. T. (2002). Morality vs. ideology: Implications for accounting ethics research. *Advances in Accounting Behavioral Research, 5*, 141–160.

Govrin, A. (2014). From ethics of care to psychology of care: Reconnecting ethics of care to contemporary moral psychology. *Frontiers in Psychology, 5*. Retrieved April 29, 2021, from https://www.frontiersin.org/articles/10.3389/fpsyg.2014.01135/full

Kohlberg, L. (1964). Development of moral character and moral ideology. In M. Hoffman & L. Hoffman (Eds.), *Review of child development research* (Vol. 1, pp. 383–431). New York, NY: Russel Sage Foundation.

Kohlberg, L. (1969). Stage and sequence: the cognitive developmental approach to socialization. In D. A. Goslin (Ed.), *Handbook of socialization theory* (pp. 347–480). Chicago, IL: Rand McNally.

Kohlberg, L. (1984). *Essays on moral development: the nature and validity of moral stages* (Vol. 2). San Francisco, CA: Harper & Row.

Krippendorff, K. (2011). *Computing Krippendorff's alpha-reliability*. Annenberg School for Communication Departmental Papers (ASC), University of Pennsylvania. Retrieved April 29, 2021, from http://repository.upenn.edu/cgi/viewcontent.cgi?article=1043&context=asc_papers

Lerkiatbundit, S., Utaipan, P., Laohawiriyanon, C., & Teo, A. (2006). Randomized controlled study of the impact of the Konstanz method of dilemma discussion on moral judgement. *Journal of Allied Health, 35*(2), 101–108.

Lind, G. (1978). Wie misst man moralisches Urteil? Probleme und Möglichkeiten der Messung eines komplexen Konstrukts. In G. Portele (Ed.), *Sozialisation und Moral: Neuere Ansätze zur Moral. Entwicklung und Erziehung* (pp. 6–49). Weinheim, Germany: Beltz.

Lind, G. (1992). Rekonstruktion des Kohlberg-Ansatzes: Das Zwei-Aspekte-Modell der Moralentwicklung. In F. Oser & W. Althof (Eds.), *Moralische Selbstbestimmung* (pp. 204–208). Stuttgart, Germany: Klett-Cotta.

Lind, G. (2008). The meaning and measurement of moral judgment competence revisited – A dual-aspect model. In D. Fasko & W. Willis (Eds.), *Contemporary philosophical and psychological perspectives on moral development and education* (pp. 185–220). Cresskill, NJ: Hampton Press.

Lind, G. (2016). *How to teach morality. Promoting deliberation and discussion, reducing violence and deceit.* Berlin, Germany: Logos.

Oser, F., Patry, J.-L., Zutavern, M., Reichenbach, R., Klaghofer, R., Althof, W., & Rothbucher, H. (1991). *Der Prozess der Verantwortung – Berufsethische Entscheidung von Lehrerinnen und Lehrern.* Bericht zum Forschungsprojekt 1.188-0.85 und 11.25470.88/2 des Schweizerischen Nationalfonds zur Förderung der wissenschaftlichen Forschung. Freiburg, Switzerland: Pädagogisches Institut der Universität.

Patry, J.-L. (1989). Evaluationsmethodologie zu Forschungszwecken – Ein Beispiel von "kritischem Multiplizismus". *Unterrichtswissenschaft, 17,* 359–374.

Patry, J.-L. (1997). The lesson interruption method in assessing situation-specific behavior in classrooms. *Psychological Reports, 81,* 272–274.

Patry, J.-L. (2000). Kaktus und Salat – Zur Situationsspezifität in der Erziehung. In J.-L. Patry & F. Riffert (Eds.), *Situationsspezifität in pädagogischen Handlungsfeldern* (pp. 13–52). Innsbruck, Austria: StudienVerlag.

Patry, J.-L. (2019). Situation specificity of behavior: The triple relevance in research and practice of education. In R. V. Nata (Ed.), *Progress in education* (Vol. 58, pp. 29–144). Hauppauge, NY: Nova.

Patry, J.-L., & Schaber, K. (2010, January 15–16). *Fürsorge versus Gerechtigkeit: Argumentieren Frauen anders als Männer? Eine Untersuchung zur Geschlechtsspezifität in moralischen Entscheidungssituationen* [Paper]. The conference "Moral und Beruf 2010", Basel, Switzerland.

Patry, J.-L., Schwetz, H., & Gastager, A (2000). Wissen und Handeln. Lehrerinnen und Lehrer verändern ihren Mathematikunterricht. *Bildung und Erziehung, 53,* 271–286.

Patry, J.-L., & Weinberger, A. (2017). Leistungsmessung im konstruktivistischen Unterricht: WALK. In K. Zierer (Ed.), *Schulische Werteerziehung* (pp. 220–230). Hohengehren, Germany: Schneider.

Peticzka, D., Weinberger, A., & Kastberger, A. (1998). *Dilemmadiskussion zur Wissensacquisition: Studie "Autobahn"* [Seminar paper]. Department or Educational Research, Paris-Lodron University Salzburg.

Pnevmatikos, D., & Patry, J.-L. (2012, November 8–10). *Teachers' values preferences assessed through pictures on biofuels* [Paper]. The 38th annual conference of the Association for Moral Education, San Antonio, TX.

Rest, J., Cooper, D., Coder, R., Masanz, J., & Anderson, D. (1974). Judging the important issues in moral dilemmas – An objective test of development. *Developmental Psychology, 10*(4), 491–501.

Rest, J., Narvaez, D., Bebeau, M., & Thoma, S. (1999). *Post-conventional moral thinking: A neo-Kohlbergian approach.* Mahwah, NJ: Lawrence Erlbaum Associates.

Rest, J., Narvaez, D., Thoma, S. J., & Bebeau, M. J. (2000). A neo-Kohlbergian approach to morality research. *Journal of Moral Education, 29*, 381–396.

Schoenwald, S. K., & Garland, A. F. (2013). A review of treatment adherence measurement methods. *Psychological Assessment, 25*(1), 146–156.

Stiggins, R., Griswold, M. M., & Wikelund, K. R. (1989). Measuring thinking skills through classroom assessment. *Journal of Educational Measurement, 26*(3), 233–246.

Verwanger, C. (1998). *Über die Auswirkungen Kohlberg'scher Dilemmadiskussionen auf das Lernverhalten von Pflichtschülern* [Seminar paper]. Department or Educational Research, Paris-Lodron University Salzburg.

Weinberger, A. (2001). *Verbindung von konstruktivistischer Moralerziehung und Wissensvermittlung* [Master's thesis]. Paris-Lodron University Salzburg.

Weinberger, A. (2006). *Kombination von Werterziehung und Wissenserwerb. Evaluation des konstruktivistischen Unterrichtsmodells VaKE (Values and Knowledge Education) in der Sekundarstufe 1.* Hamburg, Germany: Kovac.

Weinberger, A. (2016). Konstruktivistisches Lernen in der LehrerInnenbildung. Die Förderung des Professionsethos mit dem Unterrichtsmodell VaKE. *Journal für LehrerInnenbildung, 16*(2), 28–39.

Weyringer, S. (2008). *VaKE in einem internationalen Sommercampus für (hoch) begabte Jugendliche: Eine Evaluationsstudie* [Dissertation]. Paris-Lodron University Salzburg.

Zlöbl, S. (2014). *Der Umwelt-WALK-4 – Weiterentwicklung und erste Validierung eines authentischen Erhebungsinstrumentes zur Beurteilung von Umweltbewusstsein* [Dissertation]. Paris-Lodron University Salzburg.

CHAPTER 32

Research Designs for V*a*KE Studies

Jean-Luc Patry

1 Introduction

The design of a research study includes everything that is related with the acquisition of data: the sampling of the subjects, their assignments to experimental and control groups (if there are such), the arrangements of subject groups, assessments, and interventions (treatments), etc. The most important designs, pre-experimental, quasi-experimental and experimental ones, have been discussed by Campbell and Stanley (1963; see also Shadish, Cook, & Campbell, 2002, for a discussion of the background). These can be (and have been) used in studies aiming at testing hypotheses about V*a*KE. In the present chapter, I will address some non-traditional design approaches that have proven to be quite powerful in some of our studies. The aim of this chapter is to foster research on V*a*KE through such designs.

The chapter starts with the particular challenges research on V*a*KE is confronted with, then two specific types of designs – the one-group designs and the two-period cross-over design – will be discussed. Some conclusions close the chapter. Throughout this chapter, the studies by Frewein (2009) and Weinberger (2006) will be used as examples to illustrate the issues.

2 Challenges for Designing Research Studies with V*a*KE

The best design for intervention studies is the randomized control group design (randomized controlled trial) in which the subjects are assigned randomly to the experimental and control groups (experimental designs in terms of Campbell & Stanley, 1963). This can easily be done in laboratory studies. In principle, it is possible to carry out V*a*KE studies under laboratory or laboratory-like conditions. However, such studies are usually subject to biases (Gerhard, 2008) and hence may lack ecological validity (are the conclusions reached with the laboratory study also valid under natural conditions, i.e., when no study is being conducted? Patry, 1982[1]). Furthermore, only short interventions are possible in laboratories, as are done in some V*a*KE studies (for instance, Frewein, 2009, taught VaKE units of about three hours), but most interventions were longer (e.g., Weinberger, 2006: seven units over one week). Therefore, field studies would be appropriate, but such studies are confronted with several problems; some of them are of special importance in VaKE studies.

(1) To avoid *expectancy effects* (self-fulfilling prophecies, Rosenthal, 1976[2]), it would be appropriate that neither the experimenter nor the subjects know who is in the experimental group and who is in the control group (the so-called double-blind experiment), and which variables are addressed in the study. In a typical evaluation study for VaKE, however, this cannot be achieved; for instance, many researchers are also teachers and study VaKE in their own classes (e.g., Weinberger, 2006; Frewein, 2009). This is also appropriate to avoid biases due to the students being confronted with a teacher they do not know. When the researcher acts also as a teacher, he or she necessarily knows the relevant issues of the design, thus there is always the risk of expectancy effects.

(2) Some biases may occur when the students know that they are participating in a study. One possible bias is the John-Henry effect (Saretsky, 1972): If the participants of the control group know that they are "in competition" with the participants of the experimental group, they might put special effort to achieve as well as the latter, thus blurring potential effects of the treatment. On the other hand, there is the risk of contamination: The students of the different groups talk with each other about the study, so that not only the treatment has an influence, but also the informal information exchange between groups. To avoid this, Frewein (2009) asked her students not to talk with the other group about the study.

(3) When conducting research in schools, *random assignment*, as required for true experiments, may have disadvantages, if they are possible at all. Frewein (2009), for instance, randomly divided her class of 18 students into two groups of nine, which were treated separately; the inconvenience is that the groups were smaller than regular classes. Weinberger (2006), in contrast, had two parallel classes with 26 students each,[3] but the students of the two classes differed in intelligence and creativity; this would have been controlled for in a randomized group assignment.

(4) The classical MaxMinCon principle (Kerlinger, 1973) means that for optimal control, one should conceive a study in such a way to *max*imize systematic variance, *min*imize error variance, and *con*trol for confounding variables. The idea is that one should look to get high differences between experimental and control groups (i.e., powerful treatments), little variance within the groups (homogeneous groups, highly reliable assessment instruments), and that variables that might produce systematic errors should be controlled for (i.e., any factor that might have additional influences should be eliminated). This leads

to laboratory experiments in which one can powerfully demonstrate that one specific independent variable (treatment) has an influence on one specific dependent variable (which is measured). However, VaKE is not such a simple intervention, and in field research, none of the three parts (max, min, and con) can be achieved even approximately.

(5) The current tendency in the field of research on teaching is to use large samples (most extremely in the meta-analyses, such as Hattie, 2009). The problem is that only well-established teaching activities can be evaluated this way; new approaches, such as VaKE, have not yet been implemented in sufficient numbers to be considered in such studies. The confirmation of its viability is a prerequisite for the implementation because teachers and school administrations will only accept approaches that have shown that they are at least as good as the prevailing approaches. In this sense, large-sample assessments are rather an obstacle and not a promoter for progress in teaching since if they are taken seriously, they hinder the implementation of innovations. Evaluation studies, hence, can only be done with small samples, with the corresponding problems.

Critics of research on VaKE have objected that in the studies conducted on this research programme, there are too many threats of internal validity.[4] We agree that not everything could be controlled, as claimed, for instance, by the MaxMinCon principle (issue 4 above). However, we have attempted to use powerful research designs which enable, at least to some degree, to overcome the threats better than the traditional designs discussed by Campbell and Stanley (1963).

3 One-Group Designs

In some studies, it is impossible for practical reasons or inappropriate to have a control group; instead, only one group can be analysed (e.g., Weyringer, 2008; Nussbaumer, 2009; Patry & Schaber, 2010; see Chapter 31 in this handbook; Pnevmatikos & Christodoulou, 2018; see Chapter 9 in this handbook). In these cases, the hypotheses are different: They do not address comparisons between VaKE and other teaching methods (or different types of VaKE, as in Weinberger, 2006), but VaKE-specific issues.

The first question is whether VaKE is feasible under specific conditions. The first studies of VaKE were conducted in secondary schools and showed that it was quite successful. However, being successful on one level does not mean that it will also be successful on another. Therefore, it was necessary to show that VaKE works for other audiences before further, more in-depth studies could be carried out. For instance, it was important to us to show that V*a*KE can be used with refugees from Muslim countries; only after the evidence showed (Patry et al., 2016) we could conceive and execute a more differentiated study with female Muslim refugees. And in this, the aim could not be to compare the refugees participating in the study with some kind of control group because there was no comparable sample that one could reasonably motivate to participate in the study. Rather, the research question was whether the women were motivated and whether it was possible to have an impact on behaviour (Weyringer, Patry, & Diekmann, 2018; see Chapter 16 in this handbook).

Another study showed that an adapted version of V*a*KE can be used with children of grades one to three (Demetri, 2015; see Chapter 7 in this handbook). These studies can use quantitative methods. Often, however, qualitative methods are used to describe the procedures and the experiences with them.

In such studies, it is important to describe as precisely as possible what happened in the V*a*KE processes: the procedures and how the participants reacted. The workshop leader's protocol (preferably using a standardized description) and the participants' products (e.g., posters) can be used for that; furthermore, specific instruments can be used, such as questionnaires, diaries, etc. In contrast to the usual hypotheses that focus on comparisons of assessments (either between or within-subjects), in such studies, the hypotheses refer to a comparison with a theoretically justified norm, i.e., an aim for the dependent variable is set, and the assessments will show whether and to what degree this aim is achieved.

A second design to deal with one group only is to use time series with, among others, several assessments over the course of the workshop. In this case, the intra-personal variance that can be accounted for by V*a*KE is checked. The question, then, is not the difference between subjects but the differences within-subjects, mostly in function of situations (e.g., in different V*a*KE phases). A prerequisite for such studies is that indeed, the dependent variable may vary between situations (in contrast to trait assessments, which are claimed to be situation independent); this is the case for social behaviour – this discussion is directly linked with the one about situation specificity (Mischel, 1968; Patry, 2019).

For this, the Lesson Interruption Method (LIM) is an ideal assessment approach. This has been discussed more deeply in Chapter 31. Another study was conducted by Nussbaumer (2009), who analysed how the structure of arguments according to Miller (2006) evolves in a V*a*KE process; she showed that the first discussion contained already all topics but that with progressing discussion, the arguments became more differentiated.

4 The Two-Period Cross-over Design

Some of the problems from section 2 can be overcome by using the *two-period cross-over design* (Cochran & Cox, 1957; Wilk, 1963). In this design, each subject gets two periods or phases; each contains an intervention and the respective measurements. The base is a 2*2 latin square[5] in which the rows represent groups (same subjects), and the columns represent periods; the cells contain the treatments and the respective measurements (e.g., experimental and control treatments and outcome assessments). In this design, with repeated treatments and repeated measurements, the subjects of the first group get treatment and measurement A first and then treatment and measurement B second, while the order is inverted for the second group (Figure 32.1).

Again, the studies by Weinberger (2006) and Frewein (2009) will serve as examples to illustrate the issues:
– Weinberger compared VaKE with VaKE+, an extension of VaKE that includes additional steps (viability checks); one dilemma dealt with nuclear power plants, one with drugs (see Chapter 8 in this handbook for more details).
– Frewein (2009) compared VaKE with traditional teaching, using four dilemmas in two subject matters; two dilemmas were theoretical, in the subject matter business management (planning of an acquisition; copyright) and two were practical, in the subject matter Electronic Data Processing (Excel: If-then functions; diagrams).

Both studies used the cross-over design. A prototypical design for a cross-over study with VaKE is presented in Figure 32.2. We call this design *prototypical* because it can be adapted to the specific needs, i.e., it cannot be interpreted as a recipe but as a framework to be used flexibly while adhering to the relevant issues. Frewein (2009), for instance, repeated the design of Figure 32.2, thus having four phases and four topics; this complies with the general idea of the design and expands it.

The most important feature in the design is the distinction of two topics: *Within each period*, both the VaKE unit and the control unit address the same content; the two treatments should be as similar as possible with respect to *what* is taught and differ only with respect to *how* it is taught, the methods used.

Group	Period 1	Period 2
1	A	B
2	B	A

FIGURE 32.1
2*2 latin square as a base for the cross-over design;
A and B: different treatments and respective assessments

		Period 1			**Period 2**			
Group	Person trait	Pre-test *topic 1*	Intervention topic 1	Post-test topic 1	*Pre-test* *topic 2*	Intervention topic 2	Post-test topic 2	*Follow-up test*
1	Test	SET *topic 1*	VaKE	SET topic 1	SET *topic 2*	Control	SET topic 2	SET *topics 1 and 2*
2	Test	SET *topic 1*	Control	SET topic 1	SET *topic 2*	VaKE	SET topic 2	SET *topics 1 and 2*

FIGURE 32.2   Prototypical cross-over design; SET: Summative Evaluation Tool; in italics: optional

The methods (e.g., VaKE vs. traditional teaching) should only differ in the issues relevant to the hypotheses but not in other regards. For instance, the time on task should be similar. Frewein (2009), however, found that the participants in VaKE were highly motivated and voluntarily spent much more time discussing the dilemma than anticipated, therefore the time on task was much longer; but since the students' motivation was presumably due to VaKE, the spontaneous activity can be attributed to the method. When interpreting the results, such effects must be taken into consideration, e.g., by arguing that the extended time on task is due to the intervention.

Between the two periods,[6] in contrast, the topics differ. Weinberger (2006), for instance, used the following topics: nuclear power plants in period 1 and drugs in period 2. Here, two threats must be considered. (1) There is the risk of a carry-over effect (Chinchilli & Esinhart, 1996): Dealing with topic 1 (assessments and intervention) may have an impact on dealing with topic 2. For instance, if the knowledge acquired in period 1 is a condition for discussing the topic in period 2, the two periods cannot be considered as independent. The impact of treatment 2 is then confounded with the impact of period 1. Frewein (2009) used pairs of topics that were similar, due to the subject matters she was teaching (two topics from business management, and two from Electronic Data Processing), accepting that one topic may have had an influence on the other one within the same subject matter. (2) On the other hand, a certain similarity between the two contents might be necessary to avoid that topic preferences are confounded with treatment: It is possible that some students are more interested in the topics of period 1 while others are more interested in those of period 2, and hence the motivation conditions for periods 1 and 2 would be different and confounded with the treatment. For instance, in

Weinberger, students of one group may have been interested in nuclear power but not in drugs, whereas the opposite might have applied for the students of the other group; it is then not clear whether the differences between the outcomes of the groups are due to the different treatment or to the respective interests. He could have controlled for this threat by asking the students about their interests in the respective topics. This was done by Frewein with a questionnaire about interests in different fields and general motivation, as well as the average of the students' grades in the two subject matters.

Such a control addresses *person traits* in Figure 32.2. More generally, these traits refer to tests that can be used to check whether the two groups differ with respect to variables which are judged relevant. For instance, Weinberger (2006) used an intelligence test and a creativity test. This way, he found that VaKE+ (with scheduled viability checks) yielded better results than VaKE (no scheduled viability checks) for low achievers (low intelligence), whereas there were no differences between treatment and control groups for high achievers; this might indicate that the low achievers need the structure provided by the additional viability checks provided by VaKE+ whereas the high achievers perform these viability checks spontaneously and do not need to be prompted to do so (see Chapter 8 in this handbook for more details). This is an example on how an Aptitude-Treatment Interaction (ATI; Cronbach & Snow, 1977) study can be carried out with VaKE.

The *Summative Evaluation Tool* (SET) in the design (Figure 32.2) refers to instruments used to assess the dependent variable. For knowledge acquisition, this can be a teacher-made test, a WALK (see Chapter 31 in this handbook), an essay, etc. (Weinberger, 2006, used all of them). Some of these instruments cannot be used in the pre-test; the essay, for instance, builds upon the discussions in the intervention, and it does not make sense to use it before the intervention. In principle, if the assignment to the groups is randomized, a pre-test is not necessary (within one period: post-test only experimental design, design 6 according to Campbell & Stanley, 1963). If the assignment is not random, the threats to validity of the pre-experimental design static-group comparison (design 3, ibid.) must be considered: There are no formal means for certifying that differences between the groups in the dependent variable can be accounted for by the treatment because one does not know whether and how the groups differed before the intervention. If a pre-test is used, the principles of quasi-experiments, in particular the – non-equivalent control group design (design 10, ibid.), apply.

To assess the *long-term impact* of the treatment (sustainability), a follow-up assessment is recommended (Figure 32.2). However, the problem is often that the subjects are not available for some time after the study. In the case of Weinberger (2006), since the study was done in a school, the students could be asked again four weeks after the interventions; in this particular case, the two follow-up assessments were done separately, the first one was done before the second period (topic 2) began. In contrast, Frewein (2009) had no follow-up.

Depending on one's research question, one can add further elements to the design, provided these do not affect the rationales discussed above. For instance, Weinberger (2006) used also sociometric assessments in the pre- and post-tests in both phases and the Lesson Interruption Method during the treatments (four assessments in the first phase, three assessments in the second phase) with variables judged as relevant on theoretical grounds (teacher directivity; achieved viability checks; self-efficacy; cooperation; learning success; see Chapter 2 in this handbook) and teaching protocols (see above, the section on one-group designs). Frewein (2009) used questionnaires about phase-specific motivation and teaching methods at the end of each phase, an approach that comes close to the Lesson Interruption Method.

5 Conclusions

There cannot be a perfect methodology, rather all methods have their advantages and disadvantages. This is why critical multiplism has been promoted, which means to use different methods to address the same question within the same study or in different studies (Patry, 2013), with the methods choice being based on theoretical grounds (Patry, 2008). These methodological theories can come from the theoretical framework underlying VaKE, which is discussed in Chapter 2 (this handbook) or can come from different sources. One example was the theory of situation specificity as alluded to above.

Another issue is the aim to improve reliability and validity. So, for instance, Frewein (2009) repeated the cross-over design, one with theoretical topics and another with practical topics. This is a practical example of critical multiplism: First, the extension of the study increases the reliability of the study results through a conceptual replication within the study; secondly, it was a conceptual replication of earlier studies such as Patry and Weinberger (2004) – one of the first studies to compare VaKE with traditional teaching – with a different population, different topics, and accordingly different assessments. In a research field in which replications, if done at all, are rarely successful (see, for instance, Świątkowski & Dompnier, 2017), this is highly valuable.

This is an example for the concept of studying VaKE as a research *programme*: The individual studies must not be regarded as separated from, but in relation with each other. This is the aim of the present handbook. For this, some comparability between the studies needs to be given, but differences are also important. The aim of the present chapter is also to encourage conducting such research. When doing this, variation of the methods in agreement with the underlying frameworks is also recommended.

Notes

1 Other definitions of ecological validity (e.g., the one that is most cited: Bronfenbrenner, 1979) factually refer to theories that explain why ecological validity in the definition presented here is jeopardized, such as the theory of situation specificity (Patry, 2011).
2 Experimenter expectancy effect: "An experimenter-related artifact that results when the hypothesis held by the experimenter leads unintentionally to behavior toward the participants that, in turn, increases the likelihood that the hypothesis will be confirmed" (Rosenthal, 2012, p. 328).
3 Integration students (students with learning difficulties) and students who did not participate in all phases of the study are not counted (Weinberger, 2006).
4 Internal validity is high if the study provides sufficient evidence to account for the observed outcome – in VaKE studies, this is knowledge gains or increased moral competence, among others – by the treatment and only by the treatment (see Campbell & Stanley, 1963). In a very simplified way, one would say that the treatment is the cause and the outcome is the effect (see Shadish, Cook, & Campbell, 2002, for a discussion).
5 "A latin square is an arrangement of latin letters in rows and columns such that each letter appears once and only once in each row and each column" (Grant, 1948, p. 427).
6 This comparison between periods within one group corresponds to the one-group design with repeated measurements. In this regard, the cross-over design is an extension of this one-group design described in Section 3.

References

Bronfenbrenner, U. (1979). *The ecology of human development. Experiments by nature and design.* Cambridge, MA: Harvard University Press.

Campbell, D. T., & Stanley, J. C. (1963). Experimental and quasi-experimental designs for research on teaching. In N. L. Gage (Ed.), *Handbook of research on teaching* (pp. 171–246). Chicago, IL: Rand McNally.

Chinchilli, V. M., & Esinhart, J. D. (1996). Design and analysis of intra-subject variability in cross-over experiments. *Statistics in Medicine, 15,* 1619–1634.

Cochran, W. G., & Cox, G. M. (1957). *Experimental designs.* New York, NY: Wiley.

Cronbach, L. J., & Snow, R. E. (1977). *Aptitudes and instructional methods. A handbook for research on interactions.* New York, NY: Irvington.

Demetri, A. (2015). *Kombination moralischer Werterziehung mit konstruktivistischem Wissenserwerb in der Grundschule. Das Unterrichtsmodell VaKE in der Grundschule* [Dissertation]. Paris-Lodron University Salzburg.

Frewein, K. (2009). *VaKE – Die Verbindung affektiver und kognitiver Lehrziele oder Kognitive Lehrziele müssen erfüllt werden – affektive auch* [Master's thesis]. Paris-Lodron University Salzburg.

Gerhard, T. (2008). Bias: Considerations for research practice. *American Journal of Health-System Pharmacy, 65*, 2159–2168.

Grant, D. (1948). The latin square principle in the design and analysis of psychological experiments. *Psychological Bulletin, 45*, 427–442.

Hattie, J. (2009). *Visible learning*. London, UK: Routledge.

Kerlinger, F. N. (1973). *Foundations of behavioral research*. New York, NY: Holt, Rinehart, and Winston.

Miller, M. (2006). *Dissens. Zur Theorie diskursiven und systemischen Lernens*. Bielefeld, Germany: transcript.

Mischel, W. (1968). *Personality and assessment*. New York, NY: Wiley.

Nussbaumer, M. (2009). *"Argumentieren geht über Studieren". Wie Schülerinnen und Schüler im didaktischen Konzept VaKE argumentieren* [Master's thesis]. Paris-Lodron University Salzburg.

Patry, J.-L. (1982). Laborforschung – Feldforschung. In J.-L. Patry (Ed.), *Feldforschung. Methoden und Probleme der Sozialwissenschaften unter natürlichen Bedingungen* (pp. 17–42). Bern, Switzerland: Huber.

Patry, J.-L. (2008). Konkurrenz, Koexistenz, Komplementarität qualitativer und quantitativer Methoden in der Erziehungswissenschaft aus der Perspektive des Kritischen Multiplizismus. In F. Hofmann, C. Schreiner, & J. Thonhauser (Eds.), *Qualitative und quantitative Aspekte. Zu ihrer Komplementarität in der erziehungswissenschaftlichen Forschung* (pp. 133–150). Münster, Germany: Waxmann.

Patry, J.-L. (2011). Methodological consequences of situation specificity: Biases in assessments. *Frontiers in Psychology, 2*(18). Retrieved April 29, 2021, from http://www.frontiersin.org/quantitative_psychology_and_measurement/10.3389/fpsyg.2011.00018/abstract

Patry, J.-L. (2013). Beyond multiple methods: Critical multiplism on all levels. *International Journal of Multiple Research Approaches, 7*, 50–65.

Patry, J.-L. (2019). Situation specificity of behavior: The triple relevance in research and practice of education. In R. V. Nata (Ed.), *Progress in education* (Vol. 58, pp. 29–144). Hauppauge, NY: Nova.

Patry, J.-L., & Schaber, K. (2010, January 15–16). *Fürsorge versus Gerechtigkeit: Argumentieren Frauen anders als Männer? Eine Untersuchung zur Geschlechtsspezifität in moralischen Entscheidungssituationen* [Paper]. The conference "Moral und Beruf 2010" in Basel, Switzerland.

Patry, J.-L. & Weinberger, A. (2004). Kombination von konstruktivistischer Werterziehung und Wissenserwerb. *Salzburger Beiträge zur Erziehungswissenschaft, 8*(2), 35–50.

Patry, J.-L., Weyringer, S., Aichinger, K., & Weinberger, A. (2016). Integrationsarbeit mit eingewanderten Jugendlichen mit VaKE (Values *and* Knowledge Education). *International Dialogues on Education, 3*(3), 123–29.

Pnevmatikos, D., & Christodoulou, P. (2018). Promoting conceptual change through Values and Knowledge Education (VaKE). In A. Weinberger, H. Biedermann, J.-L. Patry, & S. Weyringer (Eds.), *Professionals' ethos and education for responsibility* (pp. 63–74). Leiden, The Netherlands: Brill.

Rosenthal, R. (1976). *Experimenter effects in behavioral research*. New York, NY: Irvington.

Rosenthal, R. (2012). Self-fulfilling prophecy. In V. S. Ramachandran (Ed.), *Encyclopedia of human behavior* (2nd ed., pp. 328–335). Oxford, UK: Elsevier Science.

Saretsky, G. (1972). The OEO P.C. experiment and the John Henry effect. *Phi Delta Kappan, 53*, 579–581.

Shadish, W. R., Cook, T. D., & Campbell, D. T. (2002). *Experimental and quasi-experimental designs for generalized causal inference*. Boston, MA: Houghton Mifflin.

Świątkowski, W., & Dompnier, B. (2017). Replicability crisis in social psychology: Looking at the past to find new pathways for the future. *International Review of Social Psychology, 30*(1), 111–124.

Weinberger, A. (2006). *Kombination von Werterziehung und Wissenserwerb. Evaluation des konstruktivistischen Unterrichtsmodells VaKE (Values and Knowledge Education) in der Sekundarstufe 1*. Hamburg, Germany: Kovac.

Weyringer, S. (2008). *VaKE in einem internationalen Sommercampus für (hoch) begabte Jugendliche: Eine Evaluationsstudie* [Dissertation]. Paris-Lodron University Salzburg.

Weyringer, S., Patry, J.-L., & Diekmann, N. (2018). *Schlussbericht zum Pilotprojekt VaKE mit weiblichen Flüchtlingen*. Bericht an den Österreichischen Integrationsfonds. Department of Educational Research, Paris-Lodron University Salzburg.

Wilk, R. E. (1963). The use of a cross-over design in a study of student teachers' classroom behaviors. *The Journal of Experimental Education, 31*(4), 337–341.

CHAPTER 33

Transdisciplinarity and Trans-Domain Approaches in V*a*KE

Jean-Luc Patry, Natascha Diekmann and Sieglinde Weyringer

1   Introduction

In V*a*KE, the students discuss the options of a protagonist in a concrete dilemma situation and analyse them from the points of view of values ("Ought") and description of facts ("Is") to find and justify the best way for the protagonist to act. For this, the value and fact descriptions cannot be seen independently of each other but need to be related to each other. Furthermore, given that a dilemma addresses several values, the relationships between these ("within Ought") need to be addressed. And finally, when discussing the dilemma, fact descriptions from different fields (e.g., different scientific disciplines) become relevant ("within Is"). These relationships between Is and Ought, within Ought and within Is, will be analysed in the present chapter, and for this, we use an extension of the meta-theoretical framework of transdisciplinarity which we call Trans-Domain Approaches (TDAs). In a first tentative formulation, we define TDA as *integrative reciprocal referentiality between domains*; domains are fairly homogeneous sets of statements that are used consistently across time and clearly distinct from other such sets. Disciplines can only partly be interpreted as domains in this sense, as will be argued below.

   This definition will be specified, and a concept of TDA presented in Section 2. In Section 3, this concept will be applied to V*a*KE. In the remaining sections, we will discuss specific relationships based on a concrete example for a V*a*KE process; the latter will be presented in Section 4. Sections 5 to 7 will be structured according to three central TDA topics: Is vs. Ought (Section 5), different approaches to values (within Ought; Section 6), and different frameworks for fact description (within Is; Section 7). The chapter will end with a discussion (Section 8).

   The theory of V*a*KE is also based on normative frameworks (what should be aimed at in education, and why? – Ought) and descriptive theories about learning and development, motivation, critical thinking, etc. (Is). These relationships will not be discussed in this chapter as they are addressed, at least partially, in other chapters in this handbook.[1]

2 Transdisciplinarity and Trans-Domain Approaches

Transdisciplinarity is one of those iridescent terms in science that has almost as many definitions as authors writing about it (see, for instance, Behrendt, 2004; Vilsmaier, 2010, p. 37ff.; Rousseau et al., 2018, pp. 49ff.; Weingart, 2000, p. 28).[2] The evolution of the disciplines is characterized by an increasing specialization (Bromme & Kienhues, 2014, p. 56); established disciplines split into presumably independent disciplines, new scientific disciplines arise, others vanish. Hence, the system of disciplines is not given once and for all, but it is a historically and socially grown and still developing organization of science, whose main sense is practical: to organise scientific institutions, studies, and professions, and to produce, disseminate, and apply specialist knowledge (e.g., Balsiger, 2005, pp. 51–57; Mittelstrass, 2018, p. S71; Stenner, 2014, p. 1988), etc. Therefore, disciplines are temporary and not epistemic categories; instead, we prefer the more general and stable concept of Trans-Domain Approaches (TDAS) – for a generic definition of *domains* see above.

Following Rousseau et al. (2018, p. 53) and many others, we define TDA as follows, as illustrated by Figure 33.1: A TDA consists of a scientific system of theories that includes a general theory (GT) that connects, integrates, and transcends a set of specialized (domain-specific) theories (DTs), but does not replace them. It addresses issues or problems (research topics) which cannot be satisfactorily dealt with within a single domain (see Mittelstrass, 2005/2007, p. 2). This goes beyond a simple combination of the domains;[3] rather, the general theory (GT) contains more information than can be found in the combined theories of the respective domains (DTs) alone. The GT, hence, is a superordinate theory with respect to the DTs, which each of them addresses some issues of the research topic (for the principle of super- and subordinate theories, see Patry, 2014).

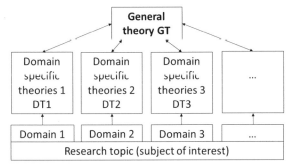

FIGURE 33.1   Trans-Domain Approach (TDA) as the relationships between general theory (GT), domain-specific theories (DT), domains, and research topic

In this definition, it is not postulated how the domains are distinguished and how the relationships between DT and GT are conceived. Since TDAs are seen as scientific concepts, however, the definition stipulates that these relationships must be scientifically justified. Although it is based on a specific theory of science (constructivist post-positivism, see, for instance, Phillips and Burbules, 2000), we do not want to restrict this definition to one way of doing science; however, we insist that one principle of the above theory of science must be adhered to, namely the principle of warranted assertibility (see Phillips & Burbules, 2000, p. 31; Putnam, 1990, p. 21),[4] which means in this context that such connections must be endorsed by arguments that are viable within the respective scientific system of reference.

Humanity is challenged by many problems, which therefore are subjects of interest; most of these problems are not limited by the borders of a specific domain (Patry, 2018); hence, scientific accounts must necessarily include several domains (Mittelstrass, 2018, p. S72). This applies even more, when practical solutions are sought, as not only the problem itself needs to be considered but also additional conditions and possible side-effects which may belong to other domains (e.g., Knapp et al., 2019; Fritz & Binder, 2020).

These principles of TDA apply to subjective theories and negotiations between participants of a VaKE discussion as well, although for them, the concept of warranted assertibility does not apply to scientific principles but to the conviction of the participants about what counts as a "good argument". However, the concept of warranted assertibility might differ from one participant to another and could be challenged within a VaKE discussion.

3 TDA and VaKE

The components of TDA can be applied to the VaKE discussions as follows: The *problem* (research topic or subject of interest in Figure 33.1) is the question "What should the protagonist of the dilemma story do?", with the relevant parameters of the story. As the very base of VaKE, two domains are addressed: (i) On one hand, given that a moral dilemma is addressed, several *values* (statements about norms, "Ought"), i.e., normative justifications of the goals the protagonist should try to achieve or of the principles he or she should apply, and possibly the justification of the ethical appropriateness of the action. (ii) On the other hand, *knowledge* about facts (descriptive statements, "Is") is required, i.e., statements about "what is the case" (in VaKE discussions, in the sense of "What I believe is the case"). In the presentation of the steps of the prototypical VaKE (Chapter 2 in this handbook), it is referred to as "information", which can be tested, at least in principle, through observation. For practical reasons, these statements will be called *contents* (or knowledge contents) below. VaKE then, is a TDA since the participants, when confronted with the dilemma address several value issues as well as several fact issues (knowledge of contents) and relate both types with each other.

Traditionally, knowledge education and values education have been provided separately, knowledge contents being taught in the STEM[5] and other knowledge-oriented disciplines (language and literature, history, psychology, history of philosophy, etc.), whereas values education is practiced in subject matters like religion, ethics and – with respect to esthetical values – arts. In contrast, we claim that it is necessary to do both values education as well as knowledge education and to relate them with each other (see Chapter 29 in this handbook for the justification of this claim). Hence, this very claim requires TDA.

Besides the TDA issue "Is vs. Ought", VaKE necessarily leads the participants to address different values as the dilemma story describes a situation in which the protagonist has two (or more) action options, each of which is related with a set of values; the values of the different sets cannot be satisfied simultaneously, therefore, the participants have to compare the values. The different values (or sets of values, or frameworks for their justification) can be regarded as domains, as they are mutually exclusive, and consequently, dealing with the different sets simultaneously is a TDA issue.

Similarly, with respect to knowledge about facts, in their information search and further discussions (in the prototypical VaKE process: from step 4 up, asking about missing information), the participant groups always address different contents, i.e., the facts they are looking for stem from different fields (often different disciplines) which are linked to each other only for the discussion of the dilemma. Under other circumstances, no relationship between them would be established, i.e., the relationship is not inherent in them but constructed for the occasion. This means that the respective contents of knowledge can be considered as domains, and hence the principles of TDA apply.

In the further sections, we will deal with these three TDAs separately: between Is and Ought, within the values systems (Ought), and within the knowledge about facts (Is) (see also Patry & Weyringer, 2019). For each of these TDAs, we will first address the issues from a theoretical point of view and then apply the outcomes of these discussions to a concrete example: sustainable consumer education, which will be presented beforehand in section 4.

In all cases, the General Theory (GT) in the sense of Figure 33.1 is linked with the dilemma story. It is a theory in that it refers to a set of theoretical relationships which have in common that they are relevant for the dilemma from the point of view of the discussants. Such a common GT that all participants in VaKE share is necessary to ensure a mutual understanding. Any participant who would remain within his or her preferred domain and not join in a common GT would not understand the others' statements, and a fruitful discussion would not be possible. The option of the protagonist in the dilemma that the participants choose, and in particular the justification of this decision, is then based on such a GT. One can regard this argumentation as a theoretical underpinning of the collaborative framework addressed in Chapters 2 and 30 in this handbook.

4   Example: Sustainable Consumer Education

In the well-received sense of the World Commission on Environment and Development (1987), sustainability means to take the needs of the present generation into account without compromising the opportunity of the future generations to meet their needs. With the release of this report (the result of a conference during the world commission for environment and development) the popularity of the concept of sustainable development increased. The next strong impetus was the Agenda 21 in 1992 as a result of a conference conducted by the United Nations (UN, 1992). Sustainability is a complex construct, which contains the consideration of environmental and social aspects in our economic system with regard to inter- and intragenerational justice (UN, 2015). Within the last few years, sustainable development became one of the most challenging deviances in the 21st century, especially when we take climate change into consideration.

The relatively new research topic *sustainability science* is a TDA per se. The aim is to solve problems that emerge in the field of sustainability, which is not limited by certain domains (like disciplines); hence, for this, domain-specific theories are insufficient. Rather, different scientific disciplines and domains are required and contribute their respective special expert concepts. Sustainability science is thus a TDA which is focusing on finding solutions (Komiyama & Takeuchi, 2006). Without integrating different domains, it is not possible to meet the challenges of sustainability (Enders & Remig, 2015). This applies even more for sustainability education, as the domain of education is added.

The most current version of political objectives from 2017 to 2030 (UN, 2015) addresses Sustainable Development Goals (SDGs). One of the 17 goals is "responsible consumption and production". VaKE was used to achieve this goal. In the following, experiences from the intervention will be given to illustrate how TDA works in a practical implementation. The intervention was a workshop of four-morning sessions within the framework of the Platon Youth Forum 2015, a summer academy for highly gifted students from Europe. Under the heading "Shopping for a Better World", six adolescents (mean age 17;7) worked together on the topic of manufacturing conditions in the textile industry. The focus was on the social aspects of sustainable consumption.

The dilemma story used in the workshop included the following key points: The protagonist is 16-year-old Philip from Germany. His father has been unemployed for a long time and finally gets the chance for a new job in the German sales department of an international textile company. Philip's life changes from a former victim of bullying to a popular teenager. At the beginning of the father's career, the whole family accompanied him on a business trip to Bangladesh. There, Philips met a boy of the same age who works in one of the textile factories, who tells him about the working conditions. After this insight, Philip does not want to wear the clothes produced in such factories anymore. Furthermore, he wants to join an NGO which fights against bad working conditions in the textile industry. The options are that Philip either switches to fair trade clothes and joins the NGO (risking jeopardizing the relationship with his father and his new friends) or carries on his life in the way he led has the last few months (and leaves bullying and loneliness behind).

5 TDA of Is and Ought

The discussion about Is and Ought has a long tradition, which we cannot discuss here. Following Hume (1739/1896), Moore (1903/1971), and subsequently many others (see also the application to moral education by Morscher, 2018), we assume that the transition from Is (descriptive statements) to Ought (prescriptive or normative statements) is *logically* impossible (a naturalistic fallacy); in our opinion, it is also *ethically* inappropriate since normative requests deserve to be discussed for their own sake, and one should not even try to reduce them to descriptive statements. In the sense of the present chapter, hence, Is and Ought represent different domains.

5.1 *Principles*
The relationship between the domains *Is* and *Ought* is addressed in several regards in VaKE.

(1) The request for the double assignment states that in education, one should do both, promoting the acquisition of knowledge (content) as well as value education, whereby the values addressed should be linked with the content. The most important relationship here is that values are not sufficient for

good action and content knowledge can be used for many different purposes, and not all of them are ethically justified ("Values without knowledge is blind; knowledge without values is irresponsible"; see Chapter 29 in this handbook). The link, therefore, is through possible actions based on the respective content knowledge and values, i.e., whether the values can be used for concrete action decisions and whether the action decisions based on the knowledge are responsible, i.e., justifiable on ethical grounds.

(2) Any action – including those of participants in V*a*KE processes and the options of the protagonist of the dilemma as discussed by the participants – is inevitably based on values since the actors aim at achieving goals and/or complying with principles, which need to be justified through normative statements. Within a teleological framework,[6] it is based on knowledge in terms of means to achieve the goals, which are based on descriptive statements with the form "if I do x, I achieve y": This contains no prescription, neither that one should achieve y nor that one should do x. The often-used formulation "if I want to achieve y, I must do x", is misleading in two regards: First, x is possibly not the only means to achieve y, so one does not necessarily have to do x to reach y. Second, and more importantly, the presumable imperative to do x ("I must do x") is only given if y is normatively required.[7] This is obvious when turning the statement around: "If I want to avoid y, I must avoid x". This time, the first issue is that avoiding x might still allow y if other reasons than x lead to it. Except for that, the message is the same as in the positive formulation, but this time it would be necessary to ethically justify why to avoid y. Neither the necessity to achieve y nor the necessity to avoid it is stipulated in the statement "if I want to achieve y, I must do x", rather this simply expresses a descriptive relationship, translated into an action option (Stranzinger, 1984). This argumentation becomes obvious in statements like "if someone wants to destroy the world, he must start a nuclear war": While the descriptive statement "if a nuclear war is started, the world will be destroyed" is acknowledged as correct by most people, no one wants to destroy the world, hence no one would claim that one must start a nuclear war. In other words, the goal y needs to be justified (with values) before the action x can become imperative.

The same kind of argumentation[8] applies in the case of a deontic justification of an action, i.e., when one decides to act following a principle that one regards as justified; such a principle could be, for instance, truthfulness, justice, respecting the other's dignity. In this case, the action must comply with the requirements addressed by the rule. However, what it means to act truthfully, just, respecting the other's dignity, etc., is an issue of descriptive claims: I am truthful *if I say what I am convinced of,* justice means that I *consider the claims of all people who are involved,* respecting dignity requires to know *in what regard the other person is sensitive*, etc. – all the statements in italics are descriptive.

When deciding what to do in a given situation with the aim to achieve goals or comply with principles, which we need to justify (normative), we use means (actions) to achieve them, based on descriptive statements. We agree with Klafki (1984) that the goals and principles and their justification (what he calls didactics in the narrow sense) must have priority over the method to achieve them. This means that one must first decide on the goals and principles and justify them, and only as a second step should one decide what means is appropriate to achieve them. In everyday practice, though, it can well be that the subjects are not aware that besides the values they actually pursue, other values might be relevant that, upon reflection, they would consider as important (or even more important) as well.

(3) In values education (including V*a*KE), the distinction between Is and Ought gets an additional dimension, because the students' dealing with values is among the educational goals. In the Kohlbergian tradition, this is not solved by conveying the values themselves; rather, the participants are stimulated to better *justify* their value choices based on their normative framework (e.g., Kohlberg's, 1984 theory of moral development). Education then means fostering the improvement of the justification pattern. And this is what is done in V*a*KE through dilemma discussions. The stage theory by Kohlberg is descriptive: It is the result of empirical research on the human development of moral judgment. But Kohlberg (1971) has argued that justifications on the higher stages are ethically better (normative statement) because they emphasise autonomy and universality more than those on the lower stages; universality means here that in higher stages, the rights and interests of more people and maybe other valuable units (organisms, inorganic nature; in the present and in the future) are considered in one's argument. This issue becomes important when the participants in V*a*KE discussions address the question of the sense of *values education* itself, as visible in Chapter 22 by Legué in this handbook: They might connect the label "values education" – erroneously – with indoctrination attempts, i.e., imposing values, which they reject on ethical grounds, instead of recognising that education focuses on fostering moral argumentation without a-priori preference of a specific set of values. To recognise the priority of justification over the values themselves is an issue of knowledge, namely about V*a*KE and the principles of constructivist values education.

(4) In argumentation – the core processes of V*a*KE – both contents and values are used. The contents are based on the inquiry of descriptive statements, while the values need to be justified. To avoid the naturalistic fallacy, such justifications can be done using some type of practical syllogism: by referring

to superordinate norms with which the subordinate norm is compatible; a superordinate norm is a norm that is more general than the subordinate norm and includes the latter. In many such justifications, the relationship between superordinate and subordinate norms ("Ought") is through descriptive statements ("Is"; factual premises, e.g., Gorecki, 1991, p. 352).

In VaKE discussions, the problem with this kind of argumentation structure is whether the participants avoid the naturalistic fallacy and justify the values by using superordinate norms. Nussbaumer (2009) has shown that the participants in her study committed the naturalistic fallacy several times; one can assume however, that in some cases they considered the values justifications that are implicit in some descriptive statements: In everyday argumentation, some assumptions may be considered to be self-evident; for a formally correct argumentation, however, the implicit argumentation must be made explicit. In the course of argumentation in a group discussion, one tacitly (and probably unconscientiously) insinuates a common understanding of the superordinate norm and the descriptive statement. In terms of the concept of TDA (Figure 33.1), as applied to VaKE (section 3), the fact that such an insinuation works for the group indicates that the participants share a (possibly implicit) General Theory GT about normative connotations of the used presumably descriptive terms.

5.2 *Example: Sustainable Consumer Education*

Regarding sustainable consumption, knowledge and values are always connected. This can be seen in the different points discussed in Section 5.1.

Ad (1): The principle "values without knowledge is blind" can be applied to the sustainability fundamentalists (for instance, in politics by some parts of the Green parties in many countries) who oppose any non-sustainable activities or laws, irrespectively of whether their action propositions are actually practicable or might have impacts in fields other than sustainability; the potential impact is a descriptive issue, whether the ensuing side-effects are relevant is a normative one. "Knowledge without values is irresponsible" refers to the possibility to act against sustainability if one knows, but does not care, about the impact of one's deeds that may be judged as negative. Sustainability issues always combine prescriptive and descriptive aspects because sustainability is a normative construct.

Ad (2: relevance of values in actions): Participants do not often know about the sustainability issue of their consumption; within the participants of the study, this knowledge (e.g., about children's work in the manufacture of textiles) triggered a sensitivity for the relevant normative issues like fairness of manufacturing conditions which they were not aware before, and corresponding actions that take these issues into account.

As to 3 (values education), from the very onset, the participants recognised that the aim of the VaKE procedure was not indoctrination (conveying a specific set of values), rather that they were supposed to justify their values choices, and they come up themselves with the priority of the values of sustainability, many of which they had already defended before. Finally, Point 4 (argumentation) was achieved as the participants used both normative and descriptive statements; for instance, in the dilemma presented, the references to values are indirect: Most people agree – once they know about the working conditions in Bangladesh – that these conditions are bad. The argument would be: (1) Human dignity has priority (superordinate norm; the norm of human dignity is concretized in some issues, like the right to decent working conditions and the prohibition of children work); (2) working conditions in Bangladesh are as described (descriptive); (3) the described conditions do not comply with the ones described in the principle of human dignity (descriptive), hence (4) the working conditions are bad (subordinate norm). Given the implicit assumptions, the argumentation string is not made explicit.

6 TDA between Values

6.1 Principles

A VaKE process starts with a dilemma that, by definition, has several values at stake: The protagonist has two (or more) action options, and whatever he or she does, some of the values will be broken. For the present purpose, two distinctions need to be made (see also Table 33.1).

- On the one hand, there is a difference between the teleological and the deontic principles. In the teleological argumentation, the *consequences* for the people who are involved in the dilemma are considered, whereas, in the deontic argumentation, the *principle underlying the decision* is crucial, independent of the consequences.
- On the other hand, one can distinguish between different topics of values, such as justice, care, and truthfulness, to mention just those that Oser et al. (1991) studied. These can also be more specific, such as life, property, human dignity, social cohesion, etc., as in Kohlberg's dilemmas. Another way to structure values might be the approach by Schwartz (e.g., 2015).[9]

The two dimensions (topics and types) are orthogonal, that is, all combinations are possible. Therefore, in the sense of the definition of TDA, the respective

TABLE 33.1   Different types of TDAs of values, as addressed in dilemmas

		Topics (justice, care, truthfulness, economics, etc.)	
		Same	Different
Types (deontic and/or teleological)	Same	1 (not TDA)	2
	Different	3	4

combinations of topic and type form domains. In Table 33.1, if a discussant uses one issue with respect to type and/or topic to justify one option the protagonist of the dilemma has but uses another issue to justify the other option (e.g., cell 3: When arguing for option 1, the participants refer to a deontic justification, whereas when arguing for option 2, they use a teleological argumentation), there are different domains, and TDA applies. This is also the case if the discussants use several arguments based on different issues to argue in favour of the same action option of the protagonist (e.g., in cell 2, in order to justify the preference for one of the action options, one discussant addresses fairness and another one care).

The cell to be applied according to Table 33.1 is already conceived in the formulation of the dilemma. Some dilemmas are *within* one domain (cell 1), such as the typical Kohlbergian dilemmas, which are deontic and focus on justice; these dilemmas do not address TDA as there are no different domains at stake. Other dilemmas are within one dimension but differ with respect to the other one (cells 2 and 3). This is the case – at least from the standpoint of the respective dilemma constructors – for many VaKE dilemmas since these are typically teleological, i.e., they address the consequences of the protagonist's decision, but they deal with different topics, for instance, economic vs. ecological consequences (cell 2). Many of the dilemmas that were used oppose the decision to favour consequences for a single person (e.g., an unemployed father needs to earn money for health care for his sick son; or bluntly hedonistic care for the protagonist him- or herself) versus the decision in favour of consequences that benefit a group of people, possibly the whole society, such as considering the danger of building a nuclear power plant. Both are teleological justifications. The theories that the participants defend (DTs in Figure 33.1) are compatible with respect to the dimension *type of argument* (teleological) but require TDA with respect to the dimension *topic* (benefit of the individual vs. of the group).

In the VaKE discussion, it is not crucial how the constructor of the dilemma conceived the values clash, but how the participants perceive it. If some of the discussants interpret the values as deontic and others as teleological (or even the same discussant considers both types), there is a difference with respect to the dimension (types, cells 3 and 4). In principle, it is possible that some participants argue in favour of a specific behaviour option for the protagonist of the dilemma from a deontic point of view, while others defend the other option based on a teleological standpoint (cell 4). In this case, the relationship will become quite complex. If the discussants do not agree on a common general theory (GT), they will not even understand each other. Recognizing the differences between teleological and deontic justification, which would be the base of such a GT, might then be an important goal of VaKE.

6.2 Example: Sustainable Consumer Education

Following the definition in the Brundtland Report (and from the United Nations), sustainability includes inter- and intragenerational justice. In our example, the dilemma refers to intragenerational justice: the well-being of individuals in the Western world versus the well-being of individuals in Southeast Asia.

In general, sustainable consumption requires balancing hedonistic values, such as buying clothes that you like or which are cheap, against universal values, such as justice for workers in textile production in third world countries. Defending the latter requires a high moral judgement ability (Thøgersen & Ölander, 2003). An investigation by Karp (1995) shows that people who consider sustainable aspects in their consumption were more likely to be oriented towards universalistic values. In terms of Table 33.1, on one hand, the dilemma addresses the topics of care for Philip himself and for his father, a teleological perspective. On the other hand, justice for the workers in the textile manufacture in Bangladesh is at stake; it is not clear whether this is a teleological or a deontic issue. Thus, the dilemma refers either to cell 2 (both options are teleological) or to cell 4 (different types).

In the discussion, the participants mentioned justice as a core value, so this value became the superordinated norm (General Theory GT in Figure 33.1), concretized in the argument that every human has the right to live a dignified life. Nevertheless, it was challenging for the adolescent to put emphasis on that GT because of its abstractness. In contrast, it was easier to talk about the conflict within the protagonist's family and friends because of the connection to daily life. All participants in other VaKE discussions with the same dilemma (which cannot be discussed here) had the same GT as the group in our example, except for those of one group at a German school who clearly focused on hedonism as the GT.

The participants of the present study were asked to elaborate the values they recognised in the dilemma. The result is a broad list that includes, among others, (international) justice; globalization; family; friendship; equal opportunity; responsibility; human rights; wealth; freedom of speech; as well as individual welfare in a hedonistic sense. All topics were addressed in the discussions, and as mentioned before (deontic and teleological values), it was also possible that participants interpreted the values differently. In our example, as it was a small group of six students, they found a common GT in the end, which was global justice (connected to the working conditions and that Philip should stand up for this issue).

7 TDA between Contents

7.1 *Principles*

Knowledge, or the contents that the students acquire, are formulated in descriptive statements: "x is the case", or "if x, then y", or "the more x, the more y". From a constructivist standpoint, knowledge acquisition means integration into one's system of subjective theories ("I think that x is the case", etc.). Hence it is necessarily theory-dependent since assimilation and accommodation – the key processes in knowledge acquisition – depend on the compatibility of the offered information with the existing subjective theories.[10]

In the literature, TDA is usually applied to descriptive statements, and the domains are the different scientific disciplines (transdisciplinarity). This makes sense for VaKE as well as information on the internet where the VaKE participants search is typically classified according to the scientific disciplines. VaKE aims explicitly at the participants collecting (viable) information from multiple sources and multiple domains. Due to the complexity of the problems – which are enhanced by the combination of issues in the dilemma description – they address different content domains. Different groups of participants try to answer different questions, which relate to different domains, yielding domain-specific theories (DTs). Then the information from the different groups is exchanged and used in further discussions; for this, the different content domains may belong to the same discipline – in this regard, TDA as used for VaKE extends the concept of Transdisciplinarity as the latter's principles (e.g., as formulated in Figure 33.1) can apply within disciplines; for instance, when discussing nuclear power plants, the participants use information from different domains from the discipline of physics, such as energy and radiation.

7.2 *Example: Sustainable Consumer Education*

The six participants in the workshop chose the information questions themselves. The topics had been formulated based on the recognition of missing knowledge during the first dilemma discussion. The following topics were addressed: (i) Needs, consumer behaviour, and consumer responsibility;

(ii) "Fair Trade"; (iii) Consumption in a globalizing world; (iv) Manufacturing conditions in a capitalistic system; (v) Alternative economic models; (vi) NGOs with a focus on production and consumption.

The first issue is connected to psychological and sociological theories as well as ethics concerning the aspect of responsibility. The other five topics are based on economics and politics. In addition, geography and history are important to understand globalization and capitalism. Furthermore, mathematical competences were used by the participants to enhance the understanding of alternative economic models (for instance, alternative taxation models to reduce unfairly traded textiles on the market were calculated). Bringing these topics together in the context of sustainable development is a successful example of TDA between contents. This confirms that sustainable consumer education is fundamentally TDA regarding the content aspect. Further, the aim of TDA in sustainable consumer education is not to become an expert in single disciplines. Instead, it is to understand the complexity of interdependencies in sustainable development (De Vries, 2013), which is a General Theory GT.

With respect to the last step of VaKE, the transferability to other issues of sustainability is crucial (De Haan, 2010). For instance, if the focus in an intervention was on working conditions in textile fabrication (like in our example), the students should be able to apply this knowledge to other production chains, like technology or food. De Haan (2010) also puts emphasis on "the independent acquisition and assessment of information" in sustainability education (p. 317). Concerning consumption and all the connected aspects, the information varies from day to day, as can be seen, for instance, in the changing rules of the prohibition of single-use plastic products in the European Union (European Parliament, 2019). All in all, flexible and transferable knowledge is in demand.

8   Discussion

TDA is a complex topic. It was not possible in this chapter to give justice to the state of the art of its basic framework, transdisciplinarity, and how to apply it to TDA. VaKE is complex as well, and as such, it is a genuine target for TDA; again, only selected issues could be addressed, be it on a general level, be it with respect to the specific dilemma on sustainable consumption. We hope that at least some impressions of the relationships between TDA and VaKE could be conveyed.

The formulation of the dilemma is such that different domains are addressed. The *values* part of the VaKE process (steps 1 to 3 in the prototypical VaKE) that follow the principle of the approach by Blatt and Kohlberg (1975) refer to different action options for the protagonist of the story that are reigned by different values (Ought). Discussions of the dilemma require the acknowledgment that the values related to the option the individual participant does not defend are at least understood. In VaKE step 4, *Exchange of arguments; what do I need to know further to be able to argue?*, the link between the normative and the descriptive statements is established (combining Is and Ought). In steps 4 to 6, multiple descriptive domains are dealt with – these are also embedded in the dilemma (Is). Step 6 establishes, again, the relationship between Is and Ought, and in the ensuing steps, the different relationships are consolidated and differentiated (Hofer, 2006; Kircher, 2008; Nussbaumer, 2009).

Further analyses of the argumentations of participants show that in all regards, more domains are addressed than the authors of the dilemmas initially anticipated, and hence the participants learn more than the teacher knew before the start of VaKE. This has been shown in several studies for all three fields, for Is, for instance, by Weinberger et al. (2005), for Ought in Patry and Schaber (2010), and for the relationship between Is and Ought by Nussbaumer (2009). In all cases, the participants could discuss with each other, hence had a common General Theory GT that enabled them to do so.

At least in this regard, the VaKE dilemmas are prototypical for the dilemmas our society is confronted with, which can only be addressed if specialists do not speak only with specialists within the same domain, but across domains – which requires a common base, a common understanding and acknowledgement of the need for a TDA, a common vocabulary, etc.: a common GT. The VaKE process, hence, can be regarded as a simulation of real problem-solving for urgent problems. TDA and a GT are also a prerequisite for the so urgently needed compromises for addressing the aforementioned problems, and lack of attempts to reach such a common understanding is an inducement to fundamentalism, as can be seen in echo chambers among like-minded friends.

As we saw in our example, sustainability is only possible as a TDA, in science as well as in education. Sustainability is about problem-solving. These problems are obviously complex, and corresponding solutions cannot be found within a single domain. The same applies for sustainable consumption and, one step further, also for sustainable consumer education.

VaKE meets that demand and worked very well in practical tests like those pursued in our example in this chapter. Dividing up sustainable consumer education into single school subjects would not work because there would be no chance for a (common) GT. Furthermore, it is not possible for a teacher to have all the knowledge needed, which originates from different domains. When teaching with VaKE, in contrast, those possible gaps are not an issue.

Regarding challenging global constructs like sustainability, an approach which includes the corporate discovery of knowledge and discusses values seems very appropriate.

Notes

1 Particularly in Chapter 29 (Need for the double assignment) for the normative part and Chapter 2 (Theory of V*a*KE) for the descriptive part with reference to some normative issues.
2 The literature on transdisciplinarity is considerable, and it is not possible in this paper to refer even to the most important contributions because of space restrictions, but we have taken many of them into consideration when developing the ideas presented here.
3 This is in contrast to *inter*disciplinarity, which refers to coexistence between disciplines or, as applied here, domains, i.e., the different domains are accepted as being relevant but no relationship is established between them.
4 The term stems from Dewey (1938), but the interpretation here is more open than in Dewey's book.
5 STEM: Science, technology, engineering, and mathematics.
6 For the distinction between teleological and deontic frameworks, see Section 7 below.
7 We do not want to give here a full account of the underlying logical framework, which is more complex than we can discuss. Instead, we refer to the reader's intuition.
8 One can use more complex patterns of argumentation, like Toulmin's (1958), as was done by Weinberger et al. (2011); this cannot be discussed here.
9 While Schwartz's system has been developed on empirical bases and is psychological in essence, it can serve as a normative framework to distinguish different topics of values on ethical grounds, which however should be made explicit – we cannot do this in the present chapter.
10 See Chapter 2 in this handbook.

References

Balsiger, P. W. (2005). *Transdisziplinarität. Systematisch-vergleichende Untersuchung disziplinenübergreifender Wissenschaftspraxis.* München, Germany: Fink.

Behrendt, H. (2004). Multi-, Inter- und Transdisziplinarität – und die Geographie? In F. Brand, F. Schaller, & H. Völker (Eds.), *Transdisziplinarität. Bestandsaufnahme und Perspektiven* (pp. 115–128). Göttingen, Germany: Universitätsverlag.

Blatt, M. M., & Kohlberg, L. (1975). The effects of classroom moral discussion upon children's level of moral judgment. *Journal of Moral Education, 4*(2), 129–161. doi:10.1080/0305724750040207

Bromme, R., & Kienhues, D. (2014). Wissenschaftsverständnis und Wissenschaftskommunikation. In T. Seidel & A. Krapp (Eds.), *Pädagogische Psychologie* (6th ed., pp. 55–81). Weinheim, Germany: Beltz.

De Haan, G. (2010). The development of ESD-related competencies in supportive institutional frameworks. *International Review of Education, 56*(2–3), 315–328.

De Vries, B. (2013). *Sustainability science*. Cambridge, UK: Cambridge University Press.

Dewey, J. (1938). *Logic: The theory of inquiry*. New York, NY: Henry Hold. Retrieved March 29, 2021, from https://archive.org/details/JohnDeweyLogicTheTheoryOfInquiry/page/n1/mode/2up

Enders, J., & Remig, M. (Eds.). (2016). *Theories of sustainable development*. London, UK: Routledge.

European Parliament. (2019). Parliament seals ban on throwaway plastics by 2021. Press release. Retrieved March 29, 2021, from https://www.europarl.europa.eu/news/en/press-room/20190321IPR32111/parliament-seals-ban-on-throwaway-plastics-by-2021

Fritz, L., & Binder, C. R. (2020). Whose knowledge, whose values? An empirical analysis of power in transdisciplinary sustainability research. *European Journal of Futures Research, 8*(3), 1–21. https://doi.org/10.1186/s40309-020-0161-4

Gorecki, J. (1991). Moral norms: The problem of justification reconsidered. *The Journal of Value Inquiry, 25*(4), 349–358.

Hofer, R. (2006). *Interkulturelles Lernen im Unterricht. Einüben in vernünftige Formen der Konfliktbewältigung anhand des VaKE-Ansatzes* [Master's thesis]. Paris-Lodron University Salzburg.

Hume, D. (1739). *A treatise of human nature* [reprinted from the original edition in three volumes and edited, with an analytical index, by L. A. Selby-Bigge. Oxford: Clarendon Press, 1896]. Retrieved August 16, 2016, from https://people.rit.edu/wlrgsh/HumeTreatise.pdf

Karp, D. (1996). Values and their effect on pro-environmental behavior. *Environment and Behavior, 28*, 111–133.

Kircher, J. (2008). *Argumentationen im VaKE-Unterricht. Dargestellt mit der Argumentationsstruktur von Max Miller* [Bachelor's thesis]. Paris-Lodron University Salzburg.

Klafki, W. (1984). Der Begriff der Didaktik und der Satz vom Primat der Didaktik (im engeren Sinne) im Verhältnis zur Methodik. In W. Klafki, G. M. Rückheim, W. Wolf, R. Freudenstein, H.-K. Beckmann, K.-C. Lingelbach, G. Iben, & J. Diederich (Eds.), *Funkkolleg Erziehungswissenschaft, Bd. 2* (pp. 55–73). Frankfurt am Main, Germany: Fischer.

Knapp, C. N., Reid, R. S., Fernández-Giménez, M. E., Klein, J. A., & Galvin, K. A. (2019). Placing transdisciplinarity in context: A review of approaches to connect scholars, society, and action. *Sustainability, 11*, 4899. doi:10.3390/su11184899

Kohlberg, L. (1971). From is to ought: How to commit the naturalistic fallacy and get away with it in the study of moral development. In T. Mischel (Ed.), *Cognitive development and epistemology* (pp. 151–235). New York, NY: Academic Press.

Kohlberg, L. (1984). *Essays on moral development: Vol. 2. The psychology of moral development*. San Francisco, CA: Harper & Row.

Komiyama, H., & Takeuchi, K. (2006). Sustainability science: Building a new discipline. *Sustainability Science, 1*, 1–6. doi: 10.1007/s11625-006-0007-4

Mittelstrass, J. (2005). Methodische Transdisziplinarität. *Technologiefolgenabschätzung – Theorie und Praxis, 14*, 18–23.

Mittelstrass, J. (2018). The order of knowledge: From disciplinarity to transdisciplinarity and back. *European Review, 26*(Suppl S2), S68–S75. Retrieved March 29, 2021, from https://www.cambridge.org/core/services/aop-cambridge-core/content/view/8ED86874D100DA377C7151A8BCEB73E0/S1062798718000273a.pdf/order_of_knowledge_from_disciplinarity_to_transdisciplinarity_and_back.pdf

Moore, G. E. (1903). *Principia ethica* (Reproduction). London, UK: Cambridge University Press, 1971.

Morscher, E. (2018). Metaethics and moral education. In A. Weinberger, H. Biedermann, J.-L. Patry, & S. Weyringer (Eds.), *Professionals' ethos and education for responsibility* (pp. 17–27). Leiden, The Netherlands: Brill.

Nussbaumer, M. (2007). *Das Unterrichtskonzept VaKE in Verbindung mit der Argumentationsstruktur von Max Miller* [Bachelor's thesis]. Paris-Lodron University Salzburg.

Nussbaumer, M. (2009). *"Argumentieren geht über Studieren". Wie Schülerinnen und Schüler im didaktischen Konzept VaKE argumentieren* [Master's thesis]. Paris-Lodron University Salzburg.

Oser, F., Patry, J.-L., Zutavern, M., Reichenbach, R., Klaghofer, R., Althof, W., & Rothbucher, H. (1991). *Der Prozess der Verantwortung – Berufsethische Entscheidung von Lehrerinnen und Lehrern*. Bericht zum Forschungsprojekt 1.188-0.85 und 11.25470.88/2 des Schweizerischen Nationalfonds zur Förderung der wissenschaftlichen Forschung. Freiburg, Switzerland: Pädagogisches Institut der Universität.

Patry, J.-L. (2014). Rivalisierende Paradigmen in der Erziehungswissenschaft: Das Beispiel der Situationsspezifität. In S. Kornmesser & G. Schurz (Eds.), *Die multiparadigmatische Struktur der Wissenschaften* (pp. 103–144). Wiesbaden, Germany: Springer VS.

Patry, J.-L. (2018). Grenzen und Übergange. Ein allgemeines Konzept, expliziert am Beispiel des Theorie-Praxis Problems. In B. Bütow, J.-L. Patry, & H. Astleitner (Eds.), *Grenzanalysen – Erziehungswissenschaftliche Perspektiven zu einer aktuellen Denkfigur* (pp. 34–61). Weinheim, Germany: Beltz Juventa.

Patry, J.-L., & Schaber, K. (2010, January). *Fürsorge versus Gerechtigkeit: Argumentieren Frauen anders als Männer? Eine Untersuchung zur Geschlechtsspezifität in moralischen Entscheidungssituationen* [Paper]. Tagung "Moral und Beruf 2010", Basel, Switzerland.

Patry, J.-L., & Weyringer, S. (2019). Transdisziplinarität bei der Unterrichtsmethode "Values and Knowledge Education": Grundlagen und die Beziehung zwischen Sein und Sollen. *itdb – Inter- und transdisziplinäre Bildung, 1*, 45–56. doi:10.5281/zenodo.2557592

Phillips, D. C., & Burbules, N. C. (2000). *Postpositivism and educational research*. New York, NY: Rowman & Littlefield.

Putnam, H. (1990). *Realism with a human face* (J. Conant, Ed.). Cambridge, MA: Harvard University Press.

Rousseau, D., Wilby, J., Billingham, J., & Blachfellner, S. (2018). *General systemology. Transdisciplinarity for discovery, insight, and innovation*. Singapore: Springer Singapore. Retrieved March 29, 2021, from https://link.springer.com/book/10.1007%2F978-981-10-0892-4

Schwartz, S. H. (2015). Basic individual values: Sources and consequences. In T. Brosch & D. Sander (Eds.), *Handbook of value perspectives from economics, neuroscience, philosophy, psychology, and sociology* (pp. 63–84). New York, NY: Oxford University Press. doi:10.1093/acprof:oso/9780198716600.003.0004

Stenner, P. (2014). Transdisciplinarity. In T. Teo (Ed.), *Encyclopedia of critical psychology* (pp. 1987–1993). New York, NY: Springer. https://doi.org/10.1007/978-1-4614-5583-7_317

Stranzinger, R. (1984). Anmerkungen zum praktischen Syllogismus. In M. W. Fischer, E. Mock, & H. Schreiner (Eds.), *Hermeneutik und Strukturtheorie des Rechts* (pp. 111–120). Stuttgart, Germany: Steiner Verlag Wiesbaden.

Thøgersen J., & Ölander, F. (2003). Spillover of environment-friendly consumer behavior. *Journal of Environmental Psychology, 23*(3), 225–236.

Toulmin, S. (1958). *The uses of arguments*. Cambridge, UK: Cambridge University Press.

UN. (1992). *Konferenz der Vereinten Nationen für Umwelt und Entwicklung. Agenda 21*. Retrieved July 7, 2019, from http://www.un.org/depts/german/conf/agenda21/agenda_21.pdf

UN. (2015). *Transforming our world. The 2030 Agenda for Sustainable Development*. Retrieved August 17, 2019, from https://sustainabledevelopment.un.org/

Vilsmaier, U. (2010). Transdisciplinarity and protected areas: A matter of research horizon. *Journal on Protected Mountain Areas Research and Management, 2*(2), 37–44.

Weinberger, A., Gastager, A., & Patry, J.-L. (2011, October 24). *VaKE in teacher education. How do preservice teachers argue?* [Paper]. The International Conference on moral education, Association of Moral Education, Nanjing, China.

Weinberger, A., Kriegseisen, G., Loch, A., & Wingelmüller, P. (2005). Das Unterrichtsmodell V*a*KE (Values *and* Knowledge Education) in der Hochbegabtenförderung: Der Prozess gegen Woyzeck. *Salzburger Beiträge zur Erziehungswissenschaft, 9*(1/2), 23–40. Retrieved March 29, 2021, from http://gw.eduhi.at/bundesarge/Verlage/Klappacher_V*a*KE.pdf

Weingart, P. (2000). Interdisciplinarity: The paradoxical discourse. In P. Weingart & N. Stehr (Eds.), *Practising interdisciplinarity* (pp. 25–42). Toronto, Canada: University of Toronto Press. https://doi.org/10.3138/9781442678729-004

World Commission on Environment and Development [WCED]/Brundtland Commission. (1987). *Our common future. World commission on environment and development.* Oxford, UK: Oxford University Press.

PART 7

Afterthoughts to VaKE

∴

CHAPTER 34

Afterthoughts to V*a*KE

Jean-Luc Patry, Sieglinde Weyringer, Frédérique Brossard Børhaug and Dimitris Pnevmatikos

1   Introduction

The idea of what was later to become V*a*KE had emerged in the late 1980s (first mentioned in Oser & Patry, 1990, p. 77; see also Brossard, 2017, for the history of V*a*KE), based on the experiences that in dilemma discussions in the sense of Blatt and Kohlberg (1975) the students were highly interested and motivated. This led to theoretical concepts, which were turned into a practical procedure, as shown in the film by Cohenian et al. (2017). At the end of the last century, a first empirical experience was made: A seminar that yielded, among others, the papers by Peticzka et al. (1998), Pürgy (1998), and Verwanger (1998), served as some kind of a trial balloon, as a first check whether this idea worked in practice. The development of V*a*KE, thus, is the product of constant interaction between practical experiences and theoretical concerns, and this process is still continuing. The present handbook testifies this constant interaction, going back and forth between the theory and the practice of V*a*KE within and between chapters.

When these first steps were done, one could not imagine that this would lead to a research programme culminating, for the time being, in the present handbook with the contribution of thirty authors from nine countries, using V*a*KE in all kinds of schools and various extracurricular settings. The different studies – and many others that could not be included in this handbook – confirm that V*a*KE is quite successful in achieving the double assignment: to combine and relate with each other values education (in the sense of fostering the judgment competence) *and* knowledge acquisition.

In this chapter, we will look at the assets, the limits and the inconveniences of the programme and then turn to its future perspectives.

2   Assets of the Programme

The double assignment satisfies an urgent societal need, according to the principle: "Values without knowledge are blind, while knowledge without values is irresponsible". Our world is full of challenges that can be overcome if the stakeholders – and these are in most cases all of us – are aware of appropriate goals (justified through values judgments) and know how to achieve them reasonably. These challenges always have a dilemma character. In our view, VaKE can provide a valuable contribution for addressing many of them. The topics of VaKE include sustainability, climate change and environmental protection; democracy and civic competence and action; fake news, conspiracy theories, and echo chambers in the social media; political misconduct; social issues in pandemics; data protection; artificial intelligence; migration, extremism, and terrorism, to name just a few, as well as curricular knowledge in relation to such issues. In many of them, research projects with VaKE have been achieved, are underway or in planning, and some have been discussed in this handbook.

VaKE procedures cannot provide responses to such challenges that everyone can agree with. However, VaKE can sensitize citizens for a clear formulation of the relevant issues, for the recognition of the perspectives of the different stakeholders, for the antinomic values (moral dilemma), for the multiple facts, circumstances and facets that are involved in the dilemmas and tentative solutions. It can foster the participants' moral competence development and hopefully the morality of their actions. VaKE does not provide the perfect response to a dilemma but a procedure that can help by improving the proposed responses and render the participants more competent to provide such responses.

Beyond satisfying an essential requirement for education – the double assignment – the research programme VaKE has several assets, many of which distinguish VaKE from other programmes. First, it has a robust theoretical fundament. This contrasts with the perception of many teachers that constructivism means giving the students too much freedom (see Patry & Schrittesser, 2016). The theory provides security to the practitioners, allowing them to justify their choices in everyday teaching practice. Hence, when using VaKE, teachers do not act arbitrarily or driven by situational dynamics. And if they encounter difficulties while proceeding in VaKE, they know the theoretical issues related to the concrete problematic situation and do not need to take the problem personally. For example, if the dilemma discussion does not proceed as expected, the teacher who knows the VaKE theory recognises in what regard the dilemma formulation might have been inappropriate for the target group and will adjust it.

Furthermore, we consider as an asset that VaKE is not based on a single theory. VaKE exploits a series of theories that are often seen separately from each other but which can be preferably regarded as a transdisciplinary approach with constructivism as General Theory (GD) in the sense of Chapter 33 in this handbook. Single, isolated theories do not provide satisfying explanatory power in practical situations, as they explain only a small amount of the total variance of what happens in actual instructional settings. For instance, as Cafri et al. (2010) have shown, the effect sizes in empirical psychological studies are disappointingly small, which may be due to the fact that they are typically addressing only single theories – the distinction between single and multiple theory bases was not made. We assume that using several theories can substantially increase the explanatory power as the different theories consider different features that may contribute different components for explaining the research results (Patry, 2013, 2022) and become relevant for practice.

These theories are essential when it comes to flexibility. Indeed, VaKE *must not* be used in the sense of a cookbook in which one applies recipes blindly, in the perspective of "what works"[1] (e.g., NCEE, 2021). Instead, the theory is a base for how we interact with each other tactfully, adapting our actions among others to the audience's needs, the circumstances, and the curriculum.

While the theories underlying VaKE may have evolved – for instance, Kohlberg's (1981, 1984) theory has been further developed to neo-Kohlbergian frameworks (e.g., Rest et al., 2000; Thoma, 2014), their core structures as far as they are relevant for VaKE have not changed for most of them. On the other hand, the research on VaKE made it necessary to expand some of them in ways that so far had not been recognised:

– Vygotsky's (1978) social constructivism is extended to *collaborative co-construction* (see Chapter 2 in this handbook), which is necessary for communication within the discussion group and, more generally, in the comprehensive societal dialogues: Without a common understanding, no communication is possible. Moreover, the general idea of the Vygotskian 'zone of proximal development' is extended to more sophisticated approaches (e.g., the Framework Theory) for the role of prior knowledge to the construction of knowledge.
– Piaget's idea for the role of the general cognitive structures that facilitate knowledge acquisition in different domains in terms of stages has been abandoned, while his idea of the disequilibrium and the individual's effort to reduce the experience imbalances between developing new schemata to restore the equilibrium, is an evident mechanism in the implementation of VaKE. However, the concept that the subject's only reaction to cognitive disequilibrium is accommodation is challenged, as Gastager (2003) has shown: She found that people can accept contradicting subjective theories simultaneously as independent concepts; they activate the one that they need depending on the situational requirements that they perceive (see Chapter 2 in this handbook). It is not clarified yet under what conditions this happens and when such contradictions lead to accommodation.

– While the Kohlbergian tradition focuses on justice and deontic value systems, in VaKE, other value domains (see Chapter 33 in this handbook) like care, truthfulness, environmental issues are taken into consideration.
– In constructivism, viability (Glasersfeld, 1980) has played an essential role as an alternative to truth (e.g., in research). However, the concept that learners within a constructivist framework need to check their constructions for viability (the so-called viability check; Patry, 2014) has received little explicit attention.[2] Weinberger (2006) has shown that systematic viability checks can play an important role in VaKE (see Chapter 8): While able students show approximately the same knowledge learning performance in VaKE processes that includes systematic viability checks ("VaKE+") and in standard VaKE without such systematic checks, less able ones acquire more knowledge in VaKE+. This is an example of Aptitude-Treatment Interaction (ATI; Cronbach & Snow, 1977), as the intervention (VaKE+) yields different results depending on the learner's aptitude (in this case: ability). The results show that systematic viability checks, such as VaKE+, can compensate for the lack of structure in open teaching; as another ATI research has shown, low achievers perform poorly in structured environments but often even worse when the teaching lacks in structure. That this is not the case with VaKE has been shown repeatedly in VaKE studies.[3]

These extensions of theories show VaKE's potential for theory development and testing. Although VaKE is not solely accountable for that, as the references mentioned above show, it provides terrain for concretising, actualising and empirically testing such developments or – as the last example shows – for opening new issues for concepts developed outside of VaKE.

The fourth asset is that within the research programme, since the first studies, the VaKE concept has been tested with many target groups, in many contexts, with variations that are in agreement with the theoretical underpinning – this could only incompletely be documented in this handbook. In terms of Sidman (1960), these are systematic replications (in contrast to direct replications, where as little as possible is changed in the replication study). These systematic replications have consistently confirmed that the students with VaKE learn at least *as much* as in traditional teaching, and *often more and on a higher level*, as well as other results discussed in this handbook. In the light of the current replication crisis (Asendorpf et al., 2013; see also Patry, 2019, pp. 71–73), such a replication result is quite exceptional.

The following assets are practical. One asset – that VaKE shares with all dilemma discussions in the Kohlberg tradition – is that values education focuses on the *justification* of the values and not on the values themselves. The consequence is, among others, that the intervention cannot be criticised for promoting values that, from the perspective of the criticising person or institution (e.g., parents, political institutions, church), are considered as wrong. It is difficult to criticise the proposition to scrutinise values, although, admittedly, VaKE has been criticised by some (e.g., a catholic instance), for fostering a disposition that is contrary to what this institution regards as a virtue, namely obedience. Indeed, blind obedience is the only value that VaKE questions explicitly. It is difficult to argue with someone who claims the primacy of obedience, as it is generally difficult to argue with fundamentalists.

The focus on arguments is also an asset as the quality of an argument is independent of the person who utters it. Quite in opposition to what can be seen in today's policy, where often people and arguments are confounded, in VaKE, there is a clear separation of people and their arguments. Good arguments are disregarded in many traditional discussions because they are brought up by the "wrong" people – in our view, this is unacceptable: The quality of an argument is evidenced through appropriate viability checks, and while in default of better criteria, the person who utters it might be useful, it is the weakest criterion one that one can think of – according to the VaKE philosophy, then, one must search for better ones. For example, politicians often discredit arguments provided by the opposite party, even if it is a good argument. It might be a good idea to be critical towards an argument that comes from the "wrong" party at first sight, but if further viability checks reveal the argument as viable, it seems appropriate to adopt it anyway.

Finally, the method is not restricted to school and specific topics, but it is flexible, including many extracurricular contexts; it is also suited for highly diverse learner groups in terms of age, learning experiences, ethnic background, language, gender and ableness. Furthermore, besides knowledge and values, the research as documented in many chapters of the present handbook shows that many other positive effects can be found, like participants' sociability, perspective taking, negotiating agreements, working in teams, and sharing workload and benefits.

3   Limits and Inconveniences

Like any concept, VaKE has limits and inconveniences. The first set refers to *research*.

One research limit is that the studies so far have only been done by proponents of VaKE. This bears the risk of researcher biases towards confirming their hypotheses, including self-fulfilling prophecies (Rosenthal, 2012), confirming biases (Wason, 1968), social desirability (Edwards, 1957), and other systematic errors. One can fear that the researchers judge too liberally instead of conservatively in the case of ambivalence and doubt (e.g., in qualitative analyses) and would rather accept the hypotheses favouring VaKE instead of questioning them. It would be important that opponents carry out research on VaKE to avoid the risk of such misinterpretation. We have tried, with good assessments and designs (see Chapters 31 and 32 in this handbook), to minimize this risk but one is never exempt from such biases.

What has been discussed above as an asset, namely the experimental designs, has its negative counterpart, the small number of subjects. Currently, the mainstream in teaching research is using large samples, most notably in Hattie (2009) but also fostered by TIMSS, PISA and other international studies that challenged the countries to do educational research to improve their pupils' performance in the international standings. VaKE does not appear in these studies because only a few classes have used VaKE and none of them have been included in the respective samples. This shows that in contrast to the claim that such large-sample studies would contribute to improving education, they rather inhibit the development of innovations as they do not permit effective alternatives as long as these have not reached a critical number of classes in which they have been implemented; in turn, the implementation is hindered by the lack of visibility through large-sample studies – this is a vicious circle in the current research in education.

With respect to *practice*, what has been an asset for research turns out to be a problem for implementation. The solid theoretical base might be a handicap for practice, particularly for the implementation part. It is difficult to convey this theory to the teachers, who are used – and might expect – directly practicable information of the type "what works"; this the promoters of VaKE cannot and do not want to provide, as argued above as an asset. In particular, practitioners are often sceptical towards theory in general (Patry, 2005).

Furthermore, it is difficult for teachers to refrain from a central element of their (implicit) traditional teaching philosophy: intervening in class when they perceive a student's reaction that they judge as erroneous. The justification of the openness of teaching is theoretical and stands in contrast to most teachers' subjective theory (Robertson & Atkins Elliott, 2020). Teachers' roles that emanate from theory (see Chapter 6 in this handbook), and executing them appropriately, require that the practitioners have understood them. We have repeatedly experienced that teachers claimed to practice VaKE, but some substantial elements were missing or achieved differently from what the theory requires. For instance, it is insufficient to address values in a relatively open discussion to call it VaKE. It is against the VaKE philosophy for a teacher to intervene with authority when participants defend a value with which he or she does not agree or when values and knowledge are not related to each other, even if the topic is discussed with an open structure.

Teachers also have to learn not to act as the powerful superior who is in complete control and knows everything, but as someone who manages the learning situation, who shifts over control and responsibility to the learners without giving up responsibility about the whole learning situation, who trusts in the willingness of the pupils to learn, in their curiosity, in their commitment with respect to ethical issues. In particular, they have to acknowledge that they are learners themselves. They might have to recognise a new system of epistemological beliefs, according to which knowledge contents and values are not established once and for all, but whose viability may depend on the circumstances (see the concept of viability as addressed in Chapter 2) and which can evolve due to new insights.

Moreover, with respect to values education, they have to refrain from the indoctrination of values they are convinced of, but trust that the students will acquire appropriate values themselves – and maybe they have to accept that they might be challenged by the students in the values they defend and may have to justify their beliefs, which they might not even have been aware of before. Some teachers feel comfortable with these roles; others do not (Haara & Smith, 2012).

Teachers are afraid the students might take advantage of the freedom they are given. Our experience is that this is not the case, with some exceptions: Ghellini (Chapter 14 in this handbook), for instance, reports that due to the large group size, the noise level in the single room that was available was high, hence the discussion groups disturbed each other. Erratic attendance (Chapter 17) or changing timetables (Chapter 10) are other challenges for the implementation of VaKE.

The structures prevailing in the institutions are also often not conducive for VaKE. For instance, in some schools, it was difficult to conceive appropriate schedules. In others, the available rooms and furniture were inappropriate or the technical support such as the availability of computers and internet (WLAN) for the information search was insufficient. Sometimes, the cooperation between teachers, though desirable, could not be achieved to a sufficient degree.

Also, VaKE is sometimes more time-consuming than traditional teaching. However, we consider that the time invested in challenges like VaKE is beneficial: We live in a society that is in a movement of increasing velocity, and time is getting scarce and essential in human life. We need to slow down the pace and think about what is important, to develop complex reflection. Since they are motivated to do so, students deliberately take this time and volunteer to spend more time discussing the dilemma even in their leisure time (Chapter 15) or ask for more VaKE units (Chapter 16). It might well be that the equivalence and often even superiority of the acquired knowledge compared with the traditional teaching is due to the increased time on task. Since this is purely voluntary, we consider it as a consequence of the students' motivation, which is an impact of VaKE.

From the students' point of view, two problems may arise. First, the students may not be ready to follow the discussion rules, in particular, to separate the argument from the person who utters it or might reinforce some stereotypical thinking at first (Chapter 23). It is necessary to train the students. Secondly, when being confronted with VaKE the first time, the students may feel insecure by the freedom they are given. However, once they have become accustomed to open teaching situations, they appreciate them. We have experienced more than once that the students sent the workshop leaders away as they were disturbing their discussions.

4   Future Perspectives

The impetus of writing this handbook can be summarized as attempts:
- to show the development of VaKE from its origins to the present to its potential development in the future;
- to address advantages and limitations of the research programme and the implementation of VaKE;
- to transform theory into practice and practice into theory;
- to combine structured school curricula with an unstructured real world;
- to include global education objectives in the concrete teaching objectives and classroom learning goals;
- VaKE is claimed to be one proposal among others for making the young generation fit for the future. Making fit includes, but is not restricted to, the goals for education and development established by supranational organisations like UNO, OECD, European Council, etc.;
- how to find and use reliable, warranted and viable knowledge – in addition to school knowledge;
- how to develop a stable but flexible personality;
- how to negotiate agreements;
- how to work in teams and share workload and benefit;
- how to handle the multi-diversity of groups regarding culture, language, age, gender, etc.

The future challenges are already visible today, but the demands on meeting them are likely to increase due to a world that becomes more and more complex. We want to mention only a few issues without prioritizing any of them:

artificial intelligence, robotics, big data-related problems and challenges, private and personal data owned by commercial companies, control, and tracing in the privacy of a whole civic society, reduction of the distance to problems due to increasing close-knit technological network, problems with alienation, with technological addiction, in global dimensions like a pandemic, climate change, and many more.

All related efforts for establishing joined global perspectives and related educational objectives aim to further develop democratic societies, sustainable living, and responsible acting – this handbook on V*a*KE wants to contribute that these objectives can be achieved.

We also have founded AV*a*KE – the Association for Values *and* Knowledge Education registered in Austria[4] to provide a virtual meeting place for all people interested in V*a*KE and providing information and exchange.

Notes

1 While earlier versions of What Works (e.g., US Department of Education, 1987), the Clearinghouse approach is more sophisticated, as it includes the full account of the respective research. Nevertheless, the risk is that the single studies are seen as an appropriate method, without taking into account the potential role of other issues that may interact with it.
2 Disequilibrium is the result of the learner's viability check and plays an important role in constructivist learning, but to our knowledge has not been investigated systematically from a theoretical point of view yet.
3 Brossard Børhaug and Harnes (2020); Brossard Børhaug and Weyringer (2019); Pnevmatikos et al. (2019).
4 www.vake.eu

References

Asendorpf, J. B., Conner, M., De Fruyt, F., De Houwer, J., Denissen, J. J. A., Fiedler, K., Funder, D. C., Kliegl, R., Nosek, B. A., Perugini, M., Roberts, B. W., Schmitt, M., Vanaken, M. A. G., Weber, H., & Wicherts, J. M. (2013). Recommendations for increasing replicability in psychology. *European Journal of Personality, 27*, 108–119.

Berry, J. (2019). *Acculturation: A personal journey across cultures.* Cambridge, UK: Cambridge University Press.

Blatt, M. M., & Kohlberg, L. (1975). The effects of classroom moral discussion upon children's level of moral judgment. *Journal of Moral Education, 4*(2), 129–161.

Bloom, B. S., Engelhart, M. D., Furst, E. J., Hill, W. H., & Krathwohl, D. R. (Eds.). (1956). *Taxonomy of educational objectives – the classification of educational goals – Handbook 1: Cognitive domain.* London, WI: Longmans, Green & Co.

Brossard, F. (2017). *VaKE: Using dilemmas for intercultural competence development.* SIETAR Europa Webinar: "Value and Knowledge Education". Retrieved May 17, 2021, from https://www.youtube.com/watch?v=hTRP2ag_HF4

Brossard Børhaug, F., & Harnes, H. B. (2020). Facilitating intercultural education in majority student groups in higher education. *Intercultural Education, 31*(3).

Brossard Børhaug, F., & Weyringer, S. (2019). Developing critical and empathic capabilities in intercultural education through the VaKE approach. *Intercultural Education, 30*(1), 1–14.

Cafri, G., Kromrey, J. D., & Brannick, M. T. (2010). A meta-meta-analysis: Empirical review of statistical power, type I error rates, effect sizes, and model selection of meta-analyses published in psychology. *Multivariate Behavioral Research, 45*, 239–270,

Cohenian, I., Briner, D., Toledano, B., Patry, J.-L., Linortner, L., Nakotechny, R., & Eichler-Maron, R. (2017). *The VaKE process* [Video]. YouTube. Retrieved June 25, 2020, from https://www.youtube.com/watch?v=VytqZ56KVIY

Cronbach, L. J., & Snow, R. E. (1977). *Aptitudes and instructional methods. A handbook for research on interactions.* New York, NY: Irvington.

Edwards, A. L. (1957). *The social desirability variable in personality assessment and research.* New York, NY: Dryden.

Gastager, A. (2003). *Paradigmenvielfalt aus Sicht der Unterrichtenden. Subjektive Theorien über Handeln in "traditionellen" und konstruktivistischen Lehr-Lern-Situationen.* Lengerich, Germany: Pabst.

Haara, F. O., & Smith, K. (2012). Increasing the use of practical activities through changed practice. A case-study examination of the influence of a value-based intervention on two teachers' use of practical activities in mathematics teaching. *The Mathematics Enthusiast, 9*(1&2), 77–110.

Hattie, J. (2009). *Visible learning.* London, UK: Routledge.

NCEE. (2021). *What works clearinghouse.* Retrieved May 1, 2021, from https://ies.ed.gov/ncee/wwc/

Oser, F., & Patry, J.-L. (1990). *Choreographien unterrichtlichen Lernens. Basismodelle des Unterrichts.* Fribourg, Switzerland: Universität Fribourg.

Patry, J.-L. (2005). Zum Problem der Theoriefeindlichkeit der Praktiker. In H. Heid & C. Harteis (Eds.), *Verwertbarkeit. Ein Qualitätskriterium (erziehungs-)wissenschaftlichen Wissens?* (pp. 143–161). Wiesbaden, Germany: VS Verlag für Sozialwissenschaften.

Patry, J.-L. (2013). Beyond multiple methods: Critical multiplism on all levels. *International Journal of Multiple Research Approaches, 7*, 50–65.

Patry, J.-L. (2014). Die Viabilität und der Viabilitäts-Check von Antworten. In C. Giordano & J.-L. Patry (Eds.), *Fragen! Antworten? Interdisziplinäre Perspektiven* (pp. 11–35). Wien, Austria: Lit.

Patry, J.-L. (2016). Thesen zur konstruktivistischen Didaktik. *Journal für lehrerInnenbildung, 16*(2), 9–17.

Patry, J.-L. (2019). Situation specificity of behavior: The triple relevance in research and practice of education. In R. V. Nata (Ed.), *Progress in education* (Vol. 58, pp. 29–144). Hauppauge, NY: Nova.

Patry, J.-L. (2022). *Theorienvielfalt*. Manuscript submitted for publication.

Patry, J.-L., & Schrittesser, I. (Eds.). (2016). Konstruktivistische Didaktik: Theoretisch unbehaust? *Journal für LehrerInnenbildung, 16*(2), 4–72.

Peticzka, D., Weinberger, A., & Kastberger, A. (1998). *Dilemmadiskussion zur Wissensacquisition: Studie "Autobahn"* [Projektseminararbeit]. Institut für Erziehungswissenschaft der Paris-Lodron Universität Salzburg.

Pnevmatikos, D., Christodoulou, P., & Georgiadou, T. (2019). Promoting critical thinking in higher education through the Values and Knowledge Education (VaKE) method. *Studies in Higher Education, 44*(5), 892–901.

Pürgy, U. (1998). *Inwiefern ist es in Unterrichtseinheiten möglich, Moralerziehung und Stoffvermittlung mit einander zu kombinieren?* [Projektseminararbeit]. Institut für Erziehungswissenschaft der Paris-Lodron Universität Salzburg.

Rest, J. R., Narvaez, D., Thoma, S. J., & Bebeau, M. J. (2000). A neo-Kohlbergian approach to morality research. *Journal of Moral Education, 29*(4), 381–395.

Robertson, A. D., & Atkins Elliott, L. J. (2020). Truth, success, and faith: Novice teachers' perceptions of what's at risk in responsive teaching in science. *Science Education, 104*, 736–761. Retrieved June 5, 2021, from https://onlinelibrary.wiley.com/doi/epdf/10.1002/sce.21568

Rosenthal, R. (2012). Self-fulfilling prophecy. In V. S. Ramachandran (Ed.), *Encyclopedia of Human Behavior* (2nd ed., 328–335). Oxford, UK: Elsevier Science.

Sidman, M. (1960). *Tactics of scientific research. Evaluating experimental data in psychology*. New York, NY: Basic Books.

Thoma, S. J. (2014). Measuring moral thinking from a neo-Kohlbergian perspective. *Theory and Research in Education, 12*(3), 347–365.

US Department of Education. (1987). *What works. Research about teaching and learning* (2nd ed.). Washington, DC: US Government Printing Office.

Verwanger, C. (1998). *Über die Auswirkungen Kohlberg'scher Dilemmadiskussionen auf das Lernverhalten von Pflichtschülern* [Projektseminararbeit]. Institut für Erziehungswissenschaft der Paris-Lodron Universität Salzburg.

Wason, P. (1968). Reasoning about a rule. *Quarterly Journal of Experimental Psychology, 20*, 273–281.

Weinberger, A. (2006). *Kombination von Werterziehung und Wissenserwerb. Evaluation des konstruktivistischen Unterrichtsmodells VaKE (Values and Knowledge Education) in der Sekundarstufe 1*. Hamburg, Germany: Kovac.

Index

achievement 18, 73, 138, 196, 335, 354
action
 definition 216, 301
 moral 33, 300, 301, 303, 304, 306, 308–310
 vs. behaviour 304, 307, 310
affect 188, 216, 294, 295, 306, 366
America/USA 167, 203, 204, 351
antinomy 58, 215, 264, 320
Aptitude Treatment Interaction (ATI) 104, 106, 365, 396
assessment
 Defining Issues Test (DIT) 351–353
 judgment 348–353
 lesson interruption method 145
 Moral Competence Test (MCT) 350, 351, 353
 qualitative 50, 81, 82, 122, 182, 205, 252, 276, 305, 362
 questionnaire 81–83, 116, 122, 157, 178, 182, 228, 233, 234, 263, 265, 267, 344, 345, 347–349, 362, 365, 366
 W Assessment of Latent Knowledge (WALK) 71–73, 80, 105–108, 178, 232, 347–349, 354, 365
attitude xv, 17, 46, 47, 49, 126, 153, 154, 159, 183, 189, 190, 193, 212, 223, 249, 253, 265, 276, 280, 283, 301, 332, 333, 337–340
Australia 8, 142–145, 150, 203
Austria 8, 13, 91, 92, 98, 104, 178, 179, 181, 183, 187, 190–194, 348, 401
autonomy 48, 123, 125, 133–136, 189, 193, 239, 250, 326, 327, 338, 377
AVaKE (Association for Values and Knowledge Education) 9, 33, 401
awareness
 of ethical values 67–69, 72, 78, 104, 125, 126, 175, 244–249, 255, 263, 264, 267, 309
 self- 178, 182, 244–249, 267

behaviour 35, 51, 52, 59, 64, 68, 69, 75, 79, 83, 92, 108, 158, 175, 177, 183, 184, 189, 190, 192–194, 196, 213, 214, 216, 231, 244, 246, 249, 261, 262, 264, 265, 276, 300–302, 304, 307–310, 313, 319, 321, 326, 333, 345, 347, 351, 352, 355, 362, 381, 382
brain-storming 21, 71, 72, 97, 169, 171, 172, 226, 286, 288, 302, 310, 335

China 162, 168
civic
 education, see education, civic
 media 294, 295, 297, 298
citizenship 10, 158, 175–178, 180, 182–184, 187, 190, 193
coaching 243–245, 248, 250
communication 25, 46, 50, 67, 68, 73, 91, 92, 94, 96, 165, 177, 179, 181–183, 192, 206, 225, 230, 231, 242–246, 249, 265, 294, 295, 306–309, 311, 312, 395
 non-verbal 238, 324
competence
 definition 46, 189
 integration 187, 189–191
 moral 20, 24, 190, 320, 344, 348, 350, 351, 353, 354, 367, 394
computer
 internet 25, 28, 30, 33, 73, 74, 136, 139, 382, 399
 search engines 73
Computer-Supported Collaborative Learning (CSCL) 33, 283–292
conceptual change 8, 27, 35, 111–113, 116
concernedness 346
constructivism
 assimilation and accommodation 8, 22, 23, 335, 382
 co-construction 23
 social 22, 35, 103, 395
criteria for
 ethical thinking 338
 morality 240, 350, 352, 354
curriculum
 foreign language 143, 155
 science 112, 114, 148, 150
 values in 60, 83, 114, 150, 154, 322

deontic   376, 379–382, 385, 396
design
    cross-over   104, 232, 233, 259, 363, 364, 366, 367
    experimental   359, 365, 398
    max-min-kon   360, 361
    one group   359, 361, 362, 366, 367
devil's advocate   53, 74, 75, 138
dignity, human   18, 196, 305, 321, 323, 379
dilemma
    characteristics   50, 59, 60
    definition   379
    Sikh   34, 162–164, 168, 236, 237, 238, 241, 245, 247
    writing   57, 60, 62, 65, 81, 83, 122, 136
dilemma-based learning (DBL)   224, 283
dilemma-based model (DBM)   33, 273–279
discussion   5–8, 12–14, 17, 19–31, 34, 45, 49, 51–54, 59–64, 67, 69, 71–76, 79–82, 92–97, 101, 102, 105, 107, 114–116, 123–125, 127, 134–138, 142, 146, 147, 162, 164–166, 168–171, 178, 180–182, 191, 192, 194, 195, 200, 203, 204, 206, 226–228, 233, 236–238, 246–248, 250, 255–257, 261–265, 267, 274, 275, 281, 285, 287–291, 297, 308–311, 319, 325–329, 339, 346, 348, 353, 362, 367, 373–375, 381–383, 393–400
    rules   29, 52, 79, 80, 191, 195, 309, 311, 400
disposition
    definition   112
    habit   307, 333
    trait   355
double assignment   319–322, 325–327, 375, 385, 393, 394

education
    civic   155, 158, 240, 295
    higher   9, 50, 153–157, 159, 162, 170, 171, 199, 200, 202, 236, 237, 244, 252, 257
    intercultural   10, 120, 158, 199, 252–254
    health   10, 116, 215, 260, 261
    peace   295, 298
    science   10, 111–115, 117, 142, 144, 145, 147–150, 323
empowerment   182, 187–190, 193, 196, 283, 291
Europe   5, 64, 120, 125, 176, 177, 179, 181, 183, 187, 254, 340, 375

feedback   xv, 6, 25, 31, 52, 102–105, 108, 122, 136, 181, 190, 195, 204, 265, 288, 301, 332, 334
foreign language   120, 121, 159, 223, 225
    classes   121, 126
France   8, 120, 163–165, 167, 168, 170, 181, 203, 236, 237, 240, 245

Georgia   8, 153–159, 203, 204
Germany   8, 181, 264, 265, 350, 375
goal
    millenium development   339, 374
    social   23, 143, 305
    taxonomy   26, 214, 285
Greece   8, 116, 137, 260

health
    care   10, 59, 215, 216, 260, 268
    professionals   215, 216, 260
hearing-impaired   32, 230–234
higher education   9, 50, 153–157, 159, 162, 170, 171, 199, 200, 202, 236, 237, 244, 252, 257
hospitality   199–202, 209

identity   5, 18, 19, 27, 156, 177, 178, 180, 190, 192, 200, 202, 238, 239, 283, 291, 295, 307
integration   19, 31, 92, 114, 156, 187–192, 194–196, 199–203, 207, 208, 285, 286, 325, 367, 382
intercultural
    creating dilemma story   252–257
    dialogue   163, 199–203, 206, 208, 209
    intercultural education   10, 120, 158, 199, 252–254
    management of cultural differences   162, 163, 171, 242, 243
    participants' identities   4, 203
Ireland   8, 199, 203, 204

knowledge
    about myself   193, 281
    acquisition   4, 8, 12, 20–22, 25, 26, 30, 46–49, 71, 80, 101, 111, 112, 117, 124, 125, 143, 232, 234, 237, 238, 297, 300, 325–327, 340, 344, 347, 365, 375, 382, 393, 395
    content   16, 142, 340, 343, 375, 376, 399
    latent   70, 72, 178, 347
    tacit   70, 72, 180, 352

INDEX

language
    foreign   120, 121, 159, 223, 225
    native   187, 203, 225–227
    sign   230, 233, 234
    skills   191, 223–228
learning
    authentic   284
    collaborative   8, 23, 33, 98, 103, 104, 113, 114, 142, 207, 283–285, 289–291
    inquiry-based   6, 8, 13, 25, 26, 112, 113, 284
    Klippert method   94, 96, 98
    lifelong   193, 211, 217, 267, 268
    method   4–6, 8, 9, 91, 92, 94, 98
    transformative   8, 211–213, 216, 217, 256
Lesson Interruption Method (LIM)   105, 145, 178, 344, 345 362, 366

MA*a*KE (Moral Action *and* Knowledge Education)   300, 301, 304, 305, 307–313
management
    globalization   237, 381, 383
    intercultural management   236, 242
    management practices   51, 163
migrants
    females   187, 188, 192, 216, 313, 362
    foreign language minors   121
    newly arrived pupils   121
    refugees   187, 188, 190–192, 194–196, 199, 200, 202, 203, 209, 216, 296, 362
    unaccompanied minors   188
mind-map   71, 72, 74, 76, 94
moral
    action   33, 300, 301, 303, 304, 306, 308–310, 313
    care   5, 213, 261, 354
    judgment   4, 8, 10, 23, 24, 32, 49, 101, 114, 116, 136, 212, 213, 303, 348–353, 377
    justice   25, 49, 212, 213, 350, 352, 354
    justification   6, 21, 28, 57, 319–323, 325, 327
    stages of development   8, 23, 24, 61, 349, 352, 377
motivation
    self-determination theory   133, 211
    self-efficacy   345, 366
Muslim   61, 70, 163, 164, 168, 193, 216, 295, 362

narrative   4, 57, 63, 182, 202, 225, 277, 294, 295, 297, 298

naturalistic fallacy   16, 320, 375, 377, 378
Norway   5, 8, 252, 254, 262
N-ST V*a*KE Prototype   116

optometrists   264–267

peer feedback   102–105, 108
personality
    creativity   6, 27, 71, 72, 166, 179, 208, 284, 334, 335, 340, 360, 365
    intelligence   27, 107, 179, 360, 365
    traits   365
Plato Youth Forum   175, 176, 178, 179, 182–184
portfolio   73, 74, 76, 225–227
potter box   51, 68–70
practice
    educational   211, 256, 322
    professional   261, 264
primary level   92–98
process   4, 13–15, 17, 20–23, 27, 29–31, 33, 34, 45–47, 50, 51, 53–55, 57, 60, 63, 65, 67–76, 78–81, 83, 84, 97, 103, 104, 111, 112, 114, 121, 122, 126, 134, 137–139, 153, 155–158, 164–166, 170, 171, 179, 180, 188–191, 193, 196, 206, 207, 209, 212, 223–225, 227, 228, 230–234, 243, 249, 252, 253, 256, 257, 261, 262, 264–268, 275, 276, 278–281, 284–286, 290, 291, 295, 297, 298, 300–309, 313, 325, 331, 332, 334, 335, 337, 339, 340, 344–347, 352–354, 362, 370, 373, 376, 377, 379, 382–384, 393, 396
psychology
    behaviourist   52, 75, 79, 83, 93, 108, 189, 190, 192, 213, 216, 246, 261, 276, 304, 307–310, 362
    cognitive   17, 23, 46, 51, 101–105, 107, 108, 182, 188, 225, 350
    social   8, 17, 20–23, 35, 188, 189, 212, 225, 238, 253, 352, 362

rational decision behaviour   64
reflection
    critical   122, 212, 214–217, 255, 261, 311, 312
    theory based   10, 137, 139, 214–216, 261, 264, 268
reflective cycle   33, 273–278
reliability   150, 339, 345, 346, 348, 366

religion   58, 101, 123, 177, 193, 194, 196, 203, 208, 236–238, 240, 245, 373
religious signs   163, 165–168, 170, 236, 237, 239
research
   bias   397
   design, *see* design
   programme   26, 355, 361, 366, 393, 394, 396, 400
   self   334
responsibility   27, 34, 35, 46, 48, 51, 53, 78, 81, 139, 143, 165, 169, 183, 200, 216, 239, 291, 298, 305, 308, 319–321, 325–327, 340, 382, 383, 399
role-play   13, 74–76, 80, 84, 157, 165, 166, 194, 233, 234, 246, 248, 265, 267, 275

search for information   6, 13, 22, 28, 51, 53, 54, 61, 73, 97, 108, 115, 136, 137, 139, 194, 263, 311, 373, 399
secularism   34, 124, 165, 170, 236, 237, 240, 241, 245
   laicism   239
situation   3, 4, 8, 12, 14, 15, 18, 19, 21, 23, 27, 32–35, 58, 59, 62–64, 69, 70, 72, 75, 79, 84, 93, 102, 121, 123, 125, 134, 137, 138, 144, 145, 164, 166, 181, 182, 187, 189–191, 195, 203, 214, 216, 224, 227, 228, 231, 239, 246, 254, 255, 257, 260, 262–266, 273, 276–278, 280, 281, 284, 287, 291, 294, 296, 297, 300, 304, 305, 307, 309, 311, 319–320, 322, 334, 335, 337–339, 344–346, 350, 355, 362, 366, 367, 370, 373, 377, 394, 395, 399, 400
   -specific   15, 27, 79, 190, 216, 264, 320, 337, 344, 346, 355, 362, 366, 367
society   3, 18, 142, 143, 144, 148, 149, 153, 154, 156, 158, 159, 167, 177, 182, 187–189, 194, 195, 200, 202, 207, 208, 211, 237, 248, 252, 253, 256, 261, 274, 306, 319, 323, 352, 380, 384, 399, 401
sociology
   anthroposociology   238
   axiological   236, 238, 241
   social context   242, 246, 307
   social practices   238
statements
   descriptive ("Is")   16, 321, 372, 375–379, 382, 384

prescriptive ("Ought")   16, 321, 375, 378
superordinate and subordinate
   norms   321, 326, 378
   theories   371
sustainability   114, 158, 182, 374, 378, 379, 381, 383–385, 394

teacher
   education   10, 142, 148, 157–159, 170, 252–254, 274, 291, 351
   guidance   82, 101, 108
   in-service   133–137, 139, 274, 287
   pedagogical challenges when using VaKE   57, 125, 184
   roles in VaKE   78–85, 108, 135, 145
   training   48, 78, 83, 133, 155, 159, 213, 264, 286, 291, 313
teaching
   meaningful   273, 275
   method   5–8, 47, 78, 82, 95, 98, 101, 140, 143, 168, 169, 172, 182, 223, 224, 228, 232, 233, 266, 292, 346, 347, 361, 366
   open   28, 51, 67, 95, 96, 195, 255, 347, 396, 400
   traditional   7, 9, 26, 33, 53, 101, 133, 138, 140, 143, 233, 250, 346, 347, 363, 364, 366, 396, 398–400
technology in education   4, 83, 234, 283, 284, 291, 323
teleological   25, 306, 376, 379, 380–382, 385
theory
   -based reflection   10, 137, 139, 214–216, 261, 264, 268
   general   371–374, 378, 381–384, 394
   of VaKE   84, 370, 385
   -practice gap   264, 265
   subjective   10, 13–17, 21–23, 28, 264–266, 372, 382, 395, 398
thinking
   anticipatory   332, 333, 335, 337, 339
   collaborative   331, 335–337, 339, 340
   complex thinking   125, 237, 238, 242, 253, 255
   creative   334–337, 339
   critical   5, 22, 27, 50, 67, 91, 92, 138, 154, 168, 182, 183, 215, 224, 231, 283–286, 288–291, 333–335, 338–340
   ethical   165, 301, 313, 331, 336, 338

INDEX 409

freedom of thought 240
reflective 114, 298, 332, 339
style 308, 331, 335–338, 340
systemic 340
trans-disciplinarity 27, 370, 371, 382, 383, 385
trans-domain approaches (TDA) 354, 370–375, 378–380, 382–384
transfer XV, 51, 62, 81, 115, 137, 175, 187, 190, 193, 194, 215, 227, 264, 266, 268, 290, 300, 301, 312, 313, 324, 337

VaKE (Values *and* Knowledge Education)
adaptation 10, 19, 28, 31–34, 47, 74, 92, 94–98, 101, 102, 115–117, 195, 230, 234
implementation 10, 28, 54, 67, 81, 83, 84, 91, 92, 94, 116, 120, 123, 124, 126, 135, 137–139, 157, 162, 163, 200, 224, 247, 248, 263, 267, 274, 291, 344, 395, 399, 400
steps 7, 13, 25, 28, 29, 31–33, 54, 59, 62, 79, 84, 85, 92, 96, 104, 108, 114, 121, 134–136, 139, 146, 150, 157, 164, 171, 172, 191, 215, 225–228, 236, 237, 247, 263–266, 268, 274, 285–290, 363, 272, 383, 384, 393
VaKE+ 33, 101, 102, 104–108, 348, 363, 365, 396
VaKE-*dis* 28, 30, 31, 79, 82, 94, 120, 121, 164, 204, 215, 252, 268, 310–312
VaKE-pr 32, 84, 91, 95–98, 232

VaKE-Tact 32, 216, 264–268
validity 48, 59, 61, 63, 105, 107, 306, 307, 340, 344, 346, 348, 359, 361, 365–367
values
creating moral dilemma stories for intercultural education 252–257
cultural 177, 244, 247
immaterial 16, 18, 67
-ladenness 142, 144, 322, 324
principle value 378, 393
value register 19, 238–240
value transformation 7, 8, 50, 211–217, 228, 239
values and development square 68, 70
viability
check 13, 14, 17, 22, 24, 28–31, 33, 102–105, 107, 108, 114, 178, 182, 214, 267, 297, 332, 363, 365, 366, 396, 397, 401
definition 13–14

W Assessment of Latent Knowledge (WALK) 71–73, 80, 105–108, 178, 232, 347–349, 354, 365
World-café 73, 74

zone of proximal development 8, 47, 103, 395